SUICIDE ACROSS THE LIFE SPAN— PREMATURE EXITS

SUICIDE ACROSS THE LIFE SPAN— PREMATURE EXITS

Judith M. Stillion, Ph.D.
Western Carolina University
Cullowhee, North Carolina

Eugene E. McDowell, Ph.D.
University of North Carolina
Asheville Graduate Center
Asheville, North Carolina

Jacque H. May, M.A.
Cullowhee, North Carolina

●HEMISPHERE PUBLISHING CORPORATION
A member of the Taylor & Francis Group
New York   Washington   Philadelphia   London

Permissions

Figures 2.1 and 2.2 from *Introduction to Psychology*, 8th Ed. (pp. 32–33), by R. L. Atkinson, R. C. Atkinson, and E. R. Hilgard, copyright © 1983 by Harcourt Brace Jovanovich, Inc., reprinted by permission of the publisher.

Table 2.5, "Maslow's Need Hierarchy and Levels of Personality Functioning" from *Personality Theories: Guide to Living* by Nicholas S. DiCaprio, copyright © 1974 by Holt, Rinehart & Winston, Inc., reprinted by permission of the publisher.

Tabular material on pp. 48–49 from table "Common Beliefs Illustrative of 'Neurotic' Behavior" from *Behavior Change Through Self-Control* by Marvin Goldfried and Michael Merbaum, copyright © 1973 by Holt, Rinehart & Winston, Inc., reprinted by permission of the publisher.

Quotation on p. 135 is from Viorst, J. (1986). *Necessary Losses*. New York: Fawcett, copyright © 1986 by Judith Viorst. Reprinted by permission of Simon & Schuster, Inc.

This book was set in Trump by Harper Graphics. The editors were Carolyn Ormes and Karla Philip. Cover design by Debra Eubanks Riffe. Edwards Brothers, Inc. was printer and binder.

Library of Congress Cataloging-in-Publication Data

Stillion, Judith M., date
    Suicide across the life span: premature exits / Judith M. Stillion, Eugene E. McDowell, Jacque H. May.
        p. cm.

    Includes index.

    1. Suicide.   2. Life cycle, Human—Psychological aspects.
I. McDowell, Eugene E.   II. May, Jacque H.   III. Title.
    [DNLM: 1. Suicide.   HV 6545 S857]
HV6545.S797   1989
362.2'8--dc20
DNLM/DLC
for Library of Congress   89-7499
                                                                                   CIP

ISBN 0-89116-630-0 (cloth)
ISBN 0-89116-951-2 (paper)
ISSN 0275-3510

Dedication

To all who have been or will be tempted to make premature exits from the stage of life, and to those who would work with them.

Contents

Preface

So many excellent books have been written on the subject of suicide that we had to ask ourselves at the outset, why should we write yet another? To answer that question, we had to focus tightly on what we thought another book on suicide, this particular book, might offer readers that is not already available in the burgeoning literature on the topic. We believe there are three major ways in which this book differs from others.

First, this book is designed with a special audience in mind. It is directed primarily toward advanced undergraduate students and secondarily toward beginning graduate students who are planning to enter helping professions. It is designed to provide these students with an introduction to the complex topic of suicide written from a life span perspective. There are many benefits in having, under one cover, a resource that contains an overview of the history of suicide in Western culture; an introduction to major psychological, sociological, and biological perspectives; reviews of statistics and factors affecting suicide across the life span; and an introduction to issues involved in suicide prevention, intervention, and postvention. Such a volume should provide prospective helping professionals with a thorough introduction to the multifaceted subject of suicide.

Second, this book, unlike any other currently available, examines suicide from a life span perspective. Not only do we review what is known about suicide at the various developmental stages across the life cycle, but we also examine seven developmental principles as they apply to suicide. In addition, we present a model suicide trajectory, which conceptualizes suicidal behavior as the product of an interactive process composed of psychological, biological, cognitive, and environmental risk factors as they contribute to the development of suicidal ideation. We also show the ways in which this model is useful in understanding the commonalities and differences that exist in suicidal behavior across the life span.

Third, we were aware that there are many aspects of suicide in which current knowledge is dated or fragmented. Therefore, when possible, we carried out original studies to be reported in this book. Three such studies are included: (1) a review of programs sponsored by the different state departments of public instruction to encourage education for suicide prevention in the public schools, (2) a similar study of postsecondary education institutions, and (3) a study of the attitudes of middle-aged adults toward suicide. While all of these studies require replication, they do provide timely information about these three subjects that is not available in print elsewhere.

As we began writing this book, we delimited the topic of suicide. We consciously chose not to include detailed analyses of suicides committed by psychotics. Although we are aware that such suicides do occur, we believe that they shed little light on the general topic of suicide from a developmental perspective. Instead, our focus throughout the book is on the interaction between developing individuals and their environments as the individuals move through predictable stages of development. Wherever possible, we have tried to illuminate our writing with case studies, newspaper reports, and examples of suicidal behavior from other sources. All case studies and examples, although based on real incidents, have been altered in order to ensure the privacy of the individuals concerned.

From the time we conceived this book in 1985, both of the senior authors took administrative positions, moving from faculty positions in the Department of Psychology at Western Carolina University. The third author, after completing her Master's degree, settled into the roles of full-time mother and part-time researcher. Because of these life changes, we find ourselves especially indebted to many people without whose help this book simply could not have been completed. We owe each of them an enormous vote of thanks.

First, Hannelore Wass encouraged this project from the beginning. She also read and critiqued an earlier version of the manuscript, completing her work in an extremely short time in order to keep us on schedule. Her insightful comments and excellent suggestions have been incorporated into the final draft.

Ron Wilder, the Acquisitions Editor at Hemisphere, has also been very helpful. He provided guidance for obtaining copyright releases, as well as support for procuring the pictures that appear in the book. His final editing and cover selection are responsible for the appearance of the book.

We owe very special thanks to Jan Scroggs, who rapidly and accurately typed every word of this book (at least three times). Her ability to transform our rough drafts into a finished product bordered on the miraculous. We also thank Becky Pope, who typed many of the tables in the book.

The staff of Hunter Library at Western Carolina University are very real partners in the production of this book. Two people, Ed Cohen and Rebecca Kornegay, were especially helpful, devoting many hours of time to finding art, government references, and other materials. Their help, as well as that of our University Librarian, Bill Kirwan, ensured that we had the necessary research support and breathed real meaning into Western Carolina University's image as a "community of scholarship." Ray Williams, of the Ackland Art Museum in Chapel Hill, was also very helpful in locating potential art for the book. In addition, we thank the many subjects who voluntarily responded to the three original studies which were conducted as part of this book.

Finally, and most especially, we thank our spouses, Glenn, Suzanne, and Jim, for their continuing support from the beginning to the end of this 3-year project. They have done far more than their share of housework, yardwork, and childcare, especially during the last 7 months as we struggled to meet final deadlines. Their patience and good humor enabled us to complete this book without experiencing separation or divorce.

1
Suicide Then and Now

Those who cannot remember the past are condemned to repeat it.
George Santayana

This book is intended to be primarily a study of issues in suicidal behavior and attitudes in the late 20th century from a life span perspective. However, suicide is a complex phenomenon which has had different meanings across time and cultures. A detailed discussion of suicide across cultures is beyond the scope of this chapter. However, in-depth examination of suicide throughout the history of Western culture will serve to show that the meaning of suicidal behavior is relative and that attitudes toward suicide have varied across time within Western culture. Such an examination will also remind us that our attitudes toward suicide are often rooted in past events and should enable us to evaluate more clearly the current situation regarding suicide.

A SUMMARY OF SUICIDE IN WESTERN HISTORY

Human beings have an ancient tradition of self-murder. Altruistic suicide (i.e., a person giving up his or her life for others or for a greater good) has existed since humans banded together in clans. It is easily seen in primitive hunting patterns in which one individual volunteered to draw the attention of a herd of animals to himself in order to turn them in a direction which would allow the tribe to trap them more easily. The probability that the hunter would survive the onrushing herd was low. The reward if he did survive must have been very high. The reward for the tribe was survival itself. Thus, the early acts of altruistic suicide clearly had survival value, and the oral legends about the bravery of such hunters became embedded in our early myths.

We find modern remnants of this urge toward altruistic suicide in battlefront accounts of people who sacrifice their lives for the lives of their fellow soldiers as well as in the 20th-century records of Eskimo tribes whose elders sacrificed their lives by

1

wandering alone into the freezing countryside when they felt they could no longer be of use to the social system in which they lived. Such voluntary deaths also had species survival value in that they freed the tribes of numbers of the elderly who would inevitably become increasingly dependent. Bromberg and Cassel (1983) reported that many primitive cultures encouraged suicide in the elderly as a means to avoid the pains of old age and earn honor from their people. These authors pointed out that cultures as diverse as those of the Norsemen, the polar Eskimos, the Crow Indians, and the Samoans all had traditions that promoted suicide with honor.

Although altruistic suicide and suicide by the elderly can be seen to have species survival value, the history of Western civilization is marked by self-killings done for other reasons. A summary of selected milestones in the history of suicide in the Western world is shown in the time line depicted in Table 1.1. It will form the framework for the historical discussion which follows. The discussion is based on several resources, including *The Cry for Help* (Farberow & Shneidman, 1961), *Essays in Self-Destruction* (Shneidman, 1967), *The Savage God* (Alvarez, 1970), *Suicide in Different Cultures* (Farberow, 1975), *Biathanatos* (Donne, 1644/ 1982), *Definition of Suicide* (Shneidman, 1985), the King James version of *The Holy Bible*, and the *World Book Encyclopedia* (Harmet, 1984). As is true in most historical research, many of these sources cited the same events and dates. Therefore, in the discussion that follows, we have not tried to identify specific sources for each event.

Suicide in the Old Testament

There are four instances of suicide recorded in the Old Testament, only two of which appear on the time line. These two took place at approximately the same time, around 1000 B.C. It is interesting to note that no judgment is expressed about either suicide, both being merely described factually. The first is the suicide of Samson. Samson killed himself after violating his faith, being captured and blinded by his enemies, and suffering a long period of physical labor as a prisoner. Those familiar with the story recognize retribution against enemies, atonement for behavior that violated deep religious beliefs, and sacrifice for principle as possible motivating elements in that suicide. It is noteworthy that his suicide resulted in the death of many of his enemies as well as the destruction of their temple.

The second suicide, that of King Saul, seems to have occurred as a reaction to loss and pain and as the end result of deepening madness. The loss involved was the death of his three sons, who had died in the same battle in which Saul was wounded. Saul apparently also sought to ward off worse wounds by his suicide, since he asked his armorbearer to kill him "lest these uncircumcised come and thrust me through and abuse me" (1 Sam. 31:4). When his armorbearer refused to kill him, Saul fell on his own

TABLE 1.1 Selected Milestones in the History of Suicide in the Western World

Event & approximate date	Description
1000 B.C. Deaths of Samson and Saul	Reported without comment. Possible causes: retribution, self-punishment, justification of God and beliefs, reaction to death of sons, despair, fulfillment of prophecy.
399 B.C. Death of Socrates	Honorable exit; rational control over death.
350 B.C. Proclamation of Aristotle	Established suicide as unlawful.
300 B.C. to 300 A.D. Development of Greek & Roman Stoicism	Concept of rational suicide is developed fully.
33 A.C. Death of Judas Iscariot	Reported without comment. Possible causes: guilt, remorse, self-punishment, fulfillment of prophecy.
33 A.D. Death of Jesus of Nazareth	Martyrdom (i.e., allowing oneself to be killed for one's faith) becomes a major moral lesson for Christians.
65 A.D. Death of Seneca and his wife Paulina	Reinforced concept of rational suicide; quality rather than quantity of life emphasized.
73 A.D. Mass suicide at Masada	960 defenders of Masada die rather than surrender to the enemy.
300–400 A.D. Donatism flourishes	Martyrdom established as a goal for fervent Christians.
400 A.D. St. Augustine condemns self-killing	Censured martyrdom to ensure future of Christianity.
533 A.D. Council of Orleans	Denied funeral rites to suicides accused of crime.
563 A.D. Council of Braga	Denied funeral rites to all suicides.
590 A.D. Council of Antisidor	Added system of penalties for suicide.
693 A.D. Council of Toledo	Adopted excommunication as punishment for suicide or attempted suicide.
1265–1272 A.D. Thomas Aquinas' *Summa Theologica*	Presented detailed arguments against suicide. Added to the idea that suicide is sinful.
1284 A.D. Synod of Nimes	Denied Christian burial to suicides.
1647 A.D. John Donne publishes *Biathanatos*	Questioned whether self-murder always a sin.
1651 A.D. Word *suicide* enters English language	
1670 A.D. Secular laws are passed against suicide	Suicide became triple crime: murder, high treason, heresy.
1763 A.D. Merian publishes medical work on suicide	Introduced concept of suicide as illness.
1783 A.D. Hume publishes *Essay on Suicide*	Argued that suicide is not a crime against God, neighbors, or self.
1838 A.D. Esquirol published chapter describing suicide as a symptom of mental illness	Added support to the interpretation of suicide as an illness.
1897 A.D. Durkheim publishes *Le Suicide*	Beginning of study of suicide as a sociological phenomenon.
1800–1900 A.D. Rise of existentialism (e.g., Kierkegaard, Nietzsche, et al.)	Stresses individual freedom to act and responsibility for that action. Suicide is merely one more decision which individuals must face throughout their lifetimes.
1917 A.D. Freud publishes *Mourning and Melancholia*	Establishes modern foundation for viewing suicide as evidence of mental illness.
1958 A.D. First suicide prevention center established in Los Angeles	Based on the view that suicidal thoughts are temporary and that intervention effects a cure.

sword. There is also an element of prophecy fulfillment understood in this suicide, since Saul's death had been foretold earlier by the witch of Endor. The third suicide, not shown on the time line, was that of Saul's servant and armorbearer, who appears to have killed himself out of a sense of loyalty to King Saul.

The last suicide mentioned in the Old Testament was that of Ahithophel, whose plan to attack and kill King David went awry. When he realized this, he went home, put his affairs in order, and hanged himself. The Scripture once again passes no judgment. The motivations in this case might have been a sense of shame and disgrace over his failure or a fear of retribution from David or from his captain, Absalom. From these four cases of suicide, which occurred during the same general period, little can be discerned about the attitudes of the populace toward the act of suicide.

Suicide in Ancient Greece and Rome

Perhaps the best known suicide in history is the next one depicted on the time line, the suicide of Socrates. Occurring in 399 B.C., this suicide is the epitome of taking one's life out of a sense of duty and an enduring loyalty to one's philosophy of life. There is every reason to believe that Socrates might have avoided the death sentence rendered against him if he had moderated his teachings at an earlier period. He also could have chosen not to take the hemlock, thus forcing his accusers to murder him. But Socrates chose to die as he had lived, teaching right up until the moment of his death and in control of his own fate until the last.

The Death of Socrates, Jacques Louis David. (The Metropolitan Museum of Art, Wolfe Fund, 1931. Catharine Lorillard Wolfe Collection, 31.45).

His death has long been regarded as an example of honorable death.

The next major milestone on the suicide time line occurred around 350 B.C., when Aristotle, the intellectual heir of Socrates via his teacher, Plato, proclaimed that suicide is or should be unlawful because it injures the community. This could be most clearly seen in the case of a suicide by a slave or servant, which would result in the deprivation of services to the master's household. It is also evident, however, that in a culture where community welfare is a strong value, the life of any one individual would be viewed as secondary in importance to the needs of the community as a whole. In such a situation, suicide would be condemned, since it would result in a weakening of the community by the loss of the talents and energies of the suicidal individual.

During the period of 300 B.C. to 300 A.D., the concept of self-murder as a rational act was developed fully by followers of the philosophy known as Stoicism. Stoicism flourished first in Greece and then in Rome. The Stoics placed a high value on reason and on control of all aspects of life, including death. Self-murder was seen as a rational act that enabled a human to have control over the time and nature of his or her death. It might even be a preferred method of dying, since it permitted a rational review of one's past life and future options as well as recognition that death is in the natural order of things. However, Stoicism had nothing to say about those humans who took their own lives in an emotional state or as a result of nonrational motivations. It would follow that the Stoics could easily understand, accept, and approve the suicide of Socrates but would reject that of Saul. One of the most famous Stoic suicides occurred in 65 A.D., when Seneca, a former teacher of the Roman Emperor Nero, was forced by his mad former pupil to take his own life. This suicide was noteworthy for two reasons. First, it seemed a fitting death for a man who had taught that it is not the quantity but the quality of life that counts. Second, it inspired the self-murder of Seneca's wife, Paulina, which further underlined the quality of life argument, since Paulina chose to die rather than experience the reduced quality of life she expected after her husband's death.

Just as I shall select my ship when I am about to go on a voyage, or my house when I propose to take a residence, so I shall choose my death when I am about to depart from life. Seneca

Suicide in Christianity

The most famous suicide in the New Testament is that of Judas Iscariot, which occurred around 33 A.D. Judas hanged himself after the priests refused to take back the "blood money" they had paid him for his betrayal of Jesus of Nazareth. Once again, the Scriptures are noncommittal about this suicide, merely recording it as a historical fact. Possible motivations for the act include remorse for the betrayal, an attempt at atonement for his breach of faith (similar to the case of Samson), and an element of fulfilling prophecy (similar to the case of King Saul). Judas had heard Jesus predict the betrayal and had heard the accompanying observation: "But woe unto that man by whom the Son of Man is betrayed! It had been good for that man if he had not been born" (Matt. 26:24). For Judas, acting emotionally, and for millions of readers of the Gospel of Matthew over the centuries, the act of self-murder described may represent just punishment for traitorous behavior.

The next entry on the time line is the most controversial by far. Occurring at almost the exact moment in history as the suicide of Judas, it is the death of Jesus of Nazareth. Donne (1644/1982) was the first to assert that this death contained many elements of suicide. Donne, a devout Christian, maintained that Jesus of Nazareth, like Socrates, could have abandoned behaviors which led to his death.

However, Donne maintained that Jesus, unlike Socrates, could also have avoided death because of his divine nature. The fact that he did not choose to avoid it makes this particular death one of the earliest in recorded Christian history that might be classified as an altruistic suicide.

An alternative and more traditional view of the death of Jesus is that he was martyred. Those who hold this view take martyrdom to be clearly different from suicide. Martyrdom occurs when an individual is put to death by others for his or her beliefs; suicide, on the other hand, occurs when an individual takes his or her own life for personal reasons. Given this distinction, the death of Jesus would not be considered a suicide.

Regardless of whether one classifies the death of Jesus of Nazareth as altruistic suicide (following Donne's reasoning) or as martyrdom (following more traditional Christian thought), we include this death on our time line because of its impact on attitudes toward suicide over the centuries. Jesus' death set in motion a series of historical events that caused the Catholic Church and, later, secular law to condemn suicide.

Because of the example of the death of Jesus, many of the early Christians sought martyrdom as a way of asserting their belief and demonstrating the strength of their faith. By 400 A.D., the problem had grown to such dimensions that it could not be ignored. Alvarez (1970) pictured the early Christians as glorifying martyrdom, often seeking even flimsy ways in which to give their lives for their faith. He concluded that "Christian teaching was at first a powerful incitement to suicide" (p. 68). The practice went so far that a sect called the Donatists killed themselves out of respect for martyrdom.

All of this activity led St. Augustine to condemn self-killing around 400 A.D., proclaiming it to be a sin. Later writers (e.g., Shneidman, 1985) have maintained that the basic reason for this condemnation was political: Augustine was concerned for the future of a religious movement that approved or even encouraged martyrdom. At the time, however, the authority for viewing self-killing as sin was found in the Sixth Commandment ("Thou shalt not kill") as well as in the argument that self-killing took the power of life and death out of the purview of the Creator and indicated a desire to avoid accepting the Divine Will in one's life.

Following Augustine's pronouncements, the Catholic Church, in a series of councils held across a period of 160 years, began to build consequences into the act of suicide by Christians. The Council of Orleans in 533 denied funeral rites to people who killed themselves while accused of a crime. The Council of Braga in 563 refused funeral rites to all suicides regardless of social position, reason, or method, and the Council of Toledo in 693 passed a ruling excommunicating people who attempted or committed suicide (Alvarez, 1970).

For the next 500 years, organized Christianity continued to regard suicide as a mortal sin and to punish attempters, completers, and their families in various ways. Survivors could not inherit an estate from a suicide victim. The victim was excommunicated from the church, and burial was conducted in nonhallowed ground. Punishments were also inflicted on suicide victims in order to impress upon others the deeply sinful nature of the act.

The next important milestone in the Church's view of suicide is found in the writings of St. Thomas Aquinas (1225–1274 A.D.). Aquinas tried to incorporate the teachings of Aristotle into prevailing Christian thought in his massive exposition, *Summa Theologica* (1265–1272/1975). In this work, Aquinas gave three reasons to support his view that suicide is wrong. The first is that it is against natural inclination and therefore violates the physical and biological laws set down by the Creator. The second reason echoes Aristotle: Suicide damages the community, both by depriving the community of the talents and energies of the suicide victim and by setting a bad example for others. The third reason is that it does not show proper respect for the most precious of all God-given gifts, life itself.

Growing out of these arguments against suicide came more specific doctrinal statements. For example, self-killing was viewed as a mortal sin because the individual who killed him- or herself could not confess the sin, atone for it, or benefit from the final sacrament of extreme unction. Suicide came to be viewed as a sin also because it revealed a lack of faith in God providing for the needs of humans. In this connection, the depression and despair often seen in suicidal people were interpreted as evidence of lack of hope brought about because of a weakened or nonexistent faith in God. The desperation accompanying impulsive suicides was viewed either as the work of the devil or as final evidence that the victim had discounted the power of the Divine Savior. In either case, the act itself was considered sinful, so sinful that in 1284 at the Synod of Nimes, Christian burial was denied to suicides and they were forced to be buried in nonhallowed ground

Suicide is the worst form of murder, because it leaves no opportunity for repentance. Churton Collins, *Aphorisms*

(Hutton & Valente, 1984). Soon after this stricture was enforced, more punitive customs began to gain popularity. For example, it was not unusual for the bodies of suicide victims to be dragged behind carts or buried at crossroads with stakes in their hearts (Farberow, 1975).

By the time John Donne wrote *Biathanatos*, in the middle of the 17th century, church teaching about suicide had become rigid, and there was no doubt that suicide was considered one of the worst sins, if not the worst, that humans could commit. In *Biathanatos*, Donne re-examined the case of self-killing and specifically argued against the points raised by the Christian church in declaring suicide a sin. It is telling that the book was shared only with a few close friends while Donne lived and that it was published only after his death. In their commentary, modern authors credit Donne with being the first to suggest that human beings have a natural desire to die as well as a desire to live (Donne, 1644/1982). For this reason, Donne, rather than Freud, should perhaps be credited as the first to explicate the concept of thanatos. To support his claim that humans are attracted to death, Donne cited examples of group suicides as well as almost two dozen individual suicides. In a wide-ranging, well-informed discussion, he highlighted the practice of suttee in India, the group suicides of Jews at Masada, suicides of New World Indians, and, perhaps most tellingly, the suicides of the early Christian martyrs. Donne's modern interpreters argue that, for Donne, this desire to die on the part of the Christian martyrs was less a wish for self-destruction than a measure of their faith, their desire to change their current pattern of existence, and their belief in the "spiritual comforts of the afterlife" (Donne, 1644/1982, p. 111).

Donne did not endorse widespread self-murder, but he did recognize that suicide occurs for many reasons, and he argued that individuals who kill themselves in order to promote the glory of God do not sin. In this way, Donne is perhaps the first author to call attention to the motivation for or intention behind a given suicide as a determining factor in whether it should be considered right or wrong. Donne also foreshadowed one side of a current ethical debate when he proclaimed that there is no moral difference between acts of omission and acts of commission in taking one's own life. Thus Donne would label as suicidal a man who allowed himself to be killed by an enemy without trying to defend himself, a woman who starved herself for a principle, a man who went without medical care for an increasingly serious physical condition, or a woman who shot or poisoned herself. He would not, however, necessarily judge any of them as sinners. Rather, the *intention* behind the act would determine the sinfulness of the act. In this context, Donne also foreshadowed some of the elements of Kohlberg's modern theory of moral development, which maintains that it is not the behavior but the reason behind the behavior that determines the level of morality of an act. In the end, however, *Biathanatos* did not argue for a legalization of suicide or even a lessening of the strictures against suicidal people and their families. Donne finally approved only one kind of suicide, that carried out for the glory of God. Suicides of all other kinds seemed to Donne to be based on the suicidal person's own desires for comfort rather than on God's will; therefore, he concluded that they should not be allowed.

The next date on the time line is 1651, which seems to be the year when the word *suicide* was introduced into the English language. There is some difference of opinion about the origin of the word. Farberow (1975) suggests two possible derivations. The first suggestion is that it derives from the word *suist*, meaning a selfish man. The second suggestion, perhaps more believable, is that it derives from the Latin word *suicidium*. The Latin roots of this word seem clear: *sui*, a pronoun meaning him- or herself, and *cedo*, a verb meaning to give up.

In 1670, under the influence of the Christian religion, legislation was passed making suicide a triple crime. It was considered not only murder but also high treason and heresy (Farberow, 1975). This was the period in which punishment became common both for the deceased and for his or her family. Aries (1981) pointed out that "men of the middle ages and of early modern times did not believe that the cause of justice or of legal action stopped with the death of the defendant. In the case of a suicide, they prosecuted the dead man in court, and his body was ejected from the cemetery" (p. 44). Alvarez (1970) cited another example of such punishment for suicide which occurred as late as 1860.

Death may be call'd in vain, and cannot come, Tyrants can tie him up from your relief: Nor has a Christian privilege to die. Alas, thou art too young in thy new faith. Brutus and Cato might discharge their souls: But we like sentries are oblig'd to stand In starless nights, and wait th' appointed hour. Dryden, *Don Sebastian*, Act II, Sc.1

A man was hanged who had cut his throat, but who had been brought back to life. They hanged him for suicide. The doctor warned them that it was impossible to hang him as the throat would burst open and he would breathe through the aperture. They did not listen to his advice and hanged the man. The wound in the neck immediately opened and the man came back to life again although he was hanged. It took time to convoke the alderman to decide the question of what was to be done. At length the alderman assembled and bound up the neck below the wound until he died. (p. 45)

Suicide in Secular Society

An important milestone in the history of suicide occurred in 1763, when Merian, a Frenchman, published a treatise which attempted to establish that suicide was neither a crime nor a sin but resulted from emotional illness (Merian, 1763). This was followed by Hume's *Essay on Suicide* (1783/1929). In this work, Hume argued that suicide was not a crime against God, neighbors, or self and therefore did not deserve the extreme punishments common at that time.

To attempt suicide is a criminal offense. Any man who, of his own will, tries to escape the treadmill to which the rest of us feel chained incites our envy, and therefore our fury. We do not suffer him to go unpunished. Alexander Chase, *Perspectives*

The Suicide, Thomas Rowlandson. Pen and watercolor drawing. (Courtesy of the Boston Public Library, Print Department.)

The 19th century witnessed writings on the topic of suicide by philosophers as well as by scientists and medical doctors. In 1838, Esquirol, writing from a medical perspective, echoed Merian's earlier sentiment that people who commit suicide suffer from a mental condition or are insane. With the rise of existentialism, philosophers such as Kierkegaard and Nietzsche (followed by Heidegger, Sartre, and Camus in the 20th century) introduced the idea that individual freedom to act and responsibility for one's acts are fundamental characteristics of the human condition. Many considered suicide merely one more act that a human being had to make a decision about (or a series of decisions over a lifetime), weighing both freedom and responsibility to self and others.

The 19th century closed with the publication of one of the most influential books of all time on the subject of suicide, Emile

Durkheim's *Suicide* (1897/1951). The content of this work is discussed in detail in Chapter 2. It remains an influential work to this day for two reasons. First, it made a case for using sociological methods to understand an individual phenomenon. According to Durkheim, when a person commits suicide, one must investigate not only the particulars of the individual situation but also the values of the society and the amount of integration or isolation the suicidal individual experienced. Second, Durkheim introduced the first widely discussed typology for classifying suicides, a practice that would proliferate in the 20th century.

The 20th century witnessed a major turnabout in attitudes toward suicide. Christianity began to consider routinely the state of mind of a suicide victim at the time of the act as an extenuating circumstance. In this way, the church could be less judgmental toward a suicide victim and the survivors, because the victim was not necessarily a sinner condemned to hell but could be regarded as someone whose mind was unclear and therefore not subject to judgment.

In addition to decreasing disapproval by the church, suicide also came to be viewed less harshly from other perspectives as much of Western society moved toward secularism. With the increase of secularism, suicide began to be regarded less as a sin and more as a sign of mental illness. This change in view was not altogether positive, however, as families of suicide victims often found themselves trying to cover up the cause of the death rather than face the disgrace of having to admit "insanity" in the family.

Freud published two important works that added to the understanding of suicide as mental illness. The first was *Mourning and Melancholia* (1917/1961), in which he introduced intrapsychic reasons for suicide. He maintained that suicide results when anger, harbored by the id toward some outside force, is turned inward upon the ego. In this work, he also laid the base for his concept of thanatos, the death instinct. In a later work, *The Ego and the Id*, Freud returned to the theme, stating in effect that suicide could be caused because the superego, for many complex reasons, could become "a pure culture of the death instinct" and turn its full strength against the ego (Freud, 1923/1961, p. 53).

At the same time that Freud's theories were spreading throughout the Western world, the influence of the scientific method was also spreading. Inevitably, that methodology was directed toward the study of suicide, and in 1958, with the aid of a 5-year grant from the U.S. Public Health Service, Shneidman and his colleagues established the first suicide prevention center in the United States. That center was designed to address the nonmedical needs of suicidal people. It had three major goals: (1) to save lives, (2) to serve as a major public health agency for the Los Angeles community, and (3) to test "various hypotheses concerning suicidal phenomena." Thus, this center had a clinical mission, a community service mission, and a research mission. The Los Angeles Center quickly became the model for suicide intervention and prevention centers throughout the United States during the last half of the 20th century.

In addition to its critical lifesaving work, this important center carried out studies and began to build a wealth of factual material. In 1961, Shneidman, Farberow, and Litman increased our understanding of suicide by debunking ten myths using data from their Los Angeles research as well as their combined knowledge of the history of suicide. These myths were as follows:

1. *People who talk about suicide won't commit suicide*. Their studies at that time indicated that a full 75% of those who committed suicide had talked about it or threatened it earlier.
2. *Suicide happens without any warning*. Their studies indicated that warnings and clues generally occur but are often overlooked until after the fact.
3. *Improvement after a suicidal crisis means that the suicide risk is over*. Their research indicated that almost half of the suicidal people whom they saw through the crisis period committed suicide within 90 days—after they seemed to be recovering well.
4. *Suicide and depression are synonymous*. While the L.A. group continued to maintain that depression remained the best indicator of suicide, they also reported instances of agitation, psychosis, anxiety, and other symptoms that led to suicide attempts.
5. *All suicidal persons are insane*. Confronting this myth was of major importance to the field. In a study of over 700 genuine suicide notes, the authors maintained that many showed rational logic. They pointed to a large minority of suicidal patients who were old, in physical pain, or both but whose notes were rational. In addition, they also detected ambivalence about the act in a majority of notes. They concluded that "the majority of persons who commit suicide are tormented and ambivalent; i.e., they are neurotic or have a character disorder, but are not insane" (Shneidman, Farberow, & Litman, 1961, p. 13).
6. *Suicide is a single disease*. Because of the multiple types of suicide seen at the clinic, the authors viewed it as a complex phenomenon rather than a single entity, and they called for "the development of a taxonomy or classification of types of suicide" (p. 14).
7. *Suicide is immoral*. The authors, familiar with the history of attitudes toward suicide, agreed with sociologists that "whether or not one thinks of suicide as immoral depends on the time and place in which one happens to live" (p. 14).
8. *Suicide can be controlled by legislation*. The authors main-

tained that you cannot legislate suicide out of existence. They pointed out that the effect of punitive legislation might be to increase the lethality of the attempt so that the individual will not face punishment or, in the case of a failed attempt, might cause the attempter not to seek out needed psychological and physical care.

9. *The tendency to suicide is inherited.* The authors rejected this assumption, claiming that there was not enough data to support such a notion and that children of suicides who later committed suicide might just as easily do so because of the modeling effect of the parental suicide as from a genetic predisposition.

10. *Suicide is the "curse of the poor" or the "disease of the rich."* The authors maintained that controlled studies indicated that "almost all strata contribute their pro rata share to the overall suicide rate."

The importance of the Los Angeles Suicide Prevention Center cannot be overstated in any history of suicide. The work begun in that center by Shneidman and his associates and expanded upon later, when Shneidman became director of the Suicide Center in the National Institute of Mental Health, changed the nation's view of suicide and suicidal behavior. The most important change was a shift away from seeing suicide as an act committed by an insane person to seeing it as an act committed by a person who felt overwhelming ambivalence toward life. Suicidal people came to be regarded as individuals who needed help to find reasons to live, and the view of "suicide as a cry for help" became common. The major implication of this new view was that an interruption in the trajectory toward suicide might result in an individual changing his or her mind about living, and as a result crisis intervention centers became commonplace in urban areas. Many were and still are staffed by volunteers, trained to handle the emergency situation until longer-term supportive therapy can be arranged.

Although the crisis intervention philosophy had already begun, attitudes toward suicide remained contradictory well after the midpoint of the century. Still officially condemned by the Catholic church as a mortal sin, suicide was also viewed as the ultimate evil by many other religious sects. For example, the Church of Jesus Christ of Latter Day Saints, one of the fastest growing denominations in the 20th century, maintained that "mortal life is a gift of God; it comes according to the divine will, is appointed to endure for such time as Deity decrees, and is designed to serve as the chief testing period of man's eternal existence. No man has the right to run away from these tests, no matter how severe they may be, by taking his own life" (McConkie, 1966, p. 771).* The treatise did go on to make the now

*Copyright © 1966 by Bookcraft, Inc. Used by permission.

common exception based on mental condition, "Obviously persons subject to great stresses may lose control of themselves and become mentally clouded to the point that they are no longer accountable for their acts. Such are not to be condemned for taking their own lives" (p. 771).

In contrast, one of the oldest non-Christian religions in the world, Judaism, has relied on its historical traditions for its interpretations. The Jewish position throughout history has been to abhor suicide and to relegate the punishment for suicide to God in the hereafter. However, the Talmudic tradition has recognized and accepted (if not approved) suicides that fit in two different categories. The first category contains suicides that occur when death is imminent and that enable people to avoid a painful or disgraceful demise. Examples of such suicides include King Saul and the deaths of 960 Jewish defenders of Masada in 73 A.D. The second category contains suicides that are committed to avoid abandoning the Jewish faith.

In 1976, Cohn reviewed suicide in the Jewish legal and religious tradition and concluded that it is difficult to prove that any given death is a suicide. Cohn (1976) stated that "suicide can be proved only by two eye-witnesses who saw the actor committing the act after having been warned by them, or after having declared to them, that it was forbidden and unlawful to do so" (p. 136). Thus, in the Jewish tradition, both the motivation for suicide and the state of mind of the individual committing the act is taken into consideration. In addition, the term *suicide* is not applied to minors (because they are not capable of forming the necessary criminal intent) or to depressed or mentally disturbed persons. Although it is difficult to determine when a suicide has occurred, the Jewish tradition still employs some punishments for the act when it can be documented:

> *Still, Jewish ritual denies the suicide certain honours due to the dead: suicides are given no funeral orations, and the mourners' clothes may not be rent for them. In many places it has become customary to set aside a particular portion of the cemetery for the burial of suicides, so as not to bury the wicked next to the righteous. The general rule is that on the death of the suicide you do everything in honour of the surviving, such as visit and comfort and console them, but you do nothing in honour of the dead apart from burying them. (Cohn, 1976, pp. 135–136, S. Karger AG, Basel)*

As the century nears its end, researchers into the chemistry of the brain are making valuable contributions to our understanding of suicide. Chapter 2 documents some of the major findings to date. Another major avenue of research and theory formation, also discussed in Chapter 2, emerged from the work of Beck and his colleagues into the cognitive state of depressives. Building upon the techniques of the behavioral school of psychology, these

therapists attempted to modify the rigid and perfectionist thinking patterns common to depressed, suicidal people.

Another influence on attitudes toward suicide in the latter
half of the 20th century has been the spectacular increase in
medical discoveries and the rapid development of medical technology. Beginning with the discovery of penicillin by Fleming in
1928, medicine has become increasingly able to prolong life. Life
expectancy increased almost 30 years from the beginning of the
20th century until now, because of improved understanding of
the disease process, improvements in childbirth procedures, advances in the prevention and treatment of disease, and technological advances in the treatment of traumas and terminal illness.
Ironically, the capability to prolong life beyond any useful function with the aid of such devices as respirators has coincided with
an increasing need for donor organs to help maintain other lives,
setting the stage for heated ethical debates about the right to die
and the rules surrounding transplantation and blurring the lines
between suicide and euthanasia.

While many people differentiate between euthanasia and
suicide, many more think the purported distinction is a matter
of "splitting hairs." The latter question whether there is any real
difference between actively taking your own life and creating the
conditions for your own death. For example, John Brantner, an
early leader in the field of death and dying, actively committed
suicide a few years ago. His suicide seemed to be a response to
the knowledge that he was terminally ill and to be based on a
wish to retain control of his life until the time of his death.
Because he had been a public figure in the so-called "death movement," his suicide was widely publicized. Some people assumed
that his suicide was a form of self-performed euthanasia, that he
had chosen what for him was "an appropriate death," that he had
indeed "died with dignity." Some critics, however, condemned
his action, stating that suicide under any circumstance is wrong
and that the principle of the sanctity of life must be defended no
matter what the situation. These same critics would insist that
a terminally ill woman who carefully arranges her affairs, enters
a hospital stating that her wish is to die, and declines nourishment
is as guilty of suicide as was Dr. Brantner, since she too arranged
the conditions of her death. To these people, terminating life or
allowing it to be terminated violates the principle that God is the
only judge of when and how one should die.

The majority of people probably hold a moderate position
on the subject. Two principles seem to be important in the thinking of the moderates. The first is that the rights of the individual
are primary in any situation. The second is that death is both
natural and inevitable and that it is not necessarily the province
of God alone. In support of these principles, over 30 states have
passed "right to die" legislation. Such legislation, while differing
in language from state to state, endorses the right of persons to

refuse treatment as well as the right to establish the conditions under which they would wish to die. Most of these states still have laws which make aiding and abetting suicide a crime. It is clear that many of the legislators in these states, since they ascribe to both of these laws, do not believe that arranging the circumstances of one's death under controlled conditions and while one is in good mental health is a form of suicide. One key to understanding the difference between suicide and euthanasia, according to the moderates, lies in the action necessary to bring about death. Passive euthanasia (i.e., allowing an individual to die by withholding treatment, food, or water) is allowable. Active euthanasia (i.e., helping an individual to die by injecting too much pain-killing drugs or by cutting off life support systems) is not allowable. Active euthanasia is covered by the laws against aiding and abetting suicide.

It is clear that in the latter part of the 20th century, the issues of suicide and euthanasia are controversial. Organizations such as Concern for Dying (formerly the Euthanasia Council) and EXIT are vocal in their insistence on the individual's right to death with dignity. The Hemlock Society, established in England, has even introduced the term *rational suicide* in their material. Thus, the ancient arguments of the Stoics are being heard again in classrooms, hospitals, and in the courts of many developed countries. The vigor of the arguments being heard internationally attests to the confusion that still exists about these topics. Clearly, the three conflicting views cannot co-exist. The most conservative view maintains that life is sacred and not to be shortened under any circumstances. The most liberal view maintains that an individual's life belongs to him- or herself and that he or she can choose to end it whenever it becomes unbearable to continue. This view incorporates a qualified endorsement of suicide. The moderate view maintains that under carefully controlled conditions, with special pre-arrangements in place, life may be shortened by passive means, but that people cannot be helped to commit suicide by active means. Although this controversy is not likely to be entirely settled in the remaining years of the 20th century, it has provoked much thought and discussion and has created the conditions for a re-examination of all facets of suicide.

THE STATISTICAL PICTURE

Even as discussion about the complexities of suicide proliferates, suicides continue to occur throughout the world. One of the central features of the information age we live in is our ability to collect reliable data about any phenomenon that occurs, at least in developed countries. Table 1.2 lists suicide rates for selected countries by sex and age group. The table shows that suicide remains an issue in the 12 countries which reported their suicide statistics between 1983 and 1985. It is clear that suicide rates vary widely among these countries, with Italy reporting the lowest

TABLE 1.2 Suicide Rates for Selected Countries by Sex and Age Group

(Rate per 100,000 population. Includes deaths resulting from self-inflicted injuries. Except as noted, deaths classified according to the ninth revision of the International Classification of Diseases [ICD].)

Sex and age	United States 1983	Australia 1984	Austria 1985	Canada 1984	Denmark[1] 1984	France 1984	Italy 1981	Japan 1985	Netherlands 1984	Poland 1984	Sweden[1] 1984	United Kingdom[2] 1984
Male												
Total[3]	19.2	16.9	40.9	21.4	36.5	32.2	9.8	26.0	15.2	23.6	27.4	11.8
15–24 yrs. old	18.8	18.8	31.9	26.9	16.1	16.3	5.0	13.0	7.0	18.2	16.4	7.5
25–34 yrs. old	25.4	23.9	42.5	27.8	37.7	33.6	8.3	23.4	18.6	36.3	36.5	14.0
35–44 yrs. old	22.7	20.1	53.6	25.3	53.2	36.7	8.9	30.5	19.0	37.0	36.5	16.5
45–54 yrs. old	23.7	22.7	56.3	28.6	57.1	43.8	14.0	49.6	22.5	39.0	42.2	18.2
55–64 yrs. old	25.7	24.3	53.9	28.8	65.5	46.1	16.3	41.4	23.7	31.2	30.5	16.8
65–74 yrs. old	31.7	24.7	71.9	25.1	48.8	64.9	24.9	42.6	28.6	29.1	37.9	17.0
75 yrs. old and over	50.7	30.4	95.3	33.0	67.3	116.7	36.4	74.8	42.7	29.7	47.5	22.5
Female												
Total[3]	5.4	5.2	15.7	6.1	21.0	12.4	4.0	13.1	9.6	4.9	11.8	5.7
15–24 yrs. old	4.2	4.4	7.9	4.3	4.1	4.5	1.7	5.9	3.7	3.8	6.2	6.1
25–34 yrs. old	6.6	6.5	10.2	7.0	12.9	11.5	3.1	9.8	10.1	5.7	15.3	3.8
35–44 yrs. old	7.9	6.7	20.5	9.2	28.3	13.9	4.3	11.9	11.1	6.6	15.3	6.4
45–54 yrs. old	8.9	10.6	19.1	10.5	41.1	17.6	5.2	17.3	14.8	8.3	20.1	9.8
55–64 yrs. old	8.3	8.2	22.4	10.7	38.1	18.4	7.8	18.6	17.3	8.0	15.0	10.7
65–74 yrs. old	7.3	6.5	31.0	8.4	37.7	25.3	9.5	29.7	21.2	7.5	17.9	10.6
75 yrs. old and over	6.1	5.7	32.2	5.8	32.2	28.8	7.7	54.3	14.6	6.4	11.7	10.0

[1]Based on the eighth revision of the ICD. [2]England and Wales only. [3]Includes other age groups not shown separately.
Source: U.S. Bureau of the Census (1988). *Statistical abstract of the United States:* (108th Edition) Washington, DC, 1987, p. 803.

18

figures for both males and females and Austria reporting the highest figures. The United States ranks 8th among the countries in its rate of male suicide and 9th among the countries in its rate of female suicide.

Table 1.2 shows also that the pattern of suicide by age varies among the countries reporting suicide statistics, a point which is pertinent to the focus of this volume. Not only are there different suicide rates for different age groups, but in general suicide tends to increase with age. Closer examination of the pattern of suicide by age shows that for males the pattern is generally linear. With only a few exceptions in the middle years, suicide increases across the age span for males in all countries. For females the pattern is more variable. In five countries (the United States, Australia, Denmark, Poland, and Sweden), suicide among women peaks during the period from 45 to 54. In two countries (Canada and the United Kingdom), suicide among women peaks during the period from 55 to 64. In the remaining five countries (Austria, France, Italy, Japan, and the Netherlands), the suicide rate of women mimics that of men, increasing in frequency across the life span. Having established that suicide is a worldwide phenomenon, we will now turn our attention to a detailed picture of suicide in the United States.

The advance report of mortality statistics for 1986 showed that suicide was the 8th leading cause of death for the general population in the United States, accounting for 30,904 deaths in that year, for a rate of 12.7 per 100,000 population (National Center for Health Statistics, 1988). In the white male population, suicide was the 7th leading cause of death, with a rate of 20.5 per 100,000 population. Among females and blacks, suicide did not rank among the top 10 causes of death. In fact, the female rate of suicide has been declining since the late 70s.

Table 1.3 provides detailed age-adjusted statistics regarding suicide rates per 100,000 by sex and race in the United States in 1986. The table shows that the suicide rate of white males is two times the rate of black males and four times the rate of white females.

Table 1.4 shows the suicide rates per 100,000 by age for 1986. The pattern, influenced heavily by the white male suicide rate,

TABLE 1.3 U.S. Suicide Rates per 100,000 by Sex and Race for 1986

	White		All other		Black		Total	
	Number	Rate	Number	Rate	Number	Rate	Number	Rate
Male	22,270	20.5	1,956	11.5	1,537	11.5	24,226	19.3
Female	6,167	5.4	511	2.7	355	2.4	6,678	5.1
Both sexes	28,437	12.7	2,467	6.8	1,892	6.6	30,904	11.9

Source: National Center for Health Statistics, *Advance report of final mortality statistics, 1986*, p. 38, Sept. 30, 1988.

TABLE 1.4   Suicide Rates Per 100,000 by Age for 1986

Age	Rate
Under 1 year	—
1–4	—
5–14	0.8
15–24	13.1
25–34	15.7
35–44	15.2
45–54	16.4
55–64	17.0
65–74	19.7
75–84	25.2
85+	20.8
All ages	12.8

Source: National Center for Health Statistics, *Advance Report of Final Mortality Statistics, 1986*, p. 38, September 30, 1988.

shows that suicide increases in frequency until age 85. However, it is important to note that the relative significance of suicide as a cause of death differs with age. For example, suicide is the 6th leading cause of death between ages 5 and 14. It is the 3rd leading cause of death between ages 15 and 24. It drops to the 4th leading cause of death between ages 25 and 44 and to the 8th leading cause between age 45 and 64. After age 65, it does not appear among the top 10 causes of death.

Suicide rates alone cannot tell the whole story about the cost of suicide to a nation. McGinnis (1987) has reported that between 1970 and 1980 there were 287,322 suicides in the United States, for an average of one suicide every 20 minutes. Each of these suicides results in years of potential life lost to our society. The National Center for Health Statistics has developed a way to estimate years of potential life lost (YPLL). The YPLL attributable to suicide by year, race, and sex in the United States between 1968 and 1983 are shown in Fig. 1.1. It is obvious from the figure that the suicides of white males were more costly in terms of YPLL than those of any other group. Also, the figure shows that the YPLL rate has increased considerably since 1968 because of the shift in the age of people committing suicide. Since the 1950s, suicide rates for young people have increased while those for older people have gradually decreased (Centers for Disease Control, 1986).

Suicide was the fifth leading cause of YPLL in the United States in 1983, accounting for a total of 631,990 years lost. A breakdown of YPLL before age 65 because of suicide for the year 1983 appears in Table 1.5. It is apparent that white males accounted for most of the YPLL (70.6%), while white females accounted for another 19.7%. The estimate of YPLL is greatly deflated because of underreporting of suicides on death certificates. As

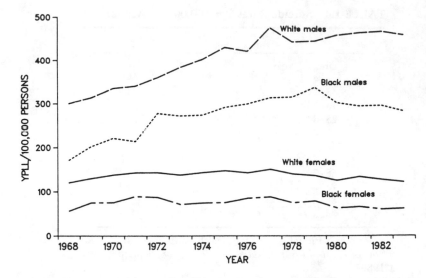

FIGURE 1.1 Suicide-attributable Years of Potential Life Lost (YPLL) by Year, Race, and Sex—United States, 1968–1983 Source: *Morbidity and Mortality Weekly Report,* **June 6, 1986, p. 338.**

reported in the *Morbidity and Mortality Weekly Report* on premature mortality, "Reasons for this underreporting include difficulties in establishing suicide intent, certifier error or bias, and the lack of awareness of a suicide because a body was never recovered" (Centers for Disease Control, 1986, p. 360).

These data, dramatic as they are, do not begin to measure the extent of suicidal behavior in the United States at this time. In a recent survey, 200 medical examiners were asked to estimate the number of suicides that are not reported as such. More than 50% indicated that the reported number of suicides was possibly less than half of the actual number (Jobes, Berman, & Josselsen,

TABLE 1.5   Years of Potential Life Lost (YPLL) Before Age 65 Because of Suicide, 1983

Sex and race	Total	Percentage	Rate per 100,000 persons
Males			
White	445,890	70.6	458.1
Black	37,524	5.9	282.6
Other	11,485	1.8	368.7
All	494,899	78.3	435.2
Females			
White	124,475	19.7	121.7
Black	9,085	1.4	61.4
Other	3,531	0.6	108.9
All	137,091	21.7	114.0
Total	631,990	100.0	270.1

Source: *Morbidity and Mortality Weekly Report,* June 6, 1986, p. 338.

1986). In addition, it is estimated that for every completed suicide there are 8 to 20 attempts at suicide that are not reported (Farberow & Shneidman, 1961; McIntosh, 1985). If one considers other forms of suicidal behavior (e.g., drug abuse, drunken driving, high-risk sports, etc.), the total picture for the United States becomes even grimmer. Suicide and suicidal behaviors will be major health issues for the population of the United States in the last decade of the century. Because of the frequency of suicidal behaviors and the cost to our society, the subject of suicide deserves detailed examination and careful analysis.

TOWARD A DEFINITION OF SUICIDE

Thus far, we have examined suicide across time and to a lesser extent across cultures. It is clear that the attitudes of others toward the act of suicide is dependent upon many factors. For example, the dominant religion of a given period may embrace martyrs for the faith, as in the early days of Christianity, or condemn suicidal persons to posthumous punishments, as in the years between St. Thomas Aquinas's writings and the advent of science in the 1900s. Also, in this century, as in the time of the Stoics, many people seek to discover the motivation of an individual who commits or tries to commit suicide before passing judgment. Is the individual aged and infirm, in the throes of terminal pain, psychotic, depressed, or emotionally overwrought and impulsive? The answers to such questions now color our reaction and response to any given suicide.

Up to this point, we have discussed suicide without giving a definition of the term. We have mentioned in our historical overview suicides that today might be viewed as active euthanasia (e.g., King Saul), forced suicides that today might be considered substitutes for murder (e.g., Socrates), and altruistic suicides, where an individual lays down his or her life for a greater good or for another person (e.g., Jesus and the early Christian martyrs). And we have regarded all of these types of self-induced death as forms of suicide.

For the purpose of the remainder of this book, we will adopt a broad definition for the term *suicide*. Shneidman (1985), devoting a whole book to defining suicide, concluded with a definition which is perhaps the clearest given to date: "Currently in the Western world, suicide is a conscious act of self-induced annihilation, best understood as a multidimensional malaise in a needful individual who defines an issue for which the suicide is perceived as the best solution" (p. 203). We accept Shneidman's definition with one addition. We believe that a broad definition of suicide should be consistent with the moderate view of euthanasia. A terminally ill person may not manifest "multidimensional malaise" as he or she seeks to actively terminate life, yet we view active euthanasia, but not passive euthanasia, as suicide.

We accept Shneidman's definition, because it clearly recognizes that any definition of suicide is "timebound" and relative to various societies. A 10-year-old child who knowingly stands in the path of oncoming traffic and is killed would be classified as a suicide according to this definition. So would an air force pilot who chooses to go down with her plane rather than to ditch it over a heavily populated area. So would an elderly man who takes an overdose of medication, hastening his death. Obviously so would people who shoot or hang themselves or find other overt ways of shortening their lives.

As we attempt to shed light on suicidal behavior across the life span, we will use the term *attempted suicide* in place of the term *parasuicide*. While we are cognizant of the movement toward using the term *parasuicide* to refer to all self-damaging behavior which falls short of death, we will not use it that way for two reasons. First, we feel it sets up a false dichotomy between suicide attempters and completers; second, we will be reviewing literature which either was written before this terminology was introduced or specifically rejects the rationale behind the use of such terminology.

A LOOK AHEAD

This book focuses on suicide from a developmental perspective. The demographics show clearly that, although suicide occurs in all age ranges but the very youngest, the pattern of suicide differs by age. For example, adolescents and young adults have shown a dramatic increase in their suicide rate during the past 30 years, while elderly adults have shown a significant decrease. The entire book will focus on patterns of suicide in different age groups, with Chapter 8 providing a synthesis from a life span perspective.

In addition to examining age differences, we will also examine the intriguing sex differences in suicidal behavior across the life span. The greatest sex differential among the 15 leading causes of death in 1985 was for suicide. In that year males completed suicide 3.8 times more often than did females (National Center for Health Statistics, 1987). However, for many years females have attempted suicide at a rate estimated to be 4 to 8 times higher than the rate of male attempts (Van Fossen, 1985). It seems plausible that suicidal actions mean different things to males and females and that the different meanings also differ by age or cohort group.

A final interesting difference in suicidal behavior is found between the races. In 1986, whites in the United States had a suicide rate of 12.7 per 100,000, blacks had a suicide rate of 6.6 per 100,000, and members of all other races had a suicide rate of 6.8 per 100,000 (National Center for Health Statistics, 1988).

It is clear that age, sex, and race are powerful factors influencing suicide and attempted suicide. However, it is our view that developmental influences also must be taken into account in trying to understand suicidal behavior. Why do males more frequently complete suicide? Did they learn somewhere in their early sex role lessons that "real males" succeed in everything they do? Did they learn that to ask for help is a sign of weakness and that decisive, aggressive behavior, even directed against oneself, is a sign of strength? Are they influenced by the view that a man's worth is proportional to his earning ability and do they thus become more susceptible to suicide after retirement or after financial reversals? Do females attempt suicide more often but complete it less often because they have been taught that help will be available when they need it? Are blacks and other minority persons in the United States somehow inoculated against suicide because of the early hardships inherent in living in a society where the majority culture is different from theirs? Are elderly suicide victims of both sexes also victims of learned stereotypes that maintain that human life is worthwhile only so long as a person is productive? If the answer to any of these questions is yes, then we must consider the messages repeated across the life span of the developing individual to have a strong influence on suicidal behavior.

In addition to examining how learning and development may contribute to suicide, we recognize that there is a major trend toward examining the biological bases of many behaviors, including suicide. In Chapter 2, we will review some of the evidence of biological involvement in suicide as well as selected psychological and sociological views of suicide.

The heart of the book lies in the review of research and writing from a developmental perspective in Chapters 3 through 6. Chapter 3 examines childhood suicide. Chapter 4 details the growing incidence of suicide among teens and young adults. Chapter 5 considers the demographics of suicide in middle adulthood from the perspective of adult development theorists. Chapter 6 reviews the growing literature on suicide among the elderly.

In Chapter 7, we present a discussion of the parameters of prevention, intervention, and postvention programs—written once again from a developmental perspective. Finally, in Chapter 8 we discuss in detail the assumptions inherent in a developmental perspective, and we draw conclusions and provide a synthesis regarding suicide across the life span from the information provided in the previous chapters.

In this book, there is a bias which runs from the first to the last page. This bias results from our belief that the study of suicidal behavior is enriched by approaching the topic from a life span perspective. Although there are many commonalities which occur in all age groups, in other important ways suicide is a phenomenon which differs from one developmental level to another. The differences have important implications for understanding suicide and for prevention, intervention, and postvention activities. A fuller understanding of suicide from a life span developmental perspective will enable us to work more effectively with suicidal individuals of all ages.

Another bias that runs throughout this book should be evident from the subtitle, *Premature Exits*. In general, with few exceptions, we believe that suicide should be discouraged, that it results in waste and unnecessary loss. We endorse the old cliche that suicide is a permanent solution to what is most likely a temporary problem. This position becomes clearest in Chapters 7 and 8; however, we believe the reader should be warned at the outset that all chapters manifest this bias. This is not a neutral book. It reviews the literature on suicide but it does so from a values position. Put most concisely, the values position holds that all of life from infancy through old age is an adventure in the development of individuality and that suicide cancels the adventure and causes premature foreclosure of a person's developing uniqueness.

SUMMARY

In this chapter we have reviewed the major milestones of the history of suicide in the Western world. We have reviewed suicide in ancient Greece and Rome, in the history of Christianity, and in historical and recent secular society, culminating in the suicide prevention movement that began in the United States in the 1950s. Several different historical and current attitudes toward suicide have been described, including views of suicide as a rational act, as a sin, as a transgression against community, as altruistic behavior, as a result of societal influence, as evidence of insanity, and as evidence of emotional distress and ambivalence toward life.

Ten modern myths about suicide, myths disproven by research growing out of the suicide prevention movement, were discussed. The importance of recent progress in research on brain chemistry and depression as well as medical advances which prolong life was noted. Special attention was given to the growing ethical dilemma regarding euthanasia and its relationship to attitudes about suicide.

Statistical data were provided regarding present suicide rates in the United States and in other developed countries. Special attention was given to sex and race differences in suicide rates over the life span.

Shneidman's definition of suicide was presented and accepted (with one modification) as a working definition to be used throughout this book. We broadened Shneidman's definition to include active euthanasia as a kind of suicide—a kind which can occur in the absence of extreme "multidimensional malaise."

Finally, the major focus of each of the following chapters was previewed. The reader was also warned about two biases

which are woven throughout this book. First, we are strongly
committed to a developmental perspective as an important way
of viewing suicide at any age. Second, we are opposed to suicide
as a solution to problems except in the most extreme circumstances.

REFERENCES

Alvarez, A. (1970). *The savage god: A study of suicide.* London: George Weidenfeld
    & Nicolson Limited.
Aquinas, T. (1975). *Summa theologica* (Vol. 38). London: Blackfriars. (Original
    work written 1265–1272.)
Aries, P. (1981). *The hour of our death.* New York: Knopf.
Bromberg, S., & Cassel, C. (1983). Suicide in the elderly: The limits of paternalism.
    Journal of the American Geriatrics Society, 31(11), 698–703.
Centers for Disease Control. (1986). *Mortality and Morbidity Weekly Report,
    35*(22).
Cohn, H. (1976). Suicide in Jewish legal and religious tradition. *Mental Health
    and Society, 3,* 129–136.
Donne, J. (1982). *Biathanatos* (M. Rudick & M. P. Battin, Trans.). New York:
    Garland. (Original work published 1644.)
Durkheim, E. (1951). *Suicide* (J. A. Spaulding & G. Simpson, Trans.). Glencoe, IL:
    The Free Press. (Original work published 1897.)
Farberow, N. (Ed.). (1975). *Suicide in different cultures.* Baltimore, MD: University
    Park Press.
Farberow, N., & Shneidman, E. (1961). *The cry for help.* New York: McGraw-Hill.
Freud, S. (1961). *Mourning and melancholia.* In J. Strachey (Ed. and Trans.). *The
    standard edition of the complete psychological works of Sigmund Freud*
    (Vol. 14, pp. 243–258). London: Hogarth Press. (Original work published
    1917.)
Freud, S. (1961). *The ego and the id.* In J. Strachey (Ed. and Trans.). *The standard
    edition of the complete psychological works of Sigmund Freud* (Vol. 19,
    pp. 3–66). London: Hogarth Press. (Original work published 1923.)
Harmet, A. R. (Ed.). (1984). *The World Book Encyclopedia* (Vol. 18, p. 770). Chi-
    cago: World Book.
The Holy Bible. (1949). (King James edition). New York: American Bible Society.
Hume, D. (1929). *An essay on suicide.* Yellow Springs, OH: Kahoe. (Original work
    published 1783.)
Hutton, C. L., & Valente, S. M. (1984). *Suicide: Assessment and intervention* (2nd
    ed.). Norwalk, CT: Appleton-Century-Crofts.
Jobes, D. A., Berman, A. L., & Josselsen, A. R. (1986). The impact of psychological
    autopsies on medical examiners' determination of manner of death. *Journal
    of Forensic Science, 32*(1), 177–189.
McConkie, B. R. (1966). *Mormon doctrine* (2nd ed.). Salt Lake City: Bookcraft,
    Inc.
McGinnis, J. M. (1987). Suicide in America: Moving up the public health agenda.
    Suicide and Life-Threatening Behavior, 17, 18–32.
McIntosh, J. L. (1985). Suicide among the elderly: Levels and trends. *American
    Journal of Orthopsychiatry, 55,* 288–293.
Merian, J. (1763). Sur la crainte de la mort, sur le mepris de la mort, sur le suicide,
    memoire [About the fear of death, about contempt for death, about suicide,
    recollection]. In *Histoire de l'Academie Royale des Sciences et Belles-Lettres
    de Berlin* (Vol. 19).
National Center for Health Statistics. (1988, September 30). Advance report of
    final mortality statistics, 1986. *Monthly Vital Statistics Report,* pp. 1–55.
Shneidman, E. (Ed.). (1967). *Essays in self-destruction.* New York: Science House.

Shneidman, E. (1985). *Definition of suicide*. New York: Wiley.

Shneidman, E., Farberow, N., & Litman, R. (1961). The suicide prevention center. In N. Farberow & E. Shneidman (Eds.), *The cry for help* (pp. 6–18). New York: McGraw-Hill.

Van Fossen, D. (1985, June). Preventing youth suicide. *Health Link*, pp. 7–10.

2
Perspectives on the Nature and Causes of Suicide

*There is but one truly serious philosophical problem, and that is suicide.
Judging whether life is or is not worth living amounts to answering the
fundamental question of philosophy.*

Albert Camus, *The Myth of Sisyphus*

As we have seen in Chapter 1, suicide has been and continues to
be a salient issue. What makes individuals take their own lives?
Some of the best thinkers in every human-oriented field have
puzzled over this question. The purpose of this chapter is to review major theoretical perspectives and their implications for the
study of suicide. We will examine four major psychological perspectives which offer some insight into the phenomenon of suicide: psychoanalytic theory, behaviorism, humanistic psychology,
and cognitive psychology. Sociologists also have speculated about
the nature and causes of suicide. The most influential sociological
theory, that of Emile Durkheim, will be explored. Although this
theory is almost 100 years old, it continues to generate thought
and empirical research today. In recent years, it has become obvious that biology plays a role in at least some suicides. Therefore,
evidence for a biological substrate or correlate of suicidal behavior
will also be presented in this chapter.

Because each of these perspectives could easily justify several books, the discussion of each theoretical perspective will be
general in nature and will focus primarily on implications for the
study of suicide. A list of suggested additional readings for each
perspective is provided at the end of the chapter.

THE PSYCHOANALYTIC PERSPECTIVE

The psychoanalytic perspective has been a strong force
throughout this century in shaping the way many people view
individual behavior. Its founder, Sigmund Freud, is still recognized as a sensitive and insightful pioneer in the investigation of
the bases of human personality. Freud's theory is so well known
as to be almost commonplace. It is summarized in every intro-
ductory psychology text and in many texts on personality and

abnormal psychology. We have included only those aspects of the theory that have implications for the study of suicide.

Freud was trained as a biologist and a physician. Every aspect of his theory is rooted in the notion that each human being is a closed energy system. He believed that humans have only a certain amount of energy, which he called *libido*, available to them at any given time. Furthermore, he believed that there is a dynamic balance between two major forces in the lives of humans. These two forces came to be known as *eros* and *thanatos*. *Eros* is the name given to the life instinct, whose purpose is individual survival and species propagation. The death instinct, thanatos, was regarded as the psychological embodiment of the drive to return to an inorganic state. Freud believed that thanatos is universal in humans and is based on the constancy principle. Simply put, the constancy principle proposes that the goal of all living beings is to return to the stability of the inorganic world (Freud, 1920/1961).

Later theorists have attached additional meanings to the constructs of eros and thanatos. They have described eros as consisting of all the positive influences in a person's life that urge that person on to become all he or she can be. Humor, compassion, altruism, and sexual intimacy are all aspects of eros. Thanatos has come to be viewed as made up of those negative traits (e.g., hatred, anger, jealousy, guilt) that cause humans to become less than they can be. The interplay between eros and thanatos represents a lifelong struggle. When individuals are growing and developing in a positive way, eros is dominant in their personalities. When, however, individuals feel stagnant, depressed, or hopeless, thanatos is in control of their lives. The implications of the eros-thanatos dichotomy for suicidal individuals are obvious: persons attempting suicide are acting under the influence of thanatos.

A second major contribution of Freudian psychology is its construction of a topography of the mind. Freud envisioned the human mind to be made up of the conscious, the preconscious, and the unconscious. Of the three components, the conscious is by far the smallest part. The conscious consists of all those things of which an individual is aware at the present moment. For example, for an individual who is engrossed in reading an absorbing novel, the conscious would include only the words on the page and the mental images those words are evoking in the reader's mind. If, however, the story begins to get less absorbing, the reader may become aware of background noises, physical sensations such as hunger or an itch, and psychological sensations such as boredom. At any given time, then, the field of attention of the conscious is narrow and subject to change. The topography of the mind is commonly likened to the topography of an iceberg. In this metaphor, the conscious is like the tip of the iceberg. It is the only part visible, but it signals that much more is hiding beneath the surface.

The preconscious is a reservoir of material that we are not aware of at present but which can become conscious given appropriate circumstances. For example, if you were asked to identify a specific song that was popular in the 60s, you might have some difficulty unless you were given more clues. If you were told that the song was made popular by a young group of male singers from Liverpool, you might begin to make reasonable guesses. If you were then told that the title of the song included the name of a color, you might well be able to guess it. Perhaps a final clue would be necessary: The name of the color preceded the name of a type of boat in the song title. At this point, you would probably guess the song was "Yellow Submarine." Freudian-oriented psychologists would probably agree that the song was buried in your preconscious just awaiting adequate environmental cues to bring it to mind. The same kind of exercise can occur when you remember nursery rhymes (e.g., The Cow Jumped Over the Moon) and fairy tales (e.g., Cinderella). The preconscious has much material stored within it that can be accessed fairly easily. Using the iceberg metaphor, the preconscious can be likened to that portion

Depression, Jacob Lawrence. Tempera on paper, 22 × 30½". (From the collection of the Whitney Museum of American Art, New York. Gift of David M. Solinger. 66.98.)

of an iceberg which is just below the surface and is made visible as tides grow lower or as waves wash up and down over the surface.

The third component of the topography of the mind is the unconscious. It is, from the point of view of Freudian theorists, the most important component of the triad. The unconscious, like the nine-tenths of the iceberg that is never seen, is the part which can present the most danger to navigation through life. The unconscious contains material that is threatening and painful to us, including perhaps memories of incidents that would cause anger, grief, guilt, or anxiety if we admitted them into consciousness or ongoing feelings such as inferiority or insecurity. In any case, people protect themselves by repressing such material and thus keeping it from being known by the conscious. Because keeping repressed material contained within the unconscious uses up some of the libidinal energy, which is limited at any point in time, less energy is available to the human being for growth and development. It follows that an excess amount of repressed unconscious negative material can lead to a strengthening of thanatos.

When thanatos threatens to envelop eros within an individual, suicide is a natural alternative, according to the Freudian view. Many psychoanalytic theorists believe that suicide is a manifestation of anger turned inward. Shneidman (1985) makes the claim that, according to Freud, suicide "was essentially within the mind. The major psychoanalytical position on suicide was that it represented unconscious hostility directed toward the introjected (ambivalently viewed) love object. Psychodynamically, suicide was seen as murder in the 180th degree" (p. 34).

The third major Freudian construct related to suicide is the concept of the triad of personality. Freud believed that personality is composed of three entities: the id, the ego, and the superego. To Freud, most mental illness comes about as a result of intrapsychic conflict between these three aspects of the personality. Once again adhering to his biological roots, Freud felt that, at birth, all energy is invested in the id, which has been described as the "spoiled brat" of the personality. The id is represented as the now-centered, demanding portion of a person which insists, "I want what I want and I want it now." Because of this emphasis on immediate gratification, the id has been described as operating according to the pleasure principle. Only gradually, as humans leave the infant stage, does the id surrender some energy to the ego.

The ego can best be viewed as the executive of the personality. The ego mediates between the id and the component of the triad that develops last, the superego. It also mediates between the id and the superego on the one hand and the realities of the outside world on the other. Among the questions which the ego asks in its mediating function are, "Is it safe? Is it available? Is it to my long term good?" Because it is the rational part of the personality, the ego is said to operate on the reality principle.

The superego, which begins to develop around 5 or 6 years of age, is composed of two components: the conscience and the ego ideal. The conscience is, of course, that part of the personality that is composed of all the "no-no's" taught at home and school and by religion and other socializing forces. It is that part of the personality that metes out psychological punishment in the form of guilt. The ego ideal, on the other hand, is that part of the personality that is composed of all we would like to be (i.e., our idealized self). It is the one part of the personality that is self-created. Each person's ego ideal is unique and changes as the person grows and matures.

Many Freudians believe that an overdeveloped superego may be implicated in some suicides. They suggest that people who have adopted perfectionist standards and whose ego ideal is out of reach set themselves up for constant intrapsychic conflict. Such conflict uses up so much of their available energy that they have less and less available for coping with everyday demands and for growth. Thus, they become even less like their ego ideal, are farther from their own standards each day, suffer more guilt and anxiety, and experience more intrapsychic conflict. This type of downward spiral may be difficult to break and may account, at least in part, for the narrow, rigid, and unrealistic thinking seen among some potential suicides. The superego is said to operate according to the perfection principle. A case in point might clarify the relationship between superego and suicide.

Marian N. was a 38-year-old married mother of two. She was also a successful career woman and had recently accepted a position as director of nursing at the local urban hospital. She had the respect of the doctors and other nurses, and many patients spoke of her with gratitude. Her 18-year marriage was stable, and her teenage children seemed happy and productive. Yet Marian N. appeared in a psychiatrist's office, deeply depressed and harboring active suicidal thoughts.

She confided that she was really a failure; that her life was not what it should be. As a young child, she had set high standards for herself in every area of life. She had wanted to be the perfect wife and mother. It was clear to her that she was neither. She had wanted to help people in her career and to excel at it in every way. She continually recalled and dwelt upon rather minor errors she had made in each of her roles. She summed up her failures by saying, "It's just never enough. I never have enough to give to everyone who needs it. I always fail everyone sometime in some way." She felt "sinful and inadequate," although she could not verbalize any real reasons for feeling this way. She felt that she could never live up to what she "should be" and that the future was bleak and hopeless. She had few avenues of pleasure in her life, and felt guilty on the rare occasions when she discovered she was having a good time.

Both in word and in her appearance, she betrayed a great deal of anger and disgust directed at herself for failing, in her own eyes, to

Our greatest foes, and whom we must chiefly combat, are within.
Cervantes, Don Quixote

live up to what she should be. When confronted with the realities of her patients' esteem and her family's love, she retorted irrationally, "It's because they really don't know the real me. If they did, they'd know the truth—that I am a failure in everything."

It is clear from the Freudian perspective that Marian suffers from unrealistic anxiety and guilt inflicted by an overdeveloped superego. Such an individual may be using rigid, perfectionist standards to cover deep-seated feelings of inferiority or self-contempt. In any case, it takes little imagination to relate to the intense negative feelings that might lead to suicidal thoughts and actions. Such negative thoughts and emotions might be addressed by trying to provide insight through therapy or by bolstering Marian's defense mechanisms.

Freud hypothesized that all of us attempt to protect our egos from anxiety and guilt by employing defense mechanisms. Defense mechanisms allow us to distort or selectively perceive reality in ways which protect our self-esteem. Table 2.1 presents the most common defense mechanisms, their definitions, and an example of each. Utilizing defense mechanisms is almost always unconscious. If we utilize defense mechanisms too often, we use up the energy available for day-to-day functioning and growth. When this happens, we become overwhelmed by the demands of the environment and/or by the material in the unconscious which we do not have energy to repress any longer. As our customary defense mechanisms begin to fail, we may become overwhelmed with feelings of helplessness and inability to cope. In the case study just presented, Marian shows a failure to cope with feelings of inadequacy and inferiority. Bolstering defense mechanisms might help temporarily—until real insight and change could be achieved. But overuse of defense mechanisms would obviously be nonproductive, since it would decrease the amount of energy left for positive growth.

The fourth major contribution of Freudian theory with implications for suicidal behavior is the concept of developmental stages. Freud was the first psychologist to popularize the existence of specific age-related stages of development. In keeping with his ideas about libidinal energy, he hypothesized that the focus of each stage was a specific erogenous zone. Table 2.2 depicts the psychosexual stages with their appropriate ages, the erogenous zone identified by Freud, and the personality outcomes that might occur if fixation or regression occurred at a given stage.

Freud described children during the first 2 years as learning about the environment through their mouths. He described people whose development became fixated at this stage or who later regressed to this stage as either oral dependent or oral aggressive. According to Freud, oral dependent people have great problems with decision making and tend to depend on others for their happiness and identity. Oral aggressive people tend to use their

TABLE 2.1   Common Defense Mechanisms

Defense mechanism	Definition	Example
Repression	Forgetting or unconsciously denying emotionally laden material	Amnesia; fugue states; missing appointments, deadlines, etc., because they were "forgotten"
Denial	Rejecting or ignoring unacceptable impulses and ideas that do reach awareness	A man who continues to smoke in spite of multiple warnings, believing that lung cancer, heart disease, etc., happen only to others
Projection	Attributing unacceptable impulses and ideas to others	A young adolescent who has overwhelming aggressive feelings and maintains that "people are out to get him"
Reaction formation	Reversing an impulse so that the original anxiety-evoking impulse is replaced by its opposite	Dealing with someone you dislike by treating him or her with exaggerated warmth and friendliness
Regression	Returning to an earlier stage of development in an attempt to cope with anxiety	Taking up thumb sucking again when a new baby is born after not sucking one's thumb for a year
Fixation	Becoming stuck at a given stage of development	A child who throws temper tantrums becomes an adult who is given to rages in anxious situations
Sublimation	Turning unacceptable impulses and ideas into socially acceptable avenues	An artist who uses repressed sexual feelings to create a statue of a beautiful nude body
Displacement	Diverting negative feelings onto innocent people or objects	A man who is scolded by his boss and comes home and yells at his wife and children
Identification	Modeling oneself on an admired person; taking on his or her valued attitudes and behaviors and making them a part of one's own personality	Children's acquisition of habits and mannerisms of their parents; students' imitation of mentor figures.

mouths as weapons, engaging in sarcasm and gossip and making vicious remarks about others. Both types have high oral needs and often use oral habits such as smoking or overeating to help them cope.

During the anal stage, children learn control over their bodily waste products. At that time, they gain pleasure, according to Freud, by consciously retaining or expelling feces. The psychological costs of becoming fixated or regressing to this stage again

TABLE 2.2   Freudian Psychosexual Stages of Development

Stage	Age	Erogenous zone	Outcome of fixation or repression at this stage
Oral	0–2	Mouth	Oral dependence Oral aggression
Anal	2–4	Anal area	Anal retentive personality Anal expulsive personality
Phallic	4–6	Genitalia	Unresolved Oedipus conflict Castration anxiety Penis envy
Latency	6–12	None	Delayed maturity Possible homosexuality
Genital	12–18	Genitalia	None

take two forms: anal retention and anal expulsive. Freud described anal retentive and anal expulsive personality types as opposites. The anal retentive personality was described as almost compulsively clean, parsimonious, and orderly, while the anal expulsive personality was pictured as generous, disorderly, and gregarious. Those familiar with the play *The Odd Couple* might recognize Freud's descriptions in the two main characters, Felix Unger and Oscar Madison.

The phallic stage presents the most danger to a child's developing personality. Freud believed that a child at this stage falls in love with the parent of the opposite sex and wishes to replace the parent of the same sex. For boys this conflict, which Freud called the *Oedipus complex*, is resolved by identification with the father, which permits a healthy boy to move into the latency period with little difficulty. A young boy who does not move through this stage appropriately will experience problems in the masculine identification process. A girl, however, has far more problems during this stage. She cannot identify with her mother because of her growing "realization" that females are inferior because of their lack of male anatomy (Freud dubbed this realization *penis envy*). The girl child, therefore, is more liable to suffer from arrested development and to have less energy available for moving into the latency stage. As a result, females, according to Freud, are more likely to have weaker superegos than males and also to be more dependent, narcissistic, and masochistic as adults. This aspect of Freud's theory has been soundly criticized by feminist writers for obvious reasons.

Freud suggested that during the latency stage of development children are freed from sexual urgings and are thus able to devote their energy to learning and to socializing. This stage, he intimated, is important for the development of sexual identity and for healthy superego development. The latency stage will be described in more detail in Chapter 3.

The final psychosexual stage begins around age 12. Its central theme is the development of procreative sexuality, which is fully achieved at approximately age 18. Although the focus is once again on the genitalia, this stage differs from the phallic stage in that the young person becomes increasingly capable of relating to nonfamily members of the opposite sex, closing the distance between the sexes that typifies the latency stage. People toward the end of this stage are able to make specific choices regarding sexual partners, build ongoing relationships, and create the next generation of human beings.

Although Freud's psychosexual stages do not in themselves relate directly to suicide, it is important to acknowledge them, as they may help us to understand children and adolescents who are considering suicide. It is also important to be familiar with these stages because so many helping professionals, in a variety of fields, use them as part of their frame of reference in dealing with troubled children and adolescents.

In summary, Freudian theory views suicide as a failure to cope. The failure may arise out of a collapse of ego defense mechanisms; out of an overdeveloped, demanding superego; out of prolonged intrapsychic conflict; or out of regression or fixation at a particular psychosexual stage. All of these causes have two things in common: They use up energy and they result in a disequilibrium between thanatos and eros, a situation in which thanatos takes command. The direct result might be a suicide attempt. The Freudian emphasis on the early years of life as all-important in determining personality makes the psychoanalytic perspective a gloomy one for those intent on helping suicidal persons. The theory suggests that only through in-depth analysis can a person obtain the insight necessary to understand and cope with unconscious material and with energy-draining intrapsychic conflict.

THE PSYCHOSOCIAL PERSPECTIVE

One exception to the generally dark picture presented by Freudian psychoanalytic theory is found in the writings of Erik Erikson, who extended Freudian theory to allow for the social nature of human beings (Erikson, 1959). Erikson did not reject most of the Freudian constructs. He did, however, suggest that Freud had not given adequate recognition to the fact that humans are social beings. Erikson also believed that human beings continue to develop in important ways throughout their lifetimes rather than culminate their development in adolescence, as Freudian theory suggests. Erikson's well-known eight stages of psychosocial development, presented in Table 2.3, portray the major tasks and dangers at each stage.

Erikson believed there are special developmental periods when specific psychosocial lessons are most likely to be learned. These periods are closely related to the developing capabilities of the individual, but they are also dependent on the conditions in the

TABLE 2.3   Erikson's Stages of Psychosocial Development

Stage	Most sensitive ages	Task	
		Positive pole	Negative pole
Sensory stage	0–2	Trust	vs.	Mistrust
Muscular development stage	2–4	Autonomy	vs.	Shame, doubt
Locomotor stage	4–6	Initiative	vs.	Guilt
Latency stage	6–12	Industry	vs.	Inferiority
Puberty stage	12–18	Identity	vs.	Role diffusion
Young adult stage	15–20	Intimacy	vs.	Isolation
Adulthood stage	30–65	Generativity	vs.	Stagnation
Maturity	65 +	Ego integrity	vs.	Despair, disgust

Source: Table adapted from Byrne, B. F. & Kelley, K. (© 1981), *An introduction to personality*, 3rd ed., Englewood Cliffs, N.J.: Prentice-Hall, p. 70. Used with permission.

environment. A physically healthy person in a positive, nurturing social environment learns each lesson well, emerging from the stage at the positive end of the continuum. People, no matter how physically healthy, who are in unhealthy social environments learn negative lessons and are less likely to learn lessons well during subsequent stages.

According to Erikson, in the first stage, between birth and age 2, infants work primarily to develop a basic sense of security in the world. Children developing positive feelings of trust view the world as more pleasant than unpleasant, more predictable than unpredictable, and they also view themselves as having some control over their own world. This developmental stage is particularly important, since it is preverbal and the child is not able to mediate with words such negative experiences as abuse, neglect, or trauma.

The development of a basic sense of autonomy (roughly equivalent to independence) or of shame and doubt is the central developmental outcome of the second stage. Children between the ages 2 and 4 are working on their growing sense of identity (or "me-ness"). All parents recognize the autonomy of the "terrible twos," for this is when healthy children insist on doing things their own way. Erikson, like Freud, recognized that conflict with parents over toilet training can lead to deeply ingrained feelings of shame. However, he also maintained that children who experience major problems in any aspect of their social world during this stage are apt to emerge with high levels of self-doubt and accompanying feelings of shame about self.

During the period from ages 4 to 6, children are involved in the process of developing either a healthy sense of initiative or feelings of guilt. During this stage, children often use their newly developed independence to move out into neighborhood, pre-school, and other group settings. Children suffering from self-doubt are not able to move with assurance in these circles and thus may feel guilty about their inability to participate as fully in their social worlds as can some of their peers.

The long childhood period, between ages 6 and 12, permits a great deal of exploration regarding the extremes of industry and inferiority. Healthy children, who have developed trust in their worlds, independence, and a positive sense of initiative are in good positions to try out new relationships, activities, and skills. Those who do not trust their world, doubt themselves, and have high levels of guilt will find it hard to develop a positive sense of industry. Instead, dragging their burdens of previous negative development, they are likely to not try very hard, to doubt their abilities, and to perceive themselves (and be perceived in turn by teachers and peers) as inferior.

Identity and role diffusion are the extremes of the next stage hypothesized by Erikson. The most sensitive period for beginning to explore the continuum is during the early teen years, although such exploration, like the earlier explorations, is likely to be re-peated at intervals throughout the life span. Identity and a positive sense of self, including both strengths and weaknesses, is the positive end of the continuum, while role diffusion leaves the adolescent lost in the worlds of school and vocation.

The next stage, with the extremes of intimacy and isolation, occurs during the middle teens and extends into young adulthood. The central goal of this stage is to develop the ability to maintain an ongoing intimate relationship with another human being that becomes more meaningful with time. Psychological isolation, with its accompanying loneliness and depression, is a significant danger.

Erikson believed that most adults, from early adulthood un-til old age, are in a period of generativity rather than stagnation. The central task of a generative period is to find ways to give back something to the society which has nurtured them. Being pro-ductive on the job, parenting, writing books, painting pictures, carrying out community service are all ways of being generative. Erikson pointed out that people who don't find ways of contrib-uting to society are likely to stop growing, to lose their zest for living, to turn inward in a futile effort to nurture themselves— in short, to stagnate.

The final psychosocial stage Erikson proposed has ego in-tegrity at one extreme and despair and disgust at the other. He viewed this stage as attainable only after a lifetime of positive or negative experiences. Those with ego integrity have developed a sense of positiveness about their life histories while those who arrive at old age at the negative end of the continuum view their lives as lacking in meaning and question the reasons for existence.

Erikson's theory provides a helpful framework for viewing suicide from a developmental perspective. It is important to note that Erikson believed that individuals are able to move back and forth across the bipolar continuum regardless of their age. In this way, young people who have developed negatively during the first few stages could, with proper attention and guidance in a changed social environment, establish a sense of basic trust in the world which would allow them to re-examine negative lessons like self-doubt, guilt, and inferiority. Thus, Erikson's theory is more hopeful than Freud's and provides a framework both for understanding and for working with suicidal persons. The following case study illustrates negative psychosocial learning.

Robin S. is a 16-year-old boy who was admitted to a psychiatric institution following a moderately serious suicide attempt. Robin took several Quaaludes and washed them down with bourbon. Upon his recovery, he admitted knowing that the combination could be fatal. He said he had learned that from reading about Karen Quinlan's case. "But," he said sadly, "I guess I wasn't as lucky as her."

Upon questioning, the following facts were revealed. Robin was born into a lower-middle-class family. He was the fourth of five children. Before the last one was born, Robin's father deserted the family. Robin's mother went to work as a carder in a local textile mill. The three older siblings also worked as soon as they were able to help out with expenses. Even as a baby, Robin's care was frequently left to his oldest sister, then 8 years old, who was at best casual in caring for him. Robin learned three specific lessons: (1) the world was not a comfortable, warm, and secure place; (2) he could not predict consequences (when he cried, he was sometimes attended to and sometimes not); and (3) he was powerless to affect the outcome of any situation in a consistent way. In short, he learned mistrust.

When Robin began talking, he lisped. As he grew older and other children made fun of him, he stopped talking almost completely. His shyness made him the butt of still more neighborhood teasing, and Robin developed a strong sense of shame and self-doubt. These feelings became overlaid with a sense of guilt over his own inadequacy as he watched his preschool friends move confidently into a world he dared not approach.

When he entered school, he was labelled as "slow" and placed in the slow-learning group. His boredom with the group, coupled with his unwillingness to talk, caused his teachers to lose patience with him, to write him off, and to communicate their convictions that Robin was stupid to parents, peers, and other teachers in a variety of ways. They also communicated them to Robin, who learned "I am inferior."

As a result of his feelings of inferiority, Robin seldom entered into any activities. He did only what was absolutely required and withdrew into himself. He had no friends and rarely even talked to his siblings. When his oldest sister suggested that he get involved in something he was good at, Robin said, "There ain't no such thing." He had no clear understanding of his strengths and weaknesses and almost no interpersonal connections. In short, he suffered from role diffusion and isolation.

Clearly, Robin is someone who, at 16, has gone through the first five stages delineated by Erikson's theory at the extreme negative end of each continuum. However, if Erikson is correct, it would be possible to work with Robin and help him regain a sense of trust in his environment by proving to be a trustworthy counselor. He could be helped to overcome his sense of shame and self-doubt by developing competence and confidence in speaking through speech therapy. He could be supported and rewarded for expressing himself in safe situations. In addition, he could be encouraged to try out new situations in which he could expect to succeed (and even be accompanied for added support). In this way, as Robin developed increasing competence, he would be likely to overcome self-doubt and feelings of inferiority and to move toward the positive poles of autonomy and industry. As his feelings of competence and self-esteem grew, he would be in a good position to move toward a self-defined identity as expressed by pursuing a vocation or developing positive relationships with others. While such developments take time, energy, and support, from an Eriksonian perspective they pay off. They allow a person to develop the psychosocial foundation on which to build an adult life of generativity and integrity. From the Eriksonian perspective, then, suicidal individuals are people who must be helped to move from the negative to the positive poles in the psychosocial tasks of life.

Erikson's theory has been the source of a great deal of rich discussion since the 1950s and has been used by many authors (e.g., Vaillant, 1977 and Levinson, 1980) as an organizational framework for analyzing research findings concerning adult development. Erikson was the first major theorist to postulate that development continues after sexual maturity is attained. Furthermore, he pointed out that age and life experience are essential if people are to successfully complete the stage of generativity and move into the stage of ego integrity in old age. Because Erikson's theory has been so influential to thinking in the latter half of the 20th century, we rely on it heavily in the developmental chapters which follow.

THE BEHAVIORAL PERSPECTIVE

The second major psychological perspective is that of behaviorism. Behaviorism traces its roots to Pavlov and his famous conditioning experiments with dogs (Pavlov, 1927). Pavlov and others showed that principles of learning could be gleaned from research with animals. These principles were later shown to be applicable to the more complex behavior of human beings. For example, certain phobic responses, such as claustrophobia, were shown to have their roots in early traumatic experiences, such as being punished by confinement. Such phobic reactions in adulthood could be traced to even a single traumatic experience in childhood, suggesting the powerful influence of classical conditioning.

Perhaps the best-known form of behaviorism in the United States is Skinnerian operant conditioning (Skinner, 1953). The most basic principle in this model is the principle of reinforcement. Skinnerians believe that reinforcement is the key to controlling behavior and that behavior can be understood by identifying the contingencies which have shaped it and maintain it. Even more than Eriksonians, behaviorists believe in the plasticity of human beings. In its purest form, behaviorism holds that all behavior is learned and that anything that is learned can be unlearned and relearned.

Social learning theory is a third type of behaviorism, one that places an emphasis on modeling and imitation as prime factors in learning. Mischel and Bandura are two of the leading exponents of this theory. Bandura, in particular, has attempted to modify learning theory to include the principles of modeling and self-efficacy as they interact within a social context (Bandura, 1977).

In accordance with most behavioral approaches to personality, social learning theory is based on the premise that human behavior is largely acquired or learned. The following case study illustrates some of the principles of suicidal behavior from the perspective of behaviorists.

Jerry W. was a 42-year-old man referred to therapy after an unsuccessful but very serious suicide attempt. He had waited until his wife and teenage children had gone to visit the grandparents. Then he had systematically sealed the windows in the garage and the air space under the door with rags and fed a hose from the exhaust pipe into the car. He had then taken the evening paper with him into the car. Only the unexpected visit of a golf partner, who was returning a borrowed club and who heard the engine running as he got out of his car, prevented the completion of this suicide.

Jerry had no obvious reason for attempting suicide. His 15-year-old marriage was a success. He was considered to be a leader in his job. He had been successful at a very young age in a computer software company and now was earning a salary of six figures. His children, while not models of adolescent development, seemed to be well adjusted and reasonably loving. Upon probing, the therapist discovered that Jerry had been feeling anxious for a couple of years, "like everything was going to go wrong." Just lately, within the last month, he had felt that everything was over, that he "was just going through the motions, that he had no right to go on living." After several therapy sessions, Jerry admitted that his father had committed suicide at exactly age 42, leaving a very confused and angry 15-year-old, Jerry, trying to understand why. After a while, he gave up trying to understand, stopped talking about his father, and went on to become a "wunderkind" in the computer software business. Jerry took quiet pride in his success, particularly when older family members told him that his intelligence and hard work reminded them of his father.

Supporters of the social learning view would claim that Jerry's suicide attempt is an example of an "anniversary" suicide attempt and that both anniversary suicides and cluster suicides are examples of suicides that result from imitation and modeling. Jerry's suicide attempt was rooted in the traumatic experience of observing his father commit suicide. Jerry's father modelled suicide as an acceptable behavior. It is worthwhile to note that the power of modeling is increased when the model performing the behavior is the same sex as the learner and is regarded as powerful by the learner. Both of these conditions were met in Jerry's case.

A special case of social learning theory is particularly appropriate in any discussion of suicide. It is the research generated by Martin Seligman, which applies learning principles originally established in the laboratory with animals to a special emotional reaction among humans, depression (Seligman, 1975). Seligman was trained as an experimental psychologist in the behavioral tradition, and his initial work followed the principles of experimental research with animals. Seligman and his colleagues carried out a series of experiments which placed dogs in a device called a shuttlebox, which is essentially a large box with two compartments. Seligman then administered a series of shocks accompanied by a tone. The dogs, in their anxiety to escape the shock, would eventually jump over the barrier dividing the box. When they did, both the shock and the tone would stop. Eventually the animals would jump over the barrier at the first sound of the tone, thus avoiding the shock altogether. In another experiment, dogs were placed in restraining harnesses in the first compartment of the shuttlebox and given a series of brief shocks that they could not escape. In subsequent trials, even with no restraint, the dogs did not attempt to escape from the compartment. They lay whimpering in the first compartment until both the tone and the shocks ended. Their response of passive acceptance of painful stimuli was labelled *learned helplessness*.

Seligman and his colleagues soon investigated this phenomenon with college students. In a series of experiments, they showed that when students were faced with unsolvable problems coupled with noxious stimuli (noise), the students were later unable to learn to escape the stimuli. In other experimental conditions, students confronted with solvable problems or with no problems quickly learned, in later sessions, to escape or avoid the noxious stimuli. Seligman pointed out that in both kinds of situations later learning was dependent on antecedent events. He drew parallels between reactive depression brought on by a major loss or failure and learned helplessness. Table 2.4 shows the features common to learned helplessness and depression. Seligman believed that at least some forms of depression that often lead to suicidal behavior could be explained as the result of traumatic events that could not be controlled or warded off, even by the

Razors pain you;
Rivers are damp;
Acids stain you;
And drugs cause cramp.
Guns aren't lawful;
Nooses give;
Gas smells awful;
You might as well live.
    Dorothy Parker,
    "Résumé," 1926

TABLE 2.4 Summary of Features Common to Learned Helplessness and Depression

	Learned helplessness	Depression
Symptoms	Passivity	Passivity
	Difficulty learning that responses produce relief	Negative cognitive set
	Dissipates in time	Time course
	Lack of aggression	Introjected hostility (hostility turned inward)
	Weight loss, appetite loss, social and sexual deficits	Weight loss, appetite loss, social and sexual deficits
	Ulcers and stress	Ulcers (?) and stress
Cause	Learning that responding and reinforcement are independent	Belief that responding is useless
Cure	Directory therapy: forced exposure to responses that produce reinforcement	Recovery of belief that responding produces reinforcement
	Electroconvulsive shock	Electroconvulsive shock
	Time	Time
Prevention	Immunization by mastery over reinforcement	(?)

Source: From Martin E. P. Seligman, *Helplessness: On depression, development, and death*, p. 106, W. H. Freeman and Company, © 1975. Reprinted with the permission of W. H. Freeman and Company.

best efforts of those involved. One approach to helping individuals who evidence learned helplessness and its accompanying depression is to teach a more "internal locus of control," that is, to help people see that they do have control over many aspects of their lives and do not have to be entirely at the mercy of the environment in all situations. Identification of controllable elements and rational acceptance of those which cannot be controlled might also help alleviate depression.

In summary, the behavioral perspective would maintain that suicidal behavior, like all behavior, is learned. Whether it is learned by imitation and modeling or through unavoidable loss (which can lead to learned helplessness), it can be manipulated. What is learned can be unlearned and re-learned. It is clear that the proper role of the therapist in the behavioral model is as a teacher, utilizing the powerful principles of learning to help clients develop new and healthier ways of coping.

THE HUMANISTIC PERSPECTIVE

The third major school of thought in psychology is called the humanistic or humanistic-existential perspective. It was developed during the middle part of the 20th century as a response to the pessimistic view of human growth held by Freudian psychoanalysts and the more mechanistic view of humans held by the early behaviorists. The basic emphasis in this school is on the human potential for growth. It also stresses essential human characteristics, those which separate humans from other animals. Thus, humanistic psychologists feel free to focus on the inner experience of the individual. They frequently use such tools as humor and visualization in working with people. Central to most humanistic-existential schools of applied psychology is the belief that the client should be at the center of the process and that the client can, with minimal intervention, approach the realization of his or her potential.

Two of the major figures early in the development of humanistic psychology in the United States were Abraham Maslow and Carl Rogers. Maslow is also known as the father of transpersonal psychology, an approach which focuses specifically on such subjective experiences as ecstasy, mystical experiences, awe, wonder, and cosmic awareness. Rogers, the father of client-centered therapy, derived his positive theory of human development from his clinical work (1961). We shall examine here only the early work of Maslow, with special reference to its similarities to Roger's therapeutic approach and to its relevance for suicidal behavior. In Chapter 8, we will examine in more detail the tenets of self-theory, since they are incorporated into our model of suicidal behavior.

Maslow conceived of human behavior as operating on a hierarchical basis (Maslow, 1954). Table 2.5 presents Maslow's now-famous hierarchy of needs, as well as conditions of deficiency and fulfillment and an example at each level. The column entitled "Conditions of deficiency" can be regarded as a summary of the feelings of suicidal people. Maslow believed in two basically different types of needs, the D or drive needs and the B or being needs. Maslow felt that we are pushed by our drive needs to eliminate a deficiency and we are pulled by our being needs to become more completely all that we are capable of becoming.

Similarities between Maslow's theory and Rogers' theory are many. In particular, both would agree that, provided basic needs are met, humans are essentially growth-oriented creatures whose nature is directed toward realizing their potential (if external conditions permit). Both theorists are also basically optimistic about human nature. That is, rather than view human development as a product of basic energies and conflicts (as do psychoanalytic theorists) or as a result of learning imposed largely by environmental conditions, these theorists believe that humans are essentially good and that there are levels of healthiness that are "more fully human" than the levels most of us achieve (Maslow, 1971). Aspiring to these levels helps humans to live "authentic" lives and to find meaning in their lives.

Inability to discover meaning in life can lead to feelings of uselessness, hopelessness, and depression. Frankl (1963), an existential neurologist, described this state as noogenic neurosis and claimed it to be one of the most widespread illnesses of Western

TABLE 2.5   Maslow's Need Hierarchy and Levels of Personality Functioning

Need hierarchy	Condition of deficiency	Fulfillment	Illustration	
Self-actualization	Alienation	Healthy curiosity	Experiencing a pro-found insight	
	Metapathologies	Peak experiences		
	Absence of meaning in life	Realization of poten-tials		
	Boredom	Work that is pleasura-ble and embodies val-ues		
	Limited activities	Creative living		B needs
Esteem	Feeling of incompetence	Confidence	Receiving an award for an outstanding per-formance on some project	
	Negativism	Sense of mastery		
	Feeling of inferiority	Positive self-regard		
Love	Self-consciousness	Free expression of emo-tions	Experiencing total ac-ceptance in love rela-tionship	
	Feeling of being un-wanted	Sense of wholeness		
	Feeling of worthlessness	Sense of warmth		
	Emptiness	Renewed sense of life and strength		
	Loneliness	Sense of growing to-gether		
Safety	Insecurity	Security	Being secure in a full-time job	
	Yearning	Comfort		
	Sense of loss	Balance		
	Fear	Poise		D needs
	Obsession	Calm		
	Compulsion	Tranquility		
Physiological	Hunger, thirst	Relaxation	Feeling satisfied after a good meal	
	Sexual frustration	Release from tension		
	Tension	Experiences of pleasure from senses		
	Illness	Physical well-being		
	Lack of proper shelter	Comfort		

Source: Adapted from Nicholas S. DiCaprio, *Personality theories: Guide to living.* © 1974. Philadelphia, PA: W. B. Saunders Company. Reprinted by permission of Saunders College Publishing/CBS College Publishing.

societies in the 20th century. People who cannot see any meaning in living are prime targets for suicide from the point of view of humanists and existentialists. The following case study exemplifies some of the elements thought to be important in suicidal behavior by proponents of the humanistic-existential school of psychology.

Lynne B. was a successful 28-year-old high school English teacher. She had always been a good student, finishing college with honors. She had taught for 6 years and described her experience in muted, solemn tones. "I guess I was convinced that the two greatest goods in the world were knowledge and helping people. That's what attracted me to teaching. I thought that was the one field where my two highest goods in life could be realized together. I guess I really bought into the old "Mr. Chips" stereotype. I thought I would go through life learning more and more and sharing it with eager young people, who would be properly appreciative. It seems funny now. My students have taught me more than I've ever taught them. They've taught me that reading poetry is a waste of time, that literature is only millions of meaningless words written by dead people who thought they had something to say. For the first few years, I thought the students were wrong. Then I began to ask what was so great about the stuff I was teaching, and it came to me that the students were right. Much of literature is as dead as the people who wrote it. It doesn't speak to humans today. Learning it is just an exercise of neurons. When we die, will it make any difference if we've read Beowulf? Or Canterbury Tales? Will it make any difference to us before we die? I see no difference in the lives of my students who take my old English course and those who don't, except maybe that the others are not so bored for one hour a day. If you ask me why I live, I guess the best answer I can give you is, 'Why not?' Sometimes it almost scares me. I'd like to believe in something again, but I know better now."

According to humanists, Lynne is in psychological trouble. If she doesn't find something that she feels has real meaning, she will go through life in a kind of fog of meaninglessness and ennui. If and when things get too difficult for her and an existential crisis of major proportions occurs, she is very likely to attempt suicide. At the very least, her life will be an emotional desert, lacking passion and commitment.

Humanists speak of self-actualization as the highest attainment of humans, the ideal mental health criterion. Self-actualization is the process whereby we each realize our own unique potential. It is a lifelong process, marked by discovering our own version of what gives life meaning and living that to its fullest. Self-actualized people are well adjusted and productive. They are also capable of having a rich inner life. Suicide is highly unlikely among self-actualized people—unless it is a response to a terminal illness.

*"Again the voice spake unto me:
"Thou art so steep'd in misery,
Surely 'twere better not to be."*

Tennyson,
The Two Voices

THE COGNITIVE PERSPECTIVE

Beginning in the late 1950s, many psychologists became disillusioned with what was the prevailing theory in psychology at that time, behaviorism. The reason for their disillusionment lay in the fact that strict behaviorists thought that psychologists should study only observable behaviors. Such topics as motivation, will, desire, even learning (except as it could be observed) were considered to be outside the purview of psychology. In fact, the behaviorism of the early and middle 20th century became known as "black box" psychology, since, in its purest form, it regarded the individual as a black box whose internal workings could never be known. Black box psychology restricted itself to studying the stimuli that acted on the black box, the behavior emitted from the black box, and the results of reinforcing or punishing that behavior.

Since the goal of psychology as a social science is to understand, predict, and control behavior, and since much behavior is rooted in motivations that are not visible, many psychologists began to broaden their field of study to include the thinking of the individual. The broadening of research has resulted in the establishment of a fourth school of psychology. This school, known as cognitive psychology, is the fastest growing theoretical perspective in psychology in the United States. It has been greatly influenced by the work of the Swiss psychologist Jean Piaget.

Piaget was the foremost 20th-century theorist regarding the development of cognitive abilities in children and young adults. Piaget proposed that cognitive development occurs in an orderly manner that is less open to environmental manipulation than the behaviorists believe. Piaget thought that all children move through stages of cognitive development in a particular order and that each stage is associated with specific qualitative aspects of thinking and problem solving (Piaget, 1926; Piaget & Inhelder, 1969). Piaget's stages of cognitive development, the ages which children typically progress through them, and some major characteristics of each stage are presented in Table 2.6.

As shown in Table 2.6, the first stage of cognitive development, the period of sensorimotor intelligence, occurs between birth and 2 years of age for most children. The sensorimotor period was so named by Piaget because children in this age group typically learn about the world through their sensory and motor experiences. The young child has little or no symbolic representation of the world until the end of this stage. As the newborn child progresses through the first 2 years of life, he or she moves from a very immature level (in which mental capabilities are limited to reflexive activities such as sucking and grasping) to a more mature level (which includes the ability to distinguish between

TABLE 2.6 Piaget's System of Cognitive Development

Period and stage	Life period	Some major characteristics
I. Period of sensori-motor	Infancy (0–2)	"Intelligence" consists of sensory and motor actions. No conscious thinking. Limited language. No concept of reality.
II. Period of preoperational thought	Early childhood (2–7)	Egocentric orientation. Magical, animistic, & artificialistic thinking. Thinking is irreversible. Reality is subjective.
III. Period of concrete operations	Middle childhood/preadolescence (7–11/12)	Orientation ego-decentered. Thinking is bound to concrete. Naturalistic thinking. Recognition of laws of conservation and reversibility.
IV. Period of formal operations	Adolescence and adulthood (12+)	Propositional and hypodeductive thinking. Generality of thinking. Reality is objective.

Source: Adapted from Wass and Corr, *Childhood and death*, p. 4, New York, Hemisphere and McGraw-Hill International, 1984.

self and others and the performance of intentional acts). A special milestone, which typically occurs about half way through the sensorimotor period, is the development of *object permanence*, which is indicated when a child searches for an object that has been moved out of his or her visual field. Object permanence is very important, because it reflects the rudiments of the capability for symbolic representation of objects in the world. Toward the end of the sensorimotor period, children show evidence of learning through trial and error and even some capacity for insight learning through mental combinations.

The second stage of cognitive development is the preoperational period, which occurs between ages 2 and 7. These preschool years are marked by very rapid development of language skills and symbolic capabilities in general. Young children are very impressive when they begin to develop language and can, for the first time, actually communicate their thoughts to another person. In some ways, however, Piaget characterized the preoperational period more in terms of what the child is unable rather than able to do. The term *preoperational* was chosen by Piaget to reflect the fact that children in this age group are typically unable to utilize certain logical thinking techniques in problem solving. For example, the preoperational child is unable to deal effectively with part-whole relationships. Also, the child has great difficulty solving conservation problems involving quantity and volume.

Preoperational children show their intellectual immaturity in other ways as well. They are, for example, very susceptible to animistic thinking, investing inanimate objects with lifelike characteristics. In addition, they are unable to understand the concept of reversibility (e.g., if $3 + 2 = 5$, then $5 - 3 = 2$). Preoperational children also tend to be incapable of understanding more than one point of view in a complex situation. This characteristic has been blamed for much of the argumentativeness and negativism of younger children who are at this stage.

The concrete operations child, between ages 6 and 12, possesses many logical thinking characteristics which younger children do not. Concrete operations children can easily solve conservation problems, have no difficulty with part-whole relationships, and show mature understandings of time, space, and causality. Their thinking and problem solving closely approximates adult reasoning except for one important limitation—their orientation is limited to that which can be experienced by the senses. The elementary school child works best in the real and the here and now. This stage has been called the stage of the natural scientist, because children's thinking is so bound to the concrete aspects of their world.

The formal operations period begins during adolescence and develops more fully in young adulthood. Unlike children in younger age groups, individuals at the formal operations stage can think hypothetically and deal with higher levels of abstraction. Also, during this period, adolescents and young adults begin intuitively to utilize certain aspects of the scientific method in solving problems. This stage has been called the stage of the philosopher, because young people can begin to ask questions regarding abstract principles, such as truth and justice, and can begin to face issues of meaning in their intellectual lives.

Piaget's detailed descriptions of the qualitative changes in thinking that occur as children develop help to explain the different ways in which various age groups view the world. Some of the developmental changes have implications for the study of suicide. For example, the child in the concrete operational period understands death differently from the adult, whose formal operational thinking is richer and more abstract. There is, in fact, evidence that children younger than age 10 have a tendency to see death as a temporary and reversible state much like sleep. This and other age-related cognitive differences described by Piaget will be discussed in detail as we explore the suicidal behavior of different age groups in Chapters 3–6.

Piaget's stages of cognitive development have done more than reveal patterns in children's increasingly sophisticated thinking. They have helped other theorists to understand the powerful influences thought and language have on the developing personality and on all types of behavior.

One of the forerunners of applied cognitive psychology was Albert Ellis. Although he was trained in traditional psychoanalytic thought, Ellis began very early to develop his own therapeutic approach for dealing with mental illness. He called it rational-emotive therapy, and, in a series of books, he pointed out how we contribute to our own psychological problems by continuously repeating messages which reinforce "neurotic" behavior (Ellis, 1962). Ellis characterized neurotic behavior as "stupid behavior." He spelled out what he called the *ABCs* of stupid behavior, where *A* refers to the antecedent condition, *B* to the belief systems of the individual, and *C* to the consequences of the antecedent condition. To Ellis, aberrant behavior was not so much a result of conditions in life as of the belief system of the individual which assigned personal meaning to those conditions. The list below shows 12 common beliefs which Ellis presented as illustrative of those which lead to neurotic or "stupid" behavior.*

1. It is a dire necessity for an adult to be loved or approved by everyone for everything he or she does.
2. Certain acts are wrong, wicked, or villainous, and people who perform such acts should be severely punished.

*Source: A. Ellis, Rational psychotherapy. In M. R. Goldfried & M. Merbaum (Eds.), *Behavior change through self-control.* New York: Holt, Rinehart & Winston, Inc., 1973.

3. It is terrible, horrible, and catastrophic when things are not the way one would like them to be.
4. Much human unhappiness is externally caused and is forced on one by outside people and events.
5. If something is or may be dangerous or fearsome, one should be terribly concerned about it.
6. It is easier to avoid than to face life difficulties and self-responsibilities.
7. One needs something other, or stronger, or greater than oneself on which to rely.
8. One should be thoroughly competent, adequate, intelligent, and achieving in all possible respects.
9. Because something once strongly affected one's life, it should indefinitely affect it.
10. It is vitally important to our existence what other people do, and we should make great efforts to change them in the direction we would like them to be.
11. Human happiness can be achieved by inertia and inaction.
12. One has virtually no control over one's emotions and one cannot help feeling certain things.

Once again, a case history might illuminate key concepts.

Jason J. was a sophomore in college. Although he made good grades, he depended on his girlfriend, Susan, to help him keep his spirits up. Finally, Susan tired of being the cheerleader for Jason's flagging self-concept and broke off the relationship. Jason attempted suicide by taking an overdose of pills (35 Seconals) and alcohol. The suicide note that he left stated that the breakup with Susan was the last straw (the entire suicide note is in Chapter 4). He did not feel that he had ever been truly loved. He had contemplated suicide for some years and now was doing what was inevitable. Quick action by his residence hall advisor saved his life, but Jason was not appreciative. He awakened in the hospital emergency room tearfully regretting that he could not even commit suicide successfully.

A rational-emotive therapist would view the situation as follows. The A (antecedent event) in this instance was Susan's breaking up with Jason. The C (consequence) of that event was Jason's suicide attempt. However, the therapist would maintain that Jason did not attempt suicide because of Susan's action. Rather, he attempted suicide because of B (his belief system), which determined the meaning that Susan's action had for his life. Many young men abandoned by their girlfriends would shrug and think "There are many fish in the sea." Some might even show relief rather than despair. That Jason did neither reveals his neurotic belief system. Ellis would maintain that Jason's self-messages probably went something like this. "Susan broke up with me. This *always* happens in *all* my relationships. Even my mother didn't love me. I must be a real loser. If no one loves me, my life will be miserable. Since Susan didn't love me, and since I am so unlovable, no one will ever love me. I shall live a wretched and pain-filled life. And it will only lead to death anyway. Why not avoid all that unhappiness? I'll kill myself."

While we will never know if these were exactly Jason's thoughts, such irrationality often characterizes the cognitions of suicide attempters. Ellis called such a train of thought "awful-izing" and maintained that through such a process we distort the events of our lives and add to the pain we feel as a result of events such as the breaking up of a relationship. What's more, we can keep that pain alive over a long period of time by reciting the internal litany over and over again whenever we begin to feel better. Ellis maintained that the essence of good therapy is to teach the individual how to dispute (D) the neurotic messages which he or she uses to increase and continue the psychological pain. Another noted proponent of this type of cognitive approach is Donald Meichenbaum. Meichenbaum has suggested that poor adjustment is maintained by negative self-talk and that positive self-talk can promote better adjustment (Meichenbaum, 1985).

A second well-known cognitive approach is that of George Kelly. Kelly called his approach *personal construct theory* and maintained that all human beings act like scientists, generating hypotheses about the world and devising ways of testing them. The results of such testing are incorporated into personal constructs unique to each individual. In all of our interactions in the world, we seek meaning. "To construe is to hear the whisper of recurrent themes in the events that reverberate around us" (Kelly, 1955, p. 76). Kelly believed that the future is more important to humans than the past and stressed that humans are motivated to organize their world as an attempt to predict the future.

Kelly devised the Role Construct Repertory Test (Rep Test), which attempts to determine how individuals organize their interpersonal worlds. In the Rep Test, an individual is asked to list the significant people in his or her life. The names are arranged in groups of three. The person then is asked to specify how two of them are alike and how they are different from the third. The end result is a grid that is supposed to show how the individual organizes his or her interpersonal world. People who have a limited repertoire of roles tend to have restricted personalities and an oversimplified view of others. Kelly's theory is useful in that it helps explain the process of awful-izing described by Ellis. Kelly would probably maintain that such negative thinking results from restrictive thinking, which cannot envision multiple futures and thus gives in to feelings of hopelessness.

A third cognitive theorist who has done a great deal of work in the area of depression is Aaron Beck. Beck described depression as a disturbance in thinking that leads to a disturbance in mood (Beck, 1967). Depressive individuals tend to have a general pessimistic attitude toward the world. In addition, they tend to engage in three types of cognitive distortion: overgeneralization, selective abstraction, and inexact labelling. Overgeneralization is similar to awful-izing. Selective abstraction occurs when the perceptual set of a depressed individual causes the individual to focus on the negative and ignore or de-emphasize what is positive in his or her life as the nurse, Marian, did in our earlier case study. Inexact labeling occurs when a person interprets a situation negatively, places a label on him- or herself as a result of the negative interpretation, and reacts to the label rather than to the situation itself. In the previous case study, Jason labelled himself a "loser," which caused him to feel more negative about his girlfriend's breaking off the relationship than was necessary or healthy.

Cognitive theory is interesting because it promises a blend of the major points of the other three perspectives. For example, Kelly's discussion of the importance of the future echoes the humanistic psychologists. Ellis considered his theory to be a humanistic one, as is evidenced by the title of one of his books, *Humanistic Psychology: The Rational-Emotive Approach* (1974). Cognitive theorists also use some behavioral constructs. Since their main emphasis is on learning and rationality, they readily relate to operant conditioning terms and techniques. Cognitive theories are optimistic in that they suggest that individuals can change their cognitive sets and thus improve their mental health. From the point of view of suicidal patients, cognitive therapy offers hope that they can be taught to see the world in a more rational, less hopeless manner and that such a change in worldview will result in a change in suicidal attitudes and behavior.

THE SOCIOLOGICAL PERSPECTIVE

Sociologists maintain that human behavior cannot be viewed outside of the context in which it is situated. As evidence, they point to the fact that people in different cultures have different psychological problems at different times. For example, hysterical symptoms, such as spontaneous blindness, deafness, or loss of feeling in a part of the body, were far more common in the early part of this century than they are today. Sociologists would maintain that greater understanding of the way the body works, coupled with widespread reading of psychoanalytic literature, has led to a decrease in the number of people presenting with this type of artificial physiological problem.

As we have seen in Chapter 1, sociology first began to examine suicidal behavior and its causes in the latter part of the 19th century. Emile Durkheim (1897/1951), a major figure in sociology, hypothesized that suicides occur as a result of the kind of "fit" that an individual experiences in his or her society. He postulated four different types of suicide. Durkheim's first type, called *egoistic suicide*, occurs when "the bond attaching man to life relaxes because that attaching him to society is itself slack.

The individual becomes remote from social life and suffers from an excess of individualism" (Taylor, 1982). Durkheim took pains to point out that the suicide rate of that time was higher among Protestants than among Catholics; his explanation was that Catholics received more support from their church while Protestants were left more to their individual devices. Other supportive evidence for egoistic suicide was that more single people committed suicide at that time than married people and that fewer married women with children comitted suicide than unmarried women. Durkheim believed that the incidence of egoistic suicide is inversely related to family density.

Durkheim labelled the second type of suicide *altruistic suicide*. According to Durkheim, altruistic suicide occurs when there is an overintegration of the individual into society. The person then kills him- or herself in an attempt to conform to social imperatives. Suttee, the ritualistic suicide that Indian widows committed by throwing themselves on their husbands' funeral pyres, is an example of such suicide. More modern examples can be found in the Japanese kamikaze pilots of World War II. These young boys, some under 15 years of age, volunteered to fly planes on one-way missions to destroy U.S. ships near the end of the war. The planes they were given did not have enough fuel for a return trip. In addition, the landing gear on some of them was even altered to dislodge on takeoff so that no safe landing could be carried out. These young idealists are good examples of people who had so thoroughly introjected their society's values that they were willing to commit suicide for love of country. The opposing side in that war offered similar examples. Many veterans remember the name Roger Young. During an attack, a grenade rolled into the foxhole he shared with several other infantrymen. Most of them flung themselves away from the grenade. Roger Young threw himself on it and was immortalized in song: "Roger Young, Roger Young, fought and died for the men he marched among. To the everlasting glory of the infantry, shines the courage of Private Roger Young." Roger Young's sacrifice was a model of altruistic suicide.

The third type of suicide discussed by Durkheim was called *anomic suicide*. This type of suicide results from a person's activity "lacking regulation." Evidence for this type of suicide is found in the fact that suicide rates rise both in depressions and in times of greater prosperity. Regardless of what is going on in the larger society, the individual feels cut off from it, "out of sync." In addition, the individual has a great deal of freedom to express him- or herself. The drug-related suicides of the late 1960s might be good examples of this type of suicide. Many of the young people during that decade were not comfortable with society's mainstream values. Their behavior lacked regulation. They experimented wildly, sometimes fatally, with toxic substances.

The final type of suicide discussed by Durkheim was fatalistic suicide. He viewed this as almost the opposite of the anomic type of suicide. It results from overregulation and oppressive discipline by a society directed at some segment of that society. Evidence of this type of suicide might be found in the suicide rates among slaves or prisoners in barbaric and punitive conditions, such as those in concentration camps or camps for prisoners of war.

The sociological view of suicide calls for a broader perspective than that found in most psychological approaches. It challenges people to look at conditions in their cultures at any given point in history as factors which can directly influence the suicide rate. In this way, sociologists provide a major service to students of suicide. An analogy that is useful in understanding the utility of this perspective is that of an ant hill. A child watching an individual ant busily wander back and forth across a path carrying a bit of sand can infer little meaning from the behavior. If, however, the child stands up and regards the broader scene, he or she may observe a nearly finished ant hill. While the individual behavior is not explainable, it becomes meaningful as a part of a larger picture. In just such a way, individual suicidal behavior may become more meaningful when examined against the social fabric of society.

THE BIOLOGICAL PERSPECTIVE

No discussion about perspectives for viewing suicide would be complete without a brief review of the remarkable progress being made in understanding the biological correlates of depression. Although depression is not synonymous with suicide (for a person can commit suicide without being depressed), the relationship between the two is sufficiently close to justify an examination of the research on the biological bases of depression.

During the past 3 decades, major insights have been gained into the way the brain functions and into how specific brain dysfunctions may relate to depression. In order to appreciate these findings, some understanding of the way the brain functions is helpful.

The nervous system of human beings is composed of two parts: the central nervous system and the peripheral nervous system. The central nervous system is made up of the brain and the spinal cord, while the peripheral nervous system is made up of all the nerves outside the brain and spinal cord. The central nervous system governs behavior by interpreting informational or sensory input that comes to it from the peripheral nervous system and by sending messages to the muscles and glands.

The most central part of the nervous system is the brain, which is composed of billions of individual nerve cells called *neurons*. Figure 2.1 depicts the anatomy of a neuron. Neurons are

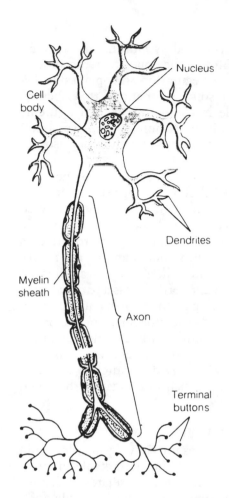

FIGURE 2.1 An idealized diagram of a neuron. Stimulation of the dendrites or the cell body activates an electrochemical nerve impulse that travels along the axon to the terminal buttons. The myelin sheath covers the axons of some, but not all, neurons; it helps to increase the speed of nerve impulse conduction. *Source:* Atkinson, R. L., Atkinson, R. C. & Hilgard, E. R. (1983).

composed of a cell body, a cell nucleus, impulse receptors (dendrites), and impulse transmitters (axons). Each neuron is capable of "firing," that is, of producing an electrical impulse in the cell body which is sent through the axon to the receptor site of the next neuron. Figure 2.2 explains the synaptic transmission processes. Chemical changes at the synaptic junction between the transmitting and receiving neurons determine if the signal will complete the connection or be stopped. The discovery of the effects of these chemicals on behavior was largely accidental.

In the 1950s, many clinicians were using the drug reserpine to control high blood pressure. They noted that a high percentage of their patients reported depressive symptoms while on the drug. At the same time, animal studies showed that reserpine depleted nerve endings in the brain of several important neurotransmitter substances. Subsequent studies over a 20-year period have determined that the substances most involved are serotonin and norepinephrine (Asberg & Traskman, 1981; Banki & Arato, 1983; Schildkraut, 1965)

A deficiency of serotonin has been found in the brains of some people who have completed suicide and in the cerebrospinal fluid of suicide attempters (Asberg, Nordstrom, & Traskman-Bendz, 1986). Since serotonin is instrumental in regulating emotion, some researchers have suggested that a deficiency of serotonin may be implicated both in depression and in suicide attempts, especially impulsive suicide attempts. One researcher found that low serotonin, as measured by one of its main metabolic products (5-HIAA), was correlated with both depression and the seriousness of suicide attempts. Furthermore, this researcher showed that, among patients who had been hospitalized in conjunction with a suicide attempt, those who had less 5-HIAA were 10 times more likely to have died from suicide a year later than were those who had higher levels of the substance (Asberg, Traskman, & Thoren, 1973).

When chemical deficiencies are found to be related to mood or behavior, a natural development is to try to erase the deficiency by means of the development of drugs. Two major groups of medication have been used on depressed patients with considerable success. The first group consists of monoamine oxidase inhibitors. The second consists of drugs known as *tricyclic antidepressants*. Both of these drug groups act in such a way as to stabilize the amount of monoamine oxidase, serotonin, or norepinephrine available to the nerves in the brain. A third type of medication, lithium, is used in cases of manic-depressive or bipolar affective illness.

A second area of research on the biological bases of suicide involves examining its genetic bases. Blumenthal and Kupfer (1986), reviewing the literature on family history and genetics, reported

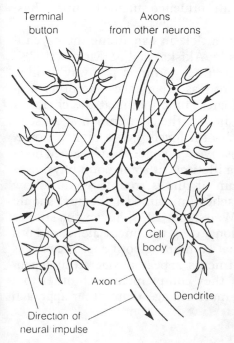

Terminal button

Axons from other neurons

Cell body

Axon

Dendrite

Direction of neural impulse

FIGURE 2.2 **Synapses at the cell body of a neuron. Many different axons, each of which branches repeatedly, synapse on the dendrites and cell body of a single neuron. Each branch of an axon ends in a swelling called a terminal button, which contains the chemical that is released and transmits the nerve impulse across the synapse to the dendrites or cell body of the next cell.** *Source:* **Atkinson, R. L., Atkinson, R. C., & Hilgard, E. R. (1983).**

that suicidal behavior is higher in relatives of persons who exhibit suicidal behavior. One study they reviewed showed that half of a sample of psychiatric inpatients who had a family history of suicide had attempted suicide themselves. They also reported a high rate of concordance (similar behavior) between pairs of identical twins. Although in the literature there were only 10 pairs of identical twins both of whom had committed suicide, there were no reported incidences of fraternal twins both of whom had committed suicide. In addition, these authors reported the findings of a study of adoptees done in Copenhagen. This study included 57 adoptees who committed suicide. Of the 269 biological relatives identified, 12 (4.5%) had committed suicide. No adopting relatives had committed suicide. Of the 57 nonsuicidal adoptees who were matched to the suicides, only 2 (0.7%) of their biological relatives and none of their adoptive relatives committed suicide.

Lester (1986), in another review of the literature on genetics, twin studies, and suicide, concluded that "it is clear that the concordance rate for completed suicide is higher in monozygotic twin pairs raised together than in dizygotic twin pairs raised together" (p. 200). While these studies are far from definitive, they are suggestive of the biological position that maintains that at least a portion of suicidal behavior may be attributed to genetic traits interacting with biology.

Although there is accumulating evidence of a biological correlate to or substrate of depression, this does not rule out environmental, cognitive, existential, or even intrapsychic factors as important in suicidal behavior. In fact, there is good evidence that all are interactively involved in precipitating and maintaining depression and therefore that all influence suicide (Teuting, Kaslow, & Hirschfeld, 1981).

Perhaps the most helpful article in explaining the psychological-physical interaction is by Akiskal and McKinney (1973). They proposed that there is a "final common pathway" which results in the transformation of loss experiences and other negative life events into physiological functioning at the chemical level in the brain. Thus, regardless of the environmental cause of depression, whether the death of a loved one, a broken home, divorce, child abuse, or the negative self-concept and learned helplessness accumulated during a lifetime, at some point physiological changes occur in the brain. If this is true, it would follow that a combination of approaches (multimodal therapy) should bring about the best results. Weissman (1978), reviewing studies which used psychotherapy alone, drug treatment alone, or both in combination, concluded that combining both approaches was most effective; the two treatments appear to operate independently of each other, and yet they complement each other to a great extent, thus producing more change than either approach by itself.

The Scream, Edvard Munch. Tempera and casein on paper. (Courtesy of Nasjonalgalleriet, Oslo. Photograph by Jacques Lathion.)

CONCLUSIONS

Examining suicide from many different perspectives pro-vides a richness impossible to achieve from a single perspective. It also establishes an appreciation of the complexities involved in any suicidal gesture. Finally, it reminds us that human beings are multifaceted creatures. Those who would work with suicidal individuals must begin to see them as persons who have internal personality needs and drives and who are placed within a society that may or may not allow for expression and satisfaction of those needs. They must also recognize that the cognitive set of the individual and his or her thoughts about the current situation can serve to increase or decrease suicide susceptibility. Helping professionals must try to understand the mind-body connections within suicidal people. Stressful environments change body chemistry. In susceptible people, increased stress can result in changes that increase the likelihood of depression. When these chemical changes occur, an increase in depression-related cognitions (Ellis's awful-izing) may result. Such negative cognitions may well increase the subjective impression of stress, which in turn will have a continuing effect on the chemistry of the brain. In short, personality, environment, biology, and cognitions may interact to produce a suicidal individual. The mind and the body are indeed a unity. We are only beginning to discover the nature of their connections, which the study of depression and of suicidal persons is helping to illuminate.

SUMMARY

In this chapter, we have reviewed the major psychological and sociological perspectives on the nature and causes of suicide and provided case studies to illustrate these perspectives. Freud's psychoanalytic perspective was presented, with emphasis on the view of suicide as resulting from an imbalance between thanatos and eros. Erikson's psychosocial perspective was discussed, stressing the importance of the social environment in contributing to the development of both healthy and unhealthy personalities. This book owes a major theoretical debt to Erikson's theory, with its emphasis on personality development over the life span.

The behavioristic perspective, which considers suicide to be a form of learned behavior, was presented in a discussion of reinforcement, modeling, and learned helplessness. The humanistic theories of Maslow and Rogers were noted, with attention given to their belief in the human potential for growth. The universal search for meaningfulness in our lives was discussed, especially on how failure to discover such meaning can lead to feelings of uselessness, hopelessness, and depression.

The cognitive perspective includes the theories of Piaget, Ellis, Kelly, and Beck. The importance of Piaget's theory for understanding the development of concepts of death and of Ellis's theory for understanding irrational cognitions was discussed. Kelly's personal construct theory and Beck's notion of how depression can result from disturbances in our thinking were introduced.

Durkheim's sociological perspective and suicide classification system were presented in detail. We noted the importance of Durkheim's work in understanding suicide, both historically and presently.

Finally, we reported several recent discoveries of biological correlates of depression. There is now a new understanding of the role of serotonin in depression and of the implications for antidepressant medications. Evidence for the role of genetics in depression is increasing. We concluded that biological factors in depression must be considered together with psychological and social factors to achieve a fuller understanding of suicide.

SUGGESTED ADDITIONAL READINGS

The Psychoanalytic Perspective

Bowlby, J. (1973). Separation. In *Attachment and loss* (Vol. 2). New York: Basic Books.

Freud, A. (1946). *The ego and the mechanisms of defense.* New York: International Universities Press.

Freud, A. (1967). *The ego and the mechanisms of defense* (2nd ed.). London: Hogarth Press.

Freud, S. (1961). *Mourning and melancholia.* In J. Strachey (Ed. and Trans.). *The standard edition of the complete psychological works of Sigmund Freud* (Vol. 14, pp. 243-258). London: Hogarth Press. (Original work published 1917.)

Horney, K. (1937). *The collected works of Karen Horney.* New York: Norton.

The Psychosocial Perspective

Erikson, E. H. (1963). *Childhood and society* (2nd ed.). New York: Norton.

Erikson, E. H. (1980). *Identity and the life cycle.* New York: Norton. (Original work published in 1959.)

Erikson E. H. (1982). *The life cycle completed.* New York: Norton.

Gould, R. L. (1978). *Transformations: Growth and change in adult life.* New York: Simon & Schuster.

Levinson, D. J., Darrow, C. N., Klein, E. B., Levinson, M. H., & McKee, B. (1978). *The seasons of a man's life.* New York: Knopf.

Vaillant, G. E. (1977). *Adaptation to life: How the best and brightest came of age.* Boston: Little, Brown.

The Behavioral Perspective

Bandura, A. (1969). *Principles of behavior modification.* New York: Holt, Rinehart & Winston.

Bandura, A. (1977). *Social learning theory.* Englewood Cliffs, NJ: Prentice-Hall.

Craighead, W. E., Kazdin, A. E., & Mahoney, M. J. (1981). *Behavior modification: Principles, issues, and applications* (2nd ed.). Boston: Houghton Mifflin.

Rotter, J. B., Chance, J. E., & Phares, E. J. (1972). *Applications of a social learning theory of personality.* New York: Holt, Rinehart & Winston.

Seligman, M. E. P. (1975). *Helplessness.* San Francisco: Freeman.

Skinner, B. F. (1971). *Beyond freedom and dignity.* New York: Knopf.

The Cognitive Perspective

Beck, A. T. (1976). *Cognitive therapy and the emotional disorders.* New York: International Universities Press.

Elkind, D. (1981). *The hurried child: Growing up too fast too soon.* Reading, MA: Addison-Wesley.

Kohlberg, L. (1969). Stage and sequence: The cognitive-developmental approach to socialization. In D. A. Goslin (Ed.), *Handbook of socialization theory and research.* Chicago: Rand McNally.

Meichenbaum, D. H., & Jaremko, M. (1982). *Stress prevention and management.* New York: Plenum Press.

Piaget, J. (1952). *The origins of intelligence in children.* New York: International Universities Press.

Piaget, J., & Inhelder, B. (1969). *The psychology of the child.* New York: Basic Books.

The Humanistic Perspective

Frankl, V. E. (1963). *Man's search for meaning: An introduction to logotherapy* (I. Lasch, Trans.). New York: Washington Square Press.

Maslow, A. H. (1967). Self-actualization and beyond. In J. F. T. Bugental (Ed.),
    Challenges of humanistic psychology. New York: McGraw-Hill.
Maslow, A. H. (1970). *Motivation and personality* (2nd ed.). New York: Harper
    & Row.
Maslow, A. H. (1971). *The farther reaches of human nature*. New York: Viking
    Press.
Rogers, C. R. (1970). *On becoming a person: A therapist's view of psychotherapy*.
    Boston: Houghton Mifflin.
Rogers, C. R. (1951). *Client-centered therapy*. Boston: Houghton Mifflin.

The Biological Perspective

Deakin, J. F. W. (1986). *The biology of depression*. Oxford: Alden Press.
Geschwind, N. (1979, September). Specializations of the human brain. *Scientific
    American, 241*, pp. 180–199.
Restak, R. M. (1984). *The brain*. New York: Bantam Books.
Rossi, E. L. (1986). *The psychobiology of mind-body healing*. New York: Norton.
Teuting, P., & Koslow, S. H. (1981). Special report on depression research. In
    Science reports. Rockville, MD: National Institute of Mental Health.

REFERENCES

Akiskal, H. S., & McKinney, W. T. (1973). Depressive disorders: Toward a unified
    hypothesis. *Science, 218*, 20–29.
Asberg, M., Nordstrom, P., & Traskman-Bendz, L. (1986, December). Cerebro-
    spinal fluid studies in suicide. *Annals of the New York Academy of Sci-
    ences, 487*, 243–255.
Asberg, M., & Traskman, L. (1981). Studies of CSF 5-HIAA in depression and
    suicidal behavior. *Experiments in Medical Biology, 133*, 739–752.
Asberg, M., Traskman, L., & Thoren, P. (1976). 5-HIAA in the cerebrospinal fluid:
    A biochemical suicide predictor. *Archives of General Psychiatry, 33*, 1193–
    1197.
Bandura, A. (1977). *Social learning theory*. Englewood Cliffs, NJ: Prentice-Hall.
Banki, C. M., & Arato, M. (1983). Amine metabolites, neuroendocrine findings,
    and personality dimension as correlates of suicidal behavior. *Psychiatry
    Research, 10*, 253–261.
Beck, A. T. (1967). *Depression: Clinical, experimental, and theoretical aspects*.
    New York: Hoeber.
Blumenthal, S. J., & Kupfer, D. J. (1986). Generalizable treatment strategies for
    suicidal behavior. In J. J. Mann & M. Stanley (Eds.), *Psychobiology of sui-
    cidal behavior* (pp. 327–340). New York: New York Academy of Sciences.
Durkheim, E. (1951). *Suicide*. (J. A. Spaulding & G. Simpson, Trans.). Glencoe,
    IL: The Free Press. (Original work published 1897.)
Ellis, A. (1962). *Reason and emotion in psychotherapy*. New York: Lyle Stuart.
Ellis, A. (1974). *Humanistic psychotherapy: The rational-emotive approach*. New
    York: McGraw-Hill.
Erikson, E. H. (1959). *Identity and the life cycle*. New York: International Uni-
    versities Press.
Frankl, V. E. (1963) *Man's search for meaning: An introduction to logotherapy* (I.
    Lasch, Trans.). New York: Washington Square Press.
Freud, S. (1961). *Beyond the pleasure principle*. In J. Strachey (Ed. and Trans.).
    *The standard edition of the complete psychological works of Sigmund
    Freud* (Vol. 18, pp. 7–64). London: Hogarth Press. (Original work published
    1920.)
Kelly, G. A. (1955). *The psychology of personal constructs*. New York: Norton.
Lester, D. (1986). Genetics, twin studies, and suicide. In R. Maris (Ed.), *Biology
    of suicide*. New York: Guilford Press.
Levinson, A. J. (1980, April). Termination of life support systems in the elderly:
    Ethical issues. Paper presented at the Scientific Meeting of the Boston
    Society for Gerontologic Psychiatry.

Maslow, A. H. (1954). *Motivation and personality*. New York: Harper & Row.

Maslow, A. H. (1971). *The farther reaches of human nature*. New York: Viking Press.

Meichenbaum, D. (1985). *Stress inoculation training*. Elmsford, NY: Pergamon.

Pavlov, I. (1927). *Conditioned reflexes*. London: Oxford University Press.

Piaget, J. (1926). *The language and thought of the child*. New York: Harcourt Brace.

Piaget, J., & Inhelder, B. (1969). *The psychology of the child*. New York: Basic Books.

Rogers, C. R. (1961). *On becoming a person*. Boston: Houghton Mifflin.

Schildkraut, J. J. (1965). The catecholamine hypothesis of affective disorders: A review of supporting evidence. *American Journal of Psychiatry, 122*, 509–522.

Seligman, M. E. P. (1975). *Helplessness: On depression, development, and death*. San Francisco: Freeman.

Shneidman, E. (1985). *Definition of suicide*. New York: Wiley.

Skinner, B. F. (1953). *Science and human behavior*. New York: Macmillan.

Taylor, S. (1982). *Durkheim and the study of suicide*. New York: St. Martin's Press.

Teuting, P., Kaslow, S. H., & Hirshfeld, R. M. A. (1981). Special report on depression research. In *Science reports*. Rockville, MD: National Institute of Mental Health.

Vaillant, G. E. (1977). *Adaptation to life*. Boston: Little, Brown.

Weissman, M. M. (1978). Psychotherapy and its relevance to the pharmacotherapy of affective disorders: From ideology to evidence. In M. A. Lipton, A. Dimascio, & K. F. Killam (Eds.), *Psychopharmacology: A generation of progress*. New York: Raven Press.

3
Suicide in Childhood

A simple child,
That lightly draws its breath
And feels its life in every limb,
What should it know of death? Wordsworth

The Downtrodden, 1900, Kathe Kollwitz. Etching on paper. (The National Museum of Women in the Arts. Gift of Wallace and Wilhelmina Holladay).

RALEIGH, N.C., April 16 (The Associated Press)—Three North Carolina children younger than 10 whose deaths in 1984 were recorded as accidental might have killed themselves, says a child psychiatrist studying the problem of suicide among very young children.

Dr. Thomas M. Haizlip, director of child psychiatry training at Dorothea Dix Hospital in Raleigh, said Monday that recent studies had exploded the long-held belief that young children were incapable of committing suicide. Many doctors fail to diagnose early childhood depression, and the state doesn't record suicides for children younger than 10, he said.

"It's much more understandable that a child might mistakenly take too much medication," Haizlip said. "But to shoot himself? . . . Even by professionals, it's going undetected."

Haizlip presented four case studies of children who might have committed suicide as a result of severe depression. . . .

The victims in the four cases he studied were boys. Three were 9 and one was 7. The 7-year-old died after taking an overdose of a medication prescribed for bed-wetting. Two of the boys died after shooting themselves in the temples. One boy died by hanging.

Haizlip said the boys were described by their parents as unusually bright and adultlike. They were given much responsibility and shared in sometimes stressful family discussions about health and financial problems.

But upon entering school, the boys failed to perform as expected in academics or sports, Haizlip said. At the same time, each boy experienced the traumatic loss of either a parent or grandparent. They began complaining of stomach aches, headaches or bed-wetting.

Though undetected at the time, the boys began to show signs of deep depression, Haizlip said.

Nationwide, accidents are reported as the leading cause of death among children younger than 12. Medical examiners tend not to document a suspected child suicide to spare the parents guilt and grief, or because states don't keep such records, said Dr. Marc Amaya, director of the Children's Psychiatric Institute at John Umstead Hospital.

The reality of suicide in childhood has only recently been recognized. Most adults in the United States find it almost impossible to contemplate a child committing suicide. As a culture, we have long shared the belief that childhood should ideally be a happy and secure time lived under the protection of parents and other caring adults, a time in which children should be free to explore actively, to learn, and to develop toward their maximum potential. However, as the article printed above indicates, child suicide is a growing reality in the United States. The purpose of this chapter is to expose the full reality of suicide in childhood, a reality in direct contrast to our cultural ideal. In order to lay the framework for the discussion which follows, we will begin with a profile of childhood from the psychological perspectives discussed in Chapter 2.

PROFILE OF CHILDHOOD

According to psychoanalytic theory, the elementary-school child is typically in the latency stage of personality development.

The latency stage was so named by Freud because libido is believed to be relatively quiet during this period, as the child represses sexual urges. Freud believed that latency children continue to work on the resolution of their incestuous wishes that arose from the Oedipus conflict during the preceding phallic period. In order to give up the parent of the opposite sex as the preferred love object, latency stage children tend to identify with members of the same sex. They often show a clear preference for interaction with their own sex and a clear disdain for the other. Children in this stage are typically concerned with making and upholding rules in their various organizations, both formal and informal. Freud believed that this appreciation for sticking by the rules helps latency children to repress their sexual urges. Children's emphasis on "playing by the rules" is also evidence of a continuation of conscience development begun in the previous stage. Freud, like all developmental personality theorists, believed that unresolved problems from an earlier stage can affect later stages. He expressed special concern for children who enter the latency period overburdened with sexual guilt from the preceding period.

Erik Erikson (1980) held that children between ages 6 and 12 are in the personality development stage that has industry and inferiority as the two extremes. Erikson believed that the major developmental task of children in this stage is the rapid accumulation of new skills and abilities associated with beginning school. When children enter school, performance expectations increase dramatically. Also, feedback concerning one's performance usually comes not only from a supporting and nurturing family but now also from teachers and peers, who tend to be more objective. The child who is able to invest energy in learning new school-related and interpersonal skills is likely to experience considerable success and become an industrious individual with high self-esteem. In contrast, the child who is unprepared for the challenges of this stage of development, because of guilt-ridden psychological baggage resulting from poor parenting and unhealthy relationships within the family, is highly likely to fail in school and with his or her peers and to suffer significant feelings of depression and inferiority. Erikson pointed out that industry during childhood is generally characterized by joining organizations, making collections of everything from coins to baseball cards, and being open to new experiences. The child on the positive end of the continuum of industry versus inferiority embarks on new experiences with enthusiasm and confidence, expects success, and interprets failure as feedback rather than as personal inadequacy. The child on the negative end of the continuum is reluctant to open him- or herself to new experiences, expects failure, and develops an ever-deepening sense of inferiority.

As discussed in Chapter 2, the behavioristic perspective focuses on reinforcement, punishment, and modeling as major influences upon behavior at any age instead of focusing on orderly stages of development. Therefore, the behaviorists would predict that children who enter the elementary school years having learned the appropriate habits and skills to meet the many challenges of this age will enjoy a great deal of success while children who begin school poorly prepared for its challenges will be very likely to fail. In addition, the inescapable punishment which failing children receive from teachers and peers tends to cause learned helplessness, which often results in depression. The modeling of parents is also very important for this age group. The child who has confident and industrious parental models at home is much better prepared for success than the child who does not. As the research literature shows, suicidal children often have parental models who are avoidant, impulsive, and suicidal.

The humanistic perspective does not specify a particular stage of development for children between ages 6 and 12. Writers such as Rogers and Maslow do believe, however, that these are important years for the development of self-concept. Healthy children in good homes and schools develop, like plants in good soil, toward their potential. The most important fruit of that development is positive self-regard. Unfortunate children who do not experience healthy, nurturing, and supportive environments may not prosper and will surely suffer very low self-esteem.

Cognitive development theory is helpful also in understanding the suicidal child. According to Piaget, the child between ages 6 and 12 is in the concrete operations stage of development. During the concrete operations years, the child shows impressive development in thinking and problem solving. Having just emerged from the preoperational period, when thinking and problem solving are characterized by an absence of logic and by egocentrism, the concrete operations child, who usually can correctly solve conservation problems, think logically, and understand time, space, and causality, is very impressive. In many ways the concrete operations child who is developing on schedule is well prepared for the challenges of this stage. Children between ages 6 and 12 are in the age of the scientist. They spend much time and energy developing an understanding of cause-effect relationships and in categorizing and classifying the external world. Their developing understandings allow them to have a growing sense of competence and control, which in turn fuels their sense of industry.

The child whose developmental pattern is delayed because of genetic factors or life experiences is likely to manifest some of the problems and failures of a younger child in this situation. Even for the child whose development is appropriate for this age, however, there are some special pitfalls associated with this stage. Although the child's logical thinking develops significantly during this period, the concrete operations child is incapable of abstraction and hypothetical thinking and therefore fails to understand fully certain concepts, such as death. It is not uncharacteristic for some children, especially those under age 10, to believe that death is a temporary and reversible state (Wass, 1984). Such thinking must surely increase a child's vulnerability to suicide when other predisposing factors are in operation.

THE STATISTICAL PICTURE

There is increasing evidence that suicide among children aged 5 to 14 is a growing phenomenon. The incidence of suicide in this age group was not officially reported by the National Center for Health Statistics until 1970. In that year, the suicide rate was reported as 0.3 per 100,000. In 1986, the last year for which official statistics were available, the comparable rate was 0.8 per 100,000, an increase of 267% in the last 15 years (U.S. Bureau of the Census, 1987). Although Canadian statistical reports do not include the same age divisions as U.S. reports, it is interesting to note that suicide rate increases among Canadians aged 10 to 19 have paralleled those in the United States since the mid-1950s (Health and Welfare Canada, 1987). In spite of the fact that these data represent only a small number of children each year who die from suicide, the mere presence of these statistics in national publications attests to the reality of childhood suicide.

It must also be stressed that, although suicide may be relatively rare among children, suicidal behavior is not. The ratio of suicide attempts to completions appears to be inversely related to age (in particular, the ratio of attempts per completions is greater for children than for adolescents or adults). Pfeffer (1981a) reported that 33% of a group of 39 children randomly selected from an outpatient clinic had contemplated, threatened, or attempted suicide. In contrast, only 10% of a group of similar children were reported to have suicidal symptoms or ideations in 1960. These findings may reflect recent trends toward more thorough clinical evaluations. However, they also undoubtedly reveal a significant change in the frequency of suicidal behavior among U.S. children in recent years. In support of this, Turkington (1983) reported that 12,000 children aged 5 to 14 are admitted to psychiatric hospitals for suicidal behavior annually, and Shaffer and Fisher (1981) found that suicidal behavior is reported in 10% of all clinic cases dealing with children. These figures are undoubtedly underestimates. Matter and Matter (1984) have stated that these figures probably represent only 5% of all attempters in this age group.

Both suicide rates and suicidal behavior are grossly underreported in all age groups (Berman & Carroll, 1984). Because there is still a stigma attached to suicide, many families hide evidence and many doctors and coroners are reluctant to classify a death as a suicide if there is the slightest doubt. This tendency to deny suicide is extremely powerful in the case of a child. Turkington (1983) has estimated that no more than 1% of the actual incidence of self-destructive behavior among children is officially reported each year.

Childhood is the kingdom where nobody dies.
Edna St. Vincent Millay,
Wine From These Grapes

One reason that the incidence of suicide in childhood is even more underreported than suicide at other ages may be found in our human tendency to defend the "just world" hypothesis. This hypothesis, held by most of us though not examined often, is that there is a natural and proper order in the universe. In this predictable and orderly universe, parents die before their children. When children precede their parents in death, the just world hypothesis is challenged. The death of a child seems all the more unnatural when it is self-inflicted.

Holmes and Rahe (1967) have suggested that the death of a child, no matter what the cause, is among the most stressful events that parents can experience. Although the data are inconclusive, many writers have suggested that the death of a child by suicide tends to cause more painful grief reactions than death from other causes. One study compared a group of 59 suicide-bereaved parents with a group of 61 parents whose children had died as a result of accident or chronic disease (Demi & Miles, 1988). Although both groups of bereaved parents had high levels of emotional distress and an increased number of negative physical symptoms, there were no significant differences between the two groups.

Perhaps the reason that parents of suicidal children did not differ in their grief reactions from parents of children who died from other causes is that there is a ceiling effect. The death of a child from any cause may evoke such enormous grief reactions that our methods of examining them may not be sophisticated enough to show differentiation at the upper extreme. It is difficult to believe that parents of children who die from suicide do not confront significant issues of guilt, remorse, regret, and anger toward the child more commonly than do other bereaved parents. Additional research is needed to determine the reality of the situation as well as to identify measures that parents use to help them cope with the reality of a child's death.

Although the Demi and Miles study found no evidence for increased parental bereavement for suicide survivors, the important issue of social support was not examined. Research is available focussing on the amount of social support available to parents of children who commit suicide. Several studies have shown that societal reactions to a child's suicide are more negative than to any other cause of death (Calhoun, Selby, & Faulstich, 1980, 1982; Rudestam & Imbroll, 1983). These studies show that parents of suicidal children are liked less, blamed more, and seen as more disturbed than parents of children who die from accidents or diseases. A recent study by Serafin, Thornton, and Robertson (1988) found that adults perceive themselves as less comfortable giving support to the parents of a child or adolescent who has committed suicide than to parents whose child has died as a result of accident or illness. It seems paradoxical that these parents, who are experiencing so much grief, are also exposed to increased external stress and lack of community support.

FACTORS AFFECTING SUICIDE IN CHILDHOOD

Many factors contribute to suicidal behavior in children. These factors can be classified into three major categories: (1) demographic characteristics, (2) home and family characteristics, and (3) psychological characteristics of the individual child.

Demographic characteristics that seem to affect suicide in childhood include sex, race, and socioeconomic status. Because the phenomenon of suicide in childhood has been recognized only recently, none of these characteristics has been studied extensively. Therefore, the relationship between these characteristics and suicide should be interpreted with caution at this time. More research into child suicide is needed to confirm each of these purported relationships.

One of the most surprising facts about child suicide concerns sex differences. In all age groups above age 14, females attempt suicide more often than do males while males complete suicide more often than do females. This is not true among children aged 5 to 14. For this age group, males both attempt and complete suicide more often than do females (Joffe & Offord, 1983; Pfeffer, 1981a). Developmental psychologists have long held that childhood is more difficult for males than for females. Females seem to mature faster than males from birth through puberty (Mussen, Conger, & Kagan, 1974). Females are also physically healthier than males. Death rates for males are higher at every age from conception onward (Stillion, 1985). In addition, the world of school seems to be a better fit for girls than for boys, perhaps because of girls' greater verbal facility (Maccoby & Jacklin, 1974). Whatever the cause, boy children seem to be at higher risk for suicide throughout childhood than are girl children.

Although there is little research relating socioeconomic factors to suicidal behavior among children, there is a general consensus among writers in the area that suicide is more prevalent among poor children (Joffe & Offord, 1983). At the very least, there is a difference in the reporting of suicidal behaviors. Suicide attempts of children from affluent families are more likely to be concealed or to be reported as accidents than are those of poor children.

The findings regarding racial factors in children's suicidal behavior show few consistent relationships. Although white adolescents and adults have a significantly higher incidence of suicide than other racial groups, these differences are not evident among children. Some studies show a predominance of suicide among white children (McIntire & Angle, 1973; Toolan, 1962). Other studies, however, show that blacks are overrepresented among suicidal children (Jacobziner, 1960; McIntire & Angle, 1971).

Joffe and Offord (1983) have pointed out that studies which show a predominance of suicide in a particular group are often difficult to interpret. For example, Gould (1965) found a higher incidence of suicide among Puerto Rican children than among other groups in New York City. Puerto Rican children in the United States frequently differ from others in socioeconomic class, educational opportunities, religion, and numerous other variables which might impact on suicide.

The family environments of suicidal children are less healthy than those of other children in a variety of dimensions. Pfeffer (1981b, 1982) has reported that the families of suicidal children tend to be inflexible and resistant to change in ways which hamper the personal growth of developing children. In addition, families of suicidal children frequently lack clear role definitions for parents and children. The relationship between the parents and children often is one of mutual dependency, almost symbiotic in nature. The children within these homes too often find themselves carrying out adult responsibilities in regard to siblings or even parents. Their own needs are often overlooked, even by themselves, as they try to gain the approval of parents who may view them with ambivalence, disfavor, or even hatred.

An increase in negative feelings among parents is undoubtedly reflected in the fact that the reported incidence of child abuse and neglect has grown annually for the past 15 years (American Humane Association, 1987). Several authors have reported that child abuse and neglect are characteristics associated with families of suicidal children (Joffe & Offord, 1983; Orbach, 1984; Pfeffer, 1981b). Perhaps the most definitive work relating child abuse and neglect to self-destructive behavior in children was carried out by Green (1978). In a study comparing the incidence of suicidal behavior among abused and nonabused children, he found that 40% of the psychologically abused children and 17% of the neglected children demonstrated suicidal behavior compared with only 7% of a group of nonabused and nonneglected children. The self-destructive behavior of the abused children often occurred in response to a beating. Another study showing a relationship between child abuse and suicide found suicide and self-destructive behavior to be the most common pathological outcome for 28 children who were sexually abused (Adams-Tucker, 1982). Pfeffer (1986) has pointed out that the victim of child abuse suffers both the stress of the abusive action and the low self-esteem associated with the belief that his or her "bad" behavior caused the abuse. We would also suggest that such children may have high levels of learned helplessness and accompanying depression. No doubt each of these consequences contributes to the relationship between child abuse and child suicide.

There are some questions, however, regarding the specific nature of the relationship between child abuse and neglect on the one hand and suicidal behavior on the other. At least two carefully controlled studies have shown that child abuse is a significant factor in the family histories of many psychologically disturbed children but that it does not specifically differentiate suicidal children from other disturbed children (Pfeffer, Conte, Plutchik, & Jerret, 1979, 1980).

In addition to blurred generational roles and the existence of abuse and neglect, the homes of suicidal children are often marked by high levels of turbulence. Family crises of all types seem to occur more often among these families, and the incidence of physical violence, divorce, and separation is greater than usual among these families (Kosky, 1983; Orbach, Gross, & Glaubman, 1981). All of these factors result in increased stress for children, whose coping mechanisms are not yet mature. With increasing stress come heightened feelings of helplessness and hopelessness, the twin harbingers of suicidal behavior. Often a child will attempt suicide when the family is in the midst of a crisis that does not directly involve the child. In retrospect, such suicidal behavior can be seen to be a product of accumulated stress, which finally overwhelms the child's endurance. The case of John P. illustrates this situation.

John was an 11-year-old only child whose family had a long history of turbulence. There had been frequent threats of separation and numerous actual separations throughout the marriage. John's younger brother had been born as a result of one of the many reunions. Social workers who became involved with the family described their situation as follows.

Most of the frequent arguments centered around money. John's father's income as a sporadically employed day laborer was never enough to support a family of four. John's mother had worked in a department store before marriage but was now forbidden to do so by her husband, who said repeatedly, "A wife's place is in the home with the children."

Although there was only occasional physical violence between the parents, shouting matches occurred weekly. During these emotional arguments—almost always witnessed by John—John's parents said terrible things to and about each other. After the arguments, John's mother often tried to persuade him to take her side against his father, to be her protector, her "little man."

As the stress increased in the home, John's mother spent more and more time in bed, abdicating her role as wife and mother. John became more a parent than a sibling to his younger brother. It was John who had to be sure that his younger brother had something to eat for dinner, took a bath, had his lunch packed, and was appropriately dressed for school.

When he was much younger, John had tearfully told a friend that when his parents argued, it "hurt his stomach and made him feel scared." He described running from the house when his parents fought—or hiding in his bedroom and using his pillow to muffle the sound of their shouting. As his parents fighting accelerated, John spent more and more time away from home, often staying away all *night. This resulted in his skipping school in order to rest during the day. When his teacher questioned him about his absences, her questions were met with stony silence. When she threatened to call his parents, John screamed, "Do it," and ran from the classroom. The teacher's call to the parents provoked a major fight, during which John's father packed his clothes and left the house. Before school the next day, on the school grounds, John set his clothes on fire.*

John's story involves many of the family characteristics typical of the homes of suicidal children. The socioeconomic status of the family was low, and money problems exacerbated the already weak relationship between the parents. The parental roles, in terms of responsibilities inside and outside the home, were inflexible. John's mother vacillated between ignoring his presence and expecting him to play an adult role in helping her deal with her husband and in raising his younger brother. The suicide attempt followed a final crisis, for which John felt partially responsible. John's choice of place, the schoolyard, represented anger with his teacher, who could have been a real source of strength in the situation. John's suicide attempt clearly marked a total collapse of his ability to cope.

It is a truism that happy, well-adjusted children do not attempt suicide. However, there is some disagreement in the literature regarding the extent of mental illness in suicidal children. One author (Ackerly, 1967) has suggested that suicide in children reflects such significant ego decomposition that the act must be a manifestation of psychosis. Following this line of thinking, it would follow that suicidal children are suffering from serious mental illness, including a break with reality.

More recent authors, however, have found that psychotic behavior is not prevalent among children who attempt suicide (Joffe & Offord, 1983). While all types of mental illness diagnoses have been present in suicidal children, depression is the one category that has consistently been shown to be related to suicidal behavior (Rosenthal & Rosenthal, 1984; Pfeffer, 1981a; Orbach, 1984). At least two studies have shown that depression is more prevalent among suicidal than among nonsuicidal children (Orbach, 1984; Pfeffer et al., 1979). Depression among children may be manifested in many ways, including increased anxiety, sleep disturbances, an increase in the acting out of aggression, low tolerance for frustration, poor impulse control, and an increase in antisocial behavior (Kosky, 1982; Orbach, 1984; Rosenthal & Rosenthal, 1984).

One element in severe depression is a sense of hopelessness. A sense of hopelessness has been shown to be a stronger predictor of suicide than is generalized depression alone. One study compared suicidal and nonsuicidal children on separate measures of hopelessness, depression, and self-esteem. The researchers found that, although all three variables were interrelated, feelings of hopelessness correlated significantly with the lethality (seriousness) of the suicide intent, even when the general level of depression was taken into consideration by using the statistical techniques of partial correlation (Kazdin, French, Unis, Esveldt-Dawson, & Sherick, 1983). These findings indicate that children who dislike themselves and are generally depressed may contemplate suicide. However, the seriousness of such contemplations is increased greatly in children who also feel hopeless about the future.

In addition to children, like John P., who attempt suicide as a reaction to stress and accompanying depression, some researchers have suggested that there are suicidal children of a second type (Pfeffer, Plutchik, & Mizruchi, 1983). They describe such children as angry and impulsive and as having a tendency to approach problems in an assaultive manner. These children often have parental models who are impulsive and show suicidal behaviors themselves. When these children exhibit suicidal behaviors, they may be manifesting a genetic predisposition or an overlearned approach to problem solving that has been observed in the home. The case of Tony L. reflects this type of suicidal behavior.

Tony, the oldest of three children, was born into a lower-middle-class home. His mother described Tony as a "live wire." He never seemed to sleep as a baby. He cried a great deal and always seemed to be hungry or uncomfortable in some way. As a toddler he was into everything. He would rummage through the cabinets, pull the cloth off the kitchen table, or demolish the linen closet. He had to be watched every waking moment or he would be into something potentially dangerous. His parents had made numerous trips to the emergency room to pump household cleaner from his stomach, to treat a burn from the iron or stove, or to have a cut sutured.

Tony's father was an aggressive and impulsive individual. Although he was a skillful carpenter and made a good salary when he worked, he had difficulty keeping jobs. He frequently developed conflicts with his foremen that resulted in his either quitting or getting fired.

The father's impulsiveness and temper caused problems at home as well as at work. Once when the family was accidentally locked out of the house, Tony's father kicked the front door down instead of searching for an unlocked window. Another time when he locked his keys in the car, he broke one of the windows rather than search for the spare key.

Tony's mother was very unhappy but felt unable to deal constructively with her family problems. She worked part-time in her father's business as a receptionist. Her husband's angry and impulsive outbursts and her son's overactive behaviors upset her greatly. She had frequent and severe headaches that sent her to bed for days at a time. She wanted to leave her husband but was afraid of what he might do in retaliation. Tony's mother was frequently depressed and cried often. Once when suffering from a particularly severe headache, she took so many aspirin that her stomach had to be pumped.

Tony's problems seemed to escalate when he entered school. He could not get along with the other children in his class. When the teacher reported that Tony fought with the other children, his mother became upset but took no action. His father spanked him.

By the time Tony entered the third grade, he had been labelled a behavior problem by teachers in the school. His relations with other students degenerated to the point where physical fighting occurred almost daily in the classroom or on the playground. One day when the teacher was scolding him for fighting, Tony broke away from her, ran to the window, and jumped from the second floor.

Children have never been very good at listening to their elders, but they have never failed to imitate them.
James Baldwin, *Fifth Avenue Uptown*

Tony's suicidal behavior can be viewed as a product of both his temperament and environment. There is evidence that Tony was "a difficult baby." Such babies seem to come into the world with more sensitive biological systems (Derryberry & Rothbart, 1984). Highly active and irritable babies are difficult for parents in the best of situations. However, in Tony's case, his parents were poor models of coping behaviors. Tony's father modeled impulsive and aggressive behaviors while his mother modeled weak, dependent, and escapist behaviors. Those two models, in combination with Tony's own tendency to act out, help to explain his suicidal reaction to the frustration of the teacher's scolding.

Tony's behavior also illustrates two other hallmarks of child suicide, impulsivity and lethality. Children differ from adults in the methods they use to attempt suicide. Some of this difference undoubtedly stems from young children's lack of access to less violent methods of committing suicide, such as toxic drugs. Some of the difference may also be related to lack of cognitive development, which will be discussed in more detail in the section to follow. However, some of the difference in method must reflect an impulsive reaction following a sudden collapse of immature coping skills. In general, children tend to use more violent methods in attempting suicide than do adolescents and adults (Joffe & Offord, 1983). They are more likely than other age groups to jump from high places and to hang, stab, or shoot themselves (Kosky, 1983).

In addition to impulsivity, Tony's case illustrates another characteristic observed in many suicidal children, poor performance in school. Many studies and clinical observations show that suicidal children tend to perform poorly in school (Connell, 1972; Joffe & Offord, 1983; Pfeffer, 1981a). There is considerable evidence, however, that the poor school performance of suicidal children is not due to low intelligence or learning disabilities. Many studies show a normal range of intelligence among suicidal children (Ackerly, 1967; Connell, 1972; Joffe & Offord, 1983; Rosenberg & Latimer, 1966). At least two studies show that some children who attempt suicide are above average in intelligence (Kosky, 1983; Shaffer, 1974).

Although the poor school performance of suicidal children is well documented, the studies typically do not examine suicidal children's school performance in comparison with other children who are psychiatrically disturbed. One study which did examine differences between these two groups found no differences in school performance between suicidal and other psychologically disturbed children (Pfeffer, 1981b). Apparently, poor school performance is associated with childhood psychopathology but is not specific to those problems associated with suicidal behavior (Joffe & Offord, 1983).

A final psychological dimension which may add to our understanding of children's suicide is that of cognitive development. Over the past 50 years, a rich body of literature has been accumulated that indicates that children's concepts of death develop slowly, in accordance with the Piagetian stages of cognitive development discussed in Chapter 2 (Gartley & Bernasconi, 1967; Koocher, 1973; Nagy, 1948; Pfeffer, 1984; Speece & Brent, 1984; Stillion & Wass, 1979; Swain, 1979; Wass, 1984; Wass & Stillion, 1988). It is generally believed that children under 7 years of age have an immature and egocentric view of death. They think of death as being a transient and reversible state. Between ages 7 and 12, most children develop increasing understanding of the facts of death. By age 12, almost all children understand that death is final, universal, and inevitable.

Some writers have suggested that the immature view which younger children have about death protects them against suicide (Gould, 1965; Shaffer & Fisher, 1981). They point to the relatively low incidence of suicide in childhood to support their position. People holding this view believe that because children do not have a clear understanding of what death is, they are reluctant to attempt suicide for fear of the unknown.

Other writers disagree with the assumption that children's immature views of death protect them from suicide (Joffe & Offord, 1983). There is evidence that suicidal children conceptualize death differently than do nonsuicidal children. Joffe and Offord (1983) have shown that suicidal children have less well-defined concepts of death. Other authors have suggested that suicidal children view death as a transient and pleasant state (McIntire & Angle, 1971; McIntire, Angle, & Struempler, 1972). Rather than protecting children against suicide, it would seem that such cognitions might make suicide a more attractive option. For children who lack a clear understanding of the finality of existence involved in death, and especially for those who believe that death is the gateway to a more pleasant existence, suicide may be less frightening than for other children.

Orbach and Glaubman (1979) have suggested that even children who have a mature view of death in general may lose that maturity when they begin to consider suicide as a personal option. Older children who understand the finality of death in the abstract may regress to earlier forms of thinking which allow them to view their own death by suicide as pleasant and even transient.

Pfeffer's (1986) clinical work with suicidal children has uncovered support for this position. She describes children in a suicidal crisis as manifesting "ego constriction" that leads to a regression in their thinking about death.

This type of ego constriction has been referred to by other authors as cognitive rigidity and has been found to characterize suicidal individuals of all ages. Cognitive rigidity is a kind of intellectual tunnel vision. The cognitively rigid individual is a dichotomous thinker who tends to see the world and its problems in terms of black and white, good and bad, right and wrong. Such individuals often have difficulty understanding the complexity of a given situation. Once a plan of action for dealing with a problem has been determined, that solution tends to be considered the only possible solution. These individuals are very unlikely to contemplate alternate plans of action which might be tried if the first possibility fails.

In a very important study, Orbach (1984) compared a group of suicidal children with a chronically ill group and a normal control group on rigidity in solving life or death dilemmas. He found the suicidal children to be significantly more cognitively rigid in problem solving in this situation than the other two groups. He found, also, that the degree of cognitive rigidity correlated positively with a measure of attraction to death among the suicidal children. Put another way, those suicidal children who were more cognitively rigid found death to be a more attractive alternative to life than suicidal children who were less cognitively rigid. Orbach concluded from these findings that cognitive rigidity is an intervening process in the relationship between the stresses of life and suicidal behavior. Cognitively rigid children tend to overestimate the seriousness of their problems, to consider too few solutions, and to exaggerate the attractiveness of suicide as a solution (Orbach, 1984; Turkington, 1983).

One final perspective in understanding the cognitive aspects of child suicide was recently developed by Orbach (1988). Orbach has proposed that understanding any child's suicidal orientation can be enhanced by a determination of his or her attraction to and repulsion from life and death. According to Orbach, every child's cognitions include measurable attitudes on each of these four dimensions. Attraction to life is influenced by personality strengths and by the support a child feels from the environment, while repulsion from life reflects characteristics growing out of experiences with pain and suffering. Attraction to death is associated with a belief in a serene and peaceful existence after life, and may also include the notion that death is reversible. As we have seen already, this type of thinking is characteristic of many suicidal children. Repulsion from death reflects a frightening expectation of irreversible cessation. We would suggest that some children in cultures that stress the concepts of heaven and hell

Whatever crazy sorrow saith,
No life that breathes with human breath
Has ever truly longed for death. Tennyson, *The Two Voices*

might also experience repulsion from death because of their belief in punishment in the hereafter.

As Orbach (1988) has pointed out, his perspective is phenomenological in orientation. Attraction to and repulsion from life and death are salient only from the child's perspective. As environmental and other factors change, the child's orientation regarding each of these dimensions will be affected.

Orbach's perspective also includes the notion of ambivalence toward suicide. Even the most seriously suicidal child shows some attraction to life. Orbach's concept of ambivalence is reminiscent of Freud's now familiar concepts of eros and thanatos. The child whose life experiences cause him or her to have a strong repulsion from life and attraction to death and a weak attraction to life and repulsion from death could be characterized as showing a pathological imbalance between eros and thanatos.

According to Orbach's perspective, happy and well-adjusted children should show very positive attitudes toward life and hold very negative views of death while depressed, hopeless, and suicidal children should view life and death in opposite ways. Orbach and his associates compared groups of suicidal and nonsuicidal children on four different measures of attraction to and repulsion from life and death in two different studies. Both studies found that suicidal children, compared with a nonsuicidal group, showed more repulsion from life, less attraction to life, more attraction to death, and less repulsion from death (Orbach, 1984; Orbach, Feshbach, Carlson, & Ellenberg, 1984). Interestingly, the smallest difference between the suicidal and nonsuicidal groups was found on the measure of attraction to life. The suicidal children in these studies remained attracted to life even under the most negative circumstances. These findings support Orbach's belief in the ambivalence of suicidal children and have encouraging implications for prevention and intervention techniques designed to move ambivalent suicidal children toward more positive views of life.

It is evident that cognitive factors are important influences on child suicide. The role which cognitive factors can play in attempted suicide is illustrated in the following case study.

Laura S. is an academically gifted 9-year-old child born to professional parents. She was a much-wanted child who was born after her mother had experienced a succession of miscarriages. Laura's parents were deeply religious people who interpreted Laura's birth as a gift from God. They vowed to do everything possible to raise this child in an atmosphere of love.

Laura was the centerpiece of the family. Her parents took her everywhere they went and included her in all activities. Her parents discontinued many of their previous social activities which did not include children. They also broke off relationships with former friends who did not share their child-centered orientation.

Garino tomb, A. Frilli. (Cemetary of Nice-Gairaut. Photograph from *Images de l'homme devant la mort* (Images of Man and Death) by Philippe Aries, Editions du Seuil, 1983, Janet Lloyd, Trans.)

Laura's parents loved and cared for her to the point of over-indulgence and overprotection. She was not allowed to have the usual kinds of experiences which promote the development of appropriate independence. She was not left in day care or with a baby-sitter, and she never stayed at other children's houses overnight.

When Laura was 8½, she and her parents took a vacation trip. While traveling there was an accident which resulted in the death of both of Laura's parents. Laura was not badly injured in the accident, and she moved into her grandparents' home, where she was loved and cared for.

Her grandparents tried to console Laura by assuring her that her parents were "happy in Jesus." As the months went on, Laura became increasingly withdrawn, spending her time alone reading Bible stories about heaven and staring at pictures of her parents. One day her grandmother found her standing on a chair with a belt around her neck in an obvious attempt at suicide. Laura tearfully told her grandmother and grandfather that, while she loved them very much, she missed her parents terribly and wanted to be with them and Jesus in heaven. She said that the Bible told her that heaven is a lovely place where she and her parents will live together in peace and happiness.

Laura's story reveals the role that lack of cognitive understanding may play in suicidal behavior. Laura, yearning for her dead parents, was attracted to death as the best way to reclaim her lost happiness. Once she considered this possibility, it seemed the only solution to her. Her thinking reflects an immature concept of death, the cognitive rigidity characteristic of suicidal children, and the attraction to death described by Orbach. Her suicide attempt also illustrates a factor often seen in child suicides, a past history of loss.

Suicidal children experience more frequent and earlier loss than others. Several studies show that these children lose parents through death and divorce before 11 years of age more often than others (Corder & Haizlip, 1984; Matter & Matter, 1984; Pfeffer, 1981b). These stresses are not, however, limited to the early years. The separation and divorce rates for parents of suicidal children of all ages are higher than the national average (Garfinkel, Froese, & Hood, 1982; Murphy & Wetzel, 1982; Tishler, McKenry, & Morgan, 1981). A study by Cohen-Sandler, Berman, and King (1982) showed that suicidal children experience more stress related to loss than others throughout their childhood and that their suicidal behavior is, to some extent, a response to accumulated loss. The relationship between loss and suicide in children was reflected in a study by Morrison and Collier (1969) which found that 76% of a group of 34 outpatient children experienced a significant family loss or the anniversary of a loss within a few weeks of a suicide attempt.

Although not true in Laura's case, another loss frequently experienced by suicidal children is loss of love. Their parents often communicate ambivalent feelings to the children, including hostility, low personal regard, withdrawal of love, or even hatred. Sabbath (1969) has observed suicidal children in these circumstances often enough to label them "expendable children."

Just as children are incapable of understanding the reality of death, many are unable to interpret parental hostility accurately. Children born to parents who dislike them and treat them with hostility are likely to introject (absorb into themselves) those feelings, turning them into self-hatred and hostility against self. Suicidal behavior may represent a natural consequence of such negative feelings turned inward. It would take the highest level of cognitive development, not to mention an enormous amount of objectivity, for a child to view hostility from the parents as "their problem" rather than as a reflection of his or her inherent "badness" or lack of worth. Young children generally are incapable of such thinking. They frequently feel responsible for parents' negative emotions and sometimes feel they should be punished for the role they play in making their parents unhappy. These types of cognitions, no doubt, contribute to suicidal ideation in children.

SUMMARY

Much of what we know about child suicide is consistent with Erikson's theory of personality development, which was discussed earlier in this chapter and in the previous chapter. According to Erikson, the elementary-school child is in the stage that has industry and inferiority as the extremes of the continuum and that includes the developmental tasks of learning many new skills associated with the elementary-school years. The fortunate child raised in a nurturant and loving family is free to invest a great deal of energy in the challenges of this stage and to function at the positive end of the industry versus inferiority continuum. The unfortunate child who grows up in a highly stressful and conflicted family environment (typically the environment of suicidal children) must utilize his or her resources in dealing with family problems and has little reserve left for the important developmental tasks which occur outside the home.

Children manifest certain characteristics in their self-destructive behavior peculiar to this age group. Children tend to be impulsive and aggressive in their suicidal acts and use more lethal techniques of self-destruction than older age groups. Fortunately, however, they are less successful than adolescents or adults. Although child suicide is rare, suicidal behavior in this age group occurs with disturbing frequency and appears to be increasing. Male children attempt and commit suicide more often than females. There are few clear-cut relationships between socioeconomic class, racial membership, or religious affiliation and suicide in children.

Many suicidal children come from pathological families where the patterns of interaction do not promote growth and development among its members. Parent role models in these families are frequently impulsive, avoidant, and aggressive. These children have often experienced early and repeated loss in the family through death, separation, or divorce. The family may be in a crisis situation, which creates a great deal of stress for the suicidal child.

Suicidal children manifest many of the characteristics that typify the emotionally disturbed, such as poor social skills and problems in school. There is, however, no particular psychiatric syndrome idiosyncratic to the suicidal child. The most predictive psychological characteristic of suicidal children is affective: Suicidal children, like their older counterparts, are often significantly depressed and often feel hopeless. Also, some suicidal children show anger and behave impulsively.

Suicidal children are more likely than their nonsuicidal age mates to view death as pleasant and reversible. They frequently hold wish fulfillment fantasies concerning death. Also, they tend to be more cognitively rigid than other children. They frequently have an inflexible and dichotomous view of life's problems and solutions.

REFERENCES

Ackerly, W. C. (1967). Latency-age children who threaten or attempt to kill themselves. *Journal of the American Academy of Child Psychiatry, 6*, 242–261.

Adams-Tucker, C. (1982). Proximate effects of sexual abuse in childhood: A report in 28 children. *American Journal of Psychiatry, 139*, 1252–1256.

American Humane Association. (1987). *Highlights of official child neglect and reporting 1985*. Denver: Author.

Berman, A. L., & Carroll, T. A. (1984). Adolescent suicide: A critical review. *Death Education, 8*, 53–64.

Calhoun, L. G., Selby, J. W., & Faulstich, M. E. (1980). Reactions to the parents of the child suicide: A study of social impression. *Journal of Consulting and Clinical Psychology, 48*, 535–536.

Calhoun, L. G., Selby, J. W., & Faulstich, M. E. (1982). The aftermath of child suicide: Influences on the perceptions of parents. *Journal of Community Psychology, 10*, 250–254.

Cohen-Sandler, R., Berman, A. L., & King, R. A. (1982). Life stress and symptomatology: Determinants of suicidal behavior in children. *Journal of the American Academy of Child Psychiatry, 21*, 178–186.

Connell, H. M. (1972). Attempted suicide in school children. *Medical Journal of Australia, 1*, 686–690.

Corder, B. F., & Haizlip, T. M. (1984). Environmental and personality similarities in case histories of suicide and self-poisoning in children under ten. *Suicide and Life-Threatening Behavior, 14*, 59–66.

Demi, A. S., & Miles, M. S. (1988). Suicide bereaved parents: Emotional distress and physical problems. *Death Studies, 12*, 297–307.

Derryberry, D., & Rothbart, M. K. (1984). Emotion, attention, and temperament. In C. E. Izard, J. Kagan, & R. B. Zajonc (Eds.), *Emotions, cognition and behavior* (pp. 132–167). Cambridge: Cambridge University Press.

Erikson, E. H. (1980). *Identity and the life cycle*. New York: Norton.

Garfinkel, B. D., Froese, A., & Hood, J. (1982). Suicide attempts in children and adolescents. *American Journal of Psychiatry, 139*, 1257–1261.

Gartley, W., & Bernasconi, M. (1967). The concept of death in children. *Journal of Genetic Psychology, 110*, 71–85.

Gould, R. E. (1965). Suicide problems in children and adolescents. *American Journal of Psychotherapy, 19*, 228–245.

Green, A. H. (1978). Self-destructive behavior in battered children. *American Journal of Psychiatry, 135*, 579–582.

Health and Welfare Canada. (1987). *Suicide in Canada: Report of the National Task Force on Suicide in Canada*. Ottawa: Department of National Health and Welfare.

Holmes, T. H., & Rahe, R. H. (1967). The social readjustment rating scale. *Journal of Psychosomatic Research, 11*, 213–218.

Jacobziner, H. (1960). Attempted suicide in children. *Journal of Pediatrics, 56*, 519–525.

Joffe, R. T., & Offord, D. R. (1983). A review: Suicidal behavior in childhood. *Canadian Journal of Psychiatry, 28*, 57–63.

Kazdin, A. E., French, N. H., Unis, A. S., Esveldt-Dawson, K., & Sherick, R. B. (1983). Helplessness, depression, and suicidal intent among psychiatrically disturbed inpatient children. *Journal of Consulting and Clinical Psychology, 51*, 504–510.

Koocher, G. P. (1973). Childhood, death, and child development. *Developmental Psychology, 9*, 369–375.

Kosky, P. (1982). Childhood suicidal behavior. *Journal of Child Psychology and Psychiatry and Allied Disciplines, 24*, 457–467.

Maccoby, E. E., & Jacklin, C. N. (1974). *The psychology of sex differences*. Stanford, CA: Stanford University Press.

Matter, D. E., & Matter, R. M. (1984, April). Suicide among elementary school children. *Elementary School Guidance and Counseling*, pp. 260, 267.

McIntire, M. S., & Angle, C. R. (1971). Suicide as seen in a poison control center. *Pediatrics, 48*, 914–922.

McIntire, M. S., & Angle, C. R. (1973). Psychological "biopsy" in self-poisoning of children and adolescents. *American Journal of Diseases of Children, 126,* 42–46.

McIntire, M. S., Angle, C. R., & Struempler, L. J. (1972). The concept of death in midwestern children and youth. *American Journal of Diseases of Children, 123,* 527–532.

Morrison, G. C., & Collier, J. G. (1969). Family treatment approaches to suicidal children and adolescents. *Journal of the American Academy of Child Psychiatry, 8,* 140–153.

Murphy, G. E., & Wetzel, R. D. (1982). Family history of suicidal behavior among suicide attempters. *Journal of Nervous and Mental Disease, 170,* 86–90.

Mussen, P. H., Conger, J. J., & Kagan, J. (1974). *Child development and personality* (4th ed.). New York: Harper & Row.

Nagy, M. (1948). The child's theories concerning death. *Journal of Genetic Psychology, 73,* 3–27.

Orbach, I. (1984). Personality characteristics, life circumstances, and dynamics of suicidal children. *Death Education, 8,* 37–52.

Orbach, I. (1988). *Children who don't want to live: Understanding and treating the suicidal child.* San Francisco: Jossey-Bass.

Orbach, I., Feshbach, S., Carlson, G., & Ellenberg, L. (1984). Attitudes towards life and death in suicidal, normal, and chronically ill children: An extended replication. *Journal of Consulting and Clinical Psychology, 52,* 1020–1027.

Orbach, I., & Glaubman, H. (1979). The concept of death and suicidal behavior in young children: Three case studies. *Journal of the American Academy of Child Psychiatry, 18,* 668–678.

Orbach, I., Gross, Y., & Glaubman, H. (1981). Some common characteristics of latency-age suicidal children: A tentative model based on case study analyses. *Suicide and Life-Threatening Behavior, 11,* 180–190.

Pfeffer, C. R. (1981a). Suicidal behavior of children: A review with implications for research and practice. *American Journal of Psychiatry, 138,* 154–159.

Pfeffer, C. R. (1981b). The family system of suicidal children. *American Journal of Psychotherapy, 35,* 330–341.

Pfeffer, C. R. (1982). Intervention for suicidal children and their parents. *Suicide and Life-Threatening Behavior, 12,* 240–248.

Pfeffer, C. R. (1984). Death preoccupations and survival behavior in children. In H. Wass & C. A. Corr (Eds.), *Childhood and death* (pp. 261–278). Washington, DC: Hemisphere.

Pfeffer, C. R. (1986). *The suicidal child.* New York: Guilford Press.

Pfeffer, C. R., Conte, H. R., Plutchik, R., & Jerrett, I. (1979). Suicidal behavior in latency-age children: An empirical study. *Journal of the American Academy of Child Psychiatry, 18,* 679–692.

Pfeffer, C. R., Conte, H. R., Plutchik, R., & Jerrett, I. (1980). Suicidal behavior in latency-age children: An outpatient population. *Journal of the American Academy of Child Psychiatry, 18,* 703–710.

Pfeffer, C. R., Plutchik, R., & Mizruchi, M. S. (1983). Suicidal and assaultive behavior in children: Classification, measurement, and intervention. *American Journal of Psychiatry, 140,* 154–157.

Rosenberg, P. H., & Latimer, R. (1966). Suicide attempts by children. *Mental Hygiene, 50,* 354–359.

Rosenthal, P. A., & Rosenthal, S. (1984). Suicidal behavior by preschool children. *American Journal of Psychiatry, 141,* 520–525.

Rudestam, K., & Imbroll, D. (1983). Societal reactions to the child's death by suicide. *Journal of Consulting and Clinical Psychology, 51,* 461–462.

Sabbath, J. C. (1969). The suicidal adolescent: The expendable child. *Journal of the American Academy of Child Psychiatry, 8,* 272–289.

Serafin, J. D., Thornton, G., & Robertson, D. U. (1988, April). The social stigma of suicide. Paper presented at the meeting of the Association for Death Education and Counseling, Orlando, FL.

Shaffer, D. (1974). Suicide in childhood and early adolescence. *Journal of Child Psychology and Psychiatry, 15*, 275–291.

Shaffer, D., & Fisher, P. (1981). The epidemiology of suicide in children and adolescents. *Journal of the American Academy of Child Psychiatry, 21*, 545–566.

Speece, M. W., & Brent, S. B. (1984). Children's understanding of death: A review of three components of a death concept. *Child Development, 55*, 1671–1686.

Stillion, J. M. (1985). *Death and the sexes: An examination of differential longevity, attitudes, behaviors, and coping skills.* Washington, DC: Hemisphere.

Stillion, J. M., & Wass, H. (1979). Children and death. In H. Wass (Ed.), *Dying: Facing the facts* (pp. 208–235). Washington, DC: Hemisphere.

Swain, H. L. (1979). Childhood views of death. *Death Education, 2*, 341–358.

Tishler, C. L., McKenry, P. C., & Morgan, K. C. (1981). Adolescent suicide attempts: Some significant factors. *Suicide and Life-Threatening Behavior, 11*, 86–92.

Toolan, J. M. (1962). Suicide and suicidal attempts in children and adolescents. *American Journal of Psychiatry, 118*, 719–723.

Turkington, C. (1983, May). Child suicide: An unspoken tragedy. *APA Monitor*, p. 15.

U.S. Bureau of the Census (1987). *Statistical Abstract of the United States: 1986* (107th Edition). Washington, DC: U.S. Government Printing Office.

Wass, H. (1984). Concepts of death: A developmental perspective. In H. Wass & C. A. Corr (Eds.), *Childhood and death* (pp. 3–24). Washington, DC: Hemisphere.

Wass, H., & Stillion, J. M. (1988). Death in the lives of children and adolescents. In H. Wass, F. M. Berardo, & R. A. Neimeyer (Eds.), *Dying: Facing the facts* (pp. 201–208). Washington, DC: Hemisphere.

4

Suicide in Adolescence and Young Adulthood

So much of adolescence is an ill-defined dying,
An intolerable waiting,
A longing for another place and time,
Another condition. Theodore Roethke, *I'm Here*

The phenomenon of suicide in adolescence and young adulthood has received much attention in recent years. Newspaper articles, books, and research reports have attempted to explain the rapid increase in suicidal behavior among people in these age groups. However, as Berman and Carroll (1984) have pointed out, the literature on youth suicide has many weaknesses. Most of these weaknesses are inherent in the subject itself and apply to all age groups. For example, it is impossible to study suicide from the point of view of those who commit it, since they are dead. This means that most of our knowledge about completed suicide is gathered retrospectively and from secondary sources. Even with improved methods for carrying out psychological autopsies (post-suicide studies), results of such research must be interpreted cautiously. In addition to the problems of carrying out research on completed suicides, there is growing evidence that the acts of attempted and completed suicide may have different meanings (Berman & Carroll, 1984). Suicidal acts vary in lethality from mere gestures to completed suicide, yet the research literature rarely controls for the level of lethality among attempters.

More recently, Berman has suggested that there are several types of adolescents who are at high risk for engaging in suicidal behavior, including "the affectively disordered, the substance abusing, the conduct disordered, the rigid perfectionist, and the socially marginal" (Berman, 1988, p. 20). However, individual types of behavior among suicidal youth have rarely been studied in depth. Intentionality has also rarely been studied. Attempters who never meant to die are grouped with those whose only desire is to die. Researchers tend to use different definitions of the term *suicidal* and frequently do not clearly operationalize them, making comparisons between studies difficult. Much of the research on youth suicide does not include comparison groups, making it difficult to know if the findings of the study apply only to suicide attempters or if they also apply to nonsuicidal youth.

Finally, studying youth suicide is made difficult by its infrequency. In spite of the fact that the incidence of suicide among young people has risen dramatically, it is still (fortunately) a rare act in most communities. Therefore, researchers find it difficult to identify a large enough sample of suicidal youth to carry out reliable studies. This is especially true for the researcher who would like to control for level of lethality, intentionality, type of at-risk behavior, etc. Also, because suicide is such a rare event, variables that have been shown through research to be associated with suicidal behavior are highly likely to result in many false positives when used in clinical practice.

Although the research literature is flawed, it does provide a starting point for the discussion of suicide among adolescents and young adults. For purposes of this chapter, we define adolescence as the period from ages 15–24, following the age grouping reported by the National Center for Health Statistics. Young adulthood is defined as the period from ages 25–34.

In this chapter, we will review the changing statistics on suicide among adolescents and young adults since midcentury in the United States and other developed countries, summarize research findings about factors contributing to suicide in these two age groups, and review what is known about the attitudes of adolescents and young adults toward suicide. In order to understand suicidal individuals, it is necessary to know about the normative events of the period of life in which these individuals are attempting to function. Therefore, we will begin each major section of this chapter with profiles of adolescents and young adults.

SUICIDE IN ADOLESCENCE

To Whom It May Concern: ?
Jason Kelvin Joyner
(July 16, 1968 - April 30, 1989)

Why?! - Because my life has been nothing but misery and sorrow for 20 3/4 years! Going backwards: I thought Susan loved me, but I suppose not. "I love you Jason" was only a lie. I base my happiness on relationships with girls—when I'm "going steady," I'm happy. When a girl dumps me (which is <u>always</u> the case) I'm terribly depressed. In fact, over the last <u>3</u> years I've been in love at least <u>4</u> times seriously, but only to have my heart shattered—like so many icicles falling from a roof. But I've tried to go out with at least 30–40 girls in the last few years—none of them <u>ever</u> fell in love w/<u>me</u>. My fate was: "To love, but not be loved."

My mother threw me out of the house in March. I guess she must really hate me; she doesn't even write me letters. I think she always hated me.

In high school, and even before that, nobody liked me. They all made fun of me and no girl would ever go to the proms with me.

I haven't anything to live for. Hope? 5 years ago I wanted to end my life—I've been hoping for 5 years! Susan was just the straw that broke the camel's back. I simply cannot take it anymore! I only wanted someone to love; someone who would love me back as much as I loved her.

Yeah, I had pretty good grades, but the way my luck runs, I wouldn't have gotten a job anyway. I got fired over the summer cause the boss said, "Jason, you don't have any common sense." Gee, that really made my day.

I walk down the streets of Madison and people call out of dorm windows: "Hey Asshole!" What did I do to them? I don't even know them!

I've been pretty miserable lately (since 1979), so I think I will change the scenery. What's the big deal? I was gonna die in 40 or 50 years anyway. (Maybe sooner: when George decides to push the button in Washington, D.C.!)

Good bye Susan, Sean, Wendy, Joe, Mr. Montgomery, Dr. Johnston, Jack, and everyone else who made my life a little more bearable while it lasted.

Jason Kelvin Joyner
April 30, 1989

P.S. You might want to print this in the campus newspaper. It would make excellent reading!

Last Will
(Only will. I never made one before.)

I probably am wasting my time, because you need a lawyer or a witness for a will to be legal, but here goes:

To Sean - go my records, tapes, cassette player, clock/radio, and my camera (in the Doctor's bag in closet).

To Wendy - I leave my car (if you want it, if not, give it to ET), my big black coat and my military school uniform - you said you wanted them.

To Joe and Wendy - All my posters, if you want them.

To Jack - Miscellaneous items left over (that's still a lot, so don't complain).

To Susan - I leave memories of nice times we had. Also my airbrush (in Doctor bag w/camera), and all my love; I'll miss you forever.

If I've forgotten anyone - I'm sorry.

Jason Kelvin Joyner
April 30, 1989

Please: No autopsy

The above is an actual suicide note of a college student, which was found in his dormitory room. Although the names, places, and dates are fictitious, the essential content is unchanged. This note reveals many of the idiosyncratic aspects of adolescent suicide which will be discussed in this section of the chapter.

PROFILE OF ADOLESCENCE

The hallmark of adolescence is physical growth. Formally, the period of adolescence begins at puberty, a point in time in which increased levels of hormones entering the bloodstream result in the appearance of the first menstrual period in girls (around 12½ years) and the first nocturnal emission for boys (around 14 years). Puberty is preceded by a period of rapid physical growth. It is not unusual for young people to grow 4 or 5 inches in a single year. Primary and secondary sex characteristics also are triggered by the increase in hormone production. In boys, such secondary sex characteristics (those not directly involved in propagating the species) include pubic, axillary (underarm), and facial hair; a deeper voice as the larynx and vocal cords lengthen; and changed body and facial contours as shoulders widen, the rib cage expands, and the face becomes bonier and more muscular. Girls at this time experience the growth of pubic and axillary hair and the rounding of the body as breasts develop and hips and thighs grow wider. Primary sex characteristics (those directly related to procreation) in boys include the development of the penis and testes and the ability to produce live sperm. Girls experience their first regular menstrual cycle, which signals their ability to conceive and bear children.

The rapid, asynchronous (uneven) growth in adolescence, coupled with the effect of relatively high levels of hormones, causes both boys and girls to become more self-conscious and introspective than they were in childhood. They focus on their changing body image and often develop negative feelings about themselves. This restricted focus can feed into a rise in adolescent egocentrism, which may result in adolescents' feeling unique, misunderstood, and lonely. The common adolescent complaint—"No one understands me"—is evidence of the kind of idiosyncratic emotions that may play a role in the rising suicide statistics among adolescents. The suicide note at the beginning of this section illustrates the egocentrism, isolation, and depressive preoccupation with self that is common among young people contemplating suicide.

The period of adolescence is considered to be formally over when the individual has become an independent adult and begins to function on his or her own without the help of parents. The period of adolescence has lengthened in the United States during this century. Puberty now occurs 2 years earlier for both boys and girls than it did at the turn of the century. In addition, many young people remain in college for a longer period of time or return

The imagination of a boy is healthy, and the mature imagination of a man is healthy; but there is a space of life between, in which the soul is in a ferment, the character undecided, the way of life uncertain, the ambition thicksighted.
Keats, *Endymion*, preface

home after college, thus re-entering the semidependent world of adolescence. (The fact that the period of dependency has lengthened at the upper end in recent years lends support to our decision to define adolescence as the period from 15 to 24 years of age.)

In the area of psychological growth, according to psychoanalytic theory, adolescents are in the final stage of personality development, the genital stage. Because Freud strongly believed that the early years are more important than later years in personality development, less has been written about the genital stage than any other. During the genital stage, in response to increased hormones, the libidinal drives reappear after the hibernation of the latency period, and sexual motivation and activity take on more adult forms. The adolescent seeks more adult sexual experiences, in dramatic contrast to the preference for one's own sex which characterized the preceding stage.

The healthy adolescent enters the adult sexual world through a variety of group experiences involving both boys and girls. Then group experiences gradually give way to deeper and more exclusive relationships with a member of the opposite sex. According to psychoanalytic theory, the poorly adjusted adolescent brings many unresolved problems from earlier stages of development into the genital period. Early conflicts related to trust (from the oral stage), difficulty with authority (from the anal stage), or sexual identification problems (from the phallic stage) all have specific implications for adult personality. As indicated in Chapter 2, when the adolescent must expend too much energy in repressing or otherwise defending against problems from earlier stages, the balance between eros and thanatos is disturbed; this creates the possibility for the strengthening of death wishes, which are sometimes manifested in suicidal behavior.

In contrast to Freud, who showed relatively little interest in this age group, Erikson described personality development in adolescence in great detail (Erikson, 1968; Thomas, 1979). Erikson proposed two stages of personality development for this age group: (1) identity versus role diffusion, for young adolescents, and (2) intimacy versus isolation, for older adolescents and young adults.

Young adolescents in the stage of identity versus role diffusion struggle to determine who they are and who they want to become while at the same time experiencing major physical changes and the development of adultlike sexual interests. They must synthesize what they have learned about themselves during the preceding 12 to 14 years and incorporate the rapid physical and psychological changes of adolescence into an understanding of self (or self-concept) which will be an important part of their adult personality.

Adolescents typically cope with this struggle toward identity by turning to peers, popular heroes, and causes. They usually engage in a process of trying out various ways of being under the critical eyes of their peers. Successful adolescents gradually glean

Don't laugh at a youth for his affectations: he is only trying on one face after another to find a face of his own. Logan Pearsall Smith, *Afterthoughts*

a growing sense of identity through this trial and error process. Unsuccessful ones become involved in the cliquish and critical world of adolescence without being able to discern what can and cannot be incorporated into their growing sense of self. As these individuals grow older they continue to show the clannishness and intolerance of adolescence. They remain confused concerning their identity and their role in life, and they are not prepared to meet the challenges of adulthood. They are likely to fail in the adult responsibilities of intimacy and generativity and to suffer low self-esteem and depression (which has repeatedly been associated with suicide).

The next psychosocial stage, intimacy versus isolation, occurs as the adolescent moves into young adulthood. In this stage the young person must deal with the issue of establishing an adult, sharing, nonexploitive relationship with another person. The young person who emerges from adolescence with a strong sense of personal identity is well prepared to establish a meaningful, loving, trusting, intimate relationship with another person. The young person who is still struggling with the issue of identity will be unable to establish a truly intimate relationship with another person and will be likely to retreat into self-absorption. These individuals tend to become increasingly isolated and unconnected as they grow older. As we will learn in the following two chapters, middle-aged and older adults who lack the support systems which develop from intimate relationships with others are a group at high risk for suicide.

While the behavioral perspective does not include specific age-related stages of development, the principle of modeling does have special significance for adolescence. Imitation and modeling are prevalent behaviors among this age group. Adolescents are especially likely to copy the dress, speech, mannerisms, and other behavior of their peers and of popular public figures such as rock stars. They are also more vulnerable to cluster suicides, a phenomenon in which a group of people who are similar demographically and live in the same general geographic location will commit suicide over a relatively short time span. Adolescents are vulnerable also to the "copy cat" suicide phenomenon, in which several suicides of a similar nature will occur following a single highly publicized suicide. Both of these phenomena can be understood as examples of modeling.

The humanistic perspective, like the behavioral perspective, does not specify stages of development. This perspective does, however, maintain that human beings are growth oriented and are continously in the process of seeking meaning and purpose in life. The search for meaning and purpose is especially prominent during the adolescent and young adult years. Young people are heavily involved in preparation for their adult lives and in setting goals and establishing a dream for lifetime accomplishments. Because of youth's heavy orientation toward the future, the existential claim that "the future determines the present" is likely to be more true for this age group than for any other. Young people who for any reason are unable to establish and work toward important lifetime goals are likely to develop feelings of uselessness, hopelessness, and depression. As discussed in Chapter 2, these individuals will be the victims of noogenic neurosis, which Frankl (1963) believed to be widespread in 20th-century Western societies.

According to cognitive development theory, the adolescent and young adult are in the formal operations stage. As discussed earlier, this stage is marked by the development of hypothetical and abstract thinking capabilities as well as by the intuitive use of the scientific method in problem solving. Piaget believed that young people's ability to form hypotheses is particularly relevant in explaining certain characteristics of adolescent thinking (Piaget & Inhelder, 1969). Adolescents, for the first time in their lives, are capable of dreaming of idealized worlds which do not exist. Because, however, their development has not yet progressed to a level where they can impose reality constraints upon their hypothetical "better" worlds, they are often disappointed with life as it really is. This type of thinking among adolescents may result in considerable disillusionment and unhappiness with the world and may also lead to the consideration of other hypothetical possibilities, one of which is death.

In summary, the adolescent years tend to be characterized by rapid physical growth and major psychological changes. Adolescents must cope not only with a rapidly changing physical body but also with hormonal changes that promote adult sexual responses and with cognitive changes that permit more abstract and hypothetical analyses. In addition, adolescents become more influenced by the behavior and attitudes of their peer group even as they strive to develop their own personal identity. The stress resulting from such major life changes undoubtedly taxes the adolescent's coping skills and contributes to the rates of suicide and attempted suicide among individuals aged 15–24.

The Statistical Picture of Suicide in Adolescence

In the United States, the incidence of suicide among adolescents has consistently risen since the middle of the 20th century. Figure 4.1 shows the age-specific suicide rates by 10-year age groups for 1955, 1965, 1975, and 1985. Clearly, adolescent and young adult suicide rates rose rapidly during this period, while the rates for older people in the population remained fairly constant or decreased. Indeed, the suicide rate among people aged 15–24 increased 132% in the 20-year period between 1960 and 1979, while the overall population rate increase was only 22% (Holinger, 1979). Between 1979 and 1985, the suicide rate for this age group continued to rise, although at a slower rate, moving

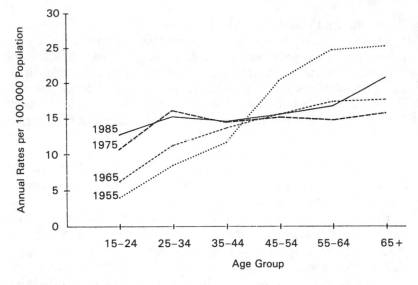

FIGURE 4.1   Age-Specific Suicide Rates by 10-Year Age Groups for
1955, 1965, 1975, and 1985. Sources: National Center for Health
Statistics, 1965, p. 43; U.S. Bureau of the Census, 1956, p. 66; 1977,
p. 174; 1987, p. 803.

from 12.4 per 100,000 in 1979 to 13.1 per 100,000 in 1986 (National Center for Health Statistics, 1987).

    More than 5,000 of the 27,000 suicides reported in the United
States each year are committed by adolescents. Suicide, which is
the 10th leading cause of death among the general population, is
the 3rd leading cause of death among those aged 15–24. Only
accidents and homicides claim more lives in this age group than
does suicide. These figures are undoubtedly low, since it is estimated that 50% or more of all adolescent suicides are incorrectly
reported as accidents (Toolan, 1975).

    The great majority of suicides among adolescents are com-
mitted by males. In 1986, the male death rate by suicide was 19.3
per 100,000, compared with a female death rate of 5.1 per 100,000.
Also, the suicide rate for adolescents increases toward the upper
end of the adolescent age range. The rate for those aged 20–24 is
15.6 per 100,000 while the rate for those aged 15–19 is 10.0 (U.S.
Bureau of the Census, 1987).

    The breakdown of suicide rates among adolescents by age,
race, and sex shows that older white males are the most likely
to commit suicide and younger black females are the least likely.
Suicide rates for white males were 17.3 per 100,000 among those
aged 15–19 and 27.4 among those aged 20–24 in 1985. The black
male incidence was 8.2 suicides per 100,000 among those aged
15–19 and 18.5 among those aged 20–24. White females had a
suicide rate of 4.1 per 100,000 among those aged 15–19 and 5.2
among those aged 20–24. Black females had the lowest suicide

rate of all groups, with 1.5 per 100,000 for those aged 15–19 and 2.4 for those aged 20–24 (U.S. Bureau of the Census, 1987).

The suicide rate for whites of all ages exceeds that of blacks by a ratio of 3 to 1 (Sudak, Ford, & Rushforth, 1984). However, black adolescents have shown the same percentage increase in suicide rates during the past 25 years as white adolescents (Gibbs, 1984). Among other minorities, Native Americans have high suicide rates, comparable to or exceeding that of whites, while Asian Americans have low rates, comparable to those of blacks (Baker, O'Neill, & Karpf, 1984).

The incidence of suicide among adolescents is dwarfed by the number of attempted suicides. Although precise information is impossible to obtain, suicide attempts are known to outnumber committed suicides by a significant margin. Farberow and Shneidman (1961) developed the most widely accepted estimate—an 8:1 ratio of suicide attempts to completions. Although this ratio appears to be realistic for the population as a whole, there is considerable variability among age groups. Curran (1987) reported that the ratio of attempted to committed suicides is inversely related to age (i.e., adolescents have a high rate of unsuccessful suicide attempts relative to successful attempts and middle-aged and older adults have a low rate). Weissman (1974) attributed 50% of all attempted suicides to persons under 30 years of age. Angle, O'Brien, and McIntire (1983) have estimated a ratio of 200:1 for attempted to committed suicides among adolescents.

It is important to note that the increasing adolescent suicide rate during the past 25 years is not confined to the United States; rather, it represents an international trend (Sainsbury, Jenkins, & Levy, 1980). Recent reports show significant increases in the adolescent suicide rate in numerous countries, including Canada (Pettifor, Perry, Plowman, & Pitcher, 1983), Great Britain (McClure, 1984), Australia (Goldney & Katsikitis, 1983), and Micronesia (Rubenstein, 1983). Other similarities between the United States and other countries include higher rates among those aged 20–24, more suicides by males, and more attempts by females.

Table 4.1 shows a comparison of suicide rates among adolescents in developed countries for the most recent year available. The United States ranks ninth in the overall rate of male suicide and tenth for female suicides. Among those aged 15–24, however, the United States ties for fourth place in male suicide (yet remains in ninth place for female suicides). It is evident that adolescent males in the United States are more likely to kill themselves than are adolescent males in any of the reporting countries except for Canada, Austria, and West Germany and that they are 2 to 5 times more likely to kill themselves than females of the same age in any of the countries reporting.

Within the adolescent population there are sub-groups who are at special risk. Statistical reports for incarcerated juveniles, for example, show elevated suicide rates. Official statistics from

TABLE 4.1 Suicide Rates for Selected Countries by Sex and Age Group
(Rate per 100,000 population. Includes deaths resulting from self-inflicted injuries. Except as noted, deaths classified according to the ninth revision of the International Classification of Diseases.)

Sex and age	United States 1983	Australia 1984	Austria 1985	Canada 1984	Denmark 1984	France 1984	Italy 1981	Japan 1985	Netherlands 1984	Poland 1984	Sweden 1984	United Kingdom 1984	West Germany 1985
Male													
Total	19.2	16.9	40.9	21.4	36.5	32.2	9.8	26.0	15.2	23.6	27.4	11.8	29.4
15–24 yrs. old	18.8	18.8	31.9	26.9	16.1	16.3	5.0	13.0	7.0	18.2	16.4	7.5	19.8
25–34 yrs. old	25.4	23.9	42.5	27.8	37.7	33.6	8.3	23.4	18.6	36.3	36.5	14.0	29.5
Female													
Total	5.4	5.2	15.7	6.1	21.0	12.4	4.0	13.1	9.6	4.9	11.8	5.7	12.7
15–24 yrs. old	4.2	4.4	7.9	4.3	4.1	4.5	1.7	5.9	3.7	3.8	6.2	6.1	5.3
25–34 yrs. old	6.6	6.5	10.2	7.0	12.9	11.5	3.1	9.8	10.1	5.7	15.3	3.8	8.9

Source: U.S. Bureau of The Census (1988). *Statistical Abstract of the United States: 1987.* Washington, DC: U.S. Government Printing Office, p. 803.

1978 show a suicide rate of 12.3 per 100,000 for children (i.e., those below 18 years of age) in adult jails and a rate of 1.6 per 100,000 for children in juvenile detention centers, compared with an overall rate of 2.7 for children in the general population at that time (U.S. Department of Justice, 1985). These findings suggest that children incarcerated in adult facilities are at special risk but those in juvenile detention centers are not.

An unpublished paper by Memory (1988) has criticized the calculation methods used in the derivation of the official suicide statistics for youth incarcerated in adult jails and juvenile detention centers. Memory has argued that the published rates are flawed for a number of reasons, including the fact that they do not take into account the small number of days a juvenile offender is typically incarcerated in a single lockup. The juvenile rates are spuriously low when compared with population statistics which include a 365-day year. Memory's recalculation of the juvenile statistics, taking into account the actual number of days of stay, resulted in the astounding rate of 2,041 juvenile suicides per 100,000 in adult jails and 57 per 100,000 in juvenile detention centers.

Regardless of whether Memory's remarkable findings or the official statistics are more accurate, it is important to note that these are high-risk groups who deviate significantly from the norm in their suicide rates. We must identify the factors that increase an incarcerated adolescent's vulnerability to suicide and take preventive measures. Research findings concerning the risk factors that contribute to adolescent suicide will be discussed in the following section.

Factors Contributing to Adolescent Suicide

There has been much speculation in recent years concerning the reasons for the dramatic increase in teen suicide. Among the factors suggested as contributing to the increase are the following: (1) an increase in the relative proportion of young people in the total population, (2) a decrease in the number of intact homes, (3) an increase in family mobility, (4) rapidly changing sex roles, (5) greater awareness of nuclear threat, and (6) an increase in social isolation.

Holinger and Offer (1982) have pointed out that the rapid growth of the baby boom generation has led to increased competition among those aged 15–24 in the recent past. One result of such competition has been more pressure, more failure, and more loss of self-esteem. These authors suggest that the press of numbers has adversely affected young people's performance in the present and their expectations for the future, thus contributing, perhaps indirectly, to the increased suicide rates.

A second result of membership in a large cohort is that the power of the peer group is enhanced. As the profile of adolescence indicated, adolescents tend to be highly imitative of their peers. Within a large, strong adolescent subculture, shared values become important and fads spring up in music, clothing, language, and behavior, even suicidal behavior, as the following article attests.

RIVERTON, Wyo., Oct. 1 (The Associated Press)—For the ninth time in less than two months a young Indian male on the Wind River Reservation in central Wyoming has committed suicide, officials said today.

A 25-year-old Arapahoe hanged himself in a closet, using a drawstring from his sweatshirt. He was found this morning by his sister, according to the Fremont County Coroner, Larry Lee. The name was withheld until relatives could be notified.

The first suicide occurred Aug. 12. The victims range in age from 14 to 25.

Since the beginning of the year, at least 48 suicide attempts have been reported on the sparsely populated two-million-acre reservation, as against fewer than 30 last year.

Spectacular and highly publicized suicide clusters, like the one described above, have occurred throughout the 1980s—in Plano, Texas; Westchester, New York; Omaha, Nebraska; and Bergenfield, New Jersey, and other locations. In all of these places, a single or group suicide served as a prelude to several others, as each became a model for self-destructive problem-solving in tragic episodes of adolescent conformity.

The suicide cluster in Plano, Texas, reflects a number of the modern-day factors that may contribute to the growing suicide problem among the young in our country. Plano is a very rapidly growing suburb of Dallas, with a highly mobile population that grew by 18,000 residents to a total of 90,000 during the 3 years preceding a 1983 suicide cluster. Plano became primarily a community of white collar families with both parents employed in middle management positions. As the town was transformed from a farming village to a metropolitan bedroom community, the incidence of divorce, substance abuse, and alcoholism also increased significantly. The dramatic influx of adolescents from success-oriented families greatly increased pressure and competition in the local high school, which included approximately 1000 students per grade level. The epidemic of teenage suicides began with the deaths of two best friends in February 1983 and grew to a total of seven suicides within a 1-year period (Coleman, 1987).

In addition to the impact of peer suicides on the behavior of adolescents, there is evidence that the media attention given to suicide also contributes to self-destructive behavior. One study by Gould and Shaffer (1986) compared the incidence of teenage suicide over 2-week periods following the television broadcasts of four fictional films about suicide with the rate during the 2-week periods preceding the broadcasts. They found that the mean incidence of adolescent suicide attempts and completions reported by area hospitals was significantly higher during the 2-

week periods following these broadcasts than during the 2-week periods preceding them.

Another study by Phillips and Carstensen (1986) examined the relationship between 38 nationally televised news or feature stories on suicide and the teenage suicide rate. They found that the number of reported teenage suicides in the United States was significantly higher than expected during the 7 days following these broadcasts.

Popular musicians and other entertainers are also powerful role models for adolescents. Suicides of famous persons, such as Marilyn Monroe, have often been accompanied by an epidemic of copy cat suicides (Phillips, 1979). Interestingly, single-vehicle motor fatalities show the same pattern of increase following famous suicides, causing some to speculate that such accidents may be disguised suicides. The numbers of copy cat suicides tend to peak bimodally at 1 and 7 days after the occurrence of the well-publicized suicide (Bollen & Phillips, 1982). It seems likely also that popular song lyrics that promote self-destructive behavior might encourage a young person with already existing suicidal thoughts to take his or her own life. Lines such as "Dance into the fire; One fatal kiss is all we need," sung by Duran Duran, could be interpreted by a disturbed adolescent as a suicidal prescription.

In addition to the sheer numbers and power of the peer group, the family plays an important role in adolescent suicide. Studies that have compared the families of adolescent suicide attempters with those of nonattempters have shown that suicidal individuals are more likely to come from families that are highly conflicted and unresponsive to the young person's needs (Berman & Carroll, 1984). Homes of suicide attempters in this age group are more likely to be disrupted by parental separation or divorce than the national average (McAnarney, 1979; and Walker, 1980). In fact, more than 50% of suicide attempters in this age group come from single parent homes. Also, even within intact families, suicide attempters see their parents as more conflicted than do nonattempters (Tishler, McKenry, & Morgan, 1981).

Although there are many exceptions, families of suicide attempters tend to be anomic (i.e., not accepting of the usual standards of conduct) more often than would be expected by chance. These families have higher incidences of medical and psychiatric problems (Garfinkel, Froese, & Hood, 1982). There is also a higher than average incidence of alcoholism and drug abuse among the parents of suicide attempters (Jacobs, 1971). In addition, these parents are likely to be depressed and to demonstrate nonproductive coping skills (Shaffer, 1974; Eisenberg, 1980). They are frequently avoidant and impulsive in their approaches to problem solving (Berman & Carroll, 1984).

In addition to creating turbulent home environments, many of these parents actively model suicidal behavior. Paulson and

Adolescents tend to be passionate people, and passion is no less real because it is directed toward a hot-rod, a commercialized popular singer, or the leader of a black-jacketed gang. Edgar F. Friedenberg, "Emotional Development in Adolescents," *The Vanishing Adolescent,* 1959

Stone (1974) reported that 50% of a group of suicidal adolescents had relatives (usually parents) who had attempted or committed suicide. Also, many suicide attempters have observed family violence related to marital discord or have experienced abuse as children (Frederick & Resnik, 1971; and Green, 1978). Based on our current knowledge about the powerful effects of modeling, it is not surprising that a young person who grows up with many family examples of violent and self-destructive approaches to problem solving would consider suicide in a crisis situation.

A third factor affecting adolescent suicide rates is social isolation. Both Seiden (1983) and Hawton (1982) suggested that today's young people do not have the support of extended families and of church and community, which previous generations enjoyed. Contributing to this sense of social isolation is the fact that family mobility is at an all-time high. Forty-six percent of all the households in the United States relocated between 1980 and 1985 (U.S. Bureau of the Census, 1985). Although 25% moved within the same geographic region, 21% relocated in a totally different place, thus breaking friendships and family ties. The greatest amount of relocation occurred in the West, which has the highest regional suicide rate. In contrast, the least relocating activity occurred in the Northeast, which enjoys the lowest suicide rate. Topol and Resnikoff (1982) endorsed the view that social isolation is characteristic of suicidal young people. They point out that adolescent suicides have a personal history of difficulty in relating to peers. They rarely have close friends and are "nonjoiners" who tend to be invisible to peers and teachers.

Still another source of feelings of isolation and insecurity is the constant threat of nuclear war. The nuclear threat and disasters from all over the world are presented nightly on our television screens. Repeated reminders of the nuclear arms buildup and of global instability have, no doubt, resulted in a more pessimistic and fatalistic outlook among young people (Newman, 1987). Recent research by Stillion (1986) shows that adolescents are significantly concerned about the possibility of nuclear war. These concerns, which begin in the elementary grades, increase in adolescence and may form a shadow that adds its impact to the anxiety and depression inherent in this period for troubled adolescents.

A fourth major factor in the high adolescent suicide rate is the easy availability of drugs and alcohol. These substances are frequently utilized in suicide attempts. Perhaps more important, however, is the fact that long-term drug and alcohol abuse is often a factor in the decision to attempt suicide (Curran, 1987). Greuling and DeBlassie (1980) reported that at least 50% of the teenagers who commit suicide have been involved in moderate to heavy use of alcohol and drugs. The downward spiral of depression and lack of control that is associated with the use of drugs and alcohol may play a very real role in suicidal behavior of adolescents. The

It is an illusion that youth is happy, an illusion of those who have lost it. W. Somerset Maugham, *Of Human Bondage,* 1915

case of Joe and Lenora illustrates many of the characteristics of adolescent suicide discussed to this point.

Joe was 18 and Lenora was 17 when they attempted suicide together. They drove their old car into a garage, closed the door, and turned on the radio. Local police patrolling the area heard the radio and saw the exhaust fumes escaping from cracks in the garage. They interrupted the suicide attempt, taking Joe and Lenora to the hospital, where they were treated for drug overdoses and for carbon monoxide poisoning. From statements made at the hospital and later at the police station, the following facts emerged.

Both Joe and Lenora came from troubled homes. Joe lived with an alcoholic father, and Lenora lived with her mother and younger sister in a run-down tenement building. She and her sister did not get along, and her mother seemed to have given up on both of them.

Joe and Lenora had become attracted to one another at a party where drugs were being used. They were both sporadic students who considered themselves to be "loners." Since they had no other friends, they soon found themselves inseparable. Joe took the responsibility for supplying the drugs for both of their growing habits. He began dealing drugs and was arrested once and put on probation. Both young people tried to stop using drugs after Joe's arrest. However, when they were not high, they were irritable and fought a great deal with each other. After several weeks of trying to be straight, they began using drugs again. Within 2 weeks, Joe was dealing again in order to supply their needs.

Joe was arrested again. This time it took several days to raise the bail. Once he was out on bail, the couple discussed their future. It was clear that Joe would be imprisoned for some time. He dreaded prison and separation from the one friend he considered loyal. Lenora would be alone once again, with a drug habit and no supplier.

The local newspaper had carried a story a few weeks before about a garage in which two sets of couples had committed suicide over a 2-year period. Joe found a copy of the article and read it to Lenora. The headline read, "Twentieth Century Technology Replaces Lovers' Leap for Suicidal Teens." The story described death from carbon monoxide poisoning as painless and portrayed the two dead couples as troubled young people who chose to die together rather than face what seemed to them to be insurmountable problems.

Joe and Lenora later reported that they knew at the same instant that this was the solution to their problems also. Joe gathered together what cocaine and marijuana he had left, and the couple located the garage from the address given in the newspaper article.

This suicide attempt contains many elements common to adolescent suicides. Drug use formed a background for this young couple, a background that became increasingly demanding and caused them to feel out of control and hopeless. Neither young person came from a stable home. Joe's alcoholic father was a model of substance abuse and Lenora's mother seemed depressed and hopeless. Both Joe and Lenora were socially isolated within their peer groups, making their relationship with each other

Lovers in the Waves, **Edvard Munch. Lithograph. (Munch-museet, Oslo Kommuns Kunstsamlinger, Norway.)**

seem even more important. Finally, when separation seemed inevitable, the young people read about an alternative way of coping—committing suicide together. The fact that others had used this method and had not been condemned in the news articles seemed to give them permission to express their hopelessness in the same way. At the same time, their suicide seemed to promise release from problems with which they could no longer cope.

The fifth area of research into adolescent suicide is that of abnormal behavior. Suicidal adolescents have been shown to exhibit many symptoms of psychopathology, including anxiety, obsessive-compulsive behavior, hostility, antisocial behavior, and depression (Berman & Carroll, 1984; Shaffer, 1974; Tishler & McKenry, 1983).

Depression is the most common pathological symptom of suicidal individuals of all ages (Goldberg, 1981; Linehan, 1981). The depressed adolescent who has suicidal thoughts is greatly at risk for suicide (Berman & Carroll, 1984; Clarkin, Friedman, Hurt, Corn, & Aronoff, 1984; Ray & Johnson, 1983; Tischler, McKenry, & Morgan, 1981; Toolan, 1975). Shaffer (1974) has found depressive symptoms to be prevalent among both adolescent suicide attempters and adolescent suicide completers. The importance of depressive symptoms in adolescent suicide was underscored in a study by Garfinkel, Froese, and Hood (1982), which found a positive correlation between the level of depression and the lethality of suicide attempts among 505 adolescents admitted to a hospital emergency room for suicide attempts. The adolescents in this study who had attempted suicide in more lethal ways showed the highest levels of depression.

Several studies that have included both adolescents and other age groups have found feelings of hopelessness to constitute an important variable linking depression to suicide (Beck, Kovacs, & Weissman, 1979; Lester, Beck, & Mitchell, 1979; Minkoff, Bergman, Beck, & Beck, 1973). These studies have shown that feelings of hopelessness determine the lethality of intent among suicide attempters more than does generalized depression.

A study by Wetzel (1976) found further that hopelessness relates to actual suicidal behavior as well as to lethality of intent. He compared three groups of hospitalized psychiatric patients on measures of depression, hopelessness, and suicidal intent. Wetzel found that a group of suicide attempters scored higher on the measure of hopelessness than either a group of suicide ideators or a nonsuicidal group. He found also that the suicide attempters with high lethality-of-intent scores felt more hopeless than attempters with low lethality-of-intent scores.

Finally, a study by Beck, Steer, Kovacs, and Garrison (1985) found that hopelessness can predict future suicidal behavior. In a 10-year follow up of 207 patients previously hospitalized because of suicide ideation, level of hopelessness at the time of hospitalization was found to differentiate the 14 (6.9%) individuals who later committed suicide from those who did not.

A final area of research regarding factors contributing to adolescent suicide focuses on cognitive development. Most adolescents, as we have seen, are in the earliest stages of the formal operations period of cognitive development. This means that adolescents are beginning to develop and to practice hypothetical thinking. They can dream of hypothetical better worlds that do not and cannot exist. This type of thinking, coupled with the absence of the ability to impose reality constraints upon what could be, creates a special opportunity for disillusionment and unhappiness. Any parent or professional who has regular contact with an adolescent is frequently perplexed by the young person's apparent lack of perspective regarding the issues that distress him or her.

In addition to the inherent cognitive characteristics of this age group, adolescent suicide attempters often manifest special deficiencies in problem solving. A study by Levenson and Neuringer (1971) compared the performances of a group of suicidal adolescents with those of a nonsuicidal psychiatric group and a nonsuicidal nonpsychiatric group on the arithmetic subtest of the

Wechsler Adult Intelligence Scale and on the Rokeach Map Reading Problems Test. The suicidal adolescents scored significantly lower than the other two groups on both of these tests. It has been speculated that the reduced problem-solving skills of suicidal adolescents are more lethal than would be the case for adults. Because adolescents have fewer life experiences than adults to draw upon in a crisis situation, problem-solving capabilities are more essential.

In addition to the problem-solving deficiencies, suicidal adolescents have been found to have a reduced future-time perspective and less goal orientation compared with nonsuicidal adolescents (Corder, Shorr, & Corder, 1974). It is easy to understand how a young person who deals with problems ineffectively and is also unable to imagine that better times are not far away might be likely to consider performing a self-destructive act when experiencing a great deal of stress. Suicide attempters also often report strong feelings of hopelessness (Topol & Reznikoff, 1982). They, like Jason, who wrote the suicide note that appears earlier in this chapter, do not believe that their situation will improve—at least not in the foreseeable future.

Sex Differences in Adolescent Suicide

Of special interest is the topic of sex differences in suicidal behavior. Males and females in the general population differ significantly in suicidal behavior. Attempted suicide is very much a female phenomenon, while males more frequently complete suicide. Actuarial data show that females attempt suicide 3 times for every single male suicide attempt. In contrast three males actually kill themselves for every one female suicide. There is evidence, however, that sex differences in suicidal behavior among young people may be greater than those for the general population. For example, 90% of all adolescent suicide attempters are female, while 80% of adolescent suicide completers are male (Berman & Carroll, 1984). The ratio of male to female adolescent suicides in the United States has steadily increased since the early 1970s (McIntosh & Jewell, 1986; Stafford & Weisheit, 1988). While both male and female adolescent suicide rates have increased, the rate of increase for males has been more than double the rate of increase for females, thus resulting in a steadily growing differential suicide rate among young people.

Several researchers have attempted to find relationships between suicide in women and hormonal changes associated with different phases of the menstrual cycle. It has been speculated that the premenstrual period, 3–5 days before the onset of menses which is accompanied by a significant reduction in the hormones estrogen and progesterone, might be associated with increases in depression and suicide.

Stillion (1985) reported three studies relating suicide in women to various stages of the menstrual cycle. One study showed a disproportionately high number of suicides in women during the second half of the menstrual cycle between days 17 and 23. The other two studies showed a high incidence of suicide among women during the premenstrual and menstrual period. In spite of the considerable speculation about female suicide and hormonal levels, no consistent findings have emerged. As Stillion (1985) concluded, human behavior as highly complex as suicide is very unlikely to show direct relationships with any single biological factor.

There are at least three well-documented behavioral differences between males and females that may be helpful in explaining sex differences in suicide: aggression, success orientation, and help seeking (McDowell, 1985).

Males are significantly more aggressive than females at all ages. Whether the measure is incidence of rough and tumble play, verbal aggression, threatening gestures, fights, violent accidents, or homicides, males are consistently rated higher (Doyle, 1983). Males use more aggressive methods in their suicide attempts than do females (Marks, 1977). Males are more likely to shoot, stab, or hang themselves; females more often take drugs or slit their wrists. It should be noted, however, that the more lethal methods of self-destruction used by males do not alone account for the large sex difference in suicide rate. Males are more successful than females with every method of committing suicide (Stillion, 1985).

Striving for success continues to be more a male than a female characteristic in our culture in spite of recent progress in reducing sex role stereotyping. The need to do things well, to be competent, to win is very much a part of male sex role socialization. David and Brannon (1976) said about this phenomenon that "success and status are the bedrock elements of the male sex role, and no man in America escapes from the injunction to succeed." (p. 89). Herb Goldberg (1977) referred to it as the "suicidal success syndrome."

Competence and achievement are responded to more equivocally by females than males in our society. Striving for success is often considered to be incompatible with some of the traditionally female characteristics such as nurturance. Susan Brownmiller (1983) suggested that "a lack of ambition—or a proposed lack of ambition, or a sacrificial willingness to set personal ambition aside—is virtuous proof of the nurturant feminine nature which, if absent, strikes at the guilty heart of femaleness itself" (p. 221). Put succinctly, ambition is not considered to be a feminine trait.

The fact that males are overrepresented in the number of suicides and underrepresented in the number of suicide attempts may be an indication that the success motive is an important aspect of suicidal behavior. Young males may regard unsuccessful suicide attempts as "failures" and may therefore be more highly motivated to complete the act than are females. Anecdotally, emergency room nurses report that male suicide attempters are much more likely than females to be distressed over the failure of their suicide attempt upon awakening in the hospital. Also males, unlike females, are likely to consider a failed suicide attempt as cowardly and unmasculine (Rosenthal, 1981).

Help-seeking behavior also tends to be scorned by males. Self-reliance and independence are very much a part of the male sex role (Doyle, 1983). Boys are taught very early not to be "cry babies" or overly reliant on help from others in difficult situations. This particular characteristic of the male sex role was epitomized by the strong, silent type often portrayed in the past by actors like John Wayne and Gary Cooper. Today's young men inherit the same type of model in Sylvester Stallone's "Rambo," Clint Eastwood's "Dirty Harry," and Arnold Schwarzenneger's "Predator."

The socialization of females in our culture predisposes them to be less self-reliant than males and more likely to seek help in a crisis situation. Role models for girls in fairy tales, on television, and even in textbooks tend to be more dependent and help-seeking than role models for boys. Sleeping Beauty, Cinderella, and Rapunzel all had two things in common: They were sexually desirable and they were dependent. Each was rescued by a handsome prince. Girls are less likely than boys to be punished for dependent behavior. Women show the effects of these socialization practices by being more likely than men to seek help in a variety of forms, such as doctor visits, hospitalizations, or psychotherapy (Stillion, 1985). Topol and Reznikoff (1982) found that female suicidal adolescents are more dependent on support from others than are male suicidal adolescents. It appears that females may view attempting suicide as a way of seeking help. If females do view attempted suicide as a "cry for help," they would be expected to engage in more suicide attempts and have fewer suicide completions than males, as is the case. As Rosenthal (1981) pointed out, suicide is in a sense a feminine act, because it often involves a combined feeling of personal helplessness with the notion of being rescued by someone else.

At least two recent studies show sex differences in levels of sympathy shown for suicidal target figures (Stillion, McDowell, & May, 1984; Stillion, McDowell, & Shamblin, 1984). In both studies a suicide attitude questionnaire was administered to adolescents and young adults between the ages of 15 and 24. The questionnaire consisted of 10 vignettes describing hypothetical situations in which an adolescent attempts suicide. The themes described in the vignettes were taken from the adolescent suicide literature and included topics such as lack of school success, loss of a loved one, parental discord, terminal illness, etc. Five males and five females were described alternately in the vignettes. Subjects were asked to respond to each of the 10 vignettes by indicating the extent to which they sympathized, empathized, and agreed with the suicide action in each case. Sex differences were found only for the sympathy scale. Females consistently scored higher than males on the sympathy scale. In addition, females scored higher on the sympathy scale when responding to the vignettes involving females than when responding to the vignettes involving males. Males showed very little sympathy for suicide regardless of the reason for suicide or the sex of the suicidal individual. Apparently females give and perhaps expect more sympathy for suicidal acts than do males. However, another interpretation was suggested in a recent study by White and Stillion (1988). These researchers found that much of the sex difference in sympathy could be traced to males who sympathize less with suicidal males. In this study, males and females did not differ significantly in sympathy for troubled, nonsuicidal individuals. However, male subjects showed significantly less sympathy for troubled males who attempted suicide. Female levels of sympathy remained constant regardless of whether the individual in the vignette was male or female and regardless of whether or not the individual attempted suicide.

In summary, female and male suicidal behavior appears to be consistent with sex role socialization. Males are more aggressive, success oriented, and self-reliant in their suicidal behavior than females. Males use more lethal techniques, are more successful, and are less likely to seek help in a suicidal crisis than females. Males appear to view suicide as a means of solving a problem in their characteristically aggressive, success-oriented, and self-reliant manner. However, they show little sympathy for other males who attempt suicide. Female suicidal behavior reflects a less aggressive, less success-directed, and more help-seeking orientation. Females use less lethal suicidal techniques, experience less success, and are more likely to seek help in crisis.

It seems reasonable to assume that as females are socialized more like males, the suicidal behavior of the two groups will become more similar. Some evidence in support of this hypothesis is available. Women who enter traditionally male occupations, such as medicine, show the same suicide rates as men in those professions (Stillion, 1985).

Adolescent Attitudes Toward Suicide

The measurement of suicide attitudes is a relatively new area of study, having been developed only in the 1980s. Although this section focuses upon adolescent attitudes, it should be noted that the seminal work measuring attitudes toward suicide involved adults; it was conducted by George Domino at the University of Arizona. Domino developed an instrument called the Suicide Opinion Questionnaire (SOQ), which includes 100 items or statements of opinion about suicide. Persons taking this questionnaire respond to items such as "Most persons who attempt suicide are lonely and depressed" by indicating their level of agreement or disagreement on a five-point Likert-type scale. The questionnaire, which was originally administered to 285 adults, yielded 15 factors that accounted for more than 75% of the total variance and underscored the complexity of suicide attitudes (Domino, Moore, Westlake, & Gibson, 1982). Subsequent work with the SOQ, which included various professional groups as well as clinical populations, has shown that suicide attitudes differ among these groups in important ways (Limbacher & Domino, 1985; Swain & Domino, 1985).

Relatively little is known about attitudes toward suicide among adolescents. Suicidal behavior is not normative for young people and is generally viewed negatively by this group, especially when related to low levels of stress. It seems logical, however, that the dramatic growth in the adolescent suicide rate during the past 25 years would be accompanied by significant attitude changes in this age group.

A Canadian study compared the attitudes of 12th graders concerning suicide and death with those of their parents (Boldt, 1982). This study showed important generational differences in conceptions and evaluations of suicide and death. The younger generation was consistently less judgmental about suicide and less stigmatizing than was the older generation. The 12th graders tended to view suicidal individuals as victims of societal malfunction, while their parents were more likely to attribute suicidal behavior to individual failings. The younger generation was much more likely to see suicide as the prerogative of any "competent" individual. Also, the 12th graders were less inclined than their parents to view suicide in religious-moral terms or to assume related calamitous outcomes (e.g., hellfire). This important study strongly indicates, consistent with actuarial data, that young people today are more accepting of suicide than previous generations.

Two studies referred to above have investigated various aspects of adolescent attitudes toward suicide (Stillion, McDowell, & Shamblin, 1984; Stillion, McDowell, & May, 1984). These studies, involving the analysis of responses of large numbers of adolescents to the Suicide Attitude Vignette Experience (SAVE) Scale and to other attitude and personality measures, identified four factors closely associated with suicidal behavior: age, intelligence, religious beliefs, and mental health status.

Older adolescents and those who scored high on tests of intelligence agreed less with all reasons for suicide on the SAVE Scale than did younger and less bright adolescents. When 9th graders, 12th graders, and college sophomores were compared, as well as gifted and nongifted students, older and brighter adolescents agreed less with all reasons for suicide than the other groups. Apparently, the cognitive changes associated with age and intelligence impact positively on attitudes toward suicide. Perhaps older and brighter adolescents, with their greater capacity for formal operational thinking, better understand the finality of death and are less likely to romanticize suicide. Rosenthal (1981) reported clinical cases in which adolescent suicide attempters expressed unrealistic notions concerning the pain and consequence of their actions. One particularly poignant example involved an adolescent female survivor of a suicide attempt by self-immolation. Incredibly, this girl later reported being surprised that her suicide attempt was so painful.

It is not unreasonable to expect strong religious beliefs to be a deterrent to suicide. As we saw in Chapter 2, the Christian religion has traditionally taught that our lives belong to God and that suicide is sinful. SAVE Scale studies conducted with Southern students, most of whom were Protestants, have shown that adolescents who reported religion to be very important in their lives agreed less with all reasons for suicide than those who reported limited or no religious influence. In addition, adolescents who had a strong belief in an afterlife agreed less with all reasons for suicide than those who did not hold such beliefs (Stillion, McDowell, & Shamblin, 1984). Finally, Boldt (1982) found that adolescents who reported attending church frequently held more negative attitudes toward suicide than infrequent attenders.

A growing body of research suggests a relationship between mental health status and attitudes toward suicide among adolescents. Our studies have shown that young people who have low self-esteem, significant depression, and self-reported suicidal intent agree more with all reasons for suicide than those who do not show such symptomatic characteristics.

Two studies have explored both ends of the mental health continuum as they relate to suicide attitudes among young people (Stillion, McDowell, Smith, & McCoy, 1986). The first study compared attitudes toward suicide between institutionalized adolescents and a group of college students. The major finding of this study was that young women who had mental health problems severe enough to require institutionalization agreed more with all reasons for suicide than did institutionalized males or males and females in a noninstitutionalized group. The second study assessed suicide attitudes among a group of college students with differing levels of mental health. The major finding of this study was that students who scored higher on a measure of self-actualization sympathized and empathized less with suicidal individuals and agreed less with all reasons for suicide than did students who scored lower on the same measure.

SUICIDE IN YOUNG ADULTHOOD

The period which we refer to as young adulthood includes the years from 25 to 34. Little empirical research is available regarding developmental changes or factors influencing suicide within this age group. However, there is a small but growing body of evidence that suggests that this 10-year period is characterized by the need to make major commitments regarding work, marriage, and parenthood as well as by rigorous re-evaluation of those commitments. The following profile of early adulthood is intended to illuminate the paradoxical and demanding normative issues of this stage of life.

Profile of Young Adulthood

Young adults have reached the peak of their development physically. Indeed, there is reason to believe that from about age 18 small but constant declines begin in sensory functioning. Hearing, in particular, begins to decline in measurable ways, but generally the changes are so small that they go unnoticed. Male sexuality also peaks around age 18, although female sexuality seems to peak later, around age 36 (Masters & Johnson, 1966). However, once again the changes are so slight that they do not affect quality of functioning or life satisfaction.

As we have seen, Freud had little to say about the pattern of development after individuals enter the genital stage. However, he did indicate that people who become fixated at or regress to earlier psychosexual stages of development because of stress or trauma are likely to be maladjusted as adults. When asked about the characteristics of well-adjusted adults, he maintained that healthy adults are capable of directing their energy toward two important adult activities: love and work (Freud, 1953).

Erikson (1980) underscored the importance of Freud's characteristics of healthy adulthood by suggesting that young adults, building upon their still-developing sense of identity, need to invest in an ongoing intimate relationship with another human being. The healthy young adult relationship is intimate both sexually and intellectually. Healthy young adult couples are able to share their thoughts, beliefs, and hopes, as well as their sexuality, with one another. Erikson reported that a counterpart of developing intimacy is "distantiation," which is the ability to defend one's beliefs, rights, and individuality. Beliefs and values that emerge from a sense of personal identity may be organized into a coherent framework for a developing philosophy of life. Thus healthy young adults are in a better position than adolescents to make permanent commitments to relationships and activities. In contrast, the young adults who continue to struggle with identity issues will be unable to develop either intimacy or distantiation.

In the cognitive realm, young adults are at their peak of performance. Because they have accumulated much knowledge in the first 2½ decades of life, they have developed many cognitive schemas that promote ease of learning. This is fortunate, because young adults typically encounter many new situations that require a great deal of learning within a short time. Marriage, pregnancy, parenthood, new jobs, and job promotions are only a few of the situations that require young adults to master new information. Young adults continue to operate at the level of formal operations in many cognitive areas. However, the novelty of this mode of thinking has worn off, freeing them to adopt a less ego-centric worldview. This development results in the ability to balance individual needs and goals with community welfare, and it frequently results in the involvement of young adults in some form of community service.

The humanistic-existential theories do not speak specifi-cally about the stage of young adulthood. However, it would ap-pear from an existential point of view that young adults seek meaning from the types of commitments they make to relation-ships, to work, and to their communities. From the point of view of Maslow, healthy young adults are working to satisfy both be-longing and esteem needs. Belonging needs are satisfied as they marry and begin their own families. As one young man said, "I knew Laura was the woman for me when I realized I felt more at home when I was with her than when I was in my old bedroom in my parents' home." Esteem needs are satisfied as young people complete school, begin their careers, and are rewarded by salaries and perhaps their first promotions. The assertion of competence helps young adults to meet their needs for self-esteem and to acquire the esteem of others.

From the behaviorist perspective, young adults continue to learn through reinforcement and modeling. Reinforcement takes on new meaning as salaries and promotions increase the young adults' buying power and make possible the visible symbols of success. A special instance of modeling that occurs primarily during the stage of young adulthood is mentoring. Studies have shown that young adults who have mentors (i.e., teacher-sponsors who guide them through the early years of their careers) get ahead more quickly and with less stress than do those without mentors (Levinson, Darrow, Klein, Levinson, & McKee, 1978; Walsh, 1983).

Contemporary Research on Young Adulthood

Three researchers who have recently added to our under-standing of young adulthood are Vaillant, Levinson, and Gould. Each researcher, drawing heavily upon Erikson's theory, con-ducted research on adults that led to the conclusion that there are identifiable themes in adult development.

Vaillant (1977) conducted a longitudinal study with a group of male Harvard students. His work suggested that the early adult years, ages 23–35, constitute a time of career consolidation in which most men are concerned with progress in their chosen profession. Vaillant characterized career consolidation as a stable and conforming process marked by assimilation into the working world. Although this period is seemingly very stable, there is an unexamined paradox in career consolidation which can be very problematic for young adults. Vaillant has pointed out that during this period difficulties often arise as young adults try to establish a proper balance between striving to get ahead and putting down roots. Progress in an individual's career often necessitates moving and thus sacrificing stable relationships. Choices between career and family welfare, as well as between financial gains and personal losses, are common causes of stress during this period (Walsh, 1983).

Vaillant has noted that both the rate and the direction of development can be affected during this stage of life by the availability of opportunities, by life events and accidents, and by the quality of the resources and relationships the individual develops. Thus, the amount of life stress experienced by young adults is a function of the fit between the life events that occur and the normative developmental processes of evaluation, commitment, and re-evaluation that characterize the young adult period. Even the best-adjusted young adults will experience stress, especially toward the end of this stage. Those who are less well-adjusted tend to experience higher levels of stress and failure to cope.

Levinson's work, based on extensive interviews with 40 middle-aged men, suggested that, in contrast to the late adolescent years, which focus on the problems of escaping parental control and leaving the family, the early adult years (ages 22–28) are characterized by the development of a mature sense of independence and by the making of basic commitments to a career and children (Levinson et al., 1978). Between the ages of 29 and 34, there is the first in a series of re-evaluations of life commitments. Levinson found that this period of evaluation, which he called the "age 30 transition," was reported by approximately 80% of the men studied. It involved a re-examination of the choices of mate, work, and lifestyle, and it sometimes resulted in divorce, return to school, change of occupation, or reorganization of priorities in other aspects of life. Levinson's subjects reported experiencing mild to moderate stress during this period. Healthy young people frequently emerged from this transitional stage with a deeper commitment to original choices or with fresh energy generated by their commitment to new and more carefully thought-out careers and relationships. Less healthy young adults, unable to establish commitments and make productive contributions, found themselves experiencing increasing stress as they realized they were on the brink of middle adulthood and had no clearly developed life goals.

Gould (1978), basing his observations on both a clinical and a nonclinical population of men and women, echoed Levinson's emphasis on stability and change. His research revealed essentially the same developmental tasks for early adulthood suggested by Levinson, but Gould added the observation that individuals who face the crises of this and other life stages and work them through are in better positions to make healthy later adjustments than those who attempt to avoid or escape the central issues of any life stage. The title of Gould's major book, *Transformations*, reveals his belief that individuals can be transformed for the better by successfully coping with the transitional periods inherent in adulthood.

As the adult development research indicates, the young adult period, especially the age 30 transition, is potentially a very stressful time of life. As shown in the next section, there is corresponding increase in the suicide rate in early adulthood as stress levels increase during the period of re-evaluation of life goals and as negative life events begin to overwhelm coping skills.

The Statistical Picture for Young Adult Suicide

The U.S. suicide rate for young adults is somewhat higher than the rate for adolescents. During 1986 the suicide rate for those aged 25–34 was 15.7 per 100,000 population, compared with a rate of 13.1 for those aged 15–24 and a rate 12.8 for the general population. Almost 7,000 young adults killed themselves in 1986, which is 1600 more than the total number of adolescent suicides in that year (National Center for Health Statistics, 1988). No data are available regarding the proportion of suicide attempts to completed suicides in this age group. The general trend of a declining ratio of attempts to completions over the entire life span entails there would be a higher percentage of completed suicides among adults than among adolescents.

Figure 4.1, presented earlier in this chapter, shows that young adults have experienced a remarkable increase in their suicide rate during the past 30 years. It should be noted, however, that the suicide rate increase for this group has not been as great as that for adolescents. Also, during the years 1979–1985, the suicide rate for young adults actually dropped 1.1 per 100,000 population, while the rate for adolescents increased .5 per 100,000 (National Center for Health Statistics, 1987). Therefore, although the rate for young adult suicide remains high, recent trends seem to indicate a closing of the gap between this group and adolescents.

The suicide statistics for young adults show the same patterns for sex and race as are found among adolescents. White males in this age group show the highest rate (25.4 per 100,000 population), followed by black males (19.6), white females (6.4), and black females (3.0). All four groups show the small decrease in suicide rates between 1979 and 1985 mentioned above (U.S. Bureau of the Census, 1987).

Although young adult suicide statistics are distressingly high throughout the world, the U.S. rate for this age group compares favorably with other developed countries. The suicide rates for male and female young adults from 13 selected countries, including the United States, are presented in Table 4.1. This table shows that the U.S. suicide rate for young adult males ranks eighth among the rates of the countries listed, with higher rates in Austria, Canada, Denmark, France, Poland, Sweden, and West Germany. Lower suicide rates are found in Australia, Italy, the

Netherlands, Japan, and the United Kingdom. Table 4.1 also shows that the U.S. rate for young adult females ranks ninth, with only Australia, Italy, Poland, and the United Kingdom showing lower rates.

In spite of findings that show a young adult suicide rate in the United States that is lower than in many other countries, and in spite of recent trends reflecting a slight reduction in the suicide rate of this age group, the overall incidence of self destructive behavior among young adults continues to be high. In the next section we will explore the research literature concerning factors that influence suicide among young adults. These findings lend support to the idea that the age 30 transition is a difficult period in the lives of young adults and that it has a significant effect on suicidal behavior.

Factors Affecting Young Adult Suicide

The research literature that attempts to determine factors related to suicide rarely studies isolated groups of young adults. Not only are adults in this age group difficult to identify and gather together for study, but also they tend to be absorbed in the demands of their stage of life and have little interest in participating in research studies. Therefore, the material in this section has been synthesized from studies that have included young adults as well as adolescents or older adults within their populations.

The first factor to emerge from suicide studies that include young adults is the now-familiar one of depression. The special stresses of the age 30 transition exacerbate depression in this age group, especially for those who may be predisposed biologically or who may have arrived at this age with much unfinished business from earlier life stages. The changing demographics of depression do indeed support the notion that the age 30 transition is a difficult period in the lives of men and women. Depression has historically been an older person's disorder. Since World War II, however, the typical age of onset has steadily decreased. Recent findings indicate that depression is now more prevalent among those aged 20–30 than among those aged 50–60 (Reich, Rice, & Mullaney, 1986). While depression continues to be more common among women than among men, the male to female ratio among people in their 30s is beginning to narrow as more young men join the ranks of the depressed. However, the incidence of depression peaks for women in their mid-30s, while it does not peak for men until the ages 55–60 (Hirshfield & Cross, 1982).

In a detailed suicide study, Goldney (1981) found that depression, hopelessness, the absence of a significant personal relationship, and a history of parental conflict were associated with suicide attempts by 110 women aged 18–30. All of the women were significantly depressed. However, the degree of hopelessness, as measured by the Beck Hopelessness Scale, was a more powerful indicator of the lethality of the suicide attempt than was the level

A young man is so strong, so mad, so certain, and so lost. He has everything and he is able to use nothing. Thomas Wolfe, *Of Time and the River,* 1935

of depression. Also, those women who had taken the most lethal doses of dangerous drugs were more likely than those taking less lethal doses to be unmarried, and they were less likely to have a supportive relationship with a significant person. As this study indicates, depression appears to be a general background factor in all suicide, while hopelessness and absence of a supportive relationship are variables which influence lethality.

Many of the risk factors for depression in women are normative life events of the young adult years. Four of the most important factors are postpartum depression (the "baby blues"), marital difficulties, the presence of young children in the home, and relocation.

Postpartum depression occurs soon after childbirth in a small percentage of young mothers. It seems to be related to the turbulent hormonal changes associated with pregnancy and childbirth but may also be associated with the change of life-style that mothers inevitably experience, at least for a while, after the appearance of a baby. New mothers frequently experience both an increase in feelings of responsibility and a decrease in their personal freedom. This shift in responsibility and freedom may provoke a crisis in young women predisposed to depression or unprepared for the realities of motherhood. Many young women today, either out of necessity or desire, plan unrealistically to return to work before their bodies and their personalities have a chance to adjust completely to motherhood. The ambivalence of leaving a loved, dependent infant, coupled with the often conflicting demands of work and parenthood and with the biological stresses of childbirth and hormonal changes, may exacerbate feelings of guilt, depression, and inadequacy and lead to suicidal ideation. Even when the postpartum period has passed, the pressures of mothering may exacerbate depression. Brown and Harris (1978) found that mothers who had three or more young children in the home, no full-time outside employment, and no supportive relationship with a husband or boyfriend were greatly at risk for depression.

Separation and divorce have been shown to be associated with depression for both women and men, although women tend to seek counseling for depression during the marital breakdown period while men rarely seek treatment until the divorce (Weissman, 1986). Maris (1971) described the prototypic young adult female suicide as married, having children, suffering from depression, and enmeshed in a marriage that has a history of conflict. Supporting the position that marital conflict is especially difficult for young females, Illfeld (1977) found that both marital stress and parenting responsibilities are special sources of depression in women; job-related stress is more likely to lead to depression among men.

Other evidence supporting the role that conflict in the home plays in adult suicide was supplied by Stephens (1985), who investigated the relationships between 50 suicidal women aged 18–63 and their boyfriends. Extensive interviews with these women, which focused on the nature of these relationships and their contribution to the suicidal act, revealed four major suicidogenic themes. The first theme included "smothering love" and the suicidal female's unrealistic expectations regarding the love relationship. The second theme involved sexual infidelity by the spouse or boyfriend that severely aggravated an already strained relationship. The third theme included physical abuse by the partner. Many of the suicide attempts by these women were followed by another battering experience as punishment for the suicidal behavior. The fourth, and most common, pattern associated with suicidal behavior involved an uncaring and emotionally indifferent relationship. Two-thirds of the women in this study characterized their partners as being unwilling to express even rudimentary affection for them. The reported feelings resulting from these relationships included loneliness, powerlessness, and low self-esteem, which led eventually to significant depression. A history of marital problems also seems to increase the tendency toward suicide among males. Rygnestad (1982), in investigating the self-poisonings of 102 males and 155 females between the ages of 13 and 88, found an increased incidence of separation, divorce, and unemployment in both men and women suicide attempters.

Occupational stress has historically been a larger factor in male suicide than in female suicide. The traditional sex role socialization of males to fulfill the instrumental role (i.e., to be the breadwinners) has placed males at higher risk for depression because of occupational failure, stress on the job, or unemployment. There is evidence that unemployment and downward occupational mobility are factors in adult suicide (Breed, 1963; Maris, 1981; Powell, 1958). The following case study illustrates the powerful influence of occupation and salary for young men.

Gary F. was only 32 when he died. Ever since he was a child, Gary had been in a hurry. His grieving parents described him as a child who "ran before he walked." Impatient, energetic, and charming, Gary had experienced almost nothing but success throughout high school and college.

Although Gary had never been a serious student, he had impressed his college teachers with his willingness to undertake a task and his political "savvy" in getting things done. He completed his bachelor of science in business administration with a respectable 2.3 grade point average (out of a possible 4.0). One of his professors wrote about him that "Gary would take a back seat to no one." Gary was hired by a major brokerage firm. He married his college girlfriend, Beth, and began to rise swiftly up the management ladder.

When the stock market crashed in 1987, Gary was among the first in his firm to be dismissed. After a few weeks of looking for work, Gary came to realize that he probably would not get work soon, certainly not as good a job as he had lost. Although Beth

worked, their debts soon reached a point where her salary could not
cover their expenses. Beth and Gary began to argue over money.

They were paying for a home in a wealthy suburb and for two
expensive cars. While Beth quietly began to figure how to get along
on her salary, Gary was busy trying to dream up get-rich-quick
schemes. Beth sold one car to make the payments for the house and
other car. From that time on, Gary became quiet and contemplative.
He no longer dreamed big or discussed material goods. He began to
refer to himself as a "loser." On the day of his death, he and Beth
argued once again about money. Gary slammed out of the house,
yelling, "We've still got my insurance policy. I'm worth more dead
than alive."

The police report filed after the accident revealed that Gary was
driving over 85 miles per hour on a narrow two-lane country road.
The car was traveling so fast that it actually became airborne. The
two front wheels were suspended over a branch of a tree 20 yards
from a curve in the road. Gary, who was not wearing his seat belt,
was thrown from the car and killed instantly.

No one will ever know with certainty whether Gary committed suicide or whether his death was a result of angry, impulsive behavior. However, Beth told her therapist that she thought
Gary had meant to die.

"At some level," Beth said quietly through her tears, "he
knew he was going to have to slow down, to take stock, to think
things through. I was trying to talk to him about having a baby
before the stock market crashed. Even that seemed to bother him.
It was as though he was afraid of what he might see if he took
time to really evaluate our life. When everything crashed, he
found it too painful to look at. He just tried to escape—from
failure, from me, from himself."

Gary's case reflects the effect that a life accident, in this
case the crash of the stock market, can have, especially when it
occurs during a period of re-evaluation. At 32, Gary might naturally have begun to examine where he was going and what he
wanted out of life. This was especially likely because Beth was
suggesting parenthood. However, faced with the disintegration of
his career and the loss of material things by which he had defined
his life, Gary probably found re-evaluation too painful. Instead,
he regressed to an earlier stage of dreaming big dreams. When
these were not realized, he became depressed and hostile. Whether
suicide or accident, Gary's death was undoubtedly due, at least
in part, to his inability to re-evaluate life choices and to set new
goals for himself when the first young dreams died.

Gary's case and others like it point up the danger of assuming
that self-worth is indicated by employment status. The literature
is less clear, however, about the relationship between occupational status and suicide.

Gibbs and Martin (1964) proposed that high-status jobs are
inherently more stressful than low-status jobs because of the re-

sponsibilities and competition inherent in the former. Breed (1963) argued that low-status jobs are more stressful because of the limited wages and the poor self-esteem which tends to be associated with them. In a definitive study, Lampert, Bourque, and Kraus (1984) examined the relationship between occupational status and suicide by calculating age-specific suicide rates for men in various occupational categories in Sacramento County, California, over 3 decades. They found a highly significant inverse relationship between occupational status and suicide rate for all age groups, including those aged 25–44 (among whom are young adults as we have defined them). In this later age group, the suicide rates were highest for the low-status occupations of laborer, farm laborer, and service worker. The lowest suicide rates occurred among the highest-status occupations, including professional-technical ones.

The final factor that increases depression is mobility. The dramatic mobility of our society, which was discussed earlier in this chapter, appears to take a special toll on women. Because young people, especially young professionals, are more mobile than other age groups, they are especially vulnerable. One study has shown that moving increases the risk for depression, especially among women, even if the move is voluntary, results in greater financial reward, and leads to a better standard of living (Hull, 1979).

In summary, we have noted in this section that depression and hopelessness are significant factors influencing suicide in young adults. Depression in this age group appears to be a frequent result of the many stressors associated with this stage of development, including problems engendered by marriage, child rearing, intimate interpersonal relationships, occupational stress, and mobility. In addition to these long-standing stressors, there is a growing threat in the world today that will surely affect the suicide rate: the growing AIDS epidemic. In the next section we will review the limited information we have concerning the impact of this terrible disease on suicide in young adults. Although AIDS is a disease that can affect people of any age, the highest incidence of infection presently is among young adults. Therefore, we have chosen to discuss AIDS and suicide in this chapter.

The Special Case of AIDS and Suicide

Acquired immune deficiency syndrome (AIDS) is a new, yet already well-known, fatal infectious disease caused by the human immunodeficiency virus (HIV). AIDS was introduced into the United States in 1976, ironically the year smallpox was eradicated worldwide. The first U.S. clinical case was discovered in 1978, and the Center for Disease Control began tracking AIDS in 1981. Today there are approximately 60,000 reported cases of AIDS, and more than half of these people have already died. It is estimated that 1.5 million people in the United States may already be infected with the HIV virus (Hostetter, 1988).

Rope and People, I, 1935, Joan Miró. Oil on cardboard mounted on wood, with coil of rope, 41½ × 29⅜ in. (Collection, the Museum of Modern Art, New York. Gift of the Pierre Matisse Gallery.)

It is well known that certain groups, especially gay men and intravenous drug users, are at great risk for AIDS. Because AIDS is a blood-transmitted disease, anal intercourse and sharing needles are especially high-risk behaviors.

Because the presence of the HIV virus can be readily detected through blood tests, people are now learning that they have this terrible disease long before the development of any symptoms. Indeed, many individuals who test HIV positive are symptom-free and remain so for periods of 2 to 5 years. It is important that we examine the impact of an HIV-positive diagnosis or of full-blown AIDS on the risk for suicide because of the implications for the treatment of AIDS patients.

Because this disease was discovered so recently, little is known about the relationship between AIDS and suicide. Fryer (1987) has speculated that there is an elevated suicide risk among people with AIDS, and he has alerted clinicians who work with these patients to be aware of this problem. He pointed out that AIDS patients constitute a high-risk group for suicide for several reasons. Certainly the presence of a condition that will result in a slow and horrible death increases the chance that a suicidal solution will be considered. Also, advanced stages of AIDS often involve a type of dementia that may affect the risk for suicide. And as Fryer has pointed out promiscuous homosexuals and intravenous drug users (groups at high-risk for developing AIDS) are especially vulnerable to suicide even before infection.

Supporting Fryer's view is a recent study, conducted in New York City, which indicates that the suicide rate among people who test HIV positive is greatly elevated (Marzuk et al., 1988). These investigators studied the suicide rates of 3,828 New York City residents who lived with a diagnosis of AIDS at some time during the year of the study. The suicide rate of this group was found to be 36.3 times higher than the suicide rate for men in the same age range (20–59) who were not so diagnosed and 66 times higher than the rate for the general population. The suicide rate of AIDS patients was also found to be significantly higher than those for other terminally ill patients, which are generally only slightly elevated. All suicides among the AIDS patients reported in this study occurred early in the disease process and before the onset of symptoms.

The investigators cautioned that only definite suicides were included in their calculations and that therefore, the resulting rate was very conservative. Inclusions of more equivocal deaths or those involving passive euthanasia would have greatly increased the reported suicide rate of this group.

Marzuk and his associates pointed out the important implications of these findings for professionals who treat AIDS patients and for the administration of large-scale screenings such as the one recently conducted by the U.S. armed services. Such screenings must be followed by appropriate counseling and followup in order to prevent a major increase in the number of suicides in the near future as the incidence of HIV positive diagnoses grows.

SUMMARY

There is a feeling of Eternity in Youth which makes amends for everything. To be young is to be as one of the Immortals. No young man believes he shall ever die.
    William Hazlitt

Although the United States has long been identified as a youth-oriented society, actuarial data on adolescent and young adult suicide indicate that many people in these two age groups are very unhappy. The suicide rate has increased more rapidly for those aged 15–24 than for any other age group during the past 25 years. The suicide rate for those aged 25–34 is higher than that of adolescents, but recent trends show a small reduction in the rate for young adults, while the adolescent rate continues to climb. Among both adolescents and young adults, suicide rates are higher for males than females and higher for whites than blacks. For adolescents, cluster suicides are a special concern.

Precipitating factors in adolescent suicide are little different from the stressors faced by many young people. There are, however, family characteristics, cognitions, and social factors which differentiate suicidal adolescents from others in this age group. In addition, suicidal young people are more likely than others to have inadequate role models, to abuse alcohol and drugs, and to be significantly depressed.

There are sex differences with respect to the suicidal behavior of adolescents; for example, there are more attempts by females and more completions by males. The higher suicide rate for males may be partly due to their tendency to be more aggressive and more success oriented than females. The higher suicide attempt rate for females may be partly due to an inclination to view suicide as a means of seeking help in a crisis. Adolescents, compared to their parents, are more accepting in their attitudes toward suicide. Research has shown adolescent attitudes toward suicide to be related to a number of variables, including age, intelligence, religious belief, and general adjustment.

Suicide among young adults, as in all age groups, is related to depression and hopelessness. The depression among young adults, which has increased significantly in recent years, appears to be related to the many stressors experienced by those in this age group. The stressors of marriage, parenting, and occupation take on special significance during the age 30 transition, when young adults are heavily involved in reviewing their previous decisions in these areas in preparation for the deeper and altered commitments that will carry them into middle age.

AIDS presents a special new concern regarding suicide among young adults. Early findings show a significantly elevated suicide rate among people with HIV positive diagnoses.

REFERENCES

Angle, C., O'Brien, T., & McIntire, M. (1983). Adolescent self-poisoning: A nine year follow up. *Developmental and Behavioral Pediatrics, 4*, 83–87.

Baker, S. P., O'Neill, B. D., & Karpf, R. S. (1984). *The injury fact book.* Lexington, MA: Heath.

Beck, A., Kovacs, M. & Weissman, A. (1979). Assessment of suicide ideation: The scale for suicide ideators. *Journal of Consulting and Clinical Psychology, 47*, 343–352.

Beck, A. T., Steer, R. A., Kovacs, M., & Garrison, B. (1985). Hopelessness and eventual suicide: A 10-year prospective study of patients hospitalized with suicidal ideation. *American Journal of Psychiatry, 142*, 559–563.

Berman, A. L. (1988). Playing the suicide game. *Readings: A Journal of Reviews and Commentary in Mental Health, 3*, 20–23.

Berman, A. L., & Carroll, T. A. (1984). Adolescent suicide: A critical review. *Death Education, 8*, 53–64.

Boldt, M. (1982). Normative evaluations of suicide and death: A cross-generational study. *Omega, 13*, 145–157.

Bollen, K. A., & Phillips, D. P. (1982). Imitative suicides: A national study of the effects of television news stories. *American Sociological Review, 47*, 802–809.

Breed, W. (1963). Occupational mobility and suicide among white males. *American Sociological Review, 28*, 179–188.

Brown, G. W. & Harris, T. (1978). *Social origins of depression*. London: Tavistock.

Brownmiller, S. (1983). *Feminity*. New York: Linden Press and Simon & Schuster.

Clarkin, J. F., Friedman, R. C., Hurt, S. W., Corn, R., & Aronoff, M. (1984). Affective and character pathology of suicidal adolescents and young adult inpatients. *Journal of Clinical Psychiatry, 45*(1), 19–22.

Coleman, L. (1987). *Suicide clusters*. Boston: Faber & Faber.

Corder, B. F., Shorr, W., & Corder, R. F. (1974). A study of social and psychological characteristics of adolescent suicide attempters in an urban disadvantaged area. *Adolescence, 9*, 1–16.

Curran, D. K. (1987). *Adolescent suicidal behavior*. Washington, DC: Hemisphere.

David, D. & Brannon, R. (1976). The big wheel: Success, status, and the need to be looked up to. In D. David & R. Brannon (Eds.), *The forty-nine percent majority* (pp. 89–160). Reading, MA: Addison-Wesley.

Domino, G., Moore, D., Westlake, L., & Gibson, L. (1982). Attitudes toward suicide: A factor analytic approach. *Journal of Clinical Psychology, 38*(2), 257–262.

Doyle, J. A. (1983). *The male experience*. Dubuque, IA: William C. Brown.

Eisenberg, L. (1980). Adolescent suicide: On taking arms against a sea of troubles. *Pediatrics, 66*, 315–321.

Erikson, E. H. (1968). *Identity: Youth and crisis*. New York: Norton.

Erikson, E. H. (1980). *Identity and the life cycle*. New York: Norton.

Farberow, N., & Shneidman, E. (1961). *The cry for help*. New York: McGraw-Hill.

Frankl, V. E. (1963). *Man's search for meaning: An introduction to logotherapy* (I. Lasch, Trans.). New York: Washington Square Press.

Frederick, C., & Resnik, H. (1971). How suicidal behaviors are learned. *American Journal of Psychotherapy, 25*, 37–55.

Freud, S. (1961). *Civilization and its discontents*. In J. Strachey (Ed. and Trans.). *The standard edition of the complete psychological works of Sigmund Freud* (Vol. 21, pp. 64–145). London: Hogarth Press. (Original work published in 1930.)

Fryer, J. (1987). AIDS and suicide. In J. D. Morgan (Ed.) *Suicide: Helping those at Risk*, Proceedings of the Conference, May 28–30, pp. 193–200.

Garfinkel, B. D., Froese, A., & Hood, J. (1982). Suicide attempts in children and adolescents. *American Journal of Psychiatry, 139*, 1257–1261.

Gibbs, J. P., & Martin, W. T. (1964). *Status integration and suicide*. Eugene, OR: University of Oregon Press.

Gibbs, J. T. (1984). Black adolescents and youth: An endangered species. *American Journal of Orthopsychiatry, 57*, 6–21.

Goldberg, E. L. (1981). Depression and suicide ideation in the young adult. *American Journal of Psychiatry, 138*, 35–40.

Goldberg, H. (1977). *The hazards of being male: Surviving the myth of masculine privilege*. New York: New American Library.

Goldney, R. D. (1981). Attempted suicide in young women: Correlate of lethality. *British Journal of Psychiatry, 139*, 382–390.

Goldney, R. D., & Katsikitis, M. (1983). Cohort analysis of suicide rates in Australia. *Archives of General Psychiatry, 40*(1), 71–74.

Gould, M. S. & Shaffer, D. (1986). The impact of suicide in television movies: Evidence of imitation. *New England Journal of Medicine, 315*, 690–694.

Gould, R. L. (1978). *Transformations: Growth and change in adult life.* New York: Simon & Schuster.

Green, A. H. (1978). Self-destructive behavior in battered children. *American Journal of Psychiatry, 135,* 579–582.

Greuling, J., & DeBlassie, R. (1980). Adolescent suicide. *Adolescence, 15,* 589–601.

Hawton, K. (1982). Annotation: Attempted suicide in children and adolescents. *Journal of Child Psychology and Psychiatry, 23,* 497–503.

Hirschfeld, R. M. A., & Cross, C. K. (1982). Epidemiology of affective disorders: Psycho-social risk factors. *Archives of General Psychiatry, 39,* 35–46.

Holinger, P. (1979). Violent deaths among the young: Recent trends in suicide, homicide and accidents. *American Journal of Psychiatry, 136,* 1144–1147.

Holinger, P., & Offer, C. (1982). The prediction of adolescent suicide: A population model. *American Journal of Psychiatry, 139,* 302–307.

Hostetter, C. (1988, April). AIDS: Its impact on the nation, the community, the family, and the individual. Paper presented at the meeting of the Association for Death Education and Counseling, Orlando, FL.

Hull, D. (1979). Migration, adaption, and illness: A review. *Social Science and Medicine, 13A,* 25–36.

Illfeld, F. W. (1977). Current social stressors and symptoms of depression. *American Journal of Psychiatry, 134,* 161–166.

Jacobs, J. (1971). *Adolescent suicide.* New York: Wiley Interscience.

Lampert, D. I., Bourque, L. B., & Kraus, J. F. (1984). Occupational status and suicide. *Suicide and Life-Threatening Behavior, 14,* 254–269.

Lester, D., Beck, A. T., & Mitchell, B. (1979). Extrapolation from attempted suicides to completed suicides: A test. *Journal of Abnormal Psychology, 88,* 78–80.

Levenson, M., & Neuringer, C. (1971). Problem-solving behavior in suicidal adolescents. *Journal of Consulting and Clinical Psychology, 37,* 433–436.

Levinson, D. J., Darrow, C., Klein, E., Levinson, M., & McKee, B. (1978). *The seasons of a man's life.* New York: Knopf.

Limbacher, M., & Domino, G. (1985). Attitudes toward suicide among attempters, contemplators, and nonattempters. *Omega, 16,* 319–328.

Linehan, M. M. (1981). A social behavioral analysis of suicide and parasuicide: Implications for clinical assessment and treatment. In J. F. Clarkin & H. I. Glazer (Eds.), *Depression: Behavioral and directive intervention strategies.* New York: Garland Press.

Maris, R. W. (1971). Deviance as therapy: The paradox of the self-destructive female. *Journal of Health and Social Behavior, 12,* 113–124.

Maris, R. W. (1981). *Pathways to suicide: A survey of self-destructive behaviors.* Baltimore: John Hopkins University Press.

Marks, A. (1977). Sex differences and their effect upon cultural evaluations of methods of self-destruction. *Omega, 8,* 65–70.

Marzuk, P. M., Tierney, H., Tardiff, K., Gross, E. M., Morgan, E. B., Hsu, M. & Mann, J. J. (1988). Increased risk of suicide in persons with AIDS. *Journal of the American Medical Association, 259,* 1333–1337.

Masters, W. H., & Johnson, V. E. (1966). *Human sexual response.* Boston: Little, Brown.

McAnarney, E. R. (1979). Adolescent and the young adult suicide in the United States—a reflection of social unrest? *Adolescence, 14,* 765–774.

McClure, G. M. G. (1984). Recent trends in suicide amongst the young. *British Journal of Psychiatry, 144,* 134–138.

McDowell, E. E. (1985). Sex differences in suicidal behavior. *Forum Newsletter, 8,* 9–11.

McIntosh, J. L., & Jewell, B. L. (1986). Sex difference trends in completed suicide. *Suicide and Life-Threatening Behavior, 16,* 16–27.

Memory, J. M. (1988). *Juvenile suicides in secure detention facilities: Correction of published rates.* Unpublished manuscript.

Minkoff, K., Bergman, E., Beck, A. T., & Beck, R. (1973). Hopelessness, depression, and attempted suicide. *American Journal of Psychiatry, 130,* 455–459.

National Center for Health Statistics, (1988, September 30). Advance report of final mortality statistics, 1986. *Monthly vital statistics report* (DHHS Pub. No. [PHS] 88–1120). Washington, DC: U. S. Government Printing Office.

National Center for Health Statistics (1987, August 28). *Monthly vital statistics report* (DHHS Publication No. [PHS] 87–1120). Washington, DC: U.S. Government Printing Office.

Newman, A.. (1987, October–November). The bomb and adolescent anxiety. *The High School Journal,* pp. 1–4.

Paulson, J. J., & Stone, D. (1974). Suicidal behavior of latency-age children. *Journal of Clinical Child Psychology, 3,* 50–53.

Pettifor, J., Perry, D., Plowman, B., & Pitcher, S. (1983). Risk factors predicting child and adolescent suicide. *Journal of Child Care, 1,* 17–50.

Phillips, D. P. (1979). Suicide, motor vehicle fatalities and the mass media: Substantive and theoretical implications of the Werther effect. *American Sociological Review, 39,* 340–354.

Phillips, D. P., & Carstensen, L. L. (1986). Clustering of teenage suicides after television news stories about suicide. *New England Journal of Medicine, 315,* 685–689.

Piaget, J., & Inhelder, B. (1969). *The psychology of the child.* New York: Basic Books.

Powell, E. H. (1958). Occupation, status, and suicide: Toward a redefinition of anomie. *American Sociological Review, 23,* 131–139.

Ray, L. Y., & Johnson, N. (1983, November). Adolescent suicide. *The Personnel and Guidance Journal,* pp. 131–135.

Reich, T., Rice, J., & Mullaney, J. (1986). Genetic risk factors for the affective disorders. In G. L. Klerman (Ed.), *Suicide and depression among adolescents and young adults* (pp. 77–104). Washington, DC: American Psychiatric Press.

Rosenthal, M. J. (1981). Sexual differences in the suicidal behavior of young people. *Adolescent Psychiatry, 9,* 422–442.

Rubenstein, D. H. (1983). Epidemic suicide among Micronesian adolescents. *Social Science Medicine, 17,* 657–665.

Rygnestad, T. K. (1982). A prospective study of social and psychiatric aspects in self-poisoned patients. *Acta Psychiatrica Scandinavica, 66,* 139–153.

Sainsbury, P., Jenkins, J., & Levy, A. (1980). The social correlates of suicide in Europe. In R. D. T. Farmer & S. R. Hirsch (Eds.), *The suicide syndrome* (pp. 38–53). London: Croom Helm.

Seiden, R. (1983). Death in the West: A spatial analysis of the youthful suicide rate. *Western Journal of Medicine, 139,* 783–795.

Shaffer, D. (1974). Suicide in childhood and early adolescence. *Journal of child Psychology and Psychiatry, 15,* 275–291.

Stafford, M. C., & Weisheit, R. A. (1988). Changing age patterns of U.S. male and female suicide rates, 1934–1983. *Suicide and Life-Threatening Behavior, 18,* 149–163.

Stephens, J. B. (1985). Suicidal women and their relationships with husbands, boyfriends, and lovers. *Suicide and Life-Threatening Behavior, 15,* 77–89.

Stillion, J. M. (1985). *Death and the sexes: An examination of differential longevity, attitudes, behaviors, and coping skills.* Washington, DC: Hemisphere.

Stillion, J. M. (1986). Examining the shadow: Gifted children respond to the nuclear threat. *Death Studies, 10,* 27–41.

Stillion, J. M., McDowell, E. E., & May, J. H. (1984). Developmental trends and sex differences in adolescent attitudes toward suicide. *Death Education, 8,* 81–90.

Stillion, J. M., McDowell, E. E., & Shamblin, J. B. (1984). The suicide attitude vignette experience: A method for measuring adolescent attitudes toward suicide. *Death Education, 8,* 65–80.

Stillion, J. M., McDowell, E. E., Smith, R. T., & McCoy, P. A. (1986). Relationships between suicide attitudes and indicators of mental health in adolescents. *Death Studies, 10,* 289–296.

Sudak, H. S., Ford, A. B., & Rushforth, N. B. (1984). Adolescent suicide: An overview. *American Journal of Psychotherapy, 38,* 350–363.

Swain, B. J., & Domino, G. L. (1985). Attitudes toward suicide among mental health professionals. *Death Studies, 9,* 455–468.

Thomas, R. M. (1979). *Comparing Theories of Child Development.* Belmont, CA: Wadsworth.

Tishler, C. L., & McKenry, P. C. (1983). Intrapsychic symptoms dimensions of adolescent suicide attempters. *Journal of Family Practice, 16,* 731–734.

Tishler, C. L., McKenry, P. C., & Morgan, K. (1981). Adolescent suicide attempts: Some significant factors. *Suicide and Life-Threatening Behavior, 11,* 86–92.

Toolan, J. (1975). Suicide in children and adolescents. *American Journal of Psychotherapy, 29,* 339–344.

Topol, P., & Reznikoff, M. (1982). Perceived peer and family relationships, hopelessness, locus of control as factors in adolescent suicide attempts. *Suicide and Life-Threatening Behavior, 12,* 141–150.

U.S. Bureau of the Census. (1985). *Statistical Abstract of the United States: 1984.* Washington, DC: U.S. Government Printing Office.

U.S. Bureau of the Census. (1987). *Statistical Abstract of the United States: 1986.* Washington, DC: U.S. Government Printing Office.

U.S. Department of Justice, Office of Juvenile Justice and Delinquency Prevention. (1985). *Children in custody: A report on the 1977 and 1979 censuses of juvenile detention, correctional, and shelter facilities.* Washington, DC: U.S. Government Printing Office.

Vaillant, G. E. (1977). *Adaptation to life.* Boston: Little, Brown.

Walker, W. L. (1980). Intentional self-injury in school age children. *Journal of Adolescence, 3,* 217–228.

Walsh, P. B. (1983). *Growth through time: An introduction to adult development.* Monterey, CA: Brooks/Cole Publishing.

Weissman, M. (1974). The epidemiology of suicide attempts 1960–1971. *Archives of General Psychiatry, 30,* 737–746.

Weissman, M. M. (1986). Being young and female: Risk factors for major depression. In G. L. Klerman (Ed.), *Suicide and depression among adolescents and young adults* (pp. 105–130). Washington, DC: American Psychiatric Press.

Wetzel, R. D. (1976). Hopelessness, depression, and suicide intent. *Archives of General Psychiatry, 33,* 1069–1073.

White, H., & Stillion, J. M. (1988). Sex differences in attitudes toward suicide: Do males stigmatize males? *Psychology of Women Quarterly, 12,* 357–366.

5
Suicide in Middle Adulthood

Anxiety seems to be the dominant fact—and is threatening to become the dominant cliche—of modern life. It shouts in the headlines, laughs nervously at cocktail parties, nags from advertisements, speaks suavely in the board room, whines from the stage, clatters from the Wall Street ticker, jokes with fake youthfulness on the golf course and whispers in privacy each day before the shaving mirror and the dressing table.

Time, March 31, 1961*

The Subway, George Tooker, 1950. Egg tempera on compositionboard, 18 × 36 in. (Collection of the Whitney Museum of Modern Art, New York. Juliana Force Purchase, Acq. #50.23.)

The years of middle adulthood bring both special opportunities and challenges. They offer perhaps more opportunities for significant accomplishments than any other period of development. However, there are associated with these years special anxieties that place men and women at significant risk for failure in coping. Middle adulthood is a time when many people begin to experience multiple losses, which increases the likelihood of negative outcomes, including suicide. In addition, there are stresses inherent in the personal lives of middle-aged adults—such as being caught between the demands of adolescent children and aging parents—that are only beginning to be recognized by researchers and theorists.

For the purpose of understanding suicide during the middle years, we will examine the changes that adults are most likely to experience during those years and their possible impact on personality and life satisfaction. The clear implication is that people who are happy with their own growth and personality and who are experiencing high levels of life satisfaction and low levels of anxiety are poor candidates for suicide, while those who are struggling with predictable midlife concerns are at risk. We will also examine the research that exists regarding suicide and attitudes about suicide among the middle aged. Because there are special problems inherent in the study of middle adulthood, we will begin this chapter by addressing methodological issues.

METHODOLOGICAL ISSUES IN RESEARCH

Middle age is truly the terra incognita of developmental psychology. There are at least four reasons why we know less about the life experience of people between ages 35 and 65 than about people in any other age group. First, developmental psychology began by studying the periods of life in which the most dramatic changes occurred—childhood and adolescence. Indeed, until recently, developmental psychologists seemed to be saying that human growth and development was completed by age 18 and that the next 50 years constituted merely a "playing out" of the learnings or mislearnings of the first 18 years. It should also be noted that the first 5 or 6 years of life were thought to be the most important by many of the early psychologists. This bias toward the earliest years probably delayed the study of normative changes in adulthood more than any other single factor, for the consensus seemed to be that once personality patterns were set during the 1st half-decade of life, little could be done to change their lifelong effects on personality.

The second reason that we know little about middle adulthood is a methodological one: It is difficult to gather data on adults between the ages of 35 to 65. Unlike children, adolescents, and even college-going young adults, middle-aged adults do not attend school on a regular basis. In addition, the middle years are typically so full of activity (e.g., parenting, establishing careers, developing leadership in community activities) that it is difficult to find groups of middle-aged adults who are willing to take the time to participate in developmental studies. In short, middle-aged adults are living Erikson's stage of generativity, and their too-full lives leave little time for participating in research.

Third, even when groups of middle-aged adults do agree to participate in research, the results are almost always less than satisfactory, because there is no one group of people that can be said to be representative of middle-aged adults. We know of no study of middle-aged adults, including a new study by the authors that is reported later in this chapter, which can claim that its sample is representative of all people in the middle years. For this reason alone, many fine researchers, loath to violate the basic tenet of representativeness in their research, have eliminated studies of middle-aged adults from their research agendas. Although the issue of representativeness also exists within the elderly population, it is less problematic because elderly people have groups organized around age (e.g., American Association of Retired Persons), and many can be found living together in retirement communities. In addition, elderly people often have more time than do the middle aged to participate in research. It is possible, then, to gather large samples of children, adolescents, young adults, and even elderly people from organized groups more easily than can be done with middle-aged adults.

The fourth major problem that exists within the literature on adulthood is the lack of comparability of age samples. Various studies operationally define middle age as starting as early as age 30 and as late as age 45. We view middle age throughout this chapter as starting at age 35 and ending at age 64. Furthermore, we suggest that within the 30-year period called middle age there should be three subdivisions: the early middle years (35–44), the middle middle years (45–54), and the late middle years (55–64). Such subdivisions are justifiable not only because the nature of individuals' lives seems to change detectably over those age ranges but also because suicide rates are reported in government statistics according to those ranges. However, many of the studies examined in this chapter do not use our age ranges. Some have studied only a segment of middle adulthood and others have not identified the ages of the adults studied. In general, then, research on suicide in the middle adulthood is scarce. It is also methodologically more flawed than the research on suicide for any other age group.

In spite of the problems inherent in studying the middle aged, a minor explosion in both the quantity and quality of research about the middle years has occurred in the last 2 decades. Much of the research is based on open-ended interviews with members of groups acknowledged to be nonrepresentative. For example, the ongoing study of Terman's sample of gifted children has followed a group of 1,000 children and adolescents into the beginning of their old age. Studies of that group, while clearly not representative of the population at large, have yielded a huge body of data. The Grant study which followed a sample of male Harvard students for 30 years, although blatantly biased with regard to sex, socioeconomic status, and education level, has also added to our understanding of the nature of middle age, as has the work of Levinson, Gould, and Vaillant. However, none of these studies specifically addresses the topic of suicide among the middle-aged population. It is the purpose of this chapter to address that topic. Utilizing the landmark studies just mentioned and reviewing the few studies available that specifically address suicide and attitudes about suicide among the middle aged, we will attempt to illuminate the circumstances of middle age that may lead individuals to consider, attempt, or commit suicide.

THE STATISTICAL PICTURE

Suicide among middle-aged people is a reality in all developed countries. Table 5.1 presents the latest statistics available for 13 countries, including the United States. The table shows that in 7 countries (the United States, Australia, Canada, Denmark, France, Italy, and the Netherlands), suicide rates for males increased from the lowest to the middle to the highest age range. In the 6 other countries (Australia, Japan, Poland, Sweden, the United Kingdom, and West Germany), male suicide rates increased from the lowest to the middle range but decreased from the middle to the highest range. For females, the rates increased across all three age ranges in 8 countries (Austria, Canada, France, Italy, Japan, the Netherlands, the United Kingdom, and West Germany). Female suicide statistics in 5 countries (the United States, Australia, Denmark, Poland, and Sweden) show an increase from the lowest to the middle range but a decrease from the middle to the highest range. Only one country, Austria, shows a decrease from the lowest to the middle range followed by an increase in the highest range. In all but 2 countries (Poland and Sweden) for males and 1 country (Sweden) for females, the suicide rates for people aged 55–64 were higher than the rates for those aged 35–44. With few exceptions, then, it seems appropriate to conclude that the general international trend is toward an increase in rates of suicide from the lowest to the highest age ranges. This seems especially true when the statistics concerning suicide among the elderly in developed countries are reviewed (see Chapter 6).

In the United States, suicide ranked as the eighth most common cause of death in 1986. Only heart disease, cancer, cerebrovascular diseases, accidents, pulmonary diseases, pneumonia and influenza, and diabetes mellitus killed more people than did suicide. In 1986, a total of 12,531 suicides were reported among persons aged 35–64. This figure represents almost 41% of all suicides reported that year. Male deaths by suicide far exceeded female deaths, a pattern that has become familiar to the reader. The age-adjusted death rate for suicide was 3.8 times higher for males than for females.

Table 5.2 summarizes the 1985 suicide rate among middle-aged adults by age, sex, and race. The table shows that the rate of suicide for those in their early middle years was 14.6 per 100,000

TABLE 5.1 Suicide Rates for Selected Countries by Sex and Age Group
(Rate per 100,000 population. Includes deaths resulting from self-inflicted injuries. Except as noted, deaths classified according to the ninth revision of the International Classification of Diseases.)

Sex and age	United States 1983	Australia 1984	Austria 1985	Canada 1984	Denmark 1984	France 1984	Italy 1981	Japan 1985	Netherlands 1984	Poland 1984	Sweden 1984	United Kingdom 1984	West Germany 1985
Male													
Total	19.2	16.9	40.9	21.4	36.5	32.2	9.8	26.0	15.2	23.6	27.4	11.8	29.4
35–44 yrs. old	22.7	20.1	53.6	25.3	53.2	36.7	8.9	30.5	19.0	37.0	36.5	16.5	31.8
45–54 yrs. old	23.7	22.7	56.3	28.6	57.1	43.8	14.0	49.6	22.5	39.0	42.2	18.2	40.3
55–64 yrs. old	25.7	24.3	53.9	28.8	65.5	46.1	16.3	41.4	23.7	31.2	30.5	16.8	36.2
Female													
Total	5.4	5.2	15.7	6.1	21.0	12.4	4.0	13.1	9.6	4.9	11.8	5.7	12.7
35–44 yrs. old	7.9	6.7	20.5	9.2	28.3	13.9	4.3	11.9	11.1	6.6	15.3	6.4	12.2
45–54 yrs. old	8.9	10.6	19.1	10.5	41.1	17.6	5.2	17.3	14.8	8.3	20.1	9.8	16.5
55–64 yrs. old	8.3	8.2	22.4	10.7	38.1	18.4	7.8	18.6	17.3	8.0	15.0	10.7	18.3

Source: U.S. Bureau of Census. (1988). Statistical Abstracts of the United States (108th Edition). Washington, D.C., 1987, p. 803.

TABLE 5.2   Suicide Rate per 100,000 Population Among Middle-Aged Adults by Age, Sex, and Race for 1985.

Age	All groups	Males	Females	White males	Black males	White females	Black females
35–44	14.6	22.3	7.1	23.5	14.9	7.7	3.6
45–54	15.6	23.5	8.3	25.1	13.5	9.0	3.2
55–64	16.7	26.8	7.7	28.6	11.5	8.4	2.2

Source: U.S. Bureau of the Census (1988). *Statistical Abstracts of the United States* (108th edition.) Washington, D.C., 1987, pp. 78 and 82.

population, for those in their middle middle years it was 15.6 per 100,000, and for those in their late middle years it was 16.7 per 100,000. Males aged 35–44 had a suicide death rate of 22.3 per 100,000, compared with a death rate of 7.1 per 100,000 for females in the same age group. Males aged 45–54 had a death rate of 23.5, compared with a female rate of 8.3. For the older middle aged (55–64), the male rate rose to 26.8 while the female rate actually dropped by 0.6 to 7.7.

Table 5.2 also shows that white males aged 35–44 had a suicide death rate of 23.5 per 100,000 while black males of the same age group had a rate of 14.9 per 100,000. White females of the same age group had a rate of 7.7, compared with a black female suicide death rate of 3.6. Among those aged 45–54, the white male suicide rate rose to 25.1 and the black male rate dropped to 13.5. The corresponding figures for females were 9.0 for white females and 3.2 for black females. Among those aged 55–64, the rate for white males rose to 28.6 and the rate for black males fell to 11.5. The corresponding rate for white females dropped to 8.4 while the corresponding rate for black females dropped to 2.2. It is obvious from these rates that the increase in suicide deaths across the age ranges is almost entirely due to increased suicides by aging white males. These data also show that the black male suicide rate peaks around age 35 and the female rates peak around age 50.

As the actuarial data show, suicide is very much a part of the midlife stage of development. Further discussions of the normative developments that occur during the middle years may help to better understand suicide in this age group.

PROFILE OF MIDDLE ADULTHOOD

Researchers in the field of adult development have engaged in an ongoing debate about continuity and change in the middle years. Some authorities maintain that development in the middle years consists primarily of continuing growth along lines begun in the young adult years (Neugarten, 1968; Vaillant, 1977). Others see the middle years as consisting of periods of intensive reflection and re-evaluation, frequently resulting in major life changes growing out of a "midlife crisis" (Gould, 1978; Jaques, 1965; Levinson, Darrow, Klein, Levinson, & McKee, 1978; Sheehy, 1976).

Perhaps the best-known research that supports the notion of a widespread midlife crisis was conducted by Daniel Levinson and his colleagues (Levinson et al., 1978). Based on interviews with 40 working and middle-class white males aged 35–45, Levinson identified specific stages, which he called the "seasons of a man's life." These seasons consist of alternating periods of stability and transition. The longer stable periods occur when appropriate developmental tasks are performed and appropriate goals pursued. The transitional periods, which tend to last approximately 5 years, occur when men review their progress toward certain goals and question the direction of their lives. Levinson found that 80% of the men he interviewed reported the midlife transition that occurs between ages 40 and 45 to be stressful. His subjects frequently expressed disappointment that they were not on schedule in realizing the dreams they had as young adults. They experienced a growing sense of aging and for the first time became keenly aware of their own mortality. Four major conflicts that seem to be central to the midlife crisis, according to Levinson, are (1) being young versus being old, (2) being destructive versus being constructive, (3) being masculine versus being feminine, and (4) being attached to others versus being separated from them.

A number of developmental psychologists are not in agreement with the "crisis" model of adult development. These writers support, instead, a model of change in which individuals progress across the life span in predictable, orderly ways, adhering reasonably well to a socially determined timetable without abrupt and tumultuous transitions. They believe that the difficulties experienced at various ages are the result of personal characteristics of the individuals interacting with environmental experiences and not universal products of a particular stage of development or transition.

George Vaillant (1977) examined data gathered by following a sample of 94 Harvard graduates across a 30-year period beginning in 1937. Vaillant found that although some men divorce, change jobs, and suffer depression at midlife, the frequency of these occurrences in this age group is no greater than at other stages of adulthood. Other research, including the California Intergenerational Studies, have found very little evidence for widespread midlife crisis among either men or women (Clausen, 1981; Haan, 1981; McRae & Costa, 1983).

Regardless of whether change occurs as crisis or in some slower, more continuous manner, the central issue of the middle years is to find ways to remain productive in the face of multiple demands and losses. Erikson (1980), describing the middle years, used the term *generativity* to include all means of giving back to or investing in society. He described the central conflict of middle age as the struggle to become productive, responsible, optimistic,

The difficulty in life is the choice. George Moore, *The Bending of the Bough*

and creative instead of psychologically stagnant. The middle-aged adult who is psychologically stagnant typically interacts in pessimistic, negative, and self-indulgent ways.

Peck (1968) added to our understanding of generativity by conceptualizing four developmental tasks or challenges for people in their middle years. First, they must shift from valuing physical capabilities to valuing wisdom. The years of middle adulthood bring the first signs of physical deterioration for most people. Unavoidable physical changes include the graying and loss of hair, the appearance of wrinkles, and a general decline in attractiveness. Speed, strength, and endurance also decline during this period, even when individuals attempt to moderate aging's effects by proper nutrition and exercise. Because of these inevitable declines, adults who are able to shift their focus from their physical appearance and functioning to their cognitive growth and development are likely to be better adjusted during the middle years. Those who cling to physical capabilities as their chief tool for coping with life and as the most important element in their value hierarchy and self-definition become increasingly depressed, bitter, and otherwise unhappy as they grow older.

The second task is to shift from sexualizing to socializing. During this 30-year period of midlife, females experience menopause, with its attendant hormonal changes and loss of childbearing possibilities, and males notice a diminishment in the urgency of their sexual drive. In addition, sexual overtures among the middle aged become less acceptable. Sometime during this period the "swinging bachelor" starts to be perceived as a "dirty old man" and the flirtatious young woman becomes the middle-aged "Mrs. Robinson" figure to be pitied for her continuing sexual overtures to others. Learning to accept people and to appreciate them for their individuality rather than for sexual possibilities permits the development of deep friendships that promote adjustment throughout middle and old age. The shift from sexualizing to socializing may not be accomplished easily, however. Frequently such changes result in the need to re-examine one's identity, and they may be perceived as a loss of a highly valued aspect of one's younger life, thus contributing to a negative self-image and deepening depression.

At thirty man suspects himself a fool;
Knows it at forty, and reforms his plan,
At fifty chides his infamous delay,
Pushes his prudent purpose to resolve,
In all the magnaminity of thought
Resolves, and re-resolves; then dies the same. Young, *Night Thoughts*

The third shift discussed by Peck is from cathectic impoverishment to cathectic flexibility. Cathectic impoverishment is a state that results from having few or no meaningful relationships, while cathectic flexibility is the ability to build new relationships as old ones are lost. As individuals move through midlife, a number of important personal relationships must be given up. Parents die, children grow up and leave home, and one's circle of friends is broken by death. The adult who is able to cope with these inevitable losses and to build new relationships is in a good position to remain optimistic and generative.

The fourth shift is from mental rigidity to mental flexibility. One of the great dangers of midlife is that a person will become increasingly rigid and set in his or her own ways. In order to grow and be productive, middle-aged individuals must avoid the tendency to become rigid in their view of the world. People who are able to remain flexible in their thinking are less likely to develop the rigid, dichotomous thinking which has been shown to be characteristic of potential suicides (Beck, Rush, Show, & Emery, 1979).

In addition to the major developmental issue of generativity versus stagnation, adults in the middle years experience other predictable changes. One of the major reliable findings about change in middle age concerns time perspective. Adult development texts consistently state that adults between the ages of 35 and 46 report that they begin to think in terms of the time remaining in their lives rather than in terms of time experienced to date (e.g., Santrock, 1985). This seemingly small change may have dramatic implications on the life satisfaction of middle-aged adults. Frequently the change in time reckoning brings with it a review of accomplishments to date that may involve thoughts like the following: "Okay, I'm 40, and I probably have only another 30 years of active life ahead. What have I done to date and what is left for me to do?"

The person who has accomplished many of his or her young dreams may have a sense of enhanced life satisfaction as a result of asking such questions, but the person whose early dreams have not been realized may become less satisfied and more susceptible to depression and suicidal ideation. Neugarten (1968) has postulated the existence of a "social clock" which helps aging people to evaluate their accomplishments with respect to their peers and those younger than they. The social clock may be superimposed over the biological clock, helping people to judge their progress in life's passage. Perception that one is "on time" with respect to one's social clock (e.g., has reached an appropriate rank in the army for the amount of enlisted time) may relate importantly to life satisfaction, while perception of great deviations or being "off schedule" may have negative psychological consequences.

A second change during this period occurs in people's experiences with death. Death, which for many fortunate people has been a stranger until the middle years, becomes first an acquaintance and then a well-known companion. Most people between the ages of 35 and 65 experience the death of their parents. With these deaths comes the clear realization that one belongs to the next generation to die. One 50-year-old reminded her five siblings at the funeral of their mother that "the next time we come together for a funeral, it will be one of us." The middle aged also become chillingly aware of deaths in their cohort group, as 40-year-old friends contract cancer and other terminal illnesses or die suddenly from heart attacks. Some middle-aged people experience the death of an adolescent or young adult child, forcing them to re-examine their concept of a just world.

Experiencing such deaths brings about the sure knowledge that time is limited, and it may fuel the sense of urgency bordering on anxiety felt by many middle-aged adults. Gould (1978) has emphasized that adults between the ages of 35 and 43 experience an urgency to attain life's goals. Their new awareness of time limitations feeds into their need to restructure their lives in more satisfactory ways. Gould, coining the term *middlescence*, suggests that middle age may be as turbulent for many adults as the period of adolescence. Certainly, the suicide statistics during this period would support such a view.

The loss of young dreams may also feed into this turbulence. Except for the fortunate few, most middle-aged people reach a point where they admit that they will never reach the high goals they set for themselves during their youth. They will never be great artists or writers or company presidents. They will never attain the perfect marriage or raise perfect children. This knowledge may be accepted in stride and be reflected in the "mellowing" that is reported to occur throughout this period. However, for many middle-aged people, the realization that they will never attain these youthful goals is regarded as further evidence of inadequacy and added fuel for personal dissatisfaction with self.

A recent popular book that attempts integration of the major studies of adult development against a background of life experiences is Judith Viorst's *Necessary Losses* (1986). In it, Viorst points out that there are many normative losses which middle-aged people experience. The "necessary losses" of midlife detailed by Viorst include several already discussed in this chapter, such as the loss of the youthful self, the loss of dreams of accomplishment, and the loss of parents and friends through death or disability. Another necessary loss of midlife discussed by Viorst is the loss of the parenting role.

The middle years are a time when children grow up and leave home, resulting in either an "empty nest" or a "child-free home," depending on the attitude of the parents. The status of parenthood can be very important to the self-definition of middle-aged people, and the loss of the parenting role can be very stressful. When children leave home, parents experience an additional shrinking of their interpersonal worlds as the children's friends and teachers also disappear. One middle-aged woman described the change in her life as follows: "It's as though someone switched the world from technicolor to black and white and turned down the volume too. Our children provided the color, noise, and activity in our life. There were always places to go, lots of friends in and out of our home, and lots of laughter. Life is calmer now, the pace is slower. It's not necessarily bad, but it certainly is different—maybe this is one of the first signs of what old age will

How beautiful is youth!
How bright it gleams
With its illusions, aspira-
tion, dreams. Longfel-
low, *Morituri Salutamus*

be like." Parents may also experience a great deal of pain as a result of relinquishing certain illusions associated with parenthood—illusions such as the belief that they can always protect their children from harm.

The special pain associated with losing one's children is closely related to the loss of other young dreams and illusions, such as the illusion of oneself as a perfect parent. The loss of this illusion is poignantly described by Viorst in the following passage:

> Our fantasy is that if we are good and loving parents, we can hold the tigers and thorns at bay. Our fantasy is that we can save our children. Reality will find us late at night, when our children are out and the telephone rings. Reality will remind us—in that heart-stopping moment before we pick up the phone—that anything, that any horror, is possible. Yet although the world is perilous and the lives of children are dangerous to their parents, they still must leave, we still must let them go. Hoping that we have equipped them for their journey. Hoping that they will wear their boots in the snow. Hoping that when they fall down, they can get up again. Hoping. (Viorst, 1986, p. 247)

Standing between the middle-aged individual and death is yet another series of losses, those associated with old age. Although these losses will be discussed in detail in the following chapter, preparation for the later years must begin at midlife. Middle-aged people know that the substantial losses of this period do not represent all that is dear and that later losses will inevitably occur. They must begin in middle age to prepare for these later losses—of spouse, companionship, occupation, status, and so on. Preparation for these later losses necessitates development of more adequate coping skills as well as a general "mellowing out" during the middle years. The individual who does not accomplish this developmental task in midlife is likely to have great difficulty coping with old age.

In summary, the literature on adult development seems to be consistent in documenting growth and change throughout the middle years. In addition, the authorities agree that the middle years are important ones in developing authenticity. People who move through these years coping well with loss and change will emerge with ego integrity. Erikson describes such integrity as follows:

> Only he who in some way has taken care of things and people and has adapted himself to the triumphs and disappointments of being, by necessity, the originator of others and the generator of things and ideas—only he may gradually grow the fruit of the seven stages. I know no better word for it than integrity. Lacking a clear definition, I shall point to a few attributes of this stage of mind. It is the acceptance of one's own and only life cycle and of the people who have become significant to it as something that had to be and that,

by necessity, permitted of no substitutions. Although aware of the
relativity of all the various life styles which have given meaning to
human striving, the possessor of integrity is ready to defend the dig-
nity of his own life style against all physical and economic threats.
For he knows that an individual life is the accidental coincidence of
but one life cycle with but one segment of history; and that for him
all human integrity stands and falls with the one style of integrity of
which he partakes. (Erikson, 1980, p. 104)

Whether attained gradually and incrementally across the 30
years of middle age or in more concentrated ways as a result of
a series of adult crises and losses, ego integrity surely is the end
achieved by well-adjusted persons. It bears more than a casual
resemblance to Maslow's concept of self-actualization, in which
an individual realizes his or her potential, and it clearly allows
for high life satisfaction in old age. Its opposite, despair, grows
just as surely out of a 30-year period in which people have not
been able to cope with the losses, deaths, and disappointments
inherent in the middle years. Feelings of regret for lost opportunities, grief over the deaths of close friends and loved ones, sorrow
over lack of time to begin anew or to realize young dreams all
feed into the sense of despair that may cause someone to attempt
or commit suicide as he or she approaches the end of the middle
years.

FACTORS ASSOCIATED WITH ADULT SUICIDE

Many of the research findings concerning suicide among
adults are consistent with the major thesis of this chapter—that
the special stresses and losses of midlife contribute to self-destructive behavior at this stage of development. Suicidal behavior
among middle aged adults has been shown repeatedly to be associated with three factors: (1) an accumulation of negative life
events, (2) an affective disorder (especially a primary depressive
disorder), and (3) alcoholism (Baraclough, Bunch, & Nelson, 1974;
Borg & Stahl, 1982; Hirschfeld & Blumenthal, 1986; Paykel, Prusoff, & Myers, 1975; Roy, 1982; Rygnestad, 1982).

The types of negative life events that accumulate prior to a
suicidal act are often the very losses inherent in midlife, including
declining health, financial reversals, reduced career opportunities,
and exit events or interpersonal losses (Slater & Depue, 1981).
These types of losses are almost universal during middle age. The
major distinction between the stresses of suicidal and nonsuicidal
adults appears to be more quantitative than qualitative. The suicidal adult is much more likely than others to have experienced
several significant losses within a relatively brief period of time.
Also, there is often an acceleration of these losses very close in
time to the suicidal event. The quantity and timing of losses may
not permit middle-aged people to work through the grief and
depression which accompany one loss before they are faced with

Americans began by lov-
ing youth, now out of
adult self-pity, they wor-
ship it. Jacques Barzun,
The House of Intellect

Suicidal Ideas, 1800s, Traviés de DeVillers. Lithograph. (Bettman Archive, New York.)

the next loss. In this way, even well-functioning adults may find themselves unable to cope at some point in the middle years, while people who began the period with marginal coping skills may find themselves contemplating suicide as a way to escape the loss-grief cycle.

The losses which occur most often among suicidal adults are interpersonal in nature. Slater and Depue (1981) found that exit events (e.g., separation, divorce, and death) differentiate suicidal depressed individuals from nonsuicidal depressed individuals more than any other kind of loss. The suicidal middle-aged adult is much more likely than others to have been recently separated or divorced, to have lost a parent, or to have had a child leave home within the year. In addition, such an individual is more likely than others to be functioning with a limited social support network. As could be predicted on the basis of Peck's view that cathectic flexibility is important for coping, suicidal adults are more likely than others to live alone or only with children and to lack a special confidante (Roy, 1982; Slater & Depue, 1981).

The losses experienced by suicidal adults are not limited to the time period just before the self-destructive act. Suicidal adults are more likely than others to have experienced early losses as well as recent ones. Several studies show that suicidal adults have a higher than expected incidence of early parental loss through death, divorce, or separation (Adam, Bouckoms, & Streiner, 1982; Richman, 1981; Shneidman, 1971; Warren & Tomlinson-Keasey, 1987). The research indicates that these individuals are especially likely to have experienced an early paternal loss, that is, the death of the father or absence of involvement by the father (Warren & Tomlison-Keasey, 1987). These repetitive experiences of separation and loss throughout the life span may interact in special ways with the stresses associated with midlife. Perhaps the sensitization created by early losses causes later losses to seem all the more unbearable, final, and devastating. The case of Beverly A. reflects the role of that negative life events can play in suicide.

Beverly A. was 43 years old when she appeared in a psychiatrist's office in March 1982. She described herself as depressed and told her psychiatrist that she was having increasing trouble resisting the urge to kill herself by crashing into a tree along the highway. "I've even picked out the tree," she confessed. "It's on a lonely strip of road between the hospital where I work and my home. The chances that anyone else would be hurt are slim, since the road is not traveled much and there's a long straight strip where I could pick up enough speed to be sure that the crash would be fatal."

In taking a history, the psychiatrist discovered the following facts about Beverly. Beverly had been adopted by a middle-class couple when she was 6. Before then she had spent time in three different foster homes. She was a wife of 21 years, a mother of two adolescent children, and a nurse with 15 years of experience at the same hospital. Her oldest child had gone away to college the previous fall. Beverly interpreted his leaving as "the beginning of the end of family life." Beverly had undergone two surgical procedures within the last year. The first was a D & C to try to avert a hysterectomy. The second, performed 6 months after the unsuccessful D & C, was a com-

plete hysterectomy to relieve excessive bleeding. On both occasions, Beverly had been given a general anesthetic. Although she was clear that she did not want additional children, Beverly viewed the surgeries with ambivalence. As a nurse, she knew they needed to be done, but she felt sadness about losing her ability to conceive children and wondered if it somehow made her "less of a woman." Her medical background did allow her to ascribe some of the depression she was feeling to the two episodes with the anesthetics (central nervous system depressants) and to the hormonal changes she was experiencing because of surgical menopause.

Beverly described herself as the sole support for her mother. Her father had died during the previous year, and her mother had developed heart trouble that necessitated bed rest. Beverly divided her time between her husband and 16-year-old daughter and her mother, who needed regular nursing care. Beverly felt both that she was "being cheated" of her daughter's last 2 years at home and that she was failing her mother by not being with her full-time.

Beverly's work at the hospital had suffered because of her lengthy absences following surgery and her depressed state. She complained that she was sleeping poorly at night as a result of worrying about her mother, her husband, her daughter, and her job. She was so exhausted during the day that she had little energy to give to her job or her home life. When asked to think of an image that would describe her life, Beverly said that she saw herself as an ant balancing the earth on her shoulders. When asked what was going to happen to the ant, she said, "She will lose her grip on the earth and will be crushed by it."

Many elements of loss and stress are evident in Beverly's story. Her foster home history revealed many interpersonal losses early in life. Her father had died within the past year. Her son's going to school portended the loss of her role as a parent. The surgeries she had not only were insults to the integrity of her body but also resulted in the loss of procreative ability. The stress of caring for her mother, of being "the good daughter," added to her feelings of being burdened, and her job also required that she nurture others even though she was exhausted herself. Clearly, Beverly had reached a suicidal crisis in her life. She was very depressed, and her imagery revealed that she thought her life consisted of nothing but burdens—burdens that would ultimately destroy her.

The second major factor related to suicide among middle-aged adults is depression. Depression has been shown repeatedly to be the most common psychiatric diagnosis associated with suicide among adults. Numerous studies have reported a diagnosis of affective disorder among suicidal individuals, with rates running from as low as 35% to as high as 80% (Borg & Stahl, 1982; Dorpat & Ripley, 1960; Guze & Robins, 1970; Silver, Bohnert, Beck, & Marcus, 1971; Weissman, 1974). After reviewing a number of the studies reported above, Pfeffer (1986) concluded that suicide is 30 times more prevalent among adults with affective disorder than among those not so diagnosed.

In an extensive study, Barraclough (1987) followed up 100 suicides in southern England over a 2-year period. Barraclough and his associates read coroner's reports, attended coroner's hearings, and interviewed at least one close relative of each suicide victim. Thorough review of each suicide case revealed considerable evidence for a diagnosis of depression in 70 of the 100 cases.

Many findings in Barraclough's study are consistent with those of other research on adult suicide. He found, for example, that widowed, divorced, and single adults were overrepresented in the group of suicide victims. This group showed a high incidence of alcoholism and prior suicide attempts. The suicide victims were 7 times more likely to live in single-person households and to have no adult confidantes than were members of a group of depressed but nonsuicidal individuals. Barraclough also found strong evidence of rapidly accelerating negative life events preceding many of the acts of suicide. Finally, Barraclough found that more than half the suicide victims had given some warning of their suicidal intentions to another person close in time to the suicide, and that 69% of the suicide victims had contacted a family physician or psychiatrist within one month of the act.

The exact nature of the relationships among negative life events, depression, and suicide are not clearly understood. It is certainly likely that negative life events, especially those involving significant loss, contribute to depression among suicidal individuals. The relationship between loss and depression is well documented. Freud wrote of this relationship as early as 1917, and more recent studies continue to show that depression is a common reaction to significant loss (Benjaminsen, 1981; Brown & Harris, 1978; Freud, 1917/1961; Roy & Linnoila, 1986). As discussed earlier, suicidal individuals often suffer more loss early in life, which may initiate depression. The depression is reinforced under the impact of later losses. However, such losses do not always result in depression and suicide for all people. There is evidence that losses interact with psychological characteristics of individuals, resulting in suicidal behavior. Shneidman (1971) carried out a study of 30 males, aged 55, who had been original subjects in the Terman gifted study; only 5 of the 30 had committed suicide. Shneidman found that trained raters, using psychological data collected over the years, could predict fairly well which men would commit suicide. Further, Shneidman maintained that these men could be identified when they were as young as 30 years of age through certain psychological constants and characteristic reaction patterns to stress. We would suggest that the psychological constants that Shneidman found among male suicides may be rooted in the biochemical changes discussed in Chapter 2.

The third factor that is clearly related to adult suicide is alcoholism. Roy and Linnoila (1986) reported the results of a group of studies which show the risk of suicide among alcoholics to be 58 to 85 times higher than that for nonalcoholics. The suicide rate for alcoholics has been estimated to be as high as 270 per 100,000 population (Miles, 1977).

Many more alcoholic suicide victims are men than women. The studies reviewed by Roy and Linnoila (1986) showed that 87% of the 349 alcoholic suicides studied were men. This ratio of almost 7 to 1 exceeds the relative proportion of male and female alcoholics in the United States, which has been reported to be between 4 to 1 and 5 to 1. It has been speculated that differences in the drinking behaviors of alcoholic men and women may affect the relative suicide rates for these groups (Rushing, 1969). Because more men alcoholics than women alcoholics drink in bars and other public places, men alcoholics may be more likely to experience alcohol-related interpersonal problems than women, who are inclined to drink alone at home. Also, because more men than women are employed outside the home, males are more vulnerable to alcohol-related job stress and to the stress of losing their jobs. It should be noted also that there are many other differences between men and women alcoholics (e.g., family history of psychiatric disorder, developmental history, and gender-related effects of alcohol) that are likely to be reflected in their suicidal behavior (Linnoila, Erwin, Ramm, Cleveland, & Brendle, 1980).

The typical alcoholic suicide is a middle-aged male between 45 and 55 years old who is currently drinking and has been abusing alcohol for as long as 25 years (Barraclough, 1987; Roy & Linnoila, 1986). Goodwin (1973) has hypothesized that the reason alcoholic suicides are often in their mid-40s or older is that the alcohol-related life problems that contribute to suicide (e.g., poor health, loss of employment, and divorce) tend to emerge only after a long history of alcoholism. In addition, Goodwin suggested that the incidence of alcoholic suicides decreases in old age because alcoholism leads to early death. Many alcoholics simply do not live long enough to commit suicide in old age.

Depression and negative life events seem to relate to suicide among alcoholics and nonalcoholics in the same manner. The dynamics of suicide among alcoholics are similar to those in nonalcoholics, but alcoholism seems to exacerbate negative life events and depression in complex ways. As is the case with nonalcoholic suicides, suicidal alcoholics are highly likely to have experienced a series of negative life events, which often involve lost relationships, close in time to the suicidal act (Dorpat & Ripley, 1960; Murphy, Armstrong, Hermele, Fisher, & Clendenin, 1979; Roy & Linnoila, 1986).

The relationship between alcoholism and depression is well documented. Alcohol acts on the central nervous system as a

She has started to drink as a way to cope that makes her less able to cope—R. D. Laing, *Knots,* 1970

depressant, provoking psychological changes that range from immediate relaxation to stupor and even to death. Roy and Linnoila (1986) reviewed several studies that indicate clinical depression rates of 28 to 59% among alcoholics. Whether the alcoholism causes depression in a direct physiological way, in a more indirect way (e.g., through the life problems and losses that a long history of alcoholism creates), or in both ways is not clear. There is strong evidence, however, that the depression associated with alcoholism is very much a part of alcoholic suicide. One study found that 78% of a group of 50 alcoholic suicides had previously been diagnosed as having affective disorder (Murphy, Armstrong, Hermele, Fisher, & Clendenin, 1979). Another study showed that the number of diagnoses of depression among a group of alcoholics who later killed themselves was significantly higher than among a group of alcoholics who did not (Berglund, 1984). Thus, when depression has been diagnosed as a correlate of alcoholism, the risk of suicide is greater.

The case of Kenneth P. illustrates the interaction between normative events of middle age, alcohol abuse, and suicidal behavior.

Kenneth P., at age 54, was brought to a hospital in an unconscious state. His wife said that she had found him in his study face down on the desk with an empty bottle of Jack Daniels on the floor and a gun near his right hand. It appeared that he had been trying to write a suicide note when he passed out.

When Kenneth awakened, his major reaction was one of dismay at surviving. He lamented, "I couldn't even do that job right. I really am no good." After emergency treatment, Kenneth was admitted to the hospital for tests, because he complained of ongoing stomach pains that he feared were the beginning of the type of cancer that had killed his father. During his discussions with his doctor, the following facts emerged.

Kenneth was a successful executive with a major computer software firm. He was also the father of three children, aged 18, 22, and 25. Only the 18-year-old daughter remained at home. His wife, to whom he had been married for 26 years, was "a typical housewife." He described his homelife as "very traditional." His wife had always stayed home and had taken care of his needs as well as those of the children. He credited her with his rapid rise in the company during his late 30s and 40s, because "she was so good at entertaining."

Kenneth had been a social drinker since his college days, and alcohol had played a major role in entertaining at home and during "business lunches." Lately, he had found that he needed a drink to "get started" in the morning. Although he maintained that his performance on the job had not been affected, he was aware that two younger employees had been promoted over him within the last year. He confessed to his doctor that he was afraid he was being "sidelined" and would never move further up in the company. As Kenneth realized that he might have reached the zenith of his career, he began to focus more on his family, only to realize that his children no

*longer needed him. Under questioning, he admitted that his homelife
had been more turbulent in the past year because his wife "kept
harping about his drinking." On one occasion, his wife and daughter
had moved to a hotel for 3 days because he had threatened to hit
them if they did not leave him alone. When asked to describe how he
felt about his behavior and his future, Kenneth responded with tears
in his eyes, "I'm ashamed of myself, Doc, and scared—real scared."*

Kenneth's case reflects many of the factors associated with
alcohol and suicide in the middle years. A history of social drinking accelerated into alcohol dependency. Feeding into this dependency were Kenneth's growing realization that his career had
probably peaked and his fear of physical illness. Undoubtedly, his
long history with alcohol exacerbated his physical symptoms, but
in a downward spiral of dependency—the more his stomach hurt,
the more he drank. Verbal and threatened physical abuse of his
family was a new behavior for him, one which did not fit his self-
image as a good husband and father. The guilt and shame he felt
from his treatment of his wife and daughter and his growing fear
that they might leave him permanently further fueled his sense
of depression and hopelessness. Kenneth's case is a good example
of the use of alcohol to try to escape the realities of middle age.
Rather than turn to his family or to professionals for help, Kenneth's traditional value system kept him from admitting his fears
about his health and his dead-ended career.

Kenneth, like many middle-aged men, began to reach out to
his family for the first time as his career began to fade. But, as in
the poignant song "The Cat's in the Cradle," this source of support
was no longer available to him. His children's need for their father's love had died long ago from benign neglect.

This case study introduces two elements involving sex differences. The first is the effect of sex role socialization on help-
seeking behavior, which was discussed in Chapter 4. Kenneth,
like many males, was reluctant to consult a physician concerning
his stomach pain or to seek professional help with his drinking
problem. He decided instead to deal with his problems alone in
a self-destructive manner. Also typically masculine was Kenneth's strong need to be successful. Males tend to assess their
self-worth in terms of their ability to compete and to be successful. Kenneth's self-esteem was adversely affected by his declining status at work. Even his "failure" at taking his own life
was a source of consternation.

ADULT INFORMATION AND ATTITUDES
ABOUT SUICIDE

The preceding section focused on the characteristics of suicidal middle-aged people. In at least one sense, however, all middle-aged people are suicidal; that is, they have considered suicide
as an option at one or more periods in their adult lives. In this

section we will examine adult knowledge about and attitudes toward suicide. As was true in the preceding section, few studies exist concerning the knowledge about and attitudes toward suicide of middle-aged adults. A major exception is a study published in 1974 which focused on age, sex, education, and ethnicity as they correlate with attitudes toward suicide (Kalish, Reynolds, & Farberow, 1974). This study was conducted by carrying out hour-long interviews with a stratified random sample of 434 people, which included equal numbers of males and females as well as equal numbers of black Americans, Mexican Americans, Japanese Americans, and Americans of European descent. The authors of the study divided their respondents into three groups: people aged 20–39, 40–59, and 60 and over. Although the 40–59 age category is not exactly the same as the middle adulthood age category being used in this chapter, the overall results of the study are informative.

When asked the main reason people have for killing themselves, two major responses emerged. In the first, respondents explained suicide as a result of insanity or mental illness. In the second, respondents described suicide as occurring as a part of a reaction to transient situations, like work-related concerns or loss of a love relationship. Older men tended to believe that impairment in mental or physical health was a major factor influencing suicide, while younger men were more likely to believe that love and psychological stress were the primary factors. College graduates were more likely than non–college graduates to describe suicide as occurring in reaction to stress and less likely to describe it as the result of insanity. Most people, regardless of age or sex, viewed people who threatened to commit suicide but did not make a serious attempt as "playing a game" or "calling for help." The least-educated respondents reacted with anger to chronic threateners and indicated most frequently that they should either be serious or stop pretending. More-educated respondents were more likely to call for professional help for chronic threateners. Older people and the less educated tended to view clergymen as more important sources of help than did younger and more educated people. All groups viewed suicide as being less tragic than accidents, homicide, and wartime killings. The authors of this study pointed out that attitudes of people toward suicide attempters and completers are important variables, since they undoubtedly affect the incidence and sequelae of attempted suicide.

A second study focused on the attitudes of health professionals toward suicide and suicide victims (Swain & Domino, 1985). A convenience sample of 128 health professionals and clergy in the Tucson, Arizona, area was asked to complete a scale designed to measure opinions about suicide and a scale designed to measure their ability to identify factors that contribute to the lethality of suicidal behavior. The study revealed that clergy differed significantly from all other helping professionals in finding suicide not acceptable. Physicians, however, found suicide significantly less acceptable than did social workers. Physicians, compared with psychologists, were more likely to describe suicide attempts as resulting from manipulation motives. The authors also found that "professionals who are more knowledgeable about lethality of suicide are less likely to impute a self-destructive drive or mental instability to suicide attempts, are more likely to see suicide as a reaction to a harsh world, see the elderly at greater risk, have a less fatalistic outlook, and see suicide attempts more as a 'cry for help' " (Swain & Domino, 1985, p. 446). Their most important conclusion was that attitudes toward suicide are complex and difficult to measure.

Finally, there have been a few studies investigating general knowledge about suicide. However, these studies have typically used college students as subjects and have therefore not measured the general population's knowledge. Two studies that measured the amount of factual information and misinformation about suicide possessed by college students found their knowledge about suicide to be generally "poor" (Leenaars, et al. 1988; McIntosh, Hubbard, & Santos, 1985). However, the students' performance on these tests (true or false) was significantly better than the results of random choosing, and it reflected more knowledge than was found by Shneidman in 1952.

Confronted with a dearth of data concerning what middle-aged adults know about suicide and what their attitudes are toward suicide, we decided to run our own small pilot study on subjects in this age range. We created a three-part instrument consisting of factual questions, a set of descriptors of suicidal people, and an open-ended interview format designed to capture people's actual words and thoughts on the topic of suicide. A convenience sample of 40 subjects (20 males and 20 females) living in a rural area of western North Carolina was selected. Participants were asked to read and respond in writing to the factual questions and the descriptors and then to respond orally to the open-ended interview questions. Subjects in the study ranged from ages 35 to 53, with a mean age of 42. Ninety percent of the males and 50% of the females were college graduates, and most were business or professional people. All were employed at the time of the study, and all fell within the middle to upper-middle income bracket. Thus, the sample is biased toward higher educational, occupational, and financial levels. Although no generalizations can be made, the responses of these subjects do provide a focus for examining middle-aged people's knowledge about and attitudes toward suicide.

In order to learn more about the knowledge adults have about suicide, all subjects were asked to complete a 20-item multiple choice test and a 12-item true or false test dealing with factual information about suicide. Specific items dealt with information concerning relative suicide rates and trends for various age, sex, and racial groups and geographic regions. Other questions dealt with characteristics of suicidal behavior, such as techniques used, time of day, and seasonal aspects. Still other questions addressed factors which have been shown to be associated with suicidal behavior (e.g., parental divorce).

All 40 subjects were also asked to complete a checklist of characteristics that might be ascribed to suicidal people. The list included items such as "crazy," "anxious," "depressed," and "unhappy." Subjects were asked to indicate which, if any, of the listed characteristics apply to suicidal people. The final and most lengthy task was to complete an open-ended questionnaire concerning attitudes toward suicide.

The adult scores on the tests of factual information concerning suicide are presented in Table 5.3. It can be seen that scores on both the multiple choice and true or false tests of factual information were generally low and consistent with those of the two previously reported studies which used college students. The typical subject in our study correctly answered only 45% of the 20 multiple choice items, 74% of the 12 true or false items, and 55% of the 32 items combined. The maximum and minimum scores show that no subjects scored exceptionally high on either test and that some subjects performed little better than they would have by random choosing. The mean scores for male and female subjects on these tests were almost identical and therefore are not reported separately.

A review of the items frequently answered correctly and the ones frequently answered incorrectly helped to establish what this group of middle-aged adults actually knew about suicide. In spite of generally low overall scores, the multiple choice and true or false items that were answered correctly by 85% or more of all subjects reflect a significant fund of general information about suicide. For example, most respondents knew that national statistics underestimate the true incidence of suicides, that the greatest increase in suicide rates has occurred among the young, and that children below the age of 10 are capable of suicide. In addition, most knew that suicide attempters are more likely than others to try again and that improvement following a suicide crisis does not necessarily mean the risk is over. Most also knew that suicide is sometimes an attempt to cope with a problem and that

TABLE 5.3 Adult Scores on Tests of Factual Information About Suicide

Tests	Mean score (%)	Standard deviation	Maximum score (%)	Minimum score (%)
Multiple choice	44.62	9.30	70	30
True or false	73.76	8.87	83	58
Both tests combined	55.25	7.11	69	40

strong religious belief is associated with negative attitudes toward suicide. Finally, most were aware of the tendency for males to use firearms and for females to use pills in suicide attempts.

The items that were missed by many of our respondents reflect some widespread misconceptions about suicide. The suicide myths which were supported by 85% or more of our respondents were the following:

1. The highest suicide rate occurs among the young (correct answer: the old).
2. There has been no decrease in suicide among any age group (correct answer: suicide rates among the old have decreased).
3. The incidence of white male suicide peaks during the teen years (correct answer: during old age).
4. The worldwide suicide rate is highest in the Western hemisphere (correct answer: in Scandinavian countries).
5. The U.S. suicide rate is highest in the Northeast (correct answer: the West).
6. The suicide rate is highest in winter (correct answer: spring).
7. Suicide occurs most often late at night (correct answer: late afternoon).
8. The rank ordering of suicide rates from highest to lowest is as follows: (1) white females, (2) white males, (3) nonwhite males, (4) nonwhite females (correct answer: [1] white males, [2] nonwhite males, [3] white females, [4] nonwhite females).

Although the test scores of our subjects were not high, the items answered correctly most of the time and the items frequently missed support a rather positive picture of adult knowledge about suicide. Our subjects showed broad general knowledge of important facts about suicide, and the majority of their errors occurred on items measuring more specific information of less importance. For example, most of our subjects knew that national suicide statistics reflect only the tip of the iceberg. They were aware of the current crisis regarding youth suicide and knew that previous suicide attempters are a high risk group. Errors made frequently by our subjects involved information concerning rates and trends among different groups, geographic locations, seasons of the year, and times of day. Although most subjects did not know the exact rank ordering of suicide rates for white males, black males, white females, and black females, they did know that in general the rate for whites is higher than for blacks.

Perhaps more important than what people do and do not know about suicide are what attributes they ascribed to suicidal people. In response to our request to select the attributes of suicidal people from a list of possible attributes, more that 85% of the subjects indicated that suicidal people are depressed, unhappy, and hopeless. More than 75% indicated that suicidal people are also upset and angry. Perhaps equally interesting, 93% indicated that suicidal people are not crazy.

It is clear that, although the adult subjects showed some misconceptions regarding the specific facts of suicide, the characteristics they ascribed to suicidal people are consistent with mainstream clinical thinking. The majority of clinicians would agree that most suicidal people are depressed, unhappy, and hopeless and that many suicidal people are upset and angry. Most clinicians would agree also that only a small minority of suicidal people are crazy or psychotic.

The above characteristics of suicidal people were chosen by both male and female respondents. The women attributed a larger number of characteristics to suicidal people than did men. The characteristics included confusion, helplessness, dependency, and ambivalence about living. These findings are consistent with those of several studies we have done regarding attitudes of other age groups toward suicide. We have found repeatedly that females respond more sympathetically to suicidal people than do males (Stillion, McDowell, & May 1984; Stillion, McDowell, & Shamblin, 1984; Stillion, McDowell, Smith, & McCoy, 1986). It has been speculated that females have more sympathy for suicidal people because they tend to view suicide as a "cry for help" and because they are more comfortable than males in seeking help in a crisis (McDowell, 1985). Males, in contrast, seem to view suicide more as a way of solving a problem, and consequently they show little sympathy for an "unsuccessful" suicide attempt, especially if the attempt is by a male (White & Stillion, in press).

Many of the attributes ascribed to suicidal people by the adults in our study are consistent with Shneidman's observations about the state of mind of suicidal people (Shneidman, 1976). Shneidman proposed that suicidal behavior is more a manifestation of a temporary state of the individual than of long-standing personality traits. Shneidman believed that the probability of a suicidal act is greatly increased when the following four characteristics are operating simultaneously: (1) heightened inimicality (increased self-destructiveness), (2) exacerbation of perturbation (a heightened negative emotional state such as anxiety or depression), (3) increased constriction of intellectual focus (tunnel vision focusing on the problem and pain), (4) the idea of cessation (thoughts of stopping consciousness and ending suffering).

The characteristics of depression, unhappiness, hopelessness, upset, and anger, which were ascribed by both male and female subjects to suicidal people, are consistent with Shneidman's prediction of increased perturbation among suicidal people; so too are the characteristics of confusion, helplessness, and dependence ascribed by the women in our study. Ambivalence about living, which women ascribed to suicidal people, is related to the idea of cessation discussed by Shneidman. Since it is unlikely that any of our subjects had read Shneidman's descriptions, it would appear that the folk wisdom about suicide is consistent with his observations.

In order to tap all dimensions of adult thinking, the third part of our study utilized an open-ended interview that focused on attitudes toward suicide. Table 5.4 presents the questions asked and the most common answers given by the adult subjects. It shows that most respondents defined suicide quite simply as the taking of one's own life. Some respondents added qualifiers, such as "deliberately," "voluntarily," or "as a result of severe depression." One respondent stated that suicide occurs when a person chooses death, then added, "even like Jesus chose death." This response echoes the discussion in Chapter 1 of Jesus' death and reveals the sophisticated level of thinking of the respondent.

The 2nd question asked respondents to describe their general feelings about suicide. The results reflect the great variety of feelings which the subject of suicide evokes. The replies commonly indicated negative attitudes toward suicide but caring feelings toward suicide victims. As shown in Table 5.4, the most common responses were that suicide is "wrong," a "tragedy," "very sad," and a "waste"; that it shows "lack of understanding," and is "not a good answer to a problem"; and that the respondent was "opposed to it," "could understand why some people do it," and found it "frightening." Adjectives used only once reflected more negative attitudes. These included "useless," "horrible," "futile," "shameful," "sinful," "sick," "selfish," "criminal," and "un-Christian." Several people admitted having mixed or ambivalent feelings about it. One said, "It's not always bad," another confessed, "I've contemplated it," and still another said that he was "not totally against it." Suicide was also characterized as the "supreme insult" and the "ultimate expression of depression."

In this sample, there seemed to be fairly widespread agreement that suicide is not always a moral issue. As shown in Table 5.4, only 40% of the sample responded with an unequivocal no when asked if there are specific instances or situations in which suicide is justifiable. The great majority of respondents indicated that suicide would be justifiable in cases of terminal illness or severe pain. Other justifiable situations mentioned included cases in which people developed AIDS; life seemed no longer worth living; the future was hopeless; an individual was wounded severely in war or was in a torture situation; it was done as an altruistic gesture (such as throwing oneself on a grenade); extreme emotional or financial pain was being inflicted on the family; and alcohol, drug abuse, family, or other problems exceeded the individual's ability to cope.

There was disagreement within this sample regarding whether suicide should be considered illegal. Table 5.4 shows that almost the same number of people agreed as disagreed with the statement that suicide should be illegal. Five of those who agreed cited the deterrent effect of such a law to defend their position. Two re-

TABLE 5.4   Questions Concerning Attitudes Toward Suicide and the Most Common Responses by a Group of 40 Middle-Aged Adults

Question	Number of Responses
1. *Define the word* suicide.	
A. Taking one's own life	38
2. *How do you feel in general about suicide?*	
A. It is wrong	6
B. A tragedy	4
C. Very sad	3
D. A waste	3
E. Lack of understanding	3
F. Not a good answer to a problem	3
G. Opposed to it	2
H. Can understand why some people do it	2
I. Frightening	2
3. *Are there specific instances or situations in which you think suicide is justifiable?*	
A. No	16
B. Yes, under special circumstances	24
4. *Suicide is illegal in at least two states. Do you think it should be? Why or why not?*	
A. Yes	13
B. No	17
C. Undecided or no response	10
5. *All states have laws against helping people to commit suicide. Do you think these laws should exist? Why or why not?*	
A. Yes	31
B. No	1
C. Undecided or no response	8
6. *Do you approve of passive euthanasia? Active euthanasia? Why or why not?*	
Active euthanasia	
A. Yes	14
B. No	15
C. Undecided or no response	11
Passive euthanasia	
A. Yes	31
B. No	4
C. Undecided or no response	5
7. *What do you think should be done with (for) suicide attempters?*	
A. Professional help for attempter	33
B. Professional help for family	6
C. No response	1
8. *If professionals know that someone is considering suicide, should they act to have him/her forcibly stopped (e.g., hospitalized)? Why or why not?*	
A. Yes	29
B. No	5
C. Undecided or no response	6

Table 5.4   Continued

Question	Number of Responses
9. *Do you have any differential feelings when you consider suicide among the following groups: women, men, young people, middle-aged people, elderly?*	
A. Yes	26
B. No	14
10. *Have you ever known anyone who attempted suicide? If yes, who?*	
A. Yes	20
B. No	11
C. No response	9
How did you feel about him/her? *How did you feel about his/her suicidal behavior?* *How did you feel toward the relatives and other survivors of the suicide victim?*	
11. *Have you ever considered suicide?*	
A. Yes	22
B. No	16
C. No response	2
Would you ever attempt suicide?	
A. Yes	11
B. No	24
C. Undecided or no response	5
If yes, under what conditions? *If no, why not?*	

spondents specifically excepted terminally ill people from the law. Others felt that such a law might lead to required counseling. Several respondents who disagreed believed that it was a person's right to commit suicide, and five maintained that a law would not be an effective deterrent. Several felt the idea of such a law was "preposterous" or "stupid." As one person said, "If the person is dead, such a law is irrelevant; if he or she survives an attempt, they need counseling and help, not prosecution." Eight respondents expressed feelings that such a law would be an infringement of individual rights. Three respondents stated that suicide should be viewed as an act resulting from mental illness rather than a crime. One person stated emphatically that such a law would "only add to a suicidal person's devastation and inability to cope," while another said, "If a man is in emotional or physical pain, he doesn't need the legal system on his back."

On the question whether there should be laws against helping people commit suicide, there was far more consensus. As shown in Table 5.4, the great majority of our sample agreed that there should be laws against helping people commit suicide. However, eight people suggested that exceptions could be made based on individual circumstances, such as the presence of terminal illness. A variety of reasons were given for the need for such laws. Five respondents felt that not having such laws could lead to an increase in murder under the guise of helping a loved one commit suicide. Others agreed that such laws were necessary for the following reasons: "You shouldn't help someone do something that is wrong," "helping would be playing off depression and an upset mental state," "because of insurance or other legal concerns," and "it's too hard for others to judge whether and when to help someone commit suicide." The respondents who disagreed with the need for such laws tended to personalize the process of helping someone commit suicide. They responded as follows: "No one should be prosecuted for what I ask them to do"; "personally, I would turn off the machine for my child if the situation were hopeless and he asked me to"; and "I'd have a hard time helping someone, but if it was me, I'd want the plug pulled." Once again, the answers of this group reflect awareness of the blurred line between suicide and euthanasia.

Question 6 directly examined opinions on passive and active euthanasia. It can be seen that passive euthanasia was strongly endorsed by the respondents, while active euthanasia was thought to be questionable. Among the reasons cited in support of passive euthanasia were the following: "It's their right," "nature should be allowed to take its course," "it's humane," and "people should have the right to die in peace." Those endorsing active euthanasia generally approved of it only in cases of terminal illness or extreme age. Even then, they frequently added qualifiers such as "if done under approved medical conditions" or "if there is a living will." One person, quoting a book title, simply said, "They shoot horses, don't they?" while another, defending the individual's right to euthanasia, asked, "Whose life is it, anyway?" People who disapproved of euthanasia generally did so on moral grounds. As one person explained, "We are not God. Only He has the right to take a life." A second person pointed out that "playing God is tricky." Two others, taking a more personal view, said, "I don't want to have to decide." In the area of euthanasia, then, this sample differentiated between passive and active euthanasia, endorsing the former far more often than the latter. It is also clear that this group of middle-aged adults had personal and moral reservations about active euthanasia and recognized the complexity of the issues involved as well as its close relationship to suicide.

Question 7 ("What should be done for suicide attempters?") yielded a high degree of agreement. The great majority of respondents recommended professional help for attempters, generally described as "counseling," "therapy," or "psychological evaluation." Several people felt professional treatment should be mandatory. In addition, six people, recognizing the interactive nature of suicide causes and effects, recommended that families of suicides or suicide attempters be required to get counseling. Other suggested options included treating with kindness, attention, and loving care; suicide prevention classes in school; involuntary commitment; and exploration of alternatives.

Question 8 also dealt with intervention in asking if suicidal people should be forcibly stopped. As shown in Table 5.4, most of the respondents believed that a suicidal person should be stopped; a few, however, disagreed. The most common comment was that suicidal people should be forcibly hospitalized. Some respondents stated that suicide is a crisis situation and may pass if there is opportunity and that we have a moral duty to help each other. Other reasons given for forcible intervention included that there can be danger to others during a suicide attempt, that suicide always affects other people, and that suicide is morally wrong. Those disagreeing with forcible intervention generally felt that it was wrong to interfere with the individual's right to self-deter-mination or privacy. Three people commented that suicidal in-dividuals should only be stopped on their first attempt; one person felt that they should be permitted to kill themselves after coun-seling; and one person felt that it is impossible to change a way of thinking forcibly, although she thought we should try. Finally, one person commented that help has to be voluntarily received; thus force would not be effective.

Of special interest for this book was question 9, which asked the respondents to note differential feelings they might have when they consider suicide done by males versus females or by people in different age groups. Table 5.4 shows that approximately two-thirds of the sample reported differential feelings regarding suicide among different groups. Two major reactions predominated among those reporting differential feelings. First, there was much higher affect and more complex reactions to suicide among young people than to suicide in other age groups. Adjectives like "more tragic," "desperate," "shocking," "appalled," and "scarier" were used in their responses. Suicide among young people was held to occur because the young generally have not developed positive coping mechanisms, and it was thought to constitute a waste of potential and a loss to society. Second, reaction to suicide among the elderly was marked by understanding. Only one person said that she thought suicide in this age group was sadder, giving as her reason that elderly people should be enjoying the fruits of their long lives. Those who viewed elderly suicide as less sad explained their stance by saying that the elderly have lived their lives; that they have more intractable problems and therefore might be better off dead; and that, because they feel lonely and hopeless, their suicide is more easily tolerated. Perhaps the most interesting finding on this question was that middle-aged respondents had few com-ments about suicide by those who were middle aged. One re-spondent seemed typical of the group as a whole when he said, "I don't know much about suicide in this group." Three pointed to aspects of midlife in their responses ("midlife crisis," "self-concepts fall apart," and "men realize that their accomplishments may be limited"). In general, however, while there was much concern about suicide among the young and resigned acceptance to suicide among the elderly, suicide among the middle-aged tended to draw little response. One person might have been speaking for the whole group when she said, "I don't have much sympathy for suicide in this age group."

The 10th question asked about personal experience with suicide among acquaintances, friends, or relatives. It was somewhat surprising that one-third of the respondents said they had never personally known anyone who attempted suicide. Among the 20 respondents who did respond positively to this question, a variety of feelings were expressed. Six expressed sympathy, five admitted anger at the selfishness involved in the suicidal act, three reported regret over the waste of life, three indicated feelings of love and compassion, and two refused to condemn the suicide attempter. Ten respondents expressed sympathy for and sadness about the relatives, while two indicated concern and compassion. Anger toward the parents of a young suicide victim for not getting him help was expressed by one person. Nine people referred to the stigma that survivors had to live with and expressed concern for the guilt, shame, and embarrassment that the families of suicides suffered.

On the final question, 22 people admitted that they had considered suicide and 16 said they never had. Eleven respondents said that they definitely would or might attempt suicide under certain conditions. The conditions listed included terminal illness, unbearable pain, loss of rationality, being a burden to the family, hopelessness, and "unbearable depression." Suicide might also be considered "if life wasn't worth the pain in a cost-benefit analysis."

Twenty-four people said they would not consider committing suicide. They gave a variety of reasons, including lack of courage, enjoyment of life, realization that things may get better in the future, the valuing of life, love of family, love of self, belief in God to see one through, and the need to meet one's responsibilities. In addition, three respondents described suicide as the weak way out and stated that they felt they should be able to cope with whatever life entails, although one person added that "nuclear war could make me consider suicide."

In reviewing the results of this small study of middle-aged attitudes toward suicide, some generalizations can be made. In spite of the homogeneity of the sample, there was a wide range of beliefs about suicide, from the extreme that suicide is always wrong for all people to the other extreme that the individual should have the right to take his or her own life at any time. Most people took more moderate positions. They generally believed that suicide is wrong, especially for young people, because it results in a waste of potential or a loss to society or violates ethical or natural laws. They tended to make exceptions to their general negative set for people who were in pain, who were suffering from terminal illness, or who were giving their lives for others. They also appreciated the fine line between suicide and euthanasia. Many were willing to cross the line and permit death to occur at a person's request as long as no action had to be taken to end the life. This group showed remarkable sensitivity toward families of suicidal people, recognizing both a need to help the family cope with suicidal members and a need for families to get help themselves after a suicide occurs. Although they did not use these terms, their high level of concern for families indicates that suicide is still *stigmatized* in our culture and that the concept of the *survivor-victim*, discussed in Chapter 7, is a valid one.

SUMMARY

Adults at midlife typically carry more responsibility than at any other period in their lives. They are parents and are guiding their children through adolescence and into young adulthood. At the same time, these parents may be caring for their own aging parents, which can create additional major psychological and financial burdens. Middle-aged adults have been characterized as a "sandwich generation" caught between responsibilities to their parents and their children. Middle adulthood typically marks the zenith of one's occupational career, at which point both professional responsibilities and on-the-job mentorship obligations are present. Civic responsibilities and the other burdens of preserving and promoting one's culture are greatest at midlife. Mature adults must care for their children and their parents, perform their work, and provide for the welfare of others in the society.

Balancing the opportunities for generativity are the normative changes in middle age, most of which involve loss. Adults at midlife become increasingly aware of their own mortality. Middle-aged adults realize that they have come more than half way and have not—and probably never will—realize many of the dreams of their youth. Middle adulthood is a time when the children begin to leave home and when men and women look around the empty nest and sometimes see less reason for prolonging their marriages. Many middle-aged adults find the increasingly evident decline in their physical attractiveness and capabilities very distressing. The loss of reproductive capability may be another blow to the middle-aged woman, while the middle-aged man may monitor with increasing anxiety his diminishing sexual drive. It takes positive coping skills and courage to face these changes with optimism and to avoid psychological stagnation and its accompanying ego absorption, depression, and cognitive rigidity.

The statistics on suicide in middle age indicate that suicide generally increases with age throughout middle adulthood. This is especially true for white males in the United States. Middle-aged males in all developed countries have higher levels of suicide than their female peers. In all nations the suicide rates for people in the late middle years are higher than in the early middle years. Much of the research concerning adult suicide is consistent with the notion that the special stresses and losses of midlife contribute to self-destructive behavior in this age group. Suicidal behavior among middle-aged adults has been shown to be associated with an accumulation of negative life events, which often involve loss, depression, and alcoholism.

A study conducted by the authors investigated the attitudes of middle-aged people toward suicide and their knowledge about it. Although the respondents did not show they possessed a large fund of detailed information about suicide, they did demonstrate an awareness of the most important facts. Also, they showed remarkable sophistication in ascribing characteristics to suicidal people. They were also asked to respond to a number of open-ended questions about suicide designed to generate additional attitudinal data. They tended to take a rather moderate view of suicide, stating that it was wrong in most situations, especially for young people. They tended to make exceptions for terminally ill people in great pain. They also expressed great concern for the families of suicidal people.

REFERENCES

Adam, K. S., Bouckoms, A., & Streiner, D. (1982). Parental loss and family stability in attempted suicide. *Archives of General Psychiatry, 39,* 1081–1085.

Barraclough, B. (1987). *Suicide: Clinical and epidemiological studies.* London: Croom Helm.

Barraclough, B., Bunch, J., & Nelson, B. (1974). A hundred cases of suicide: Clinical aspects. *British Journal of Psychiatry, 125,* 355–373.

Beck, A. T., Rush, A., Show, B., & Emery, G. (1979). *Cognitive therapy of depression.* New York: Guilford Press.

Benjaminsen, S. (1981). Stressful life events preceding the onset of neurotic depression. *Psychological Medicine, 11,* 369–378.

Berglund, M. (1984). Suicide in alcoholism—a prospective study of 88 alcoholics: The multidimensional diagnosis at first admission. *Archives of General Psychiatry, 41,* 888–891.

Borg, S. E., & Stahl, M. (1982). A prospective study of suicides and controls among psychiatric patients. *Acta Psychiatrica Scandinavica, 65,* 221–232.

Brown, G., & Harris, T. (1978). *Social origins of depression.* London: Tavistock.

Clausen, J. A. (1981). Men's occupational careers in the middle years. In D.H. Eichoun, J. A. Clausen, N. Haan, M. P. Honzik, & P. Mussen (Eds.), *Present and past in middle life* (pp. 321–351). New York: Academic Press.

Dorpat, T. L., & Ripley, H. S. (1960). A study of suicide in the Seattle area. *Comprehensive Psychiatry, 1,* 349–359.

Erikson, E. H. (1980). *Identity and the life cycle.* New York: Norton.

Freud, S. (1961). *Mourning and melancholia.* In. J. Strachey (Ed. and Trans.). *The standard edition of the complete psychological works of Sigmund Freud* (Vol. 14, pp. 243–258). London: Hogarth Press. (Original work published 1917.)

Goodwin, D. (1973). Alcohol in suicide and homicide. *Quarterly Journal of Studies on Alcohol, 34,* 144–156.

Gould, R. L. (1978). *Transformations: Growth and change in adult life.* New York: Simon & Schuster.

Guze, S. B., & Robins, E. (1970). Suicide and primary affective disorder. *British Journal of Psychiatry, 117*, 437–438.

Haan, N. (1981). Common dimensions of personality development: Early adolescence to middle life. In D. H. Eichoun, J. A. Clausen, N. Haan, M. P. Honzik, & P. Mussen (Eds.), *Present and past in middle life* (pp. 117–151). New York: Academic Press.

Hirschfeld, R. M. A., & Blumenthal, S. J. (1986). Personality, life events, and other psychosocial factors in adolescent depression and suicide. In G. L. Klerman (Ed.), *Suicide and depression among adolescents and young adults* (pp. 213–254). Washington, DC: American Psychiatric Press.

Jaques, E. (1965). Death and the mid-life crisis. *International Journal of Psychoanalysis, 146*, 502–514.

Kalish, R. A., Reynolds, D. K., & Farberow, N. L. (1974). Community attitudes toward suicide. *Community Mental Health Journal, 10*, 301–308.

Leenaars, A. A., Balance, W. D., Pellarin, S., Aversano, G., Magli, A., & Wenckstern, S. (1988). Facts and myths of suicide in Canada. *Death Studies, 12*, 195–206.

Levinson, D. J., Darrow, C., Klein, E., Levinson, M., & McKee, B. (1978). *The seasons of a man's life.* New York: Knopf.

Linnoila, R., Erwin, C., Ramm, D., Cleveland, P., & Brendle, A. (1980). Effects of alcohol on psychomotor performance of women: Interaction with menstrual cycle. *Alcoholism: Clinical and Experimental Research, 4*, 302–305.

McDowell, E. E. (1985). Sex differences in suicidal behaviors. *Forum Newsletter, 8*, 9–11.

McIntosh, J., Hubbard, R., & Santos, J. (1985). Suicide facts and myths: A study of prevalence. *Death Studies, 9*, 267–281.

McRae, R. R., & Costa, P. T., Jr. (1983). Psychological maturity and subjective well-being: Toward a new synthesis. *Developmental Psychology, 19*, 243–248.

Miles, C. (1977). Conditions predisposing to suicide: A review. *Journal of Nervous and Mental Disease, 164*, 231–246.

Murphy, G. E., Armstrong, J., Hermele, S., Fisher, J., & Clendenin, W. (1979). Suicide and alcoholism. *Archives of General Psychiatry, 36*, 65–69.

Neugarten, B. L. (1968). The awareness of middle age. In B. L. Neugarten (Ed.), *Middle age and aging: A reader in social psychology* (pp. 93–98). Chicago: University of Chicago Press.

Paykel, E. S., Prusoff, B. A., Myers, J. K. (1975). Suicide attempts and recent life events: A controlled comparison. *Archives of General Psychiatry, 32*, 327–333.

Peck, R. C. (1968). Psychological developments in the second half of life. In B. L. Neugarten (Ed.), *Middle age and aging: A reader in social psychology* (pp. 88–92). Chicago: University of Chicago Press.

Pfeffer, C. R. (1986). *The suicidal child.* New York: Guilford Press.

Richman, J. (1981). Suicide and the family: Affective disturbances and their implications for understanding, diagnosis, and treatment. In M. R. Lansky (Ed.), *Family therapy and major psychopathology* (pp. 145–160). New York: Grune & Stratton.

Roy, A. (1982). Risk factors for suicide in psychiatric patients. *Archives of General Psychiatry, 39*, 1089–1095.

Roy, A., & Linnoila, M. (1986). Alcoholism and suicide. In R. Maris (Ed.) *Biology of suicide* (pp. 162–191). New York: Guilford Press.

Rushing, W. (1969). Suicide and the interaction of alcoholism (liver cirrhosis) with the social situation. *Quarterly Journal of Studies on Alcohol, 30*, 93–103.

Rygnestad, T. K. (1982). A prospective study of social and psychiatric aspects of self-poisoned patients. *Acta Psychiatrica Scandanavica, 66*, 139–153.

Santrock, J. W. (1985). *Adult development and aging.* Dubuque, IA: William C. Brown.

Sheehy, G. (1976). *Passages: Predictable crises of adult life.* New York: Dutton.

Shneidman, E. S. (1971). Suicide among the gifted. 4 vols. *Life-Threatening Be-havior, 1*, 23–45.

Shneidman, E. S. (1976). A psychological theory of suicide. *Psychiatric Annals, 6*, 51–66.

Silver, M. A., Bohnert, M., Beck, A. T., & Marcus, D. (1971). Relation of depression of attempted suicide and seriousness of intent. *Archives of General Psychiatry, 25*, 573–576.

Slater, J. & Depue, R. A. (1981). The contribution of environmental events and social support to serious suicide attempts in primary depressive disorder. *Journal of Abnormal Psychology, 40*, 275–285.

Stillion, J. M., McDowell, E. E., & May, J. H. (1984). Developmental trends and sex differences in adolescent attitudes toward suicide. *Death Education, 8*, 81–90.

Stillion, J. M., McDowell, E. E., & Shamblin, J. B. (1984). The suicide attitude vignette experience: A method for measuring adolescent attitudes toward suicide. *Death Education, 8*, 65–80.

Stillion, J. M., McDowell, E. E., Smith, R. T., & McCoy, P. A. (1986). Relationships between suicide attitudes and indicators of mental health among adolescents. *Death Studies, 10*, 289–296.

Swain, B. J., & Domino, G. (1985). Attitudes toward suicide among mental health professionals. *Death Studies, 9*, 455–468.

Vaillant, G. E. (1977). *Adaption to life*. Boston: Little, Brown.

Viorst, J. (1986). *Necessary losses*. New York: Fawcett.

Warren, L. W., & Tomlinson-Keasey, C. (1987). The context of suicide. *American Journal of Orthopsychiatry, 57*, 41–48.

Weissman, M. (1974). The epidemiology of suicide attempts, 1960 to 1971. *Archives of General Psychiatry, 30*, 737–746.

White, H. & Stillion, J. M. (1988). Sex differences in attitudes toward suicide: Do males stigmatize males? *Psychology of Women Quarterly 12*, 357–366.

6

Suicide Among the Elderly

Old age, more to be feared than death— Juvenal, *Satires XI*

Elderly people have shown high suicide rates relative to other age groups throughout history. Hudson Bay Eskimos pitched themselves from cliffs when they could no longer negotiate the harsh physical conditions of the long winters. Aging Crow Indians dressed themselves in their finest clothes and single-handedly attacked their enemies in suicidal fashion. Aged Samoans were buried alive at their own request. Dying of natural causes in these cultures after a long, debilitating old age was considered a major embarrassment to the individual and his or her family (Bromberg & Cassel, 1983). Although longevity is not considered an embarrassment in the United States today, the suicide rate among people over 65 remains the highest of any age group.

In their classic work, *Aging and Mental Health* (1982), Butler and Lewis divided old age into two periods: early old age (65–74) and advanced old age (75 and older). Even as they made this division, however, they reminded us that chronological age is an "inaccurate indicator of a person's physical and mental status and must not be relied on too heavily for evidence about human beings" (p. 5). Gerontologists frequently point out that elderly people, because they have spent relatively long lifetimes developing their unique potential, are more different from each other than people at any other stage of life; that is, the process of individuation has had time to mature and bear fruit. In spite of this, we in the United States tend to treat all people over 65 as if they constituted a homogeneous group and to make generalizations about them. In doing so, we lose much of the richness of their individual lives and may distort the reality of being elderly more than we do for any other age group. While we recognize these cautions, we believe that many factors influencing suicide among the elderly may be inherent in this stage of life. Therefore, an understanding of the normative events and changes that occur in old age may be helpful in understanding the high incidence of suicidal behavior among the elderly.

PROFILE OF OLD AGE

One of the major realities of old age is biological change. Elderly people experience many physical changes, including loss of acuity in all the senses. The loss of hearing and eyesight are perhaps the most debilitating. Not only do these losses affect people's psychological sense of wholeness, they also isolate elderly people from normal life. In addition, poor hearing may increase the incidence of paranoia, as older people may begin to think that they are being deliberately excluded from conversations or that others are talking about them. The loss of vision prevents the elderly from having the benefit of television, which often is a friendly window to the world for those in failing health, and it also makes reading and therefore learning more difficult. Additional normative changes in old age include the impairment of motor abilities (which affects balance), the development of brittle bones, increased graying and loss of hair, and loss of teeth. There are many other changes that negatively affect day-to-day functioning as well.

In addition, up to 86% of all elderly people develop chronic illnesses accompanied by some degree of pain and incapacitation (Butler & Lewis, 1982). Elderly people go to medical doctors more often and spend more time in the hospital than do younger people. Even the most healthy older person will admit to a diminished energy level and to the need to rest more often than in younger years. Although people over 65 can do much to retain their good health throughout the early years of old age, at some time during this period they will confront physical loss.

Years following years, steal something every day; At last they steal us from ourselves away.
Pope, *To a Lady,* Epistle II, Book II

The principle of entropy is useful in understanding this loss. This principle, established in physics, maintains that there is an inevitable, progressive disorganization that occurs in living organisms and in physical systems and that leads to the collapse of the steady state system (Rifkin & Howard, 1980). There is a marked resemblance between the principle of entropy and the Freudian suggestion that a major goal of all life is death (thanatos).

In the psychological sphere, the principle of entropy was also addressed by Carl Jung, who stated, "Aging people should know that their lives are not mounting and expanding but that there are inexorable inner processes that enforce the contraction of life. For a young person it is almost a sin, or at least a danger to be too preoccupied with himself; but for the aging person it is a duty and a necessity to devote serious attention to himself" (Jung, 1960, p. 96, © 1960, 1969 by Princeton University Press. Excerpt reprinted with permission of Princeton University Press.)

Jung was the first to note a transition from concentration on external events and activities to a more internal focus. Later researchers have confirmed this psychological shift, generally referring to it as "increased interiority" (Buhler, 1961; Frenkel-Brun-swik, 1963; Lowenthal, Thurnher, & Associates, 1975; Neugarten, 1968).

Two other psychological changes that seem to occur in old age are a shift in sex role perceptions and a shift in coping styles (Neugarten, 1968). Traditional sex roles, no longer needed for childbearing and child rearing, seem to disappear or even to undergo a slight reversal. Women's behavior becomes more author-itarian and less submissive, while elderly men evidence less dominance and more often engage in tasks previously labelled "women's work," perhaps out of necessity or boredom. The shift in coping styles is from active mastery to passive mastery, which is in keeping with a lowered energy level and less need to compete in the outside world.

In addition to these shifts in personality, healthy older people must maintain positive self-concepts and high levels of self-esteem in order to realize high levels of life satisfaction. Kalish (1975) has suggested that "if the older people have a reasonably stable recent history, an anticipated standard of living, and no strong fear of being left alone, their self-esteem rises with age" (p. 47). Thus, even in a very youth-oriented culture, it is not nec-essarily inevitable that aging will entail negative self-concepts or low self-esteem. Neugarten, Havighurst, and Tobin (1961) have identified six variables that they believe are important for devel-oping a positive sense of life satisfaction in the elderly: zest, resoluteness, fortitude, a positive self-concept, an optimistic mood tone, and a strong relationship between goals and achievements.

A final psychological area in which changes occur in old age is cognitive functioning. The voluminous research on cognitive functioning in the elderly is often confusing and contradictory. There are methodological problems inherent in both cross-sec-tional and longitudinal measures of change in intellectual func-tioning over the life span (Schaie & Willis, 1986). It does appear, however, that elderly people do not suffer massive declines in intelligence. In fact, one type of intelligence, crystallized intel-ligence, continues to grow until shortly before death in people who maintain an active intellectual life and who are free of or-ganic illness. Crystallized intelligence, which was first described by Raymond Cattell and later elaborated by John Horn, concerns the learning of facts and vocabulary and the accumulation of information. Older adults do less well than younger people on measures of fluid intelligence, which involves associations and pattern recognition (Horn, 1982). They also seem to do less well than younger people on tests of classical conditioning of reflexes (perhaps because of changes in the central nervous system [Gen-dreau & Suboski, 1971; Schonfield, 1980]) and on certain problem solving tasks. In addition, older adults seem to have difficulty in the encoding and retrieval stages of learning. Encoding is the moving of new information into long-term memory while retrieval is the recalling of information. Deficiencies in these areas may be related to the rate at which older adults are able to learn or recall information. Perhaps the best generalization that can be made at present regarding cognitive functioning in the elderly is that, although there appears to be some decline in certain aspects of learning and intellectual functioning among healthy elderly people, the decline rarely if ever interferes with their daily functioning.

One exception to this generalization is the phenomenon known as the *terminal drop in intelligence*. Noted as early as 1962, the terminal drop is the marked decline in measured intelligence that occurs shortly before death (Kleemeier, 1962). The cause of the terminal drop is debatable. Perhaps it is a reflection of cardiovascular disease, depression accompanying terminal illness, or general apathy signifying a psychological withdrawal from involvement in the world's activities—similar to the depression stage in the dying trajectory (Kubler-Ross, 1969). Whatever the cause, major declines in the intelligence of the elderly, especially in verbal abilities, have proven to be better predictors of mortality than has chronological age (Blum, Clark, & Jarvik, 1973).

In the psychosocial dimension, Erikson described the major task of old age as the achievement of ego integrity; otherwise, one risks facing despair. As described in Chapter 5, ego integrity has a great deal in common with self-actualization. It represents the highest level of adjustment in human beings, and Erikson felt it could not be attained before the age of 65. At the other end of the elderly mental health continuum is despair that is rooted in an awareness of an unfulfilled life and in the knowledge that time will not permit new beginnings.

Peck (1968), who expanded on Erikson's notion of a continuum between integrity and despair, suggested that there are three challenges involved in coping with this final stage of development. The first is to develop ego differention rather than be preoccupied with the work role. Because retirement diminishes work-role opportunities, individuals must develop other meaningful activities in order to remain healthy. Individuals whose whole sense of identity came from their work may be ill-prepared to use the newly found leisure time offered by retirement and may find themselves lamenting their lost identity. The second challenge is to reduce preoccupation with the body and to increase body-transcendence. As the physical losses of old age accumulate, healthy individuals must find creative outlets for their energies rather than focus on their declining biological capabilities. The third challenge is to reduce ego preoccupation and to increase ego transcendence. By ego transcendence, Peck means the ability to take pride in accomplishments that will live on after one's inevitable death. Individuals who believe that their lives have accomplished little and that their imminent deaths will also be meaningless may well develop an abiding sense of despair.

In the social realm, most elderly people experience major changes. Retirement results in the loss of the socializing that occurs on the job. Although seldom reflected on during employment, the world of work provides most individuals with a great deal of interpersonal contact. There is often daily and extended interaction with coworkers and intermittent contact with customers, clients, or supervisors. The loss of daily work-related contacts can be a significant stressor for which the retiree is unprepared. Women who have followed the more traditional role of maintaining the home and nurturing the family may experience more continuity in their social relationships in old age. In fact, their loneliness may be alleviated, at least for a while, as a result of their retired husbands' spending more time with them. Changes in women's participation in the work force may make retirement a more salient factor in the social lives of elderly women for future cohorts. Although many elderly people use the leisure time that comes with retirement to engage in social activities such as volunteer work in their communities, these activities often must be curtailed as they grow older and develop incapacitating conditions. Deaths—the death of the spouse and the deaths of close friends—become normative events during old age, resulting in further isolation. Relationships with siblings, adult children, and grandchildren are generally the most important social ties for elderly people. However, in our mobile society, even these relationships tend to diminish during old age.

In summary, the period of old age, beginning around age 65 and continuing until death, can be a period of increased life satisfaction and ego integrity or one of dissatisfaction, despair, and disgust. Older adults who are able to stay on the positive end of Erikson's continuum may achieve wisdom during this stage. However, the principle of entropy ensures that sometime during this period individuals will experience sudden or gradual declines in health, will have to deal with the loss of friends and relatives, and will eventually face their own deaths. The special stresses of this final stage of development undoubtedly affect the suicide statistics in old age.

THE STATISTICAL PICTURE

In every developed country that reports suicide statistics, the rate of suicide among elderly people remains higher than for any other age group. Table 6.1 shows suicide rates for selected countries by age and sex. As shown in Table 6.1, France, Austria, West Germany, and Japan reported the highest suicide rates for elderly men, while Japan, Austria, Denmark, France, and West Germany reported the highest rates for elderly women. The United States ranked 6th and 11th for males and females respectively. It is apparent that the rates of suicide among both males and females aged 65–74 are much higher than for younger age groups. In addition, suicide rates among the oldest male cohort (age 75 and

*First our pleasures die—
and then
Our hopes, and then our
fears, and when
These are dead, the debt
is due,
Dust claims dust—and
we die too. Shelly,
Death*

TABLE 6.1 Suicide Rates for Selected Countries by Sex and Age Group
(Rate per 100,000 population. Includes deaths resulting from self-inflicted injuries. Except as noted, deaths classified according to the ninth revision of the International Classification of Diseases.)

Sex and age	United States 1983	Australia 1984	Austria 1985	Canada 1984	Denmark 1984	France 1984	Italy 1981	Japan 1985	Nether- lands 1984	Poland 1984	Sweden 1984	United Kingdom 1984	West Germany 1985
Male													
Total	19.2	16.9	40.9	21.4	36.5	32.2	9.8	26.0	15.2	23.6	27.4	11.8	29.4
65–74 yrs. old	31.7	24.7	71.9	25.1	48.8	64.9	24.9	42.6	28.6	29.1	37.9	17.0	50.2
75 yrs. and over	50.7	30.4	95.3	33.0	67.3	116.9	36.4	74.8	42.7	29.7	47.5	22.5	79.4
Female													
Total	5.4	5.2	15.7	6.1	21.0	12.4	4.0	13.1	9.6	4.9	11.8	5.7	12.7
65–74 yrs. old	7.3	6.5	31.0	8.4	37.7	25.3	9.5	29.7	21.2	7.5	17.9	10.6	24.7
75 yrs. and over	6.1	5.7	32.2	5.8	32.2	28.8	7.7	54.3	14.6	6.4	11.7	10.0	24.6

Source: U.S. Bureau of the Census (1988) *Statistical Abstracts of the United States*. (108th edition). Washington, DC, 1987, p. 803.

older) range from being less than 2 times more frequent than those of the youngest cohort (in Australia) to being over 7 times more frequent (in France). In the United States the oldest males are almost 3 times more likely to kill themselves than are males aged 15–24. For females, the same pattern occurs, although the overall rates are much lower. Females over age 75 are from 1.5 to 9 times more likely to kill themselves than are females aged 15–24. Table 6.1 also shows that the oldest males in all countries reporting have a much higher suicide rate than the oldest females. In every country males show an increase in suicide between the age category of 65–74 and that of 75 and older. Among women, more than three-fourths of the countries report a decreasing suicide rate between the same age categories.

There are four important generalizations that can be made concerning suicide among the elderly. First, the elderly, compared with other age groups, are overrepresented among the nation's suicides. As the decade of the 1980's began, people over 65 years of age constituted 11% of the U.S. population but committed 17% of the suicides (McIntosh, Hubbard, & Santos, 1981; Miller, 1978a; Resnick & Cantor, 1970; Seiden, 1981; Sendbuehler & Goldstein, 1977). Second, the attempt-completion ratio continues to be different for the elderly compared with younger people. Elderly people complete suicide more often while making failed attempts less often than people in all other age groups. The ratio of suicide attempts to completions in the general population has been estimated to be as low as 8:1 and as high as 15:1. The ratio among the young may be as high as 200:1 (Farberow & Shneidman, 1961; McIntosh, 1985). The ratio among those 65 and older, however, is only 4:1 (McIntosh, 1985). Third, the ratio of male to female suicides among the elderly is greater than in the general population. The elderly male-female ratio is 5:1 compared with the general population ratio of approximately 3:1. This ratio increases from the young elderly to the old elderly. Among 65-year-olds there is a 4:1 male-female suicide ratio, while those over 85 show a ratio of 12 male suicides for every single female suicide (U.S. Bureau of the Census, 1987). Finally, it should be noted that suicides among the elderly are even more underreported than for other age groups. The cause of death among the elderly is often more difficult to determine. Older people can, for example, take overdoses of prescription medications, mix drugs, fail to take essential medicine, or even starve themselves. It has been estimated that as many as 10,000 people over 60 years of age kill themselves each year, many more than the 6,000 elderly suicides officially reported (Miller, 1978b; Osgood, 1985; U.S. Bureau of the Census, 1987).

The U.S. suicide rates for three age groups of elderly males and females in 1985 are presented in Table 6.2. Table 6.2 shows that the male suicide rate among those aged 65–74 was 33.3 per 100,000 population in 1985. Among males aged 75–84 the rate

TABLE 6.2   Suicide Rates per 100,000 Population for Three Age Groups of Elderly Males and Females in 1985

Age	Males	Females
65–74 yrs. old	33.3	6.9
75–84 yrs. old	53.1	6.8
85 yrs. and older	55.4	4.6

Source: U.S. Bureau of Census, (1988). *Statistical Abstract of the United States* (108th Edition) Washington, DC, 1987, p. 78.

rose sharply to 53.1 per 100,000, and it continued to rise to a peak of 55.4 per 100,000 for those 85 and older. Corresponding rates for females were much lower. Falling from the female peak of 8.3 per 100,000 for those aged 45–54, female rates dropped to 6.9 per 100,000 for those aged 65–74, to 6.8 per 100,000 for those aged 75–84, and to a low of 4.6 per 100,000 for women over 85. This last rate is the second lowest rate of suicide for women; the lowest rate is for women aged 15–24.

Although the suicide rate among the elderly remains the highest of all age groups, there has been a decrease in the rate over the last 50 years. Figure 6.1 shows the overall suicide and elderly suicide rates per 100,000 since 1900. The figure shows that the suicide rate for the overall population has remained relatively stable since the mid-1940s. However, the rate for the elderly has gone from a high of more than 50 per 100,000 to the current relatively low rate of 20.3 per 100,000. McIntosh (1984) analyzed trends within the elderly age group itself. Figure 6.2 shows the suicide rates among the young old and the old old by sex and race from 1933 to 1985. As shown in Fig. 6.2, the suicide rate decline among the elderly has been predominantly a white male phenomenon, while white females and nonwhites have consistently had low rates which have declined little. Figure 6.2 also shows that the elderly white male suicide rates for both the young old and the old old declined over the 45-year period studied, although the decline among the young old was slightly greater than that among the old old. Clearly, the overall decline in the suicide rate among the elderly during the last half century is mainly attributable to a decrease in white male suicides.

There are at least three major hypotheses that may help explain the declining elderly suicide rate over the last 50 years (McIntosh, 1984, 1985). First, differential longevity between the sexes has increased by approximately 7 years during this century (Stillion, 1985). In contrast to the past, when men and women were more equally represented in the elderly population, women currently constitute 60% of the population over 65 years of age in the United States. Because women have lower suicide rates than men, their greater representation in this age group would naturally reduce the overall incidence.

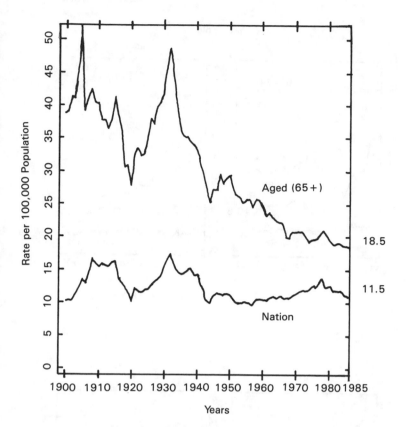

FIGURE 6.1 Overall and Elderly Suicide Rates since 1900. Adapted from McIntosh, J. L., Hubbard, R. W., and Santos, J. F. 1981, Suicide among the elderly: A review of the issues with case studies. *Journal of Gerontological Social Work, 4,* p. 66.

A second widely accepted hypothesis is that the decline in suicide rate reflects a cohort difference among the elderly. The present elderly generation came of age and lived their young and middle adult years under significantly different circumstances than their predecessors. The present generation has moved into its older years in better health, with more education, and with more social benefits of all types than previous generations. No doubt some of these factors which differentiate the present elderly generation from earlier ones have affected the suicide rate positively.

A third hypothesis is that economic gains among the elderly during the past 40 years have contributed to the decline in suicide rate for this age group. Financial security, while important to everyone, is perhaps the major factor influencing the quality of life for older men. Marshall (1978) investigated the relationship between four different indices of economic well-being among the elderly and the suicide rate for older white men between 1947 and 1972. The economic indicators were (1) the employment rate of the aged, (2) the

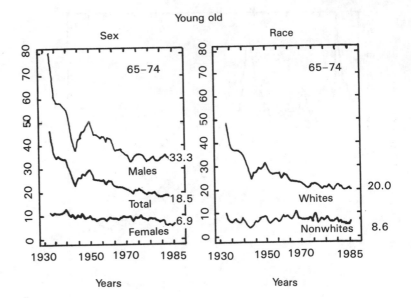

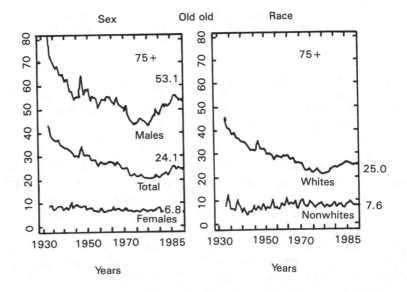

FIGURE 6.2   Suicide Rates per 100,000 Among the Young Old and
the Old Old by Sex and Race, 1933–1985. Adapted from McIntosh, J.
L., 1984. Components of the decline in elderly suicide: Suicide among
the young-old and old-old by race and sex. *Death Education, 8* (Suppl.),
p. 118.

availability of income security for older people, (3) the portion of the labor force covered by Social Security, and (4) the average monthly husband-wife income for the elderly. It was found that each of these four variables was related to the suicide rate in the manner expected. In fact, these variables collectively accounted for more than 90% of the variance in suicidal behavior among older white men during the period of the study. These findings led Marshall to conclude that economic factors are the most significant variables influencing suicide rates among older white men and are far more important than social or political issues.

The declining suicide rate among the elderly over the last 50 years is very encouraging, especially considering the fact that most of the improvement has occurred among white males, the group most at-risk. In spite of this encouraging trend, however, there are some disturbing projections which indicate that the number of suicides among the elderly will not continue to decline much longer and that the suicide rate reduction among this group will reverse itself as we enter the 21st century (Haas & Hendin, 1983).

There are two major factors that lead to the prediction of a rise in elderly suicide early in the next century. Both factors relate to the dramatic increase in our population that began after World War II and is commonly known as the "baby boom." Figure 6.3 depicts the effect the baby boom will have on the elderly population of this country beginning around the year 2000. If we assume that the suicide rate among the elderly will remain at its current relatively low level, the size of the baby boom population alone will result in the largest number of self-inflicted deaths by this age group in history. For example, the present rate of 18 suicides per 100,000 elderly results in 8,500 suicides per year for this age group. As the elderly population grows, the same suicide rate would result in 12,500 elderly suicides by the year 2000, 14,000 suicides by the year 2020, and an unprecedented 18,500 suicides by the year 2040 (Haas & Hendin, 1983).

However, there is reason to believe that the suicide rate among the elderly baby boom cohort may not remain stable. Historically, the suicide rate has fluctuated relative to any age group's representation as a part of the total population. Groups that constitute larger portions of the total population tend to have higher suicide rates than groups that constitute smaller portions (Holinger & Offer, 1982). Perhaps this phenomenon is related to the fact that the resources and opportunities available to any generation are limited. Because larger groups must spread these resources more thinly, there is greater competition and more likelihood of failure. In addition, it is more difficult to maintain positive self-esteem and visible status within a group where resources and opportunities are limited.

Another important factor in understanding elderly suicide is race. As Fig. 6.2 shows, suicide rates among elderly blacks and white females have been low relative to elderly white males since 1933.

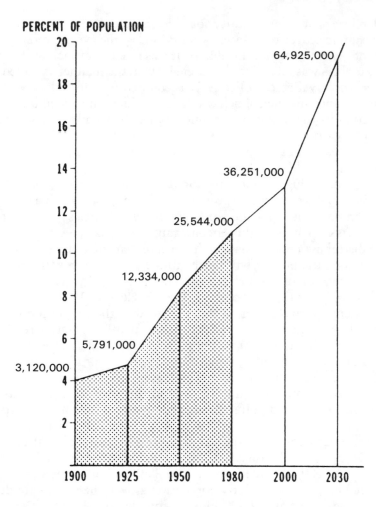

PERCENT OF POPULATION

FIGURE 6.3   U.S. Population Age 65 and Older, 1900–2030 (1985–
2030 figures are projections) Source: Cox, H. (1984). *Later life: The
realities of aging*, Englewood Cliffs, N.J.: Prentice-Hall, Inc., p. 3,
adapted from U.S. Bureau of the Census.

Differences in suicide rates for black and white elderly men have
been discussed in detail by Seiden (1981). Seiden has proposed that
racial differences in family arrangement may account for some of
the suicide rate differences between whites and nonwhites. The
nuclear family tends to be the predominant arrangement among
whites in the United States, while the extended family, with several
generations living together, is more prevalent among nonwhites.
The extended family arrangement often provides useful roles for the
elderly, such as child care and domestic services. In contrast, the
nuclear family, which is reduced to husband and wife when the
children are grown, rarely provides such opportunities for useful
work after formal retirement. If, as many believe, the absence of
purposeful activity is one factor that contributes to suicide in old

age, a minority elderly person in an extended family may be less at risk than the lonely survivor of a white nuclear family.

Minority families are more likely than white families to hold traditional values, including respect for age and appreciation for the wisdom of experience. These values especially tend to predominate in extended families with strong church affiliations. White nuclear families, on the other hand, more often reflect secular values, including a greater appreciation for education and productivity than for age and experience. These differences in values must surely provide more status and high self-esteem among elderly people in minority families than for those in a white middle-class environment.

Seiden has also pointed out that the motives for suicide may differ significantly between whites and nonwhites, especially among the elderly. The loss of financial and employment status following retirement may be a much more relevant motive for whites than for nonwhites. White men, especially, often lose power and influence as they grow old. Black men and black and white women have long been accustomed to low status because of racism and sexism. Although few would argue that the majority of white elderly people are poorer or suffer lower status than the majority of nonwhite elderly people, the contrast between pre- and post-retirement status is probably more dramatic for whites than for minorities. Because of their former higher status and power, whites have farther to fall in retirement than nonwhites. As Dick Gregory once said about the plight of minorities, "You can't kill yourself by jumping out of the basement."

It would appear that the nonwhite elderly show higher morale than whites in spite of the racism and poverty this group has endured. Perhaps there is some natural selection operating, in that those nonwhites who make it to old age have already shown considerable strength and adaptability. It also seems likely, however, that the purposeful and meaningful activity, family support, and status more available to nonwhite elderly people are important factors in mitigating some of the adversities of old age.

Although in using government statistics, we have referred to the nonwhite population as though it were homogenous, McIntosh (1984) has pointed out that this practice leads to inaccuracy in interpreting suicide rates for all minority elderly people. Because blacks constitute the great majority of the nonwhite population of the United States, their rates tend to skew the overall statistics and to mask different trends in other minority groups in the same way that the white male suicide statistics skew the overall suicide rates for the entire United States population.

McIntosh, examining identifiable subgroups within the population, has pointed out that the pattern of suicide among American Indians parallels that of blacks, with a high rate among young males that peaks around age 30 and then declines steadily with increasing age. Asian Americans, in contrast, have the highest rate of suicide among minority elderly. Although the data are limited, it appears that elderly Chinese, Japanese, and Filipino Americans have suicide rates similar to those of whites.

In summary, elderly people commit suicide at higher rates than young people the world over. In the United States, the overall elderly suicide rate of 20.3 per 100,000 population reflects a decrease in the incidence of suicide for this age group, although the present rate remains disturbingly high. Much of this rate can be accounted for by suicide among elderly white males. Although there are no simple answers explaining the high rate of suicide among the elderly, research has suggested several factors that seem to add to the probability of death by suicide.

FACTORS AFFECTING SUICIDE IN OLD AGE

There are at least four major factors that have been shown to be related to elderly suicide. These are cumulative loss, alcohol and drug dependence, retirement with its financial and social concomitants, and social isolation resulting in loneliness.

In our profile of old age, we suggested that losses are normative events for the elderly. The nature of loss in old age is different from that of younger ages, in that loss is more frequent and final. The pattern of increasing loss has led to using the term *cumulative loss* to describe the case in which elderly people must cope with a rapid succession of losses that does not allow sufficient time for resolution of the grief inherent in each loss. Evidence exists that there is a discernable pattern in grieving, called the grief trajectory, which must be experienced before an individual can invest time and energy on new activities and relationships (Raphael, 1983; Rando, 1985; Worden, 1982). The grief trajectory includes the following emotions: (1) shock and denial; (2) disorganization; (3) anger, resentment, and guilt; (4) depression; and (5) resolution (Stillion, 1985). It is important to note that depression is a normal part of the grieving process. When many losses are experienced within a relatively short period of time, as often occurs among the elderly, depression may become a chronic state. Indeed, depression has been found to be the most common of all illnesses among the aged (Butler & Lewis, 1982). Many researchers have estimated that a large majority of elderly suicides, perhaps as many as 80%, involve significant depression (Benson & Brodie, 1975; Lyons, 1984; McIntosh, Hubbard, & Santos, 1981). Thus, cumulative loss must be regarded as a significant factor influencing suicide among the elderly.

One type of loss that is inevitable in old age is the loss of physical capabilities. Suicide among the elderly is often committed by individuals suffering from chronic illness accompanied by excessive pain and the loss of independence. One study found that 85% of a group of suicide completers over age 60 were physically ill at the time they killed themselves (Dorpat, Anderson,

& Ripley, 1968). Miller (1979) found extreme illness to be associated with 60% of the cases in his extensive study of suicide
among elderly Arizona men. Additional support for the involvement of physical deterioration as a factor in elderly suicide can
be found in certain studies showing that 70% or more of elderly
people who kill themselves visit a physician within one month
of the suicide and that as many as 10% consult a physician on
the actual day of the suicide (Barraclough, 1971; Miller, 1978a;
Rockwell & O'Brien, 1973).

The second important factor in elderly suicide is alcohol and
drug abuse, which may be a corollary of the loss of physical capabilities. Many elderly people self-medicate with alcohol to ease

Blind Botanist, Ben Shahn, 1963. Lithograph in colors, 26¾ × 20½ in.
(New Jersey State Museum Collection, Trenton. Purchase. Photograph
by Geoffrey Clements.) Used by permission of Mrs. Ben Shahn.

their aches and pains and to elevate their spirits. Unfortunately, the depressant effects of alcohol are likely to be exaggerated in old age because of reduced metabolic processes that slow the detoxification process. The elderly also tend to experience over-medication as drugs prescribed by physicians are mixed with self-prescribed over-the-counter drugs. The sedating effects and metabolic problems associated with alcohol abuse and the interactions of over-the-counter and prescription drugs may result in a clouding of consciousness and increase the likelihood of depression and suicidal behavior in this age group (Butler & Lewis, 1982). Miller (1979) found that approximately 25% of a group of elderly male suicides were alcoholic or had significant drinking problems and that 35% of this group, whether alcoholic or not, were addicted to or heavily dependent on drugs.

Retirement is the third category of loss that may be related to suicide among the elderly. Although no definitive studies exist that show a direct cause and effect relationship between retirement and suicide, there is evidence that, especially for white males, retirement can be associated with decreased life satisfaction. There is also evidence that early retirement (e.g., resulting from special incentive programs) is especially likely to produce anger and depression in retirees (Alsop, 1984). The retirement research to date has focused only on males, because the majority of females in elderly cohorts have followed the traditional role of wife and homemaker. Life in retirement is not necessarily a utopian existence for everyone. Many individuals have significant difficulties adjusting to the "golden years."

There is some evidence of a pattern of adjustment in retirement. Atchley (1976) contended that recent retirees often experience a certain amount of enthusiasm and excitement about their new status. This euphoria, which usually lasts approximately 1 year, gradually gives way to a sense of letdown during the 2nd year as the novelty fades and the realities of the new status become more evident. Ekerdt, Bossé, and Levkov (1985) compared groups of 1st- and 2nd-year retirees on a number of measures of adjustment. They found that the 2nd-year retirees indicated significantly lower levels of life satisfaction and reported less involvement in leisure and physical activities than 1st-year retirees. Also, the recently retired showed much greater optimism and future orientation than those who had been removed from active service for more than 1 year. The declining optimism that usually occurs during the 2nd year of retirement may be related to the growing realization of the losses which are often part of retirement life. These losses include income, status, power, and prestige as well as purposeful and meaningful activity (Benson & Brody, 1975; Breed & Huffine, 1979; Lyons, 1984; McIntosh, Hubbard, & Santos, 1981; Miller, 1978b).

Inadequate income is stressful at any age. Poverty seems to be particularly traumatic in old age, however, especially after a lifetime of seemingly adequate income prior to retirement. Useui, Keil, and Durig (1985) conducted a survey of persons over 60 years of age to determine the relationship between a number of demographic characteristics and adjustment. The findings showed that the retiree's self-perceived financial status was more important to life satisfaction than any other factor, including functional health, age, sex, race, marital status, or education.

The financial impact of retirement appears to take the greatest toll on men whose preretirement income was marginal. Fillenbaum, George, and Palmore (1985) examined data from two longitudinal studies to measure the impact of retirement on the morale of men at different economic levels. They found that men at the marginal economic level were more negatively affected by retirement than those who were at the poverty level or who were financially comfortable. In addition, they found that only retirees at the marginal economic level reported reduced life satisfaction and decreased happiness in retirement. These results may occur because of the change in socioeconomic status that often accompanies retirement. Unlike those at higher socioeconomic levels, those with marginal income are unable to save for their retirement and thus face economic reversal. Those individuals who have lived most of their lives below the poverty level may actually improve their financial status in old age through income maintenance programs for the elderly.

While financial security and independence are important employment benefits sometimes lost in retirement, other work-related factors that influence life satisfaction may also be lost simultaneously. Many workers enjoy a significant amount of meaningful and purposeful activity in their daily work lives. In addition, a significant amount of status, power, and influence are inherently provided through holding certain privileged positions. Loss of meaningful and purposeful activity in retirement can be very distressing. Retirees often complain about boredom and inactivity. Some individuals deal with this situation by diving into hobbies and taking on new projects. Other find the inactivity of retirement so stressful that they seek re-employment, usually in lower status jobs that often lead to the sacrifice of already-earned retirement benefits.

Men who have been previously employed in high-level positions may experience significant depression related to status and power changes associated with their retirements. They may become significantly distressed to learn that former employees show them less deference than before or that their organizations are doing well without them. The following case study illustrates some of the health- and retirement-related problems faced by the elderly.

W. D. Henshaw killed himself on his 81st birthday. He carefully spread a newly purchased tarpaulin on the concrete floor of his ga-

rage, lay down upon it and shot himself in the head. The terse suicide note that he left said simply, "It's time."

W. D. was a self-made man. He often bragged to his children and grandchildren that he had come from a small dirt farm in the South, worked his way through college, and worked hard all his life. He had risen to a position of responsibility in an agricultural wholesale business by age 32. He then resigned and started his own wholesale business. Working night and day, he was personally responsible for the success of his business. It was at this time in his life that he developed the habit of working from 5:30 A.M. until 7:30 P.M., a habit which lasted almost his entire lifetime.

W. D. married at age 36. His wife was from a wealthy family, and her wealth provided even more security for the business. Although Mrs. Henshaw was 34 when they married, they had two children. The Henshaws appeared to have a stable, if unexciting, marriage. However, Mrs. Henshaw developed breast cancer at age 52 and died within 6 months. W. D. never remarried, devoting himself instead almost totally to his business.

W. D. bragged often about his reputation for hard work and honesty. As he grew older, his son and daughter tried to get him to slow down, to develop hobbies, to take vacations. They had little success. When W. D. turned 70, his son tried to talk him into retiring. The two men argued violently, and W. D. stayed on the job, although he did cut back his customary work day from 14 hours to 10.

In spite of his iron determination, W. D. found himself napping during the day, sometimes even in important meetings. He also complained to his daughter that he had constant indigestion and that food had lost its taste. At age 78, he agreed to have his hearing tested and was fitted with a hearing aid. In general, however, his health remained good until he began to have a series of small strokes at age 79. Between hospitalizations, as his health permitted, he continued to go to the office but was aware that it was running well without him and that he could no longer remember many of the details of the business. He had a long talk with his son, admitting his growing confusion and weakness. W. D. officially resigned from the presidency of his company. He spent several months putting his affairs in order. In an uncharacteristic gesture, he invited his family and the executives of his company to a cookout on his 81st birthday. His children commented after the party that they had been impressed with W. D.'s renewed energy. His daughter had felt that it was a sure sign of physical improvement, while his son felt it was caused by removal of the stress of the job. After the party, W. D. straightened the house, piled the dishes neatly in the sink, and wrote his two-word note.

This case study reflects a number of the special losses which old people who have highly identified with their work may experience in retirement. Retirement for W. D. resulted in the loss of the high level of daily activity which was such an important part of his life for many years. He obviously gained a great deal of pride and self-esteem from his accomplishments and from his critical position within the company. These were lost in retirement. The loss of physical capabilities accompanying his retirement was a significant stressor, which steadily worsened with his strokes and ultimately precipitated his suicide. It should be noted that the renewed energy shown by W. D. is characteristic of many suicides. Once the final decision to commit suicide is made, many people experience a surge of energy, probably traceable to a decrease in ambivalence about life and the future.

Social isolation, along with its accompanying loneliness, is the final factor that is closely related to suicide among the elderly. The loss of close friends and relatives in old age may contribute more to unhappiness than any other factor. Darbonne (1969) found that suicide notes of the elderly included more references to loneliness and isolation than those of any other age group. Miller (1979), comparing a large group of elderly suicidal men with a nonsuicidal group, suggested that the presence of a confidante was very important in preventing suicide. He found that the older men who committed suicide were 3 times less likely to have a

Garden of Memories, Charles Burchfield, 1917. Crayon and watercolor, 25¾ × 22½ in. (Collection, the Museum of Modern Art, New York. Gift of Abby Aldrich Rockefeller, by exchange.)

confidante or close friend than those who died of natural causes. In addition, he found that the older men who committed suicide had fewer visits from friends and relatives and that the time interval between visits was significantly longer than for those who died of natural causes. The social isolation inherent in institutional living may help explain the increased suicide rate among the elderly in nursing homes (Butler & Lewis, 1977).

Undoubtedly, widowhood is the major source of social isolation among the elderly (Bock & Webber, 1972a). The loss of a spouse represents many losses to an elderly person, including the loss of a best friend and confidante and the loss of a shared history. To an elderly woman, the husband may be the only person alive who remembers her as a bride, who suffered through her pregnancies, and who takes the same pride in her children as she does. To the elderly male, his wife may be the only person who has seen him in both victory and defeat and with whom he has constantly shared his inner thoughts. Toynbee (1984) reflected some of the pain involved in the loss of a spouse when he said, "There are two parties to the suffering that death inflicts; and in the apportionment of this suffering, the survivor takes the brunt" (p. 14).

Widowhood has been shown to increase the risk of suicide, especially among elderly males during the first 6 months of bereavement (Benson & Brodie, 1975; Berardo, 1968; Bock & Webber, 1972b; MacMahon & Pugh, 1965; Miller, 1978a). Those widowed by suicide have especially high suicide rates (Osterweis, Solomon, & Green, 1984). In addition, widowed people who are socially isolated are at greater risk for suicide than those less socially isolated. In a study comparing suicidal widowed elderly with nonsuicidal widowed elderly people, Bock and Webber (1972b) found that those who were suicidal were more socially isolated than those who were nonsuicidal.

Some controversy exists regarding the relative amount of stress that widowhood imposes on males and females (Glick, Parkes, & Weiss, 1975; Kart, 1981; Osterweis, Solomon, & Green, 1984). Since males are less likely than females to have developed intimate relationships with a number of people, widowhood may be particularly stressful for them, especially during the first year or two. Females may suffer less role discontinuity when they are widowed than males do. Females are more likely to be familiar with the routines of keeping house and cooking, while males must often learn new skills in order to thrive in the role of widower. Females also tend to have a more diverse set of relationships than do males. In addition, there is evidence that females "practice widowhood" in an attempt to prepare themselves for their spouse's deaths and may therefore be more prepared to face the reality of the loss (Lopata, 1973). It is also true that widowhood is a normative state for most older women, since women on average live nearly a decade longer than do men. In addition, since women in our culture traditionally marry men older than themselves, most can expect to live as widows for at least a dozen years or more. Since this is true, females may find more support among other widowed females than men do among the fewer widowed males. In spite of all these factors, however, it can be argued that, while widowers may have more difficulty in the initial adjustment to widowhood, widows suffer more over the long term (Barrett, 1979; Stillion, 1984, 1985). Since women traditionally have invested more of their identity in marriage than men, a widowed woman may actually lose a greater part of her identity with the death of her spouse. This phenomenon is best seen in widows who were the wives of rich and famous men and who vicariously profited from their husbands' status and power, but it is undoubtedly a reality at some level for most women. Women are also much more likely to suffer financial loss in widowhood than are men. Many more widows than widowers live below the poverty level. Widows are also less likely to remarry. Half of all widowers remarry within 5 years, while only one-fourth of widows remarry (Barrett, 1979). The following case study illustrates some of the special losses of widowhood in old age.

Elena Mercado was widowed after 42 years of marriage, when she was 66 years of age. Her husband, "Merk," who had worked as a machinist for 33 years, had died of cancer after a long, expensive illness. Elena found herself facing a debt-filled widowhood. Elena had raised seven children. She and Merk had always taken pride in the fact that he earned enough to permit her to be a full-time wife and mother. Although Elena's seven children were concerned about their mother's financial situation, none of them was able to help very much. Elena gave up her apartment in an effort to cut down on expenses and spent her time divided among the children's homes. She confided to an old friend that she felt like an intruder at every home, because she always took a bed from one of the grandchildren and sometimes felt that her presence deprived the family of food as well as privacy. Elena actively investigated low-cost housing programs, but each one she examined seemed beyond her means. In addition to trying to make small payments on her husband's medical bills, Elena tried to help out with the grocery bills at whatever home she was visiting. She was never able to put aside any money.

Shortly after Elena moved in with her oldest son for the second time, she received notice that her brother was dying in New Mexico. Although she could not afford to make the trip, she sent as much money as she could to help with the funeral expenses. A week later her oldest son lost his job and told her she would have to leave his home. When Elena told her daughter she would have to move in with her sooner than expected, the daughter came to her brother's home to express her unhappiness. The resultant argument between the siblings was bitter. Elena, not knowing what else to do, began to pack. While doing so, she discovered a bottle of old barbituates left from her husband's illness. Elena left the house, saying she was going for a walk to clear her head. She walked to a nearby park, stopping to buy a

*coke at a corner deli. She took all of the pills in the bottle. Her body
was discovered early the next morning when the police made their
routine swing through the park.*

This case study illustrates some of the problems that may
result from the poverty many women experience in widowhood.
Attempts to deal with the unaccustomed poverty without occupational skills and experience can be humiliating and devastating for many women and can necessitate living arrangements
that lead to other problems. In these and other ways widowhood
often multiplies the cumulative losses of old age and/or increases
their rate of occurrence.

SPECIAL ASPECTS OF SUICIDE AMONG THE ELDERLY: DOUBLE SUICIDES AND EUTHANASIA

There are two special issues that deserve attention in any
discussion of elderly suicide: double suicide and euthanasia. While
both double suicide and euthanasia can occur at any time in the
life span, they tend to occur more often among people over 65
years of age.

Double suicides or suicide pacts have occurred throughout
history and even today they receive a great deal of media attention.
Pioneer scientific investigation of double suicides in England and
Wales by Cohen (1961) and subsequent work by others (Mehta,
Mathew, & Mehta, 1978; Noyes, Frye, & Hartford, 1977; Young,
Rich, & Fowler, 1984) have proven a number of commonly held
beliefs about double suicide to be incorrect. We have learned, for
example, that double suicide is a rare phenomenon. Cohen (1961)
uncovered only 65 cases (only 58 of these cases were suicide pacts
in the technical sense) in England and Wales between 1955 and
1958. The stereotypic "Romeo and Juliet" syndrome of young
lovers committing suicide in response to opposition to their relationship was also found to be unusual. Such a scenario occurred
in only 10% of Cohen's cases. Cohen's findings showed the prototypic double suicide to involve an older married couple. They
were more likely than other couples to be childless, retired, and
unoccupied. Also, one or both partners were very likely to be
physically ill.

Research has shown that couples who commit suicide manifest many of the characteristics associated with elderly suicide
in general. At least one member is likely to be physically ill and
to have visited a physician close in time to the suicide. One or
both are likely to use alcohol heavily. Also, contrary to popular
belief, elderly couples often communicate their suicide intent to
others. Their suicide ideation is not the carefully guarded "grim
secret" of the commonly held stereotype about suicide pacts (Young,
Rich, & Fowler, 1984).

*He first deceased, she for
a little tried
To live without him,
lik'd it not, and died.
Sir Henry Wotton, On
the Death of Sir Albert
Morton's Wife*

Older couples who commit suicide manifest additional characteristics which appear to be idiosyncratic. They are, for ex-

ample, more likely than others to have experienced early loss of close relatives through suicide. Also, their personalities tend to interact in ways that increase each member's depression and lower self-esteem, probably accounting in part for the fact that double-suicide attempts rarely fail. These couples tend to be interdependent and isolated from other sources of support (Mehta, Mathew, & Mehta, 1978; Young, Rich, & Fowler, 1984).

There seems to be a "special chemistry" between couples who commit suicide together. Typically, the more suicidal partner tends to be dominant and the more ambivalent partner tends to be passive in the relationship. This type of relationship has been described as "lock and key" pathology, where the dynamics of the interactive characteristics of the couple tend to increase the likelihood of suicide occurring (Santy, 1982). Sometimes, however, double suicide can occur as a result of realistic appraisal of present and future life circumstances and need not involve pathology, as in the following news story.

HIGHLAND PARK, Texas (The Associated Press)—After a loving 50-year marriage and successful medical careers, Don and Betty Morris couldn't bear the thought of some day being separated or finishing out their lives in a nursing home.

So the couple, both 76, indulged in scrambled eggs with cheese, lots of bacon, ice cream and corn chips—all of which they had been forbidden to eat. They sipped their favorite sherry and drank lethal doses of a depressant, then lay down in each other's arms until the poison took effect.

"The two of them together could function well, but not alone. If Dad had another heart attack, that would have put Mom in a nursing home. They didn't want that. They had seen too many friends who had been placed in nursing homes," said Don Morris, Jr., 49, one of the couple's three surviving children.

The elderly Morris, a semiretired psychiatrist, and his wife, a retired psychologist, were found dead in their bedroom July 14 by police after the Southwestern Medical School in Dallas, where Morris was a faculty member, received a letter from them describing their suicide.

A pair of suicide notes was found in the couple's bedroom, along with a menu of the couple's last meal and a list of poems reflecting on death.

"The problem of many deteriorating old people is obviously a new one—everybody used to die too soon," Morris said in his note. "Therefore, as a society, we have not learned to deal with it in a decent and respectable manner."

The Morris's children said their parents told them they would eventually commit suicide. But in his suicide note, Morris said he regretted taking his life "surreptitiously . . . under cover of darkness."

The above news story reflects many of the characteristics shown to be associated with double suicide among the elderly. Both the husband and wife were retired and surely less occupied than during their previous professional careers. They were quite interdependent, and both feared the prospect of coping alone. The husband had suffered debilitating heart attacks and the wife was in very poor health. Also, as is often the case in double suicides, the couple had previously communicated their suicide intent to family members.

Although a major review of euthanasia is not within the scope of this book, some consideration of this phenomenon among the elderly is important. Recent advances in medical technology have created the possibility of sustaining life long after death is inevitable and the chance of improvement nonexistent. Elderly terminally ill patients and their families often face very difficult choices concerning the continuation of life-support systems or the institution of heroic treatment procedures. Advances in medical technology have recently progressed more rapidly than medical ethics, leaving us with difficult choices and no clear-cut guidelines for decision making.

You will recall that in Chapter 1 we made a distinction between active and passive euthanasia. In our opinion, active euthanasia, which involves taking specific steps, such as the injection of lethal doses of drugs, to prematurely end the life of a terminally ill individual, is a suicidal act or murder. Passive euthanasia, which involves the willful rejection of heroic life-sustaining procedures by a fully informed terminally ill individual, we think should not be labelled suicide.

Passive euthanasia procedures are much more widely accepted than in the past. Living wills, in which individuals decree that no heroic procedures or exceptional life-sustaining measures be employed in the event of their incapacitation with a terminal illness, are considered valid in an increasing number of states. Recent court decisions in cases of terminal illness involving termination of life-support systems or refusal of treatment reflect a more pro-euthanasia trend (Baron, 1980). Many of these decisions are consistent with the view that physicians may or should withhold or withdraw treatment in cases of terminal illness upon the request of the patient, provided that the patient has been fully informed of the potential benefits of treatment procedures and the probable consequences of refusal or discontinuation (Cassem, 1980; Levinson, 1980).

There are many indications that the attitudes of the general public toward euthanasia are more positive than in the past. For example, a Gallup poll conducted in the 1950s showed that 36% of the respondents approved of euthanasia in cases of terminal illness. A similar poll conducted in the 1980s showed that 59% of the general public approved of euthanasia under the same conditions (Jorgenson & Neubecker, 1981). White males, especially, approve of euthanasia in cases of terminal illness. In contrast, women and blacks, as well as Catholics and Jews, tend to be more negative in their attitudes toward euthanasia (Jorgenson & Neubecker, 1981; Kalish, 1963).

At the door of life, by the gate of breath, There are worse things waiting for men than death. Swinburne, *The Triumph of Time*

A study of particular relevance for this chapter involved asking a group of elderly Florida residents what efforts they thought should be made to keep seriously ill elderly persons alive. Seventy-three percent of the respondents indicated that an individual in such a situation should be permitted to die a natural death and that no artificial means should be employed to keep such a person alive (Wass, 1977). A similar study conducted with retirees in California revealed even more dramatic results. Ninety-six percent of a large group of elderly respondents indicated their preference for not prolonging the life of a terminally ill individual through artificial means (Mathieu & Peterson, 1970).

Wass (1979) has surmised that many older individuals become more accepting of death as they near their end. She pointed out that young people do not readily comprehend that someone may not only passively accept death but actually desire it because he or she is tired of living, is depleted of physical strength and vital energies, wishes to be released from pain, has no goals to strive for, or simply feels that life has been fully lived. Wass suggested that these feelings are widely held by elderly individuals, especially when they are seriously ill.

I am ready to meet my Maker. Whether my Maker is prepared for the great ordeal of meeting me is another matter. Winston Churchill, *on his 75th birthday*

It is only a small step from accepting passive euthanasia to considering circumstances in which active euthanasia might be acceptable. In fact, many doctors will admit privately that they are currently practicing active euthanasia when they administer large, potentially lethal doses of narcotics to terminally ill patients. It is clear that medical ethicists will be under increasing pressure to develop guidelines for both passive and active euthanasia as our population ages. Involving elderly people in the development of such guidelines is essential if we are to incorporate their worldviews fairly.

ATTITUDES TOWARD ELDERLY SUICIDE

It is widely known that the elderly in America do not enjoy a great deal of status and prestige relative to other age groups. In fact their status is lower than persons of other age groups, except for those who have outstanding attributes, such as wealth and power, which overrule the negative prejudice toward age. Attitudinal research has shown there is an inverted U distribution for age and status in our culture: The middle aged are given maximum prestige and lower status is reserved for the young and the old (Baker, 1985).

Several studies have shown that societal attitudes toward the elderly influence suicide rates for this age group. Lyons (1984) and Stenback (1980) described a study by Yap that compared the elderly suicide rates for two cultures with very different attitudes toward old age. Yap found the elderly suicide rate to be the same as that of all other age groups in the 1917 Peking culture, which promoted respect for elders. In contrast, the elderly suicide rate was found to be significantly higher than the rate for all other age groups in the 1950s Hong Kong culture, which witnessed disruption of traditional values, including a reduction of respect for old age.

Many of our society's negative attitudes toward aging are held by the elderly as well as by younger generations. Robins, West, and Murphy (1977) found that negative attitudes toward old age held by the elderly tend to be associated with suicidal ideation and suicide attempts in this group. The particular beliefs found to relate directly to suicidal ideation and behavior among the elderly included (1) the belief that there is no reason for pride in old age, (2) the belief that relatives would not treat them well when elderly, (3) and the belief that suicide is sometimes justified.

A recent study compared adolescent and older adult attitudes toward suicide by adolescents and older adults (Stillion, White, McDowell, & Edwards, in press). Twenty male and 20 female college students (mean age 20 years) and 20 male and 20 female older adults (mean age 72 years) completed attitude questionnaires concerning adolescent suicide and questionnaires concerning elderly suicide. The Suicide Attitude Vignette Experience-Adolescents (SAVE-A) Scale and the Suicide Attitude Vignette Experience-Elderly (SAVE-L) Scale were completed by both age groups.

The SAVE-A Scale, which was described in Chapter 4, includes 10 vignettes depicting dilemmas resulting in an adolescent suicide attempt. The particular problems facing the young people in the vignettes are those which have been shown to be associated with adolescent suicide, including school failure, lost relationships, peer and parent conflict, divorce, drugs, grief, and guilt. The SAVE-L Scale includes 16 vignettes describing suicide themes for older persons. The particular suicide motives include problems associated with retirement, widowhood, grief, isolation, health problems, alcoholism, and terminal illness. Subjects complete the SAVE-A and SAVE-L scales by indicating the extent to which they sympathize and empathize with the suicidal individuals and agree with each reason for a suicide attempt on a five-point, Likert-type scale.

It was found that adolescents and older adults, both male and female, agreed more with all reasons for suicide among old females than for suicide among any other group. Also, adolescent females in the vignettes received the most sympathy and empathy for suicidal behavior, and suicidal elderly females received the least sympathy and empathy. These findings are generally consistent with the literature on attitudes toward the elderly. Because the elderly are viewed more negatively than the young by all groups, it is not surprising that suicidal elderly females received less sympathy and empathy than any other group and their reasons for suicide were agreed with more. The fact that suicidal elderly females received less sympathy and empathy and their reasons more agreement compared with suicidal elderly males may be related to the fact that males are generally more highly valued in our culture than females. Another possible explanation for the sex differences is that elderly men may be considered to be more valuable from a supply and demand perspective, that is, there are many more old women than old men in our society. Apparently many older women suffer the double burden of age and sex discrimination.

SUMMARY

Suicide among elderly people is a major problem in our society. They have the highest suicide rate of any age group. It has been estimated that each year as many as 10,000 deaths among the elderly may be the result of suicide. Elderly people are quite serious and strongly committed to suicide once a self-destructive decision is made. The old do not make suicidal gestures; their ratio of suicide completions to attempts is the highest of any age group.

Elderly suicide is very much a white male phenomenon. Elderly white females and elderly members of minority groups of both sexes have very low suicide rates, with the possible exception of Asian Americans. Although the elderly white male suicide rate in the United States has declined significantly during the past 50 years, elderly white males continue to kill themselves in greater numbers than members of any other group.

Elderly suicide is closely related to the many losses that are an inevitable part of aging. Major losses that are often a part of the elderly suicide syndrome include (1) loss of physical capabilities and increasing illness; (2) loss of employment and its associated reduction of purposeful activity, financial security, and prestige; and (3) loss of social interaction through the deaths of friends and spouses. Losing a spouse appears to be particularly debilitating socially.

Double suicide, which is somewhat rare, occurs more often among elderly couples than in any other age group. Double suicide is more likely to occur among couples who are highly interdependent and isolated from other sources of social support and in situations where special suicidogenic personality dynamics exist between the partners. Passive euthanasia, which we do not consider to be a form of suicide, is much more widely accepted in cases of terminal illness than in the past, especially among the elderly. Active euthanasia is a subject that must be considered more carefully in the immediate future.

Negative attitudes toward old age are widely held in our society, even among the elderly. Societal attitudes toward aging have been found to be related to suicide rates among the elderly. A study comparing adolescent and elderly attitudes toward suicide by adolescent and elderly subjects showed less sympathy and empathy with suicidal elderly women and more agreement with their reasons than was shown for any other group.

REFERENCES

Alsop, R. (1984, April 24). As early retirement grows in popularity, some have misgivings. *The Wall Street Journal*, p. 1.

Atchley, R. C. (1976). *The sociology of retirement*. New York: Halstead Press.

Baker, P. M. (1985). The status of age: Preliminary results. *Journal of Gerontology*, *40*, 506–508.

Baron, C. H. (1980, April). Termination of life support systems in the elderly. Discussion: To die before the gods please: Legal issues surrounding euthanasia and the elderly. Paper presented at a Scientific Meeting of the Boston Society for Gerontologic Psychiatry.

Barraclough, B. M. (1971). Suicide in the elderly. In D. W. Kay & A. Walk (Eds.), *Recent developments in psychogeriatrics* (pp. 89–97). Kent, England: Headly Brothers.

Barrett, C. J. (1979). Women in widowhood. In J. H. Williams (Ed.) *Psychology of women: Selected readings* (pp. 496–506). New York: Norton.

Benson, R. A., & Brodie, D. C. (1975). Suicide by overdose of medicines among the aged. *Journal of the American Geriatrics Society*, *23*, 304–308.

Berardo, F. M. (1968). Widowhood status in the United States: Perspective on a neglected aspect of the family life-cycle. *The Family Coordinator*, *17*, 191–203.

Blum, J. E., Clark, E. T., & Jarvik, L. F. (1973). The New York State Psychiatric Institute Study of Aging Twins. In L. F. Jarvik, C. Eisdorfer, & J. E. Blum (Eds.), *Intellectual functioning in adults: Psychological and biological influences* (pp. 13–20). New York: Springer.

Bock, E. W., & Webber, I. L. (1972a). Social status and relational systems of elderly suicides: A reexamination of the Henry-Short Thesis. *Suicide and Life-Threatening Behavior*, *2*, 145–159.

Bock, E. W., & Webber, I. L. (1972b, February). Suicide among the elderly: Isolating widowhood and mitigating alternatives. *Journal of Marriage and the Family*, pp. 24–31.

Breed, W., & Huffine, C. (1979). Sex differences in suicide among older white Americans: A role and developmental approach. In O. J. Kaplan (Ed.), *Psychopathology of Aging* (pp. 289–309). New York: Academic Press.

Bromberg, S., & Cassel, C. K. (1983). Suicide in the elderly: The limits of paternalism. *Journal of the American Geriatrics Society*, *31*(11), 698–703.

Buhler, C. (1961). Old age and fulfillment of life with consideration of the use of time in old age. *Acta Psychologica*, *19*, 126–148.

Butler, R. N., & Lewis, M. I. (1977). *Aging and mental health: Positive psychological approaches*. St. Louis, MO: Mosby.

Butler, R. N., & Lewis, M. I. (1982). *Aging and mental health: Positive psychosocial and biomedical approaches* (3rd ed.). St. Louis, MO: Mosby.

Cassem, N. H. (1980, April). Termination of life support systems in the elderly: Clinical issues. Paper presented at the Scientific Meeting of the Boston Society for Gerontologic Psychiatry.

Cohen, J. (1961). A study of suicide pacts. *Medical Legal Journal*, *29*, 144–151.

Darbonne, A. R. (1969). Suicide and age: A suicide note analysis. *Journal of Consulting and Clinical Psychology*, *33*, 46–50.

Dorpat, T. L., Anderson, W. F., & Ripley, H. S. (1968). The relationship of physical illness to suicide. In H. L. P. Resnik (Ed.), *Suicide: Diagnosis and management* (pp. 209–219). Boston: Little, Brown.

Ekerdt, D. J., Bossé, R., Levkov, S. (1985). An empirical test of phases of retirement: Findings from the normative aging study. *Journal of Gerontology*, *40*, 95–101.

Fillenbaum, G. G., George, L. K., & Palmore, E. B. (1985). Determinants and consequences of retirement among men of different races and economic levels. *Journal of Gerontology*, *40*, 85–94.

Frenkel-Brunswik, E. (1963). Adjustments and reorientation in the course of the life span. In R. G. Kuhlen & G. G. Thompson (Eds.), *Psychological studies of human development* (pp. 554–564). New York: Appleton-Century-Crofts.

Gendreau, P., & Suboski, M. D. (1971). Intelligence and age in discrimination conditioning of eyelid response. *Journal of Experimental Psychology, 89,* 379–382.

Glick, I. O., Parkes, C. M., & Weiss, R. (1975). *The first year of bereavement.* New York: Basic Books.

Haas, A. P., & Hendin, H. (1983). Suicide among older people: Projections for the future. *Suicide and Life-Threatening Behavior, 13,* 147–154.

Holinger, P., & Offer, C. (1982). The prediction of adolescent suicide: A population model. *American Journal of Psychiatry, 139,* 302–307.

Horn, J. L. (1982). The theory of fluid and crystallized in relation to concepts of cognitive psychology and aging in adulthood. In F. J. M. Craik and S. Trehub (Eds.), *Aging and cognitive processes.* New York: Plenum.

Jorgenson, D. E., & Neubecker, R. C. (1981). Euthanasia: A national survey of attitudes toward voluntary termination of life. *Omega, 11,* 281–291.

Jung, C. G. (1960). The structure and dynamics of the psyche (R. F. C. Hull, Trans.) In G. Adler (Ed.), *The Collected Works of C. G. Jung* (Bollingen Series 20. Vol. 8, pp. 749–795). Princeton, NJ: Princeton University Press.

Kalish, R. A. (1963). Variables in death attitudes. *The Journal of Social Psychology, 59,* 137–145.

Kalish, R. A. (1975). *Late adulthood: Perspectives on human development.* Monterey, CA: Brooks/Cole.

Kart, C. S. (1981). *The realities of aging.* Boston: Allyn & Bacon.

Kleemeier, R. W. (1962). Intellectual change in the senium. *Proceedings of the Social Statistics Section of the American Statistical Association* (pp. 290–295).

Kubler-Ross, E. (1969). *On death and dying.* New York: Macmillan.

Levinson, A. J. (1980, April). Termination of life support systems in the elderly: Ethical issues. Paper presented at the Scientific Meeting of the Boston Society for Gerontologic Psychiatry.

Lopata, H. (1973). Self-identity in marriage and widowhood. *The Sociological Quarterly, 14,* 407–418.

Lowenthal, M. F., Thurnher, D. C., & Associates (1975). *Four stages of life.* San Francisco: Jossey-Bass.

Lyons, M. J. (1984). Suicide in later life: Some putative causes with implications for prevention. *Journal of Community Psychology, 12,* 379–388.

MacMahon, B., & Pugh, T. F. (1965). Suicide in the widowed. *American Journal of Epidemiology, 81,* 23–31.

Marshall, J. R. (1978). Changes in aged white male suicide: 1948–1972. *Journal of Gerontology, 33,* 763–768.

Mathieu, J., & Peterson, J. (1970, November). Some social psychological dimensions of aging. Paper presented at the annual meeting of the Gerontological Society, Ontario, Canada.

McIntosh, J. L. (1984). Components of the decline in elderly suicide: Suicide among the young-old and old-old by race and sex. *Death Education, 8,* 113–124.

McIntosh, J. L. (1985). Suicide among the elderly: Levels and trends. *American Journal of Orthopsychiatry, 55,* 288–293.

McIntosh, J. L., Hubbard, R. W., & Santos, J. F. (1981). Suicide among the elderly: A review of the issues with case studies. *Journal of Gerontological Social Work, 4,* 63–74.

Mehta, D., Mathew, P., & Mehta, S. (1978). Suicide pact in a depressed elderly couple: Case report. *Journal of the American Geriatrics Society, 26,* 136–138.

Miller, M. (1978a). Geriatric suicide: The Arizona study. *The Gerontologists, 18,* 488–495.

Miller, M. (1978b). Note: Toward a profile of the older white male suicide. *The Gerontologists, 18,* 80–82.

Miller, M. (1979). *Suicide after sixty: The final alternative.* New York: Springer.

Neugarten, B. L. (1968). The awareness of middle age. In B. L. Newgarton (Ed.), *Middle age and aging: A reader in social psychology* (pp. 93–98). Chicago: University of Chicago Press.

Neugarten, B. L., Havighurst, R. J., & Tobin, S. S. (1961). The measurement of life satisfaction. *Journal of Gerontology, 16,* 168–174.

Noyes, R., Frye, S. J., & Hartford, C. E. (1977). Conjugal suicide pact. *Journal of Nervous and Mental Disorders, 165,* 72–75.

Osgood, N. J. (1985). *Suicide in the elderly: A practitioner's guide to diagnosis and mental health intervention.* Rockville, MD: Aspen.

Osterweis, M., Solomon, F., & Green, M. (Eds.) (1984). *Bereavement: Reactions, consequences, and care.* Washington, DC: National Academy Press.

Peck, R. C. (1968). Psychological developments in the second half of life. In B. L. Neugarten (Ed.), *Middle age and aging: A reader in social psychology* (pp. 88–92). Chicago: University of Chicago Press.

Rando, T. A. (1985). *Loss and anticipatory grief.* Lexington, MA: Lexington Books.

Raphael, B. (1983). *The anatomy of bereavement.* New York: Basic Books.

Resnik, H. L. P., & Cantor, J. M. (1970). Suicide and aging. *Journal of the American Geriatrics Society, 18,* 152–158.

Rifkin, J., & Howard, T. (1980). *Entropy: A new world view.* New York: Bantam.

Robins, L. N., West, P. A., & Murphy, G. E. (1977). The high rate of suicide in older white men: A study testing ten hypotheses. *Social Psychiatry, 12,* 1–20.

Rockwell, D., & O'Brien, W. (1973). Physicians' knowledge and attitudes about suicide. *Journal of the American Medical Association, 225,* 1347–1349.

Santy, P. A. (1982). Observations on double suicide: Review of the literature and two case reports. *American Journal of Psychotherapy, 36,* 23–31.

Schaie, K. W., & Willis, S. L. (1986). *Adult development and aging* (2nd ed.). Boston: Little, Brown.

Schonfield, A. E. D. (1980). Learning, memory, and aging. In J. E. Birren & R. B. Sloone (Eds.), *Handbook of mental age and aging.* Englewood Cliffs, NJ: Prentice-Hall.

Seiden, R. H. (1981). Mellowing with age: Factors influencing the nonwhite suicide rate. *International Journal of Aging and Human Development, 13,* 265–284.

Sendbuehler, J. M., & Goldstein, S. (1977). Attempted suicide among the aged. *Journal of the American Geriatrics Society,* 245–248.

Stenback, A. (1980). Depression and suicidal behavior in old age. In J. C. Birren & R. B. Sloane (Eds.), *Handbook of mental health aging.* Englewood Cliffs, NJ: Prentice-Hall.

Stillion, J. M. (1984). Women and widowhood: The suffering beyond grief. In J. Freeman (Ed.), *Women: A feminist perspective* (pp. 282–296). Palo Alto, CA: Mayfield.

Stillion, J. M. (1985). *Death and the sexes: An examination of differential longevity, attitudes, behaviors, and coping skills.* Washington, DC: Hemisphere.

Stillion, J. M., White, H., McDowell, E. E., & Edwards, P. (1989). Ageism and sexism in suicide attitudes. *Death Studies, 13*(3), 247–261.

Toynbee, A. (1984). The relationship between life and death, living and dying. In E. S. Shneidman (Ed.), *Current perspectives* (3rd ed., pp. 8–14). Palo Alto, CA: Mayfield.

U.S. Bureau of the Census. (1988). *Statistical abstract of the United States: 1987.* Washington, DC: U.S. Government Printing Office.

Useui, W. M., Keil, T. J., & Durig, K. R. (1985). Socioeconomic comparisons and life satisfaction of elderly adults. *Journal of Gerontology, 40,* 110–114.

Wass, H. (1977). Views and opinions of elderly persons concerning death. *Educational Gerontology, 2,* 15–26.

Worden, J. W. (1982). *Grief counseling and grief therapy: A handbook for the mental health practitioner.* New York: Springer.

Young, D., Rich, C. L., & Fowler, R. C. (1984). Double suicides: Four model cases. *Journal of Clinical Psychiatry, 45,* 470–472.

7

Prevention, Intervention, Postvention

The man, who in a fit of melancholy, kills himself today, would have wished to live had he waited a week. Voltaire: "Cato," *Philosophical Dictionary*, 1764

No book on the subject of suicide can be considered complete if it does not address the general topic of suicide prevention. However, it is impossible to do justice to the subject in one chapter. Many fine books exist that are designed to increase the knowledge and skills of helping professionals who work with suicidal people. Because this is so, we have chosen to present an overview of the prevention, intervention, and postvention of suicide, with particular emphasis on developmental issues. The purpose of this chapter is to explore ways in which caring societies and individuals can reach out to those whose life trajectories put them at risk for suicide.

One of the guiding principles of this book is that suicide is an act that should be prevented whenever possible. This principle is based on the premises that human life is valuable and should not be taken prematurely and that suicide is not a desirable solution to problems of any kind. However, as we have seen in Chapter 1, not all people in every society across history have accepted these premises. Even today, there are voices that defend the individual's right to take his or her own life (Battin, 1984; Lester, 1969, 1970, 1987; Noyes, 1970; Szasz, 1986). Before we begin looking at methods for prevention, intervention, and postvention, we will review the case against suicide prevention as made by selected contemporary writers.

Lester (1987), for example, has argued that "completed suicide may be a desirable act for a person, given his life circumstances and expectations for the future. Furthermore, we all have to die, and it is important to consider what would constitute an appropriate death for a person" (p. 69). To illustrate his point, he cited the case of a terminally ill man who killed himself rather than face escalating pain and uselessness.

Battin (1984), a philosopher, has made a thoughtful case for rational suicide in four different situations. First, she noted that suicide may be considered to be rational when it meets the expectations of the society in which the individual lives. Thus, ancient Scandinavians practiced suicide because of their belief that it assured them of a place in Valhalla, a belief that seems to be echoed in modern times by some of the Moslem faith. A second basis for rational suicide, according to Battin, is avoidance of harm, such as the pain that attends certain terminal illnesses. A third type of rational suicide was characterized by Battin as "in accordance with fundamental interests." People who commit suicide for a belief or allow themselves to die for a cause provide examples of this type of rational suicide. Finally, Battin delineated a type of rational suicide that she called "expressive suicide," in which individuals kill themselves to express an emotion, such as remorse for some action that they have taken which they now find reprehensible. The suicide of Judas Iscariot illustrates this type of suicide.

Szasz, an original thinker in the field of psychology, has argued against suicide prevention for two reasons. First, suicide prevention often requires stripping people of their individual rights and compelling them against their will to remain alive. Second, it requires professionals to engage in "therapeutic paternalism," which violates the maxim that people are responsible for their own behavior. Szasz warned that therapists who are willing to take the responsibility for preventing suicide are open to lawsuits in cases where therapy fails and suicide occurs. He pointed out that "because, in fact, it is virtually impossible to prevent the suicide of a person determined on killing himself or herself, and because forcibly imposed interventions to prevent suicide deprive the patient of liberty and dignity, the use of psychiatric coercion to prevent suicide is at once impractical and immoral" (Szasz, 1986, p. 809). Szasz noted that because children are typically subject to paternalistic and coercive techniques, they should be exempted from this generally permissive policy. He did not, however, exempt people who might be psychotic, depressed, or otherwise mentally ill. Instead, he reminded his readers that people in the United States are considered sane until proven insane and therefore should be free to take their own lives unless they voluntarily seek treatment. He advocated that suicide should be given the "status of a basic human right" and that "power of the state should not be legitimately invoked or deployed to prohibit or prevent persons from killing themselves" (p. 811).

In spite of well reasoned arguments from authorities like Battin and Szasz, the evidence seems to be mounting that suicide is generally a highly ambivalent act committed by an individual who is reacting desperately to both external and internal circumstances in an attempt to avoid emotional pain. Shneidman's four general psychological features, which were mentioned in Chapter

When even despair ceases to serve any creative purpose, then surely we are justified in suicide. Cyril Connolly, *The Unquiet Grave*

5, shed light on the state of mind of many suicidal people. Most experience (1) an increase in their general troubled state, which Shneidman termed *acute perturbation*; (2) an increase in negative emotions such as self-hatred, guilt, shame, etc., which he called *heightened inimicability*; (3) a sharp, sudden constriction of the thinking processes marked by rigidity and the inability to consider multiple options; and (4) the continuing presence of the idea of cessation as the way to end emotional pain. What Shneidman described so well is what Freudian thinkers might designate as an imbalance between thanatos and eros in which thanatos has the upper hand. Such an imbalance, however, is temporary, and if suicidal action can be delayed until one or more of those four conditions abate, death need not occur. The belief that suicidal action is generally the product of a temporary, reversible, ambivalent state of mind is the basic tenet of crisis intervention centers worldwide.

Kiev (1984), adding his voice to those who advocate active intervention, has stated that "there is considerable evidence in the biological and neurophysiological work now going on at the National Institute of Health and elsewhere that fundamentally we are dealing with a stress-related phenomenon which has a biological basis. What one needs is time, a reduction of stress, or major antidepressant medications" (p. 28).

Regardless of whether one views suicidal behavior as stemming from convergent conditions in the environment, as a reflection of emotional problems, as a reaction to stress, or as evidence of a biological imbalance, the prevailing crisis intervention approach to suicide seems sound. In spite of eloquent arguments about rational suicide and the freedom of the individual, suicidal behavior seems to us to cost too much. It replaces one individual's pain with the pain of many survivors, and it cuts off potential growth while giving nothing in return. Therefore, we believe that in all but the most extreme cases of terminal illness, suicide prevention and intervention are warranted.

SUICIDE PREVENTION

There are at least three types of prevention that should be considered in any discussion of general suicide prevention. The first consists of attempts to ameliorate the societal conditions that lead to suicide. The second is general education directed at increasing children's ability to cope with life's stresses. The third type is education directed specifically toward suicide prevention. We will turn our attention first to the need to change social conditions that foster suicide.

Recommendations for Social Changes

The report of the National Task Force on Suicide in Canada, recognizing the need to ameliorate social conditions that lead to suicide, included seven specific recommendations aimed at de-

To wish for death is a coward's part.
Ovid, *Metamorphoses,*
4.1.115

creasing the suicide rate by changing social conditions (Health and Welfare Canada, 1987). These recommendations, although designed for the Canadian culture, seem equally applicable to the United States. They are as follows:

1. Mental health professionals should consult with the media when suicide occurs to decrease the modeling effect that has been shown to result from widely publicized suicides and thus decrease the likelihood of cluster or "copycat" suicides.
2. Mental health professionals and the media should work together to decrease the stigma attached to seeking help for suicidal ideation, to inform the public of the warning signs of suicide, and to increase the use of positive coping skills.
3. In keeping with the evidence that limited accessibility to methods of committing suicide leads to decreases in the suicide rate, "measures should be taken to reduce the lethality and availability of instruments of suicide" (p. 41). Specifically, the report called for more stringent gun control and control of medications as well as limited access to attractive hazards, such as high bridges.
4. Governments should provide assistance for universities and colleges to incorporate suicide prevention programs into their curricula for health care professionals.
5. Workshops on suicide prevention should be instituted for all personnel in custodial and correctional services.
6. Additional suicide prevention training materials directed to specific groups of helping professionals (e.g., physicians, clergy, teachers) should be developed by leaders in each group.
7. Teachers should be trained to detect and assess suicidal risk among their students and should be aware of community referral services for potential suicides.

In addition to the specific recommendations regarding prevention of suicide, this report is important because it highlights a nation's recognition of suicide as a major social problem and focuses on education as one of the most important tools for addressing that problem. In the United States, voices have also been raised suggesting that a new commitment to suicide prevention should be made. Selkin (1983) has pointed out that, since the suicidology branch of the National Institute of Mental Health was closed in 1973, the federal government has made only minimal contributions to suicide prevention. Selkin maintained that the U.S. government has endorsed and continues to endorse a number of public policies that promote suicide, including "free and easy access to handguns, lack of vocational and educational opportunity for youth, racial discrimination and divisiveness, moral condemnation of welfare benfits, and a philosophy of punishment for those convicted of crimes without accompanying concern for their human needs" (p. 10). Selkin recommended that a computer-based model of suicide prevention be developed that would include software that could be placed in every school and suicide prevention center to help diagnose, project a lethality rating, and recommend a followup schedule for suspected suicides.

Hudgins (1983), echoing some of Selkin's suggestions, called for more social changes to prevent suicide. He pointed out that the rise in suicide in the last 3 decades can be accounted for almost entirely by the rise in deaths caused by handguns. Explaining that suicide rates are lower in states that have strict handgun laws, Hudgins called for practical measures to decrease suicide, including adopting tighter gun control laws, limiting the number of prescription drugs given at one time, fencing dangerous high places, and, in general, making suicide less convenient.

Education for Coping

On a less global level, it is clear from the suicide statistics in the United States that our society is failing to teach young people (especially young white males) how to cope in a healthy fashion with the stresses inherent in living in a complex technological society. While an in-depth discussion of coping techniques is beyond the scope of this chapter, it is important to summarize the minimum content of a general curriculum designed to prepare young people to live out their full life spans.

First, students should be made aware of the complexities involved in living and of the inevitability of experiencing some failure, disappointment, and loss in life. Because caring adults want to protect children whenever possible from harsh realities, some children may come to adolescence with little expectation of encountering adversities in life and may therefore be unprepared to face such adversities. On the other hand, some children born into turbulent homes or growing up in conditions of poverty may face severe problems before having an opportunity to learn how to cope. Thus, there is a need to teach healthy coping techniques to children from both extremes. The school may be their last best chance to observe competent models and learn these important skills.

The way in which teachers handle failure experiences is particularly crucial. Students should be specifically taught not to internalize failure in such a way that they denigrate themselves and weaken their own self-esteem. Educators interested in developing positive coping techniques will help students to view failure as a form of feedback that can lead to future success and to view disappointment as a temporary state that can, with effort and understanding, lead to greater accomplishment.

Second, specific coping techniques should be explored with young people. Such exploration might include an examination of coping strategies presently used by students when they feel depressed. An exercise conducted recently with a group of academically gifted ninth graders yielded no less than 23 coping mechanisms they employed to help themselves feel better. Coping mechanisms mentioned frequently included exercising, eating, talking with friends, listening to music, writing out their feelings in diaries or in letters to friends, composing poetry, taking long walks, focusing on the pluses in their lives, and talking with parents, counselors, and other adults (Stillion, 1985). It is important to help students see that they already have a repertoire of coping techniques and therefore a base for developing stronger and more varied approaches to coping with stress.

Among the additional coping techniques that can be taught is the skill of critical thinking. Support for teaching critical thinking has been spreading during the 1980s. The rationale for teaching this skill is generally economic (i.e., our society needs people who are good problem solvers and who can critically analyze situations and products and can contribute new ideas). We believe that training in critical thinking is also training in flexible thinking. Cognitive constriction often accompanies suicidal thought patterns. Students who form a habit early of analyzing situations from a variety of perspectives, of asking appropriate questions, and of testing the realism of their own thinking are far less likely to settle easily into the cognitive inflexibility that focuses on suicide as *the* solution.

Encouraging students to develop a sense of humor is another technique for preventing suicide. People who can laugh at themselves and at many of life's problems are in a good position to avoid the deadly serious type of thinking involved in suicide. It is difficult to remain depressed if you can see humor in a situation. Young children generally appreciate humor. Interested adults and school curricula that build upon this natural appreciation for the humorous are inoculating children against suicide.

Helping children and adolescents to set high but attainable goals for themselves is another technique that promotes coping. In recent years, this technique has been shown to be associated with achievement in the classroom (Goode & Brophy, 1984). We think it is also a powerful deterrent to suicide. Young people, who experience a wide gulf between who they are and who they want to become, are at risk for low self-concepts, self-hatred, depression, and suicidal behavior. Helping adults can encourage growing children to set short-range, realistic goals and can support them as they work toward reaching these goals. Achievement enhances self-esteem and helps students appreciate their own worth and uniqueness.

As students come to view themselves as increasingly competent, they will be less likely to develop on the negative end of Erikson's latency stage, with its extremes of industry versus inferiority. In this way, achievement and competence become two powerful tools of suicide prevention.

Other skills that can be taught to children to help them cope with stress include specific techniques such as systematic relaxation, imagery techniques, meditation, and positive self-talk. All such techniques help students attain control over stress, and they also arm them with behavioral choices other than giving in to depressed or suicidal feelings.

Education for Suicide Prevention

The second major education need is for suicide prevention education. The public schools in the United States have always been expected to provide many services in addition to the education of our youth. In the past 30 years, however, the number of these special, nonacademic responsibilities has increased. The public schools have been asked to address concerns ranging from the mundane (e.g., a "swish and spit" program of oral hygiene) to the momentous (e.g., the racial integration of our society). During the 1980s, many school districts have been charged with the responsibility of developing curricula and procedures that will specifically address suicide prevention among children and adolescents in the United States.

At the beginning of the decade, few school-based suicide prevention programs existed. A few pioneer programs, such as those of the Cherry Creek school system in Denver and the Fairfax County public schools in Virginia, were in the process of being developed (Wiley, 1987). These programs have now become well established and are viewed as national models. By the mid-1980s, the increasing awareness of the growing adolescent suicide problem and the special risk of cluster suicides among this age group led to the rapid development of many school-based programs. Community health professionals, parent groups, legislators, and educators themselves lent their voices to the growing advocacy for suicide prevention programs in the public schools. Their requests gained in salience when parents of suicide victims in several states (e.g., California and Oregon) sued school districts over the lack of suicide prevention training for teachers. Although the legal issues regarding school liability are far from settled, a landmark decision in a federal court in 1985 held that parents of a youth suicide may sue a school if the death allegedly resulted from inadequate staff training in suicide prevention (*Kelson v. City of Springfield, Oregon* 767 F.2d 651 [Ninth Circuit Court of Appeals]). Also, legislation mandating the establishment of suicide prevention programs in the schools has been passed in at least six states: California, Florida, Louisiana, Maryland, New Jersey, and Wisconsin. Many other states, including Kentucky, Rhode Island, Missouri, Minnesota, Pennsylvania, and Oregon, have commissioned special task forces to study the youth suicide problem and to develop guidelines for suicide prevention to be used in developing programs for individual school systems.

In an attempt to discover how organized the increased interest in education for suicide prevention had become at the state level, we planned and carried out a survey of the 50 state superintendents of public instruction in the United States during the fall of 1987. The brief survey sent to these offices included questions concerning the development of materials and the availability of curriculum guidelines for teaching about suicide and questions about the development of policies and procedures for dealing with the response to a student suicide or suicide attempt among peers. Although the survey was primarily designed to gather information concerning activities at the state level, respondents were also asked to provide information concerning delegation of these responsibilities to individual school systems. The findings from the surveys, which were returned by 46 of the 50 state departments of public instruction, are summarized in Table 7.1.

Table 7.1 shows that although much ongoing suicide prevention activity exists in the public schools, responsibility for these activities falls heavily on individual school systems, with only limited direction from the state departments of public instruction. Only 37% of the state education offices provide individual school systems with materials for teaching about suicide, and only 20% provide curriculum guidelines for suicide prevention. The table also shows that even fewer statewide systems (11%) are involved in the development of policies and procedures for dealing with the student response to a suicide or a suicide attempt.

All state departments of public instruction were asked to include with the completed questionnaire a copy of any suicide prevention guidelines developed by their offices. We received such materials from only 15 states. Of the sets of guidelines received, 11 dealt specifically with suicide prevention and 4 contained general health curriculum guidelines.

The following outline provides a summary of the typical contents of the suicide prevention guidelines received from the state departments of public instruction.

TABLE 7.1   Suicide Prevention Activities of Statewide and Local School Systems in the United States

Prevention activities and materials	Provided by statewide education offices	Developed by individual school systems
1. Materials for teaching about suicide	17 (37%)	32 (70%)
2. Curriculum guidelines for suicide prevention	9 (20%)	35 (76%)
3. Policies and procedures for dealing with student response to a suicide crisis	5 (11%)	38 (83%)

I. Facts about youth suicide
   A. National statistics
   B. Statewide statistics

II. Curriculum development guidelines for teaching students
   A. The youth suicide problem
   B. Individual coping skills
   C. Helping and referral skills for use with friends

III. In-service training guidelines for school faculty and staff
   A. Prevention procedures
   B. Intervention procedures
   C. Postvention procedures

IV. Pupil services guidelines
   A. Identification of suicidal students
   B. Assessment of suicide risk
   C. Referral procedures
   D. Crisis response procedures

V. Appendix materials
   A. Descriptions of model programs
   B. Suicide prevention bibliography
   C. Suicide prevention media resources
   D. List of community resources
   E. Sample referral and reporting forms

Although the specific contents of these guidelines differed from state to state, most programs included guidelines for classroom instruction and for teacher and staff training workshops. The in-service training guidelines addressed issues associated with prevention, intervention, and postvention.

The materials from the state education offices included guidelines for pupil services also. The outline shows that the recommended guidelines included procedures for identification of suicidal students and risk assessment. Recommendations for risk assessment included using procedures such as the SAL method of inquiry with suspected suicidal youth (specificity of plan, availability of means, and lethality of method). The guidelines also included referral procedures (e.g., keep the student with a responsible adult, inform the parents). Finally, many guidelines included crisis response procedures to reduce the likelihood of cluster or copy cat suicides (e.g., establish a crisis management team before a tragedy occurs, meet with high-risk students in small groups or individually, designate one person to talk to the press).

In addition to curriculum, in-service training, and pupil services guidelines, the materials provided by the state departments of public instruction usually included descriptions of model programs, bibliographical material, a list of community resources,

referral and reporting forms, and a list of suicide prevention resources. A sample list of suicide prevention resources from the
Wisconsin Department of Public Instruction is included at the
end of the chapter.

As the contents of the above outline show, the suicide prevention program guidelines received from the state education offices were well prepared, complete, and very helpful for individual
school systems preparing their own programs. In spite of the quality of the materials received, however, the fact that so few state
departments of public instruction provide direction for individual
school systems is a matter of continuing concern. Too often individual school systems are mandated to develop comprehensive
programs to deal with the youth suicide problem without adequate directions and guidelines from the state. While respect for
the autonomy of individual school systems is praiseworthy, absence of direction from and lack of accountability to the state
education offices result in unevenness of quality and fragmentation of efforts.

Moving from the state level to the level of individual schools,
a special task force of the American Association on Suicidology
recently conducted a survey of 158 school-related suicide programs in the United States and Canada (Smith, Eyman, Dyck, &
Ryerson, 1987). The survey showed few differences between U.S.
and Canadian school-based suicide programs. In fact, the only
consistent difference found between programs in the two countries was one of emphasis. The Canadian programs tend to focus
on education while U.S. programs emphasize both education and
crisis intervention.

Sixty percent of the 158 school-related suicide prevention
programs surveyed included units about youth suicide designed
for teachers to use in classroom instruction. Although some programs included curricula for all 12 grades, the majority focused
on junior high school and high school students. Most curricula
emphasized giving students practical information, such as facts,
signs, symptoms, and referral sources. Most of the curricula also
included help in developing coping skills, such as the identification and acceptance of one's own feelings, and techniques for
responding to a friend's suicidal crisis. Approximately one-third
of the school-related suicide programs surveyed included an in-
structional component containing materials to be used with school
nurses, counselors, school social workers, and parents. One quarter
of the programs surveyed included a peer support component. The
"peer counseling" activities usually involved student-to-student
tasks designed to identify, stabilize, or refer troubled students.
These programs recommended instructing peer counselors in befriending, listening, identification, and referral skills. Approximately half of the training programs for peers were taught by
school personnel and approximately half by outside mental health
professionals. Seventy-three percent of the programs surveyed in-

cluded crisis intervention components for dealing with the aftermath of suicide or a suicide attempt. Most programs included a
crisis management team of four to seven individuals, who were
given specialized training. These teams reported that the majority
of their activities in a crisis situation involved dealing with other
students, especially those previously identified as being at risk.

The survey findings showed that many public school systems are heavily involved in positive suicide prevention activities.
The findings also showed, however, that there are a number of
weaknesses in the procedures used by many school-related suicide
prevention programs. For example, some of the peer support programs had no provisions for monitoring the participants' behavior.
Also, many of the peer counselors received no training in referral
procedures. A number of these well-intentioned suicide prevention programs that lack monitoring procedures have been implemented in ways that make them as potentially dangerous as helpful.

Perhaps the most widespread criticism of the school-related
suicide prevention programs surveyed is the absence of adequate
evaluation. Very few of the 158 programs included an evaluation
component. The few programs which did include evaluation components tended to emphasize skills learning rather than changes
in the incidence of suicidal behavior. Although the procedures
used in most suicide prevention programs seem likely to be helpful, their effectiveness has not been demonstrated empirically. It
is possible that many of the programs designed to reduce the
incidence of youth suicide may be ineffective or perhaps even
harmful.

A number of writers have recently criticized the current
"broad brush" approach to suicide prevention, in which groups
apply a variety of procedures at the same time without sound
theoretical bases and no measures of specific treatment-related
outcomes (Berman, 1987; Garland, 1987; Streiner & Adam, 1987).
The critics point out that specific outcome goals should be established for target groups. In addition, sound theories of suicide
prevention must be operationalized and implemented in a manner
that will allow the precise measurement of outcomes. Finally,
experimental procedures such as the randomized assignment of
subjects to various treatment conditions, the measurement of
clinically important outcomes, long-term followup, and statisti-
cally significant results must be employed (Streiner & Adam,
1987).

Because the liabilities and potential contributions of school-
related suicide programs are so great, there is a significant need
to develop standards for the content and supervision procedures
of these programs. Beginning efforts are underway to develop standards for school-related suicide programs. The American Association of Suicidology recently appointed a 26-member task force
to develop a model for suicide prevention programs in the nation's
public schools. This task force, composed of eminent suicidolo-

gists, educators, and researchers, met in a working session in 1987 at what has come to be called the Wingspread Conference. The final report of this task force will provide guidelines which should be helpful in both establishing and reviewing suicide prevention programs in the public schools.

It is important that school personnel not become overly discouraged by criticisms of current practice. As Cantor (1987) explained, we are in a crisis situation and our young people cannot wait. Progress has been made, in that some help is available where none existed 10 years ago. However, it is now time to refine our procedures through research, for this will lead to intervention strategies better able to achieve desired outcome goals.

Parents have been largely overlooked as a potential resource for suicide prevention in the past. Parents can help both as educators and by becoming educated. Survivors of Suicide (SOS) groups, many of whom are parents, have been organized in cities across the United States. Generally, members of these groups are willing to share their first-hand experience of suicide with other groups. Parent-Teacher Association (PTA) meetings are excellent opportunities for educating both parents and teachers about the realities of suicide and the methods of coping with suicidal behavior. Such programs ideally should be done by authorities in a well-planned series rather than one 30- to 60-minute session; this will ensure adequate time to discuss the complexities of child and adolescent suicide and give parents a chance to digest material and to raise questions that occur to them between sessions. Informed parents are invaluable as supporters of suicide education programs in the schools and as members of crisis intervention teams.

SUICIDE INTERVENTION

When prevention efforts fail, it is necessary to employ intervention techniques. The success of such techniques frequently depends upon the skill and commitment of caring adults. Often, suicidal people will make their intentions known to friends or relatives untrained in crisis intervention. In such cases, the untrained individual may be overwhelmed with the responsibility inherent in serving as a confidant. The following general principles are recommended by a variety of sources and designed to help untrained individuals respond to a person who may be suicidal (e.g., Berger, 1984; McBrien, 1983; Shaughnessy & Nystul, 1985).

At the outset, it is important to determine the seriousness of the suicide intent. Direct questioning is generally the quickest method to ascertain this. A thoughtful confidant will recognize the distress of the individual and build upon this recognition, for example, by making comments like the following: "I can see that you're very upset. How bad are you feeling? Bad enough to consider harming yourself?"

Despair, Robert Godfrey, 1984. Oil on linen, 84 x 43 in. (Courtesy of Blue Mountain Gallery, New York, New York and Art Gallery, Ltd., New Bern, North Carolina. Photograph by Cathryn Griffin.)

A positive response to the last question should lead the confidant to ask for specifics (e.g., "Have you considered how you would do it? When you might do it? Where?"). Obviously, the suicidal girl who has secured a gun and keeps it under her pillow or the man who has accumulated 100 barbituates and is planning to take them before his 60th birthday next month is at higher risk than the individual who expresses a death wish but has no clear plans for suicide. This process of assessing the current level of danger, sometimes called the *level of lethality*, is important in preventing suicide.

Having ascertained the immediate danger level, the untrained helper should ensure that the suicidal person is not left alone. Especially in cases of emotional upset, where impulsive action is likely, individuals should not be left alone even for brief periods until help can arrive. Victoroff (1983) gave an example of a woman hospitalized for physical and emotional problems who was left alone in a hospital room for the moment it took the attending physician to write the orders for transfer to a psychiatric wing. The woman jumped out the window to her death while the physician was standing just outside the room.

A final principle for untrained people dealing with potential suicides is to secure qualified help as soon as possible. Confidants should try to determine who would be most acceptable to their suicidal friend. Some of the types of referrals that can easily be made include referrals to medical doctors, psychologists, counselors, pastors, social service agencies, police and fire departments, and crisis intervention centers. The important thing is to contact some agency that can give support to the confidant and share the responsibility of staying with the suicidal person until ongoing professional help can be secured.

Crisis Intervention

One of the most helpful referrals that can be made is to a crisis intervention center. Such centers are staffed 24 hours a day and have volunteers specifically trained in suicide prevention techniques. Many centers are patterned on the model pioneered in Britain in 1953 by the Samaritans and established in the United States in 1958 by Shneidman and others.

The Samaritan organization, now part of a worldwide movement entitled *the Befrienders*, was begun by a group of volunteers in central London. It started as a 24-hour hotline center based on the principle of "one-to-one befriending." From the beginning, the principle of anonymity was respected, but individuals were free to drop into the center to talk without "being preached at, counseled or therapeutized" (Fox, 1984, p. 46). The centers adopted the principle of offering unconditional friendship without regard to race, class, or creed. Volunteers are still taught to be unshockable and nonjudgmental during 7 nights of preparation classes. The centers have a consultant available in both family medicine and psychiatry. Interestingly, the growth of the Samaritan centers in England coincided with a dramatic decrease in suicide. However, careful analysis of suicide rates in towns with Samaritan groups and towns that did not have such groups has revealed no significant differences in the incidence of suicide (Jennings, Barraclough, & Moss, 1978). Some authorities (e.g., Lester, 1987) have suggested that the overall decline in British suicide rates was caused by the detoxification of household gas, which occurred at the same time that the Samaritan chapter began to spread. Whatever the reason, the decrease in the suicide rate promoted acceptance of the crisis intervention model in many developed countries.

The American version of the crisis intervention center, as we saw in Chapter 1, emphasized research and community service as well as individual intervention. Indeed, much that we know about suicide, as well as many of our theories about it, has come from the seminal work begun at the Los Angeles Suicide Prevention Center. Figures to date in the United States do not show a clear pattern of suicide reduction in cities with suicide centers (Lester, 1971). Nevertheless, the availability of caring, trained volunteers who are willing to respond to suicidal people is a mark of a humane society.

Berger has described the work of a staff member in a crisis intervention center well. "The first task confronting the therapist in the phone contact situation is to keep the patient talking and then assess the lethality of the situation. The second task is to obtain some idea of the particular state of mind or of the diagnostic picture. The task is much different in dealing with one who is severely depressed than in dealing with a schizophrenic or an individual in a state of high panic. All of these will commit suicide, but each will respond differently to the kinds of communications that the therapist is likely to deliver" (Berger, 1984, p. 69). In addition to determining the state of mind of a potential suicide, it is important to identify the sex, family constellation, available support systems, level of religious commitment, recent loss history, and adequacy of past coping behaviors as soon as possible. From the point of view of this book, one of the most salient factors in determining how to work with a suicidal person is his or her developmental level.

Crisis intervention is not equivalent to suicide prevention. It at best buys time for the suicidal patient. Its goal is to defuse the current situation, ensuring time for subsequent ongoing therapy. In order to move from crisis intervention to therapy, Schoonover (1982), the director of an inpatient psychiatric unit, has recommended that an active and directive stance should be taken by the therapist. He further recommended that therapists of suicidal people remain maximally available to them, for example, by making home visits to nonhospitalized clients, by providing 24-hour telephone access, and by increasing availability for therapy sessions, especially during the acute crisis. Encouragement of client responsibility, mutual setting of time limits, and explicit setting of therapeutic goals are also recommended techniques for dealing with people in a suicidal crisis. Schoonover (1982) further suggested that specific techniques such as "correction of cognitive distortions and ventilation and labelling of feelings" are necessary for the treatment of many suicidal people (p. 54). He summarized the crisis approach to suicidal behavior as one that "refocuses the patient from intrapsychic issues to his actual roles and relationships in the world" (p. 55). While these general guidelines may be helpful as background, it is important to review the specifics of suicide in different age groups and note the special circumstances and techniques that may affect the course of intervention.

DEVELOPMENTAL ISSUES IN WORKING WITH SUICIDAL PEOPLE

Special Issues in Helping Suicidal Children

As we have seen in Chapter 3, suicide and suicide attempts have increased among children across the last 30 years. Pfeffer (1984a) has pointed out that, in spite of this documented increase, the statistics underestimate the extent of the problem for several reasons. First, many adults deny that children are capable of attempting suicide. Such denial may stem from the belief that children under age 10 cannot understand the finality of death and therefore cannot really knowingly attempt suicide. It may stem from a desire to avoid the anxiety and guilt that adults would feel if they admitted that children they know are attempting suicide. Or it may stem from the same general social pressures that result in underreporting of suicide at all ages—exacerbated by family pressures to withold the real cause of death. The basic parental imperative is to keep children safe. Parents whose children commit suicide may feel doubly guilty. Not only have they failed to keep their children safe, they have also failed to see the signs leading up to suicide and may even have contributed knowingly or unknowingly to conditions often associated with it. For these reasons, it is important that helping professionals be alert to the conditions associated with child suicide and be willing to help parents see that their children may be at risk.

My mother does not love me
I feel bad
I feel bad because she does not love me
I am bad because I feel bad
I feel bad because I am bad
I am bad because she does not love me
She does not love me because I am bad. R. D. Laing, *Knots*, 1970

Chapter 3 noted that the family situations of suicidal children are often turbulent and that depression is a frequent concomitant. Separation, divorce, death, parental psychopathology, and family violence, including physical and psychological child abuse, are all correlates of suicidal behavior in children (Pfeffer, 1984a). Parental depression and suicidal thoughts or attempts are also associated with an increased risk of suicide among children, as is childhood depression. Caring adults should be aware that depression in children may be expressed differently from the classical adult symptoms, which include appetite and sleep disturbances, sexual dysfunction, self-reproach, feelings of despair, and loss of pleasure in life. Although suicidal children may show many of the adult symptoms, they may also act out more, refuse to go to school or make failing grades in school, and become disobedient, self-mutilating, and aggressive toward others. These reactions represent unsuccessful attempts to cope with painful feelings of worthlessness, hopelessness, and helplessness. The use of these inappropriate coping techniques only increases the painful feelings, thus feeding into a downward spiral of emotions that may end in a suicide attempt.

Compounding the problem of treating suicidal children is the issue of children's understanding of death. As we have seen in Chapter 3, the bulk of developmental literature across the last 50 years shows that young children (under age 10) do not have a clear understanding of the finality of death. Because this is true, children may fantasize that suicide will replace the pain and depression they are experiencing with a more pleasurable state. Pfeffer (1984b) illustrated this kind of immature cognitive state in a discussion of the case of an 8-year-old boy who was hospitalized because of suicidal tendencies. When questioned closely, it became clear that the boy believed that he would be reunited with his loving grandfather, who had recently died, if he committed suicide. Furthermore, he thought suicide would provide escape from an extremely stressful family situation. Such incentives are often a part of children's fantasies about suicide. Adults working with at-risk children should explicitly determine what children think death is and what their expectations are for existence after death.

Another common fantasy children have about suicide is that suicide (like running away from home) will punish the parents. While this fantasy is undoubtedly true in most cases, the unspoken expectation among children is that, like Tom Sawyer, they will be around to witness the grief and remorse of survivors. Once again, an incomplete understanding of the finality of death might make suicide seem more tempting.

Suicidal action among children may also be a cry for help, an attempt to manipulate or control family members or friends, or the expression of a wish for relief from internal psychic pain. Since children do not have mature coping techniques, they may find themselves overwhelmed by their life circumstances and react with what may appear to be an impulsive suicidal action. Pfeffer (1984a) cautioned caregivers to review the entire life circumstances of suicidal children. She pointed out that suicidal children generally "have been enduring chronic, extreme external and intrapsychic stress, stimulation, and pressure" (p. 94). Since this is true, people working with suicidal children must either be competent in or have access to family therapy. From a family systems perspective, it is difficult, if not impossible, to effect change in a depressed, hopeless child unless parents and siblings become aware of the conditions causing the depression and are willing to work together to alter them.

Young children often have trouble expressing their emotions in words. Although they may be experiencing sadness, helplessness, and anxiety, they may be unable or unwilling to verbalize their feelings. Complicating their lack of verbal ability is the fact that many children, especially those from troubled homes, may feel insecure about exposing their home life. Therefore, helping adults working with suicidal children may wish to become familiar with several therapeutic approaches designed especially for children. Traditional play therapy (Axline, 1947) has a distinguished history, especially when used with younger children. Art therapy with children helps many to express strong emotions like hopelessness and despair that they might not be able to express in words (Alshuler & Hattwick, 1947).

Dream work with children is also an effective therapeutic approach. Rosenn (1982) reported the dream of a depressed and suicidal child as follows: "An 8½-year-old reported dreaming that the floor of his bedroom suddenly sank, leaving him hanging on an overhead lamp. He received an electrical shock and fell, leaving part of his arm attached to the light" (p. 204). Rosenn pointed out that the sinking floor could be interpreted as the "child's feeling of lack of support and groundedness in his family" and the loss of the arm might symbolize "the painful absence of a sustaining and anchoring relationship" (p. 205). Common themes appearing in dreams of depressed children include abandonment, emptiness, fragmentation, and loss, as well as generalized anxiety, physical punishment, and aggression.

Generally, dream therapy, art therapy, and play therapy are based on psychoanalytic theory. A major assumption underlying each of these types of therapy is that a child knows more than he or she can express and that expression of such knowledge not only helps the therapist understand the child's world but is curative in itself, because of the catharsis it brings. In order to become skilled in such therapeutic approaches, graduate study is required. However, unskilled, caring adults can often help a child to experience some relief from painful emotions simply by encouraging the child to express his or her emotions in play or in art work.

A final approach to working with suicidal children is closely related to cognitive theory (discussed in Chapter 2), namely, explicit teaching. Children are natural learners if emotional blocks can be removed. Indeed, many trained therapists describe their work as one-on-one teaching. Adults need to teach children coping techniques such as those mentioned earlier in this chapter. Such techniques, taken together, constitute what Jaco (1986) has called education for social functioning. In a thoughtful article on suicideproofing youths, Jaco emphasized the need to teach children to communicate effectively, to develop self-awareness of emotional states, and to increase their relationship skills, including such specifics as the ability to empathize and to analyze the effect of one's own behavior on others. Other elements of education for social functioning include the ability to solve problems, to see the connections between means and ends, to do realistic planning, to make decisions, and to take responsibility for one's own behavior. Each of these abilities will help children to cope more effectively and will decrease the likelihood of attempted suicide.

In summary, although suicidal behavior in childhood may appear to be impulsive, it is generally grounded in family conditions of turbulence, loss, and psychological or physical abuse. It is especially important in working with suicidal children to understand their developmental level (paying particular attention to their knowledge about death); to attend to family constellation and functioning; to help children find multiple ways for communicating their concerns and feelings; and to inventory children's coping skills. Specific techniques well suited for working with children include play therapy, art therapy, family therapy, dream analysis, and the specific teaching of positive coping skills.

Issues in Helping Suicidal Adolescents

Adolescence has long been recognized as a period of *sturm und drang* (storm and stress) (Hall, 1904). The statistics about adolescent suicide and suicide attempts reviewed in Chapter 4 reinforce this view and suggest that the stress associated with the period seems to be increasing rather than decreasing in today's society. People confronted by suicidal adolescents should remember that adolescence is a bewildering time, a time during which every aspect of the young person is undergoing radical change. Adolescents shed their childish bodies, often growing several inches in a single year. The growth spurt is accompanied by hormonal changes that produce the development of the primary and secondary sex characteristics, not all of which may be welcome. Many girls' bodies look and function like women's bodies long before their minds become equally mature. Menstruation, the threats of pregnancy and venereal disease, and methods for responding to male advances are only some of the issues that adolescent girls face. Boys also face issues involved with becoming sexually active, but in addition, for most boys, there is relatively more pressure to perform sexual feats and to explore the riskier aspects of what is viewed as the adult world in order to prove their masculinity. High-risk behaviors like speeding, indulging in cigarettes, alcohol, or hard drugs, and practicing unsafe sex are often norms of the male adolescent culture.

Hormonal changes in adolescence also affect the brain, and young people may find their newly established cognitive skills to be a mixed blessing. Now that they can reason at the formal operational level, they are confronted with the complexities of the world. No longer is this a safe world of right and wrong, black and white, unquestioned obedience to law and order. Now they see the technicolor adult world. Many adolescents are both attracted by its promises of freedom and independence and afraid of its demands. Also, as we discussed in Chapter 4, their newly developing capability for hypothetical thinking allows adolescents to dream of idealized worlds and creates the opportunity for disillusionment with the world as it is.

In addition to the physical and cognitive changes, there is pressure on many adolescents to become independent of their families—to choose careers, to excel in school, athletics, and so on. This pressure and the attendant stresses are not new to today's adolescent. What is new is that they are occurring against a background of loss and lack of support unprecedented in modern history.

Today's young people are not strangers to loss and the insecurity it causes. Many have experienced divorce and the accompanying loss of one full-time parent. In addition, many have moved several times during childhood, losing friends as well as familiar places and routines with each move. Another area of concern is the knowledge possessed by young people about nuclear issues. Research shows that American youngsters, like their European counterparts, know much about nuclear threat by the time they are 10 years of age (Blackwell & Gessner, 1983; Stillion, 1986; Stillion et al., 1988). This knowledge shatters their illusion of safety and adds to the insecurities inherent in the adolescent period. All of these factors need to be kept in mind when working with suicidal adolescents.

Many of the therapeutic techniques used with children, such as art therapy and family therapy, also work well with adolescents. The evidence suggests that adolescent suicide often occurs within the context of a dysfunctional family. Therefore, a reexamination of family structure and function, an inherent part of the family systems therapy approach, is particularly helpful. In addition, many adolescents experience real relief from stress and depression by expressing themselves in writing. Keeping journals or sharing poetry are often helpful adjuncts to therapy. Psychodrama is also a natural therapeutic approach at this time, since teenagers almost universally experience a heightening of egocentrism (Elkind, 1967; Inhelder & Piaget, 1958). One result of this increase in egocentrism is the creation of an imaginary audience, which makes adolescents feel highly self-conscious. They are themselves on center stage and think that everyone watches and judges their appearance, behavior, and achievements. Research has shown that such self-consciousness peaks around age 13 for girls and age 15 for boys (Elkind & Bowen, 1979; Gray & Hudson, 1984). Because adolescents are used to performing for an imaginary audience, however, most will easily understand and accept the principles involved in psychodrama.

Adults working with at-risk adolescents may also want to avail themselves of the power of the peer group. One of the ironies of adolescence is that, as young people try to become independent of their families, they become increasingly dependent on their peer group for understanding and support. This interdependence strengthens the power of the group as a technique for reaching adolescents. Elkind (1967) has suggested that many adolescents create for themselves a "personal fable," a script in which they feel unique and misunderstood, and, at the same time, indestructible. Group work helps to counteract the intensive feelings of separateness, uniqueness, and aloneness that adolescents often experience, because one of the key healing elements in group therapy is experiencing universality (Yalom, 1975). Adolescents in a group cannot avoid the realization that many others in the group share their feelings and concerns. This insight, coupled with the support, warmth, respect, concern, and positive interactions that occur in well-run groups, may bring about more positive change in less time than many other therapeutic techniques used with adolescents.

In late adolescence and young adulthood, a significant number of persons are involved in higher education. In recent years, the typical college student, aged 18–22, has been joined by increasing numbers of adults over 30, raising the average age of college students to the late 20s on many campuses. Older groups have been shown to have higher suicide rates, as we have seen in preceding chapters. However, the college years provide a final opportunity for society to offer systematic education for suicide prevention. In addition, since colleges and universities must cope with suicide attempts and completions, they should be in a position of leadership with respect to other segments of society in developing models of suicide prevention, intervention, and postvention. Because of the important roles that institutions of higher learning play in the lives of older adolescents and young adults, we conducted a study to determine what is currently happening on college and university campuses with regard to education for suicide prevention and how colleges and universities react to suicide attempts and completed suicides on their campuses.

College Suicide Study

Letters and questionnaires were sent to the vice-presidents of student affairs at a number of colleges and universities throughout the United States. The two-page questionnaire included questions about the types and numbers of courses devoted to suicide prevention; noncredit types of suicide prevention education; procedures followed when a suicide is threatened, attempted, or completed; and an estimate of the numbers of suicide attempts and completions occurring on campus each year.

In order to ensure a representative sample of colleges and universities in the United States in the fall of 1987, we purchased a list of all such institutions from the American Council on Education. The list was subdivided into six categories of schools based on school type and size: (1) 2-year private, (2) 2-year public, (3) 4-year private (small), (4) 4-year public (small), (5) 4-year private (large), (6) 4-year public (large). In the categories which had many schools, we selected at random two schools from each state. The two categories of large schools did not have sufficient schools to permit random selection by state, so all schools in these categories were used. A total of 659 questionnaires were distributed. Completed returns were received from 262 institutions, for a response rate of 40%. Letters were addressed to vice-presidents of student affairs and were accompanied by the two-page questionnaire described above.

Table 7.2 shows the number of responses received for each category of school. It is clear that the largest number of responses came from large 4-year public institutions and the smallest number from the large 4-year private institutions.

In response to the question about courses offered for credit, only 26 (10%) of the institutions offered any courses dealing with suicide prevention, and only 1 institution offered a course that included the word *suicide* in the title. That course was Suicide and Society and was offered by a large 4-year public institution. The other courses "aimed at the prevention, intervention, or postvention of suicide" were identified as follows: Death and Dying, Crisis Intervention, Pastoral Counseling, Stress Management, Health, Nursing, Sociology, Psychology, Stress Management, and Helping Relationships. It is obvious that there is little or no organized course work devoted exclusively to suicide prevention being offered at this time by our nation's institutions of higher education. Instead, where the subject of suicide is addressed at

TABLE 7.2 Numbers and Types of Institutions Responding to a Suicide Survey

Type of Institution	Number in U.S.	Number of institutions receiving surveys	Number of institutions returning surveys	Percentage of total institutions responding
Two-year private	356	109	20	6%
Two-year public	972	133	38	4
Four-year private (small)	1,291	117	45	3
Four-year public (small)	445	130	59	13
Four-year private (large)	26	26	9	35
Four-year public (large)	144	144	91	63
Total	2,359	659	262	11

all within the curriculum, it appears as a unit within more general courses.

The picture looked considerably brighter regarding the question about other services on campus that deal with suicide prevention. Of those responding to this question, 111 (43.4%) offered groups through the campus counseling center and 131 (51.2%) provided groups through the local mental health center. The importance of suicide prevention for the responding institutions was reflected in the facts that 60.2% of the respondents said they sponsored in-service training for their professionals and 63.8% said they sponsored in-service training for their staff personnel. Almost 65% of the responding institutions reported using multiple community referrals in addition to campus resources in their suicide prevention services.

When asked to describe the units that were responsible for responding to a suicide attempt within the campus community, the four most frequently named were counseling, student development, security, and health services. Generally, all of these units were used in combination. This study showed that in the case of attempted suicide on campus, all relevant university units tend to work cooperatively and to respond quickly and responsibly.

The procedures described in the case of an attempted or threatened suicide varied widely. By far the most common response was to refer for counseling, often in conjunction with notifying some administrative office on campus ($n = 162$, or 62%). Fifty-three schools (20%) mentioned hospitalization as a routine option, 21 (8%) mentioned security, and 26 (9%) mentioned some type of administrative action, including administrative withdrawal of the student. Parents were informed of attempts or threats by only 16 colleges (6%).

In the case of very serious suicide attempts or completed suicides, medical personnel and the police usually became more involved. Police were mentioned 58 times (22%) either alone or in conjunction with other helping agencies. Medical facilities and personnel, including college health services, mental health personnel, hospital emergency rooms, paramedics, and hospitals, were mentioned 88 times (34%) as first-line resources, often in conjunction with other services. It was clear in these more serious cases that higher education in general acts in socially responsible ways. Even in these cases, however, families were notified by only 60 of the schools reporting (23%). This low rate of family notification probably reflects a change in the status of students. Since the 1960s, when the doctrine of *in loco parentis* (in place of parents) was struck down by the courts, institutions of higher learning have treated students as adults. Thus, in the case of serious or fatal suicide attempts by students, families are generally notified by civil authorities, just as they are when middle-aged or older adults attempt or commit suicide. Thirty-seven institutions (14%) confronted by serious suicide attempts reported taking administrative action (generally withdrawing the student).

Most reporting institutions indicated that postvention procedures were in place for responding to a completed suicide. Almost 57% of the institutions reported that they had an organized procedure for dealing with the victim's family, 56% had a procedure for the victim's close friends, 50% had a procedure for acquaintances, and 31% had a procedure for the student body as a whole. As expected, smaller schools more often reported a campuswide response, such as a campuswide memorial service. Types of responses included attendance at the funeral by university officials, sending flowers, holding memorial services, writing to families, offering support groups, and using outreach services (e.g., brochures, educational programs, newspaper articles, hall meetings). The majority of institutions reporting seemed to understand the need for addressing the topic of suicide with those groups most at risk (e.g., close friends and those sharing the same housing facilities) and seemed to be willing to use campus resources in working with these groups. Some respondents indicated awareness of "cluster suicides," while others spoke of the need to lessen the modeling effect on other at-risk students.

The number of suicide attempts reported by the respondents ranged from a low of 0 per year to a high of over 100 per year, with the highest frequencies reported by the largest institutions. Almost 31% of the colleges responding ($n = 81$) reported no attempts each year. The mode was 1 attempt and the median was 14 attempts per year. The number of completed suicides reported ranged from 0 to 7 per year, with a mode of 1 and a median of 3. It is obvious from the frequencies reported that neither attempted nor completed suicides are major problems for most of the institutions reporting. Nevertheless, most colleges are aware of the seriousness of suicidal behavior on campus and are prepared to respond in an organized way to suicidal threats or action.

The findings of our study parallel those of a smaller study (Webb, 1986). This study sampled 50 colleges and universities in upper New York State in the fall of 1984. The 25 schools responding reported 15 suicides and 108 attempted suicides during the 3-year period preceding the study. The awareness of possible "ripple effects" was a major factor in the postvention efforts by the respondents in this study. The colleges in general had professional people on the staff who were trained in suicide prevention, intervention, and postvention. The authors of the study recommended that all colleges prepare written guidelines to be used by campus personnel in cases of attempted or completed suicide. They also recommended annual training sessions for residence hall and other support staff personnel and for peer counselors. They suggested that the content of the training should include information about depression, presuicidal behavior, and normal grieving reactions and provide guidelines for referral. We would add the following to their list of information needed by college staff people: myths and facts about suicide, signs and signals specific to suicidal behavior, information about cluster suicides, and specific guidelines for dealing with persons in acute suicidal states.

In summary, postsecondary institutions have an important role to play in responding to suicidal behavior exhibited by the older teenagers and young adults enrolled on their campuses. While most colleges seem to understand the importance of the topic (as evidenced by staff development programs on suicide prevention), very little suicide prevention education seems to be occurring at the postsecondary level. Given the increasing rates of suicide throughout adulthood and the fact that college represents the last organized educational opportunity for many in our culture, it would seem important to find ways to include the topic of suicide in required courses in the college curriculum. Such courses as Health, Human Behavior, Introduction to Psychology, and Introduction to Sociology would be appropriate vehicles for suicide prevention education at the postsecondary level.

Issues in Working with Suicidal Young Adults

For the many young adults who did not attend institutions of higher learning, as well as for those who did, the period between ages 25 and 34 is marked by major life decisions. Commitments to work, to a spouse and family, and to a life-style are all initially made and often re-evaluated at least once during these years. Sheehy (1976) called the common re-evaluation that occurs around age 30 "catch 30," and she suggested that many young adults use this period to reflect upon their accomplishments to date and to chart a new course or re-commit to their earlier decisions.

There are three special issues that helping professionals should recognize when working with suicidal young adults. The first is the continuing need for young adults to prove their independence and competence to the world. This need may inhibit young adults from seeking required help, and it may even add to the suicide statistics of that age group, especially in the case of males, since it will motivate attempters to make sure their suicide attempts are successful. In U.S. culture currently, competence tends to be judged by the person's position at work and by the amount of money earned. Therefore, young adults may experience increased stress levels as they accept external definitions of their worth in terms of salary and job titles. In pursuing success as defined for them, they may become workaholics or compulsive spenders. Debt incurred during the early adult years in an effort to authenticate success often merely adds to the stress of that period. As one 26-year-old told his therapist, "It seems I work to pay for things that I don't have time to use. I look around my apartment and it's filled with *things*, nice things, but they don't make me happy. I hate my job. I have no time to make friends and, until I decided to see you, I had no one to talk to. I don't understand it.

I've got what everyone says is a good job. I've got money and lots of things, but none of it seems to really matter. If this is all there is to life, why bother?" People in the helping professions may have to be extremely sensitve in order to detect suicidal predispositions in young adults and to get them to discuss their problems openly.

Second, sexuality issues may impede therapy, especially group therapy, during this period. Because interest in the opposite sex is at a peak during young adulthood, and because young adults typically review life choices (e.g., their choice of a spouse), group therapy for suicidal young adults may be more difficult than for adolescents and older adults. Young adults may not be willing to expose suicidal weaknesses to those whom they might regard as potential mates. In addition, young adults often need more privacy than do adolescents. For these reasons, helping professionals may want to discuss the relative merits of group and individual therapy with young adults before deciding on the type of referral.

The third major issue to be considered in working with suicidal young adults is the issue of parenting. The years between 20 and 34 have traditionally been the peak parenting years in the United States. While the trend in recent years has been toward having babies at a later age, parenting concerns remain major sources of anxiety during the young adult years. For some couples, the anxiety stems from wanting children and being unable to conceive, with accompanying feelings of inadequacy and loss. For others, anxiety and division may occur when one mate wants children while the other does not. Still others may experience disruption at the birth of a child, especially if the mother experiences postpartum depression. Other couples may adjust to the addition of an infant easily only to find their lives increasingly strained as the child matures and arguments ensue over child-rearing practices. All of these conditions related to parenting require special consideration from helping professionals. Couples therapy or family therapy are referral alternatives when a suicidal young adult identifies the area of parenting as a major source feeding into his or her suicidal ideations. Suicidal young adults also need to be taught about the long-term effects of completed suicide on loved ones, especially children, a point that will be covered in depth in the section on postvention.

Issues in Working with Suicidal Middle-Aged Adults

As we have seen in Chapter 5, there are many issues adults must struggle with between the ages of 25 and 64. Such issues include redefining their identities, finding ways to be nurturant and creative, and developing a positive philosophy of life. However, the central issue of middle age, beginning as a whisper in the busy years of young adulthood but gradually increasing to a roar in late middle age, is that of continuing to be generative in the face of mounting losses.

Losses are frequent throughout the middle adult years. Primary losses (those that cannot be avoided) include the loss of one's youthful appearance (as a result of getting wrinkles, gray hair, etc.), the weakening of muscles, and the development of problems with sight and hearing. Many people develop chronic illnesses, which cause pain and a further loss of physical functioning. Such chronic illnesses may necessitate medications, which sometimes have side effects that increase anxiety or depression. Physical losses are paralleled by others, such as the loss of the young dreams of high achievement and the loss of the parenting role. Often there are still other losses, including divorce and the deaths of parents, siblings, and friends. Yet another loss of midlife is the loss of time remaining; research indicates that a central factor in midlife crises is a sense of time running out.

Helping professionals working with suicidal adults should consider taking a loss history. Such a history generally includes a listing of all losses that an individual has experienced, the age at which the loss occurred, the effect the loss had on the individual, and the methods and resources the individual used to cope with the loss. Loss histories help not only in assessing the burden of cumulative loss suffered by the suicidal adult but also in pinpointing past coping skills and available resources.

Since middle age is also the time of menopause, suicidal females may respond well to drugs, including estrogen therapy. Therefore, it is essential for helping professionals working with middle-aged adults to be aware of the drugs being used by their clients and to work in close communication with their clients' medical doctors.

Helping professionals should also attend to the middle-aged person's level of sociability. Many middle-aged people have difficulty beginning new relationships. During their early adult years, they may have been so busy with their careers and families that little time was available for investing in friendships. Many find themselves lonely at age 50—with their children grown and friends from their youth dead or living elsewhere. For these individuals, group therapy may prove very effective, since groups provide opportunities for practicing rusty interpersonal skills in addition to providing specific therapeutic benefits. However, helping professionals should expect to find initial resistance to the idea of working within a group setting.

As shown in Chapter 5, alcohol abuse is often associated with suicide among middle-aged adults. Alcoholism and its related problems tend to exacerbate the losses of this stage of development, particularly those losses associated with health, occupation, and family. Alcoholics Anonymous, a worldwide organization, has experienced a great deal of success in helping alcoholics to stop drinking. It is also likely that the group support and social interaction provided by the weekly meetings and the 24-hour emergency services of this organization significantly reduce suicide among alcholics.

Helping professionals working with middle-aged adults are also more likely than those who customarily work with younger people to encounter patients who are considering suicide because of life circumstances not realistically changeable. By the time adults have reached the middle years, many have developed chronically painful, life-threatening conditions; experienced overwhelming failure; or are facing imminent death. Adults who are terminally ill present special challenges to helping professionals. Because this is true, it is doubly important that helping professionals are very clear about their own attitudes toward suicide.

Barry (1984) has suggested that all helping professionals need to be aware of the "cultural, personal, and professional baggage we bring into suicide-related situations" (p. 17). He described eight different positions that helping professionals may take with regard to suicide, including viewing suicide as a cry for help or as heresy, sin, tragedy, duty, an act of cowardice or heroism, a threat to one's own professional reputation and feelings of competence, or a rational solution to an otherwise insoluble problem. We would agree with Barry that helping professionals, particularly those working with suicidal middle-aged and elderly adults, need to be very clear about their own views of suicide and honest about these views with the people with whom they work. Without such honesty, the helping relationship may easily become colored by the biases of the therapist and may actually result in clashing values obstructing the therapeutic process.

Is it Sin.
To rush into the secret
house of death
Ere death doth come to
us? Shakespeare, *An-*
thony and Cleopatra

Although not specifically addressing suicide, Weisman (1972) introduced the concept of appropriate death as a goal to be achieved whenever possible. Appropriate death was defined as death that is consistent with the way in which someone has lived, the kind of death that the individual would choose if in control of the conditions of his or her death. Obviously, such a definition includes the possibility of suicide, especially for those who are painfully and terminally ill. Nelson (1984) has suggested that there might be "circumstances under which mental health professionals might consider the option of death as appropriate to the individual who wishes to die and, having done so, neutrally stand aside or not actively intervene in the termination of that person's life" (p. 177). While such a position is likely to be viewed as extreme by most of the mental health community, Nelson maintains that for some people suicide may be a realistic choice. For helping professionals working with middle-aged clients whose lives may appear to be barren of satisfaction and full of pain, whose coping skills may be negligible or totally exhausted, and for whom the future may in reality be limited and bleak, the question of the morality of suicide becomes salient.

A final problem facing professionals working with middle-aged adults is related to the change in time perspective that we discussed in Chapter 5. Many middle-aged individuals do not believe they have much time remaining. They also feel that, because their present problems are the result of many years of ineffective coping, the time remaining is not adequate to improve their life situation substantially. In addition, many middle-aged adults experience a decrease in energy levels. As one wag put it, "Middle age is the time when a man is always thinking that in a week or two he will feel as good as ever." More seriously, perceptions of middle-aged people that their accumulated problems cannot be resolved within the remaining time and with their energy levels are significant factors that must be addressed by any helping professional working with suicidal individuals in this age group.

Issues in Working with The Suicidal Elderly

Of all suicidal patients, those over 65 may be the most difficult to work with, for various reasons. As we have seen in Chapter 6, elderly people tend to be devalued in our culture. The suicide of a 70-year-old seems infinitely less sad to many than the suicide of a 17-year-old. Common wisdom holds that the 70-year-old had a chance at life while the 17-year-old never really did. Such "commonsense" assumptions undoubtedly affect the way elderly people view their own suicides and, perhaps as important, the way caregivers react or fail to react to suicidal signs among the elderly. Osgood, Brant, and Lipman (1988–1989) documented that suicide among elderly people living in nursing homes was more than 4 times the rate reported among elderly people living independently. Such a finding highlights the need for increased awareness of the following special issues relating to suicide among the elderly.

The first issue concerns case-finding procedures. The elderly are overrepresented among suicides but underrepresented among the clientele of suicide prevention centers (Farberow & Moriwaki, 1975; Rachlis, 1970; McIntosh, Hubbard, & Santos, 1981; Resnik & Cantor, 1970). Because the elderly do not use hot lines and other conventional services, a number of writers have recommended establishing special suicide intervention centers for the elderly that would be staffed with older counselors and be in locations frequented by the elderly (Farberow & Moriwaki, 1975; McIntosh, Hubbard, & Santos, 1981; Rachlis, 1970; Resnik & Cantor, 1970). New case-finding methods are needed with outreach programs in order to provide services before tragedies occur (Butler & Lewis, 1977; McIntosh, Hubbard, & Santos, 1981).

The second issue concerns depression. Depression is easily the most prevalent mental illness among elderly people (Butler & Lewis, 1982). It is more likely to go untreated in this age group, either because the depressive symptoms are confused with those of normal aging or because of fear that the treatment may interact with other drugs the elderly person is taking. Nevertheless, the relationship between depression and suicide documented in other age groups is just as real for the elderly, and it undoubtedly contributes to the very high suicide rates among people over age 65. Helping professionals working with this age group must work in close cooperation with medical doctors to ensure that underlying symptoms of chronic depression are treated.

A third issue that should be recognized when working with the elderly concerns cumulative loss. Chapter 6 reviewed the normative losses elderly people endure, including physiological losses, losses of interpersonal relationships, the loss of meaningful activity, the loss of roles in life, and the loss of status. While losses may occur at any time during the life span, they are the rule rather than the exception in old age. Therefore, the elderly find themselves dealing with cumulative losses. They often do not have time to work their way through grief over one loss before they are confronted with another loss. In addition, loss may breed loss. A woman whose husband dies may give up her home to move in with her daughter. In giving up her home, she loses her independence, the security of a well-known routine, her neighbors, and her roles as home owner and hostess. Thoughtful helping professionals working with suicidal elderly people should consider taking a loss history. Such a history will show the extent of loss a person has suffered and the timing of the losses. It will also, in the hands of a sensitive professional, help the elderly person to understand why he or she may be feeling depressed and to identify (and perhaps mobilize) coping techniques used in the past.

Sensory deficits have also been shown to be related to depression among elderly people. Butler and Lewis (1982) have pointed out that failing eyesight and hearing add further to the social isolation elderly people experience. Even in the midst of a warm, supportive family, a person who cannot see or hear is not a part of the scene. Loss of taste is another normative change among elderly people. Since the loss of taste makes eating less pleasant, elderly people may eat less or may eat only certain types of food. Helping professionals should observe the eating habits of elderly persons, since preliminary evidence suggests that nutritional status may be related to depression.

Elderly people also often suffer from a lack of touching. Living alone or in impersonal nursing homes, many elderly people go for weeks or months without the loving touch of a caring human being. In recent years, a variety of programs have been started to address the essential loneliness of the elderly. Some programs match young children with elderly in nursing homes. Young children tend to be spontaneous in touching as well as naturally social and curious. Such programs can be mutually beneficial, since they help children understand and accept the aging

*When all the blandish-
ments of life are gone
The coward sneaks to
death, the brave live
on.*
Martial, *Epigrams*

process and at the same time decrease the isolation and loneliness of the elderly. There are many other examples of intergenerational programs designed to build social ties between the elderly and other segments of society and thus combat loneliness in elderly people. For example, the Elder Neighbor program in western North Carolina promotes healthy interaction by assigning volunteers to call or visit elders at specific times each day. The national Meals on Wheels program provides both nutrition and social contact for homebound elders. A program called "Age-Link" attempts to match healthy elders with school-age children during after-school hours in order to meet the needs of both groups for positive social interaction. Other programs, like Daniel Levitan's exercise program at the University of Maryland, promote intergenerational socializing while developing healthy habits of exercise and nutrition. One San Francisco-based program designed specifically to prevent elderly suicide has created a "Friendship Line" for the elderly, which is staffed by volunteers on a 24-hour basis. These volunteers take calls from and place calls to elders, and they also disseminate information about elderly suicide to a wide range of professional groups. Most communities have programs like these available. Anyone working with suicidal elderly should examine community resources and make appropriate referrals. Perhaps the most important question that can be asked an older suicidal person is, "What differences would have to occur in your life to make you feel that life is worthwhile again?"

Finally, helping professionals working with suicidal elderly persons should be aware of what Erikson called the task of developing ego integrity instead of despair and disgust. Elderly suicidal people frequently are on the negative end of this bipolar continuum. They have lived most of the years they can expect to live, and now, as they review them in their minds, they find little meaning or value in them. Butler and Lewis (1982) have described an approach called reminiscence therapy, which provides an opportunity for elderly people to search for themes that once gave meaning to their lives. Done individually or in groups, reminiscence therapy involves evoking memories about specific events in younger years; these memories help elderly people to focus on times when their self-esteem was higher and their self-concepts were more positive than currently. Reminiscence therapy can also help elderly people to validate their existence by highlighting their past ability to cope and their survivorship. In addition, if the suicidal elderly can be helped through reminiscence to discuss critical events in their lives and the meanings of those events, they may be helped to see patterns of values in their lives. Finally, reminiscence therapy may help alleviate some of the hopelessness suicidal elderly experience by helping them to take pride in past accomplishments. Although called reminiscence therapy, this approach is more a technique than a full-blown therapy, and it can be used by caring individuals without intensive training. The power of the technique can be seen in the following story, which was told to the authors by the social worker involved.

Ms. Benson was a social worker who often led groups of elderly people in remininscence therapy. She was asked to include in a new group an elderly widow, Mrs. Langley, who had become depressed and almost totally nonresponsive to people in her nursing home. Ms Benson formed a group of eight elderly widowed women that met in the "parlor" of the nursing home twice a week. Ms. Benson started each session by playing music from earlier times. She encouraged the women to share their memories of those times. In one session she suggested they talk about their wedding days. In other sessions she suggested they discuss the birth of their firstborns, the ways in which they coped during the Depression, the day World War II ended, and so on. Mrs. Langley tended to sit passively through the sessions, sometimes weeping quietly. When Ms. Benson played the song "Don't sit under the apple tree with anyone else but me" to begin the session on memories of World War II, Mrs. Langley began to cry and then to talk about her life during the war, her marriage to a naval officer, and her work with the U.S.O. From that time on, she participated actively in the sessions.

When all the sessions were over, the social worker talked to Mrs. Langley in private. She said, "I envy you. Here I am at 30, just starting out. I don't know if I'll accomplish anything in the next 50 years or if I'll stick to my principles and live a productive life. There you are, almost 80 years of age. You've raised four children, been active in your church and community, did so many good things, were a part of so much history, and you did it all with such patience and caring."

Mrs. Langley just smiled.

A major element for success in working with the suicidal elderly is respect. All caregivers must sincerely respect the life experiences of elderly persons and help them retain or develop respect for their own life histories. As Erikson defined it, ego integrity, the last stage in positive mental health, consists of the elderly realizing that they had only one life to live and that, considering their opportunities, they lived it pretty well. Anyone who comes to that realization is unlikely to commit suicide. On the other hand, people who reach old age deprecating themselves and finding little meaning in their lives are prime candidates for suicide. Despair and hopelessness undoubtedly contribute to the elderly suicide statistics. Caregivers would do well to remember that when elderly people attempt suicide, they are much more likely to complete it than are younger people. In addition, caregivers may have less warning about elderly suicides. Elderly people who choose suicide generally do so without fanfare. Any suicide threat by an elderly person must be taken very seriously. For these reasons, caregivers who work with elderly people must be positive forces in promoting a sense of ego integrity and combatting a sense of despair and disgust if the elderly suicide statistics are to decrease in the future. Finally, the promotion of integrity among the elderly necessitates more and better public education. There needs to be greater awareness of the special stresses experienced by the elderly and their special vulnerability to suicide. Perhaps most important, there is a great need to foster among all age groups cultural attitudes toward the elderly that are more positive.

POSTVENTION

The final topic to be discussed in this chapter is postvention. Shneidman (1984) has defined postvention as consisting of "activities that reduce the aftereffects of a traumatic event in the lives of the survivors. Its purpose is to help survivors live longer, more productively, and less stressfully than they are likely to do otherwise" (p. 413). The term postvention is used in the literature to refer to two slightly different types of actions taken after death by suicide; one is diagnostic and the other is therapeutic.

The first and less well-known type of postvention is intended to determine that the cause of death was suicide. At its best, this type of postvention involves securing the services of a suicide team that will investigate the circumstances around an equivocal death to determine if suicide has occurred. The suicide team conducts a psychological autopsy by interviewing people who knew the deceased in an attempt to reconstruct his or her state of mind in the days preceding the death. The team examines in particular information about earlier suicide attempts, symptoms of depression, morbid communications, behavior indicating low self-esteem or self-hatred, and other evidence that may indicate an intention to commit suicide.

The reason that such an investigation is termed *postvention* is that the results can have a major impact on the survivors. As Curphey (1961) has noted, "The statement 'your father committed suicide,' made to a child may cause genuine anguish and even severe trauma for years to come" (p. 114). If there is even a small chance that an equivocal death might not be a suicide, such an investigation is worthwhile. However, even when the death is deemed a suicide, the process of conducting a psychological autopsy may be helpful to the survivors. The investigation may help the survivors to understand better the "why" behind the suicide. In addition, survivors have acknowledged that the interviews themselves have been therapeutic (Curphey, 1961). Many survivors of suicide do not routinely have caring professionals with whom to discuss the death of a loved one. Merely venting anger, sorrow, guilt, and anxiety to a trained member of a suicide team may promote adjustment.

The National Task Force on Suicide in Canada (Health and Welfare Canada, 1987) reported that "the procedures for performing a psychological autopsy are much less threatening than the quasi-judicidal procedures of an inquest, which have been shown to only aggravate the distress of the bereaved." The task force recommended that psychological autopsies should be performed in "all cases of equivocal or causally undetermined deaths, as well as in suspected cases of suicide in psychiatric and general hospitals, prisons, community clinics, and probation services" (p. 50). Table 7.3 presents the categories which the task force suggested should be included in the psychological autopsy. It is obvious from the breadth and depth of the information requested that psychological autopsies carried out according to these standards will yield a rich base of new information for understanding both the dynamics of suicide and its effects on survivors.

The second and more common type of suicide postvention is to be systematically involved with the survivors over several months in order to help them work through their special kind of grief. The death of a loved one is always a traumatic event that engenders a grief reaction. Evidence is accumulating that grief can cause physiological changes that may endanger the health of bereaved people (Berardo, 1988; Parkes, 1972; Rando, 1985; Raphael, 1983). When the cause of the death is suicide, the trauma experienced may be greatly increased.

Numerous studies have shown that bereavement following suicide differs from bereavement following death by natural causes (Dunn & Morrish-Vidners, 1987; Sheskin & Wallace, 1976; Wrobleski, 1984). Although not all studies agree, there is evidence that

TABLE 7.3   Contents of the Psychological Autopsy

Categories	Descriptions
Identification	Name, age, sex, marital status, residence, religious practices, employment status
Details of death	Cause, method, time, place, rating of lethality
Personal history	Medical history, psychiatric history, family history (medical illnesses, psychiatric illnesses, deaths, other suicides)
Personality & behavioral profile	Personality, life style, typical reaction to stress, nature of interpersonal relationships, attitudes toward death (accidents, suicide, and homicide), extent of use of drugs and alcohol and their possible role in the death
Precipitating events	Circumstances immediately preceding death, changes in routine prior to death (habits, hobbies, sexual behavior, eating, work, etc.), incidence of positive influences in life (e.g., success, satisfaction, enjoyment, plans for the future), crises during past 5 years
Assessment of intentionality	
Reaction of informant to the death	
Comments	

Distress: A ship-wrecked crew tossing in a small boat on a stormy sea, Thomas Rowlandson, R. A. Watercolor with pen and brown ink over pencil on heavy wove paper, 12¼ × 17⅛ in. (Yale Center for British Art, Paul Mellon Collection.)

the grief of survivors of a suicide seems to differ both in kind and in intensity from the grief following a death by natural causes. Besides the feelings of sorrow and loneliness common to grief, the suicide survivor characteristrically feels higher levels of guilt, shame, and anger toward the deceased. In addition, Cain (1972) observed the following reactions among survivors of suicide: reality distortion, problems with object relations, disturbed self-concept, identification with the suicide, self-destructiveness, search for meaning, and incomplete mourning. Dunn and Morrish-Vidners documented the following responses among a group of 24 suicide survivors. Their initial reactions included the shock and disbelief common to survivors of many types of death. In addition, however, these survivors reported feelings of fear and anger. They also reported a great need to talk to people about the death, a need which was difficult to meet, because so many potential listeners were uncomfortable with the subject of suicide. In addition, the authors suggested the presence of several interrelated psychological reactions might account for the intensity of grieving among suicide survivors, including feelings of utter powerlessness; feelings of deep rejection and punishment as a result of willful abandonment by the suicide; feelings of responsibility, self-blame, and guilt; and feelings of uncertainty as to the cause of the death.

Rudestam (1977) conducted a study with 39 families of suicides. He found that the survivors continued to experience physical and psychological symptoms 6 months after the death of the loved one. It is interesting to note that Rudestam did find some families whose relationships had actually been strengthened as a result of working together to understand the suicide and its meaning in their lives. Other studies have not shown such positive findings. A study by Cain and Fast (1972) showed that children of parents who have committed suicide have shown increased incidence of emotional problems. Osterweis, Solomon, & Green (1984) reviewed the literature on the impact of suicide on survivors. They pointed out that studies of children who experience the suicide of a parent show evidence of a wide range of psychological problems, including "psychosomatic disorders, obesity, running away, delinquency, fetishism, lack of bowel control, character problems and neurosis" (p. 126).

Problems seem to be more severe in children who survive a parental suicide than in children whose parents die from other causes. In addition, problems of guilt, depression, and self-destructive behavior seem to last a long time, at least as long as 16 years after a parental suicide. For adults, the effects of suicide may be less devastating but they still present special problems for survivors. In addition to feelings of rejection, guilt, and anger at the deceased person, adult suicide survivors often feel some degree of responsibility for the suicide and some degree of social stigmatization (Osterweis, Solomon, & Green, 1984). Even if we agree that individuals have the right to take their own lives, we would champion suicide prevention, intervention, and postvention techniques in order to avoid the high price the survivors of suicide pay in emotional pain and prolonged suffering. In short, suicide is an event dangerous to the mental and physical health of surviving loved ones, and it therefore requires special awareness and sensitivity from helping professionals.

In 1969, Shneidman estimated at least 750,000 persons each year are affected by the suicide of loved ones. More recently, he pointed out that the largest public health problem in dealing with suicide is the need to provide postvention efforts for survivors of suicide "whose lives are forever changed and who, over a period of years, number in the millions" (Shneidman, 1984). Postvention efforts need to be mobilized both to deal with the needs of individual survivors and to change the conditions in society which exacerbate their grief. In addition to individual and group therapy approaches, survivors can be helped by breaking down the stigma attached to suicide. This can only be done by education. Other authors have suggested that educational efforts should be directed at helping people understand the destructive effects that suicide has on survivors and on their ability to interact positively with others (Dunn & Morrish-Vidners, 1987). Education programs that discuss suicide without moralizing are also needed if the social stigma is to be removed from suicide survivors. Such programs need to stress the complexity of any suicidal action and to publicize the growing literature that illuminates the biological-social-psychological-cognitive bases of suicide.

Postvention efforts often merge into prevention efforts. As we have seen, many school districts are developing or already have in place suicide prevention programs. Many schools are also adopting a policy on postvention. When a suicide occurs in a school, a crisis team responds, mobilizing the combined energies of teachers and informed students and even reaching out to parents in an attempt to involve them as partners in suicide prevention. One Wisconsin school sends out the following letter* to all parents after a suicide occurs among the student body:

Dear Parents:

On [date], one of our [name of school] students committed suicide. Student reaction has been filled with both confusion and grief.

A crisis center has been established in the high school guidance office to assist students in their struggle to cope with this tragedy. Counselors from [name of city] Mental Health and [name of specialist], a local specialist on issues of death and dying, have been assisting our school counselors in working with students all day today, and will continue to be available in the days to come.

This is a tragedy that has affected our entire school community, and the administration and staff is very concerned about the continued effects it could have on the student body.

Please encourage your son or daughter to talk with you about this incident. Encourage them to share their feelings. If you notice any change in what you could consider their normal behavior or habits, i.e., sleeplessness, loss of appetite, moodiness, please notify their school counselor immediately. The crisis center and counselors will continue to provide assistance to students and their families as long as the need exists.

As of this writing the school has been informed that funeral services for the student will be held [date, time, and place]. Students wishing to attend these services are encouraged to travel as a group on a school bus. Parental permission slips will be needed for students who wish to go on the bus.

The school staff will continue to monitor student reaction on a daily basis, and adjustments will be made as needs arise. If we can be of any further assistance to you or your child please contact us.

Sincerely,
(School Official)

---

*Courtesy of Jeanne Harper.

Proponents of this broad community postvention effort maintain that such open communication reassures parents that school personnel care, provides opportunities for dialogue about suicide with parents and between parents and their children, and sets the stage for more complete suicide prevention programs.

We have come full circle in this chapter. In discussing postvention, we find that we are once again discussing the need for education about suicide. Indeed, as Shneidman (1984) has said, "Postvention can be viewed as prevention for the next decade or for the next generation; . . . and a comprehensive total health program in any enlightened community will include all three elements of care: prevention, intervention and postvention" (p. 419).

SUMMARY

The important topics of suicide prevention, intervention, and postvention were discussed in this chapter. It was pointed out that suicide prevention can be done by implementing education programs for helping professionals; by changing conditions in society which foster suicide; by establishing programs in the public schools to promote healthy coping; and by planning and implementing explicit suicide prevention programs in middle schools, high schools, and colleges.

Intervention programs discussed included the Samaritan program and the American model of crisis intervention. Basic principles of crisis intervention were examined. Special issues that might impact on suicidal persons of different ages were presented as an aid to helping professionals select the types of therapy that might be most appropriate from a developmental perspective.

Two types of postvention were described. The psychological autopsy was explored as a technique to establish the cause of death and the state of mind of the deceased. The importance of working with suicide survivors was emphasized. Finally, it was suggested that good postvention is actually equivalent to prevention and that many of the educational techniques reviewed in the prevention section are equally applicable in postvention efforts.

APPENDIX: SAMPLE SUICIDE PREVENTION RESOURCE LIST*

Audiovisual Materials
But Jack Was a Good Driver
McGraw-Hill Films
Box 641
Del Mar, CA 92104

---

* *Source: Suicide Prevention: A Resource and Planning Guide* (1986) Wisconsin Department of Public Instruction, pp. 86–88.

Did Jenny Have to Die? Preventing Teen Suicide
Sunburst Communications
39 Washington Avenue
Pleasantville, NY 10570-9971

Sudden Adolescent Death—How to Prevent It
Human Relations Media
175 Tompkins Avenue
Pleasantville, NY 10570

Suicide
Burea of Audio/Visual Instruction
University of Wisconsin Extension
1327 University Avenue
Madison, WI 53706

Teens Who Chose Life: The Suicidal Crisis
Sunburst Communications
39 Washington Avcnuc
Pleasantville, NY 10570-9971

Books and Booklets

Suicide of a Child
Joy Johnson, Marvin Johnson, & Adina Wrobleski
Centering Corporation
Box 3367
Omaha, NE 68103-0367

Suicide: Questions and Answers
Adina Wrobleski
5124 Grove Street
Minneapolis, MN 55436-2481

Suicide: The Danger Signs
Adina Wrobleski
5124 Grove Street
Minneapolis, MN 55436-2481

Suicide: Your Child Has Died
Adina Wrobleski
5124 Grove Street
Minneapolis, MN 55436-2481

What About Depression?
Channing L. Bete Co., Inc.
200 State Road
South Deerfield, MA 01373

What About Suicide?
Channing L. Bete Co., Inc.
200 State Road
South Deerfield, MA 01373

What About Self-Esteem?
Channing L. Bete Co., Inc.
200 State Road
South Deerfield, MA 01373

Program Materials
Adolescent Suicide Awareness Training Manual
New Jersey State Department of Education
225 West State Street
Trenton, NJ 08625

*Fairfax County Public Schools: The Adolescent Suicide
    Prevention Program*
Myra Herbert, Social Worker
Fairfax County Public Schools
Department of Student Services & Special Education
Belle Willare Administration Center
10310 Layton Hall Drive
Fairfax, VA 22030

*Prevention of Teenage Suicide: A Comprehensive, Proactive
    Program*
Southwest Community Health Centers, Inc.
199 South Central Avenue
Columbus, OH 43223

Project Alive
Family and Children's Service of Lancaster County
630 Janet Avenue
Lancaster, PA 17601

Suicide Prevention Training Manual
Merck, Sharp and Dohme
North Wales Press, Inc.
P.O. Box 1486
North Wales, PA 19454

Youth in Crisis: Seeking Solutions to Self-Destructive Behavior
Sopris West
1120 Delaware Avenue
Longmont, CO 80501

Pamphlets
Before It's Too Late

Suicide and How to Prevent It

*Suicide in Youth and What You Can Do About It—A Guide
    for Students*

Suicide in Young People

Suicide—It Doesn't Have to Happen

Suicide in Youth and What You Can Do About It—A Guide for School Personnel

All the pamphlets above are published by:
North Wales Press, Inc.
P.O. Box 1486
North Wales, PA 19454

REFERENCES

Alschuler, R., & Hattwick, L. B. W. (1947). *Painting and personality: A study of young children*. Chicago: University of Chicago Press.

Axline, V. A. (1947). *Play therapy: The inner dynamics of childhood* (L. Carmichael, Ed.). Boston: Houghton Mifflin.

Barry, B. (1984). Perceptions of suicide. *Death Studies (Supplement)*, 8, 17–26.

Battin, M. P. (1984). The concept of rational suicide. In E. Shneidman (Ed.), *Death: Current perspectives* (3rd ed., pp. 297–320). Palo Alto, CA: Mayfield.

Berardo, D. H. (1988). Bereavement and mourning. In H. Wass, F. M. Berardo, & R. A. Neimeyer (Eds.), *Dying: Facing the facts* (pp. 279–300). Washington, DC: Hemisphere.

Berger, M. (1984). Intervention with potential suicides. In N. Linzer (Ed.), *Suicide: The will to live vs. the will to die* (pp. 55–70). New York: Human Sciences Press.

Berman, A. L. (1987, November). *Suicide prevention: A critical need and a critical perspective*. Paper presented at the First National Conference on Suicide Prevention and the Public Schools, Orlando, FL.

Blackwell, P. L., & Gessner, J. C. (1983). Fear and trembling: An inquiry into adolescent perceptions of living in the nuclear age. *Youth and Society*, 15(2), 237–255.

Butler, R. N., & Lewis, M. I. (1977). *Aging and mental health: Positive psychological approaches*. St. Louis, MO: Mosby.

Butler, R. N., & Lewis, M. I. (1982). *Aging and mental health: Positive psychosocial and biomedical approaches* (3rd ed.). St. Louis: Mosby.

Cain, A. (Ed.) (1972). *Survivors of suicide*. Springfield, IL: Charles C Thomas.

Cain, A. C., & Fast, I. (1972). Children's disturbed reaction to parent suicide: Distortions of guilt, communication, and identification. In A. C. Cain (Ed.) *Survivors of suicide* (pp. 93–111). Springfield, IL: Charles C Thomas.

Cantor, P. (1987, November). *During and after a suicidal crisis: What educators need to know*. Paper presented at the First National Conference on Suicide Prevention and the Public Schools, Orlando, FL.

Curphey, T. J. (1961). The role of the social scientist in the medicological certification of death from suicide. In N. L. Farberow & E. S. Shneidman (Eds.), *The cry for help* (pp. 110–117). New York: McGraw-Hill.

Dunn, R. G., & Morrish-Vidners, D. (1987). The psychological and social experience of suicide survivors. *Omega*, 18, 175–215.

Elkind, D. (1967). Egocentrism in adolescence. *Child Development 38*, 1025–1034.

Elkind, D., & Bowen, R. (1979). Imaginary audience behavior in children and adolescents. *Developmental Psychology*, 15, 38–44.

Farberow, N. L., & Moriwaki, S. Y. (1975, August). Self-destructive crisis in the older person. *The Gerontologtist*, pp. 333–337.

Fox, R. (1984). The Samaritans: An alternative approach to suicide prevention. In N. Linzer (Ed.), *Suicide: The will to live vs. the will to die* (pp. 43–53). New York: Human Sciences Press.

Garland, A. (1987, November). *Prevention programs: Evaluation guidelines*. Paper presented at the First National Conference on Suicide Prevention and the Schools, Orlando, FL.

Goode, T. L. & Brophy, J. E. (1984). *Looking in classrooms*. New York: Harper & Row.

Gray, D., & Hudson, L. (1984). Formal operations and the imaginary audience. *Developmental Psychology, 20*, 619–627.

Hall, G. S. (1904). *Adolescence* (Vol. 1). New York: D. Appleton.

Health and Welfare Canada. (1987). *Suicide in Canada: Report of the National Task Force on Suicide in Canada.* Ottawa: Department of National Health and Welfare.

Hudgens, R. W. (1983). Preventing suicide. *New England Journal of Medicine, 308*, 897–898.

Inhelder, B., & Piaget, J. (1958). *The growth of logical thinking from childhood to adolescence.* New York: Basic Books.

Jaco, R. M. (1987). Suicide-proofing youth: A survival technique for the eighties. In J. D. Morgan (Ed.), *Suicide: Helping those at risk. Proceedings of the Conference* (pp. 103–111). London, Ontario: King's College.

Jennings, C., Barraclough, B., & Moss, J. (1978). Have the Samaritans lowered the suicide rate? A controlled study. *Psychological Medicine, 8*, 413–422.

Kiev, A. (1984). Suicide and depression. In N. Linzer (Ed.), *Suicide: The will to live vs. the will to die* (pp. 23–34). New York: Human Sciences Press.

Lester, D. (1969). Suicide as a positive act. *Psychology, 6*(3), 43–48.

Lester, D. (1970). The concept of an appropriate death. *Psychology, 7*(4), 61–66.

Lester, D. (1971). The evaluation of suicide prevention centers. *International Behavioral Scientist, 3*(2), 40–47.

Lester, D. (1987). Preventing suicide: Past failures and future hopes. In J. D. Morgan (Ed.), *Suicide: Helping those at risk. Proceedings of the conference* (pp. 69–78). London, Ontario: King's College.

McBrien, R. J. (1983). Are you thinking of killing yourself? Confronting students suicidal thoughts. *The School Counselor, 31*, 75–82.

McIntosh, J. L., Hubbard, R. W., & Santos, J. F. (1981). Suicide among the elderly: A review of issues with case studies. *Journal of Gerontological Social Work, 4*, 63–74.

Nelson, F. L. (1984). Suicide: Issues of prevention, intervention, and facilitation. *Journal of Clinical Psychology, 40*, 1328–1333.

Noyes, R. (1970). Shall we prevent suicide? *Comparative Psychiatry, 11*, 361–370.

Osgood, N. J., Brant, B. A., & Lipman, A. (1988–1989). Patterns of suicidal behavior in long-term care facilities: A preliminary report on an ongoing study. *Omega, 16*, 69–77.

Osterweis, M., Solomon, F., & Green, M. (Eds.) (1984). *Bereavement: Reactions, consequences, and care,* Washington, DC: National Academy Press.

Parkes, C. M. (1972). *Bereavement: Studies of grief in adult life.* New York: International Universities Press.

Pfeffer, C. (1984a). Recognizing and treating suicidal youngsters. In N. Linzer (Ed.), *Suicide: The will to live vs. the will to die* (pp. 87–100). New York: Human Sciences Press.

Pfeffer, C. (1984b). Death preoccupations and suicidal behavior in children. In H. Wass & C. Corr (Eds.), *Childhood and death* (pp. 261–279). Washington, DC: Hemisphere.

Rachlis, D. (1970, Fall). Suicide and loss adjustment in aging. *Bulletin of Suicidology, 7*, 23–26.

Rando, T. A. (1985). *Loss and anticipatory grief.* Lexington, MA: Lexington Books.

Raphael, B. (1983). *The anatomy of bereavement.* New York: Basic Books.

Resnik, H. L. P., & Cantor, J. M. (1970). Suicide and aging. *Journal of the American Geriatrics Society, 18*, 152–158.

Rosenn, D. W. (1982). Suicidal behavior in children and adolescents. In E. L. Bassuk, S. C. Schoonover, & A. D. Gill (Eds.), *Lifelines: Clinical perspectives on suicide* (pp. 195–224). New York: Plenum Press.

Rudestam, K. E. (1977). Physical and psychological responses to suicide in the family. *Journal of Consulting and Clinical Psychology, 45*(2), 162–170.

Schoonover, S. C. (1982). Crisis therapies. In E. L. Bassuk, S. C. Schoonover, & A. D. Gill (Eds.), *Lifelines: Clinical perspectives on suicide* (pp. 49–57). New York: Plenum Press.

Selkin, J. (1983). The legacy of Emile Durkheim. *Suicide and Life-Threatening Behavior, 13*, 3–14.

Shaughnessy, M. F., & Nystul, M. S. (1985). Preventing the greatest loss—suicide. *The Creative Child and Adult Quarterly, 10*(3), 164–169.

Sheehy, G. (1976). *Passages: Predictable crises of adult life.* New York: Dutton.

Sheskin, A., & Wallace, S. (1976). Differing bereavements: Suicide, natural and accidental death. *Omega, 7*, 229–242.

Shneidman, E. S. (1984). Postvention and the survivor-victim. In E. S. Shneidman (Ed.), *Death: Current perspectives* (3rd ed., pp. 412–419). Mountain View, CA: Mayfield Publishing Co. (Reprinted from Shneidman, E. S., *Deaths of Man*, 1973).

Smith, K., Eyman, J., Dyck, R., & Ryerson, D. (1987, December). *Report of a survey of school-related suicide programs.* Paper prepared for the American Association of Suicidology, Denver, CO.

Stillion, J. M. (1985). *Exploring coping techniques among ninth grade academically gifted students.* Unpublished raw data.

Stillion, J. M. (1986). Examining the shadow: Gifted children respond to the nuclear threat. *Death Studies, 10*(1), 27–41.

Stillion, J. M., Goodrow, H., Klingman, A., Laughlin, M., Morgan, J. D., Sandsberg, S., Walton, M., & Warren, W. G. (1988). Dimensions of the shadow: Children of six nations respond to the nuclear threat. *Death Studies, 12*(3), 227–251.

Streiner, D. L., & Adam, K. S. (1987). Evaluation of the effectiveness of suicide prevention programs: A methodological perspective. *Suicide and Life-Threatening Behavior, 17*, 93–106.

Szasz, T. (1986). The case against suicide prevention. *American Psychologist, 41*, 806–812.

Victoroff, V. M. (1983). *The suicidal patient: Recognition, intervention, management.* Oradell, NJ: Medical Economics Books.

Webb, N. B. (1986). Before and after suicide: A preventive outreach program for colleges. *Suicide and Life-Threatening Behavior, 16*, 469–480.

Weisman, A. (1972). *On dying and denying: A psychiatric study of terminality.* New York: Behavioral Publications.

Wiley, J. (1987). *Report to the Children's Services Commission regarding teenage suicide.* Unpublished report of the Missouri Children's Services Commission, Columbia, MO.

Wrobleski, A. (1984). The suicide survivors grief group. *Omega, 15*, 173–184.

Yalom, I. (1975). *The theory and practice of group psychotherapy* (2nd ed.). New York: Basic Books.

8

Suicide Across the Life Span

All the world's a stage,
And all the men and women merely players;
They have their exits and their entrances;
And one man in his time plays many parts. Shakespeare, *As You Like*
It, Act I, Sc. 7

We chose to begin this chapter with one of Shakespeare's most famous quotes because we believe that it accurately depicts movement throughout life. From birth through maturity and up to the point of death we continuously try out new roles and drop roles we have outgrown. For example, we drop the role of dependent infant as we, under the influences of maturation and environment, become toddlers and then children. During the stage of childhood we take on the roles of student, friend, and group member in a variety of activities. We leave behind our childhood roles as we move, first tentatively and then with more assurance, toward independence and adulthood, where we take on still other roles—mate, parent, and productive worker. Finally, we move into old age, where we take on a final series of roles. We may play retiree, grandparent, patriarch or matriarch of the family, and a variety of other roles as we move toward the end of this period. At some point, however, we must make an exit from the stage of life. This chapter is intended to help readers gain insight into the perspectives of those who may be considering, at one or more points in time, whether to exit prematurely. The central theme of this book is that our understanding of suicide is enriched by examining suicidal behavior from a life span perspective. We will amplify that theme in four major ways. First, we will define the major principles that make up a life span perspective and show how these principles relate to suicidal behavior. Second, we will introduce a model of a suicide trajectory that will both reflect the complexities involved in suicidal behavior and present an organized framework for understanding them. Third, using this conceptual framework, we will discuss commonalities and age differences in suicide across the life span. Finally, we will summarize the ways in which a life span developmental perspective illuminates the study of suicide.

PRINCIPLES OF LIFE SPAN DEVELOPMENT

One important principle of our view of human development is that genetics is a core component. The genetic information inherited from our parents at conception affects subsequent development in two major ways. First, it sets limits beyond which an individual cannot go, regardless of stimulation or education. For example, a child who is born with a genetic disease that causes severe retardation will not become a college graduate. Second, it establishes thresholds for reacting to the environment. For example, Brazelton (1969) has shown that even newborn babies exhibit differences in startle responses to the noises in their environment. Infants seem to have built-in levels of arousal and irritability. These biological thresholds probably account for individual differences in endurance of pain and stress and may well contribute to differential predispositions to depression and, indirectly, to suicidal behavior. Development at any stage from conception onward can only be understood as a product of these biological limits and thresholds as they interact with a changing environment.

A second important principle of life span psychology is that change is a constant throughout life. Terenzini (1987) defines *change* as a value-free term which refers to alterations that occur over time in the affective and cognitive characteristics of an individual. It is important to note that merely recognizing that change is a constant does not allow one to infer the direction or rate of change, nor, most importantly, does it set a value on the changes that occur. There is evidence, however, that change by itself, regardless of whether it evokes positive or negative reactions, is a stressor and that rapidly accumulating change, especially of a negative nature, enhances the anxiety and depression which frequently accompany suicide attempts (Holmes & Rahe, 1967).

The third principle is that development is a continuous process. Unlike simple change, development is an organized, systematic process. Many developmental psychologists take the term *development* to have an evaluative connotation and assume that development involves a movement from immaturity to maturity and that such movement is inevitably positive. Development is also often thought to consist of a succession of changes that have survival value for the individual. Life span theorists, however, do not necessarily agree that the term *development* always connotes positive growth. They point out that development in the later years may involve loss of earlier modes of functioning in some areas, whereas other areas may continue to show improvement. Some characteristics, such as crystallized intelligence, may continue to grow over the entire life span; other traits, such a short-term memory, may have a normal distribution across time, increasing during the early years and then declining. In our life span model, we use the term *development* to include changes that lead to more complex and mature functioning as well as changes that reflect the principles of entropy, including deterioration in both structure and function.

A fourth basic tenet of developmental psychology is known as the *dialectic principle*. According to this principle, all development occurs as a result of imbalance. Freud endorsed this principle when he pointed out that children grow from one psychosexual stage to another as a result of being frustrated by the external environment. Perfect satisfaction at any given stage, Freud maintained, could lead to fixation, because there would be no incentive to grow. Piaget and Kohlberg also recognized this principle in the intellectual and moral development of children. They believed that development is dependent on external stimulation that confronts the child with unknown material and challenges him or her to master new knowledge. Piaget pointed out that there are two modes of learning: assimilation and accommodation. Assimilation involves taking in new information and adding it to already existing categories of knowledge, whereas accommodation involves changing existing knowledge structures to incorporate conflicting information. Both assimilation and accommodation occur when an individual reacts to a stimulus or intellectual challenge from the environment. Building on Piaget's theory, Kohlberg believed that people pass from a lower stage in moral development to a higher one by being confronted with moral dilemmas or examples of moral reasoning that require higher levels of cognitive functioning than they currently possess (Kohlberg, 1976). Adult developmental theorists like Gould (1978) recognize this principle when they suggest that development occurs as short periods of equilibrium give way to periods of turbulence. Implied in the concept of passages or transformations is the idea that advanced development occurs from working one's way through a challenging period and that the balance attained as a result of such work is delicate, transient, and subject to assault from new environmental demands, life accidents, opportunities, and challenges.

The dialectic principle lends credence to Shneidman's view that suicidal behavior is the result of a temporary crisis rather than an internal personality trait of the individual (1976). The principle also supports crisis intervention as a method for reestablishing balance temporarily until the individual can marshal his or her coping skills and move to a more mature level of functioning. Furthermore, the dialectic principle suggests that a suicidal crisis, once resolved, may actually cause the person to become stronger and better equipped to meet the stresses of life. The principle also recognizes that suicidal crises may recur at other periods in an individual's live and that these later recurrences may be resolved through growth or may lead to death.

The fifth principle of development, based on humanistic theories, is that there is a central organizing force within every person that governs change proactively. That force is known as the *self*. Of all the developmental principles presented in this chapter, we believe that the organization and operation of the self is the most critical for thoroughly understanding suicidal behavior. Therefore, we will devote more space to this topic than to the other developmental principles.

Figure 8.1 depicts our understanding of the way in which the self develops and regulates behavior across the life span. At birth, the self consists only of those inherited traits and tendencies that set genetic limits and establish thresholds of reaction. This

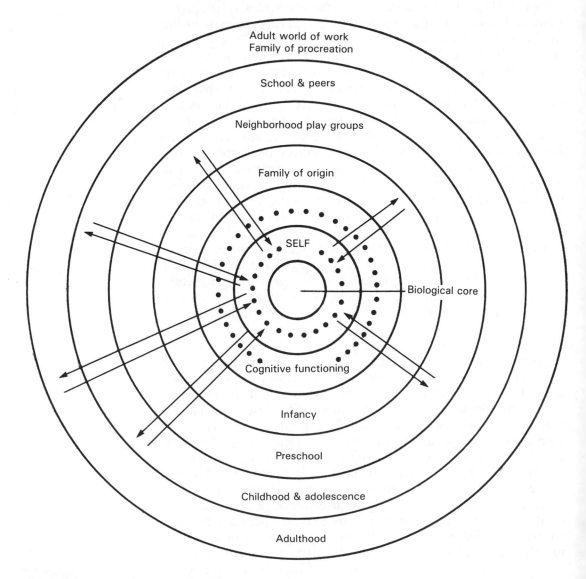

FIGURE 8.1 Development of Self

dimension is labelled the biological core in our figure. As the child grows and develops, the environment starts to impact on the self through widening circles of influence, beginning with the family of origin and later spreading to neighborhood groups, then to the school environment, and finally to the adult world of work and the family of procreation. It is important to note that the self does not merely react to the stimuli in the environment. Instead, the self acts on the environment in increasingly complex and organized ways. As the self begins to become more firmly established, it provides a consistent core for interpreting and acting on the environment (Lecky, 1973).

One major element shaping the self is the expanding cognitive repertoire that the growing child achieves. Messages from the environment are mediated by the cognitive processes and accepted or rejected based on goodness of fit. As the child grows, he or she learns to accept some of these messages and ignore others. This is called *selective perception*. Perhaps initially because of genetic predispositions and later also because of environmental experiences, humans tend to perceive the world differentially and assign different meanings to the same stimuli.

Cognitive theorists point out that one's belief system is important in establishing and maintaining a consistent picture of oneself (e.g., Ellis, 1962). This belief system is an accumulation of perceptions about oneself and one's place in the world that are consistent with one's experience of self. As Kelly's theory suggests (see Chapter 2), we create personal constructs for important events and activities (Kelly, 1955). Those constructs then become our own unique way of viewing the world. Other theorists suggest that, once established, our belief systems and view of self are maintained by the self-talk we engage in to interpret the external world meaningfully (Meichenbaum, 1985). By suggesting this, they are essentially asserting the importance of cognition in helping to maintain or enhance our self-concepts. In the same way, an individual's potential behaviors, including suicidal behavior, are mediated by cognitive processes, and these processes determine which actions the individual chooses to engage in.

Three other elements shaping the self should be noted. These include the processes of imitation, modeling, and identification. Behaviorists have shown that humans imitate the behavior of other humans. They have even discovered some rules that govern the process. For example, humans are more likely to imitate the behavior of models who are powerful, attractive, and of the same sex (Bandura, 1977). Throughout our lives we focus on other people as important sources of learning. As children, we may blindly imitate the gestures or actions of adults. As teens, we engage in idol worship. Much of faddish adolescent behavior is imitative of a style set by an admired performer, sports star, or local teen leader. Young adults continue imitating others in the process of being mentored. A young adult will focus on a successful person in his or her occupational field, develop a relationship with that person, and attempt to become as much like the mentor as possible. Every academic recognizes this behavior as basically imitative. New male graduate students, advised by a powerful, attractive male faculty member who has a beard and long hair, are apt to sprout beards and long tresses themselves before the end of the first semester. The process of imitation not only allows us to try out different types of behaviors and ways of being and to learn from them, it also forms the basis for the deeper process of identification. Identification is the taking on of qualities which others possess and making them a part of us. In this process we incorporate admired, respected, or even negative qualities that are modeled by others into our growing concept of self.

All three of these elements (imitation, modeling, and identification) have been shown to be important in suicidal behavior. The incidence of suicide increases after a powerful role model commits suicide. Parents who model suicidal behavior often have children who imitate their actions. Finally, suicidal behavior as a coping technique can be incorporated into our sense of who we are. Like Jerry W. in Chapter 2, whose suicide attempt occurred when he was the age at which his father killed himself, we may identify with a suicidal parent so completely that we feel compelled to attempt suicide ourselves at a certain age.

As the self becomes an identifiable entity, it also assumes an organizing function. The major organizing principle of self theory is that at any given time a person acts so as to maintain or enhance his or her self-concept (Lecky, 1973). Because this is true, the person's individual view of self becomes the guiding force in determining the direction of future development. Once established, a view of self as competent and worthy is strengthened by acting on the environment and accepting messages from the environment that maintain or enhance that positive self-concept. Unfortunately, the opposite is also true. Many suicidal individuals, like Marian in Chapter 2, have such poor self-concepts that they cannot accept positive feedback from those around them.

A final important concept in self theory is that of self-esteem. Self-esteem refers to the value that an individual places upon him- or herself. At any given time across the life span, an individual's behavior can be understood as a function of the way in which the individual views him- or herself and by the assessment of worth that such a self-concept inspires. The literature which we have reviewed in this book clearly links suicidal behavior to depression. We would maintain that it is impossible to have a positive self-concept, value oneself highly, and be depressed enough to consider suicide. Therefore, we suggest that a positive self-concept and high self-esteem are important variables inoculating individuals against suicide at any age and, conversely, that people with low self-esteem are at higher risk for committing suicide. Indeed, the literature of depression frequently defines depression in terms of low self-esteem, which is almost a tautology.

A sixth principle of development is the principle of individuation. According to this principle, people develop toward their unique potentials across the life span. Carl Jung, who has been called the father of adult development, was the first to popularize the term. Jung believed that the process of individuation begins during the decade of the 40s. He described it as a process that requires us to recognize the complexities of our inner selves and to try to find a balance between competing forces (Jung, 1960). Erikson (1959) interpreted this process of individuation as movement toward ego integrity. Levinson, Darrow, Klein, Levinson, and McKee (1978) recognized it as a process of clarifying the boundaries between our inner selves and the external world as well as a process of balancing conflicting internal demands. To Levinson et al., individuation is a process of coming to know who we are, what we want, what the world is really like, and how much we value these things. Proponents of the humanistic school of thought would recognize the principle of individuation in the drive toward self-actualization. Although their point of view is more clearly evaluative than some, the basic idea is the same. Individuation helps a person to move toward his or her uniqueness, to become more clearly the person he or she is capable of becoming.

The principle of Individuation contains the idea of unfolding. Walt Disney's film *The Living Desert* showed us in a spectacular way the process by which a plant breaks through the soil, attains full growth, buds, comes to full flower, fades, and disintegrates. According to the principle of individuation, this process applies to humans in all their complexity. The analogy holds up well. Just as the full beauty of the blossom depends on both the caliber of the seed planted and the characteristics of the environment (e.g., soil, sun, and rain), the quality of an individual life depends on both the genetic inheritance and the external demands, opportunities, and nurturance available. Suicidal behavior is generally the result of the accumulation of environmental insults to predisposed individuals who have not been able to develop adequate self-concepts and coping techniques.

The seventh important principle of a life span perspective is that cohort differences should be taken into account when trying to understand and explain the behavior of any age group. A cohort is a group of people who live through a particular time in history at a particular developmental stage. For example, people who were adolescents during the depression learned a dramatic lesson about limited opportunity and harsh economic reality. People who were children at the time may not have been affected so heavily, whereas middle-aged people, perhaps reacting to the lack of time for beginning anew, committed suicide at unprecedented rates. In order to understand fully the reasons for an individual suicide, characteristics of the cohort of which the suicide is a part should be examined.

In summary, the life span developmental perspective we endorse views development as the product of genetics and biology interacting with the social and physical environment as it is mediated by increasingly sophisticated cognitive skills. The gyroscope in the process of development, the factor that accounts for the consistency we see in personalities across time, is the self. We believe that all behavior can best be understood by taking into account biology; psychological development; cognitive abilities and habits; and environmental pressures, challenges, and opportunities. Suicidal behavior is no exception. In the remainder of this chapter, we will suggest a model for viewing suicidal behavior that incorporates each of these categories.

THE SUICIDE TRAJECTORY

Figure 8.2 presents our model of the suicide trajectory. There are four major categories of risk factors that contribute to suicide: biological, psychological, cognitive, and environmental. It is im-

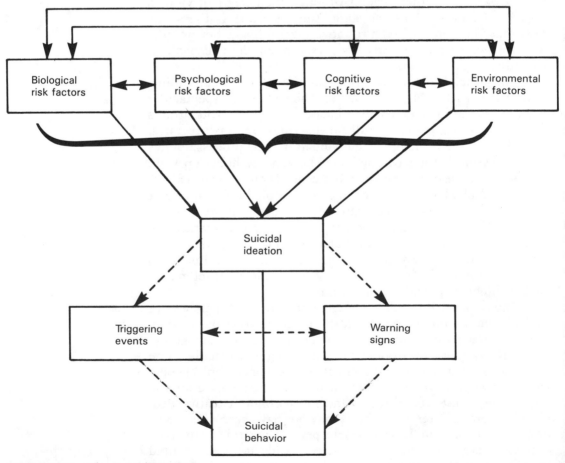

FIGURE 8.2 The Suicide Trajectory

portant to note that each of these categories can influence every other category, as indicated by the interconnecting arrows. For example, having a biological inclination toward depression can cause an individual to develop low self-esteem, to selectively interpret the environment in a negative fashion, and to engage in the type of cognitive rigidity that may promote suicidal ideation. Likewise, poor environmental conditions, such as an abusive home, may be the starting point for a poor self-concept and negative self-talk, which may eventually result in chemical changes in the neurotransmitters at the synapses of the neurons in the brain, leading to a biologically based depressive episode. The bracket below the four risk factors in Fig. 8.2 indicates that these factors work together, lending their accumulated weight to the development of suicidal ideation.

Suicidal ideation, including the making of specific suicide plans, is an essential phase in all but the most impulsive suicides. The period of suicidal ideation may last only minutes or it may go on, intermittently or constantly, for years.

Suicidal ideation may or may not become visible in warning signs, as indicated by the dotted line in Fig. 8.2. In most cases, after the suicide has been completed, people can retroactively point to warning signs. For example, Maria, a young artist, sought out one of her former professors just one week before she killed herself. She spent an hour reviewing her life and thanking the professor for her mentorship. She spoke only vaguely and rather disconsolately about the future. After the suicide, it was easy for the professor, trained in death and dying, to interpret that visit as completing unfinished business by saying goodbye. However, if Maria had not killed herself, the visit would have been inter preted as one of those rare occasions when teachers become aware that their efforts have been appreciated. Although warning signs such as this are often equivocal, they have important implications for survivors, in that failure to recognize warning signs leads to more regret than any other component of the suicide trajectory.

It is important to note that warning signs may come about as a result of a specific triggering event that solidifies the suicide plan. For example, a young couple of our acquaintance recently separated after several months of increasingly bitter arguments. The separation triggered an alcoholic bout in the husband, which ended when he called his wife and threatened suicide. Clearly, the triggering event in this instance was the separation, and the warning signs were the drunken episode and the telephone call.

It is equally possible that warning signs may lead to trig gering events, indicated by the bidirectional dotted line in Fig. 8.2. For example, a high school counselor recently shared this account of one of her experiences with a suicidal adolescent. Anna confided to her counselor that she was considering dropping out of school because she was very depressed. The counselor threat-ened to inform her parents unless she sought treatment immediately. Before the counselor had an opportunity to follow through, the girl drove to a secluded location and took an overdose of anti-depressants. Clearly, in this case the warning sign (the admission of depression and of the intent to drop out of school) led to the triggering event (the threatened intervention). The dotted line with two arrows that stands between warning signs and triggering events in our model indicates the possible interaction of the categories.

Triggering events, like warning signs, are not universally present in suicidal behavior. Therefore, we have shown the categories connected by dotted lines. Triggering events should be considered "last straw" phenomena; that is, they need not be dramatic or particularly traumatic to lead to suicidal behavior. It is helpful to conceive of life at any given time as a balanced scale in which the positive and negative events, attitudes, and self-perceptions are roughly in equilibrium. In this analogy, the risk factor categories lend their weight to a growing imbalance which manifests itself in suicidal ideation. The delicate balance between positives and negatives in a person's life may be totally destroyed by one more argument, one more failing grade, one more insult from an adolescent peer, one final broken relationship—in short, any type of last straw triggering event.

The model of the suicide trajectory should be helpful in promoting understanding of suicide across the life span. The use of the model enables us to organize the discussion of special issues in suicidal behavior at different stages across the life span more intelligibly. In addition, the model permits us to note commonalities in suicidal behavior across the life span.

COMMONALITIES AND DIFFERENCES IN THE SUICIDE TRAJECTORY ACROSS THE LIFE SPAN

Table 8.1 summarizes commonalities and differences in the suicide trajectory across the life span. The table presents information about the model's four categories of risk factors as well as specifics about warning signs and triggering events by age group. The commonalities in suicidal behavior, those aspects that re main constant in their influence on suicide across all ages, are shown in the first row of the table (life cycle commonalities). There are two biological risk factors that are constant across the life span. The first is a genetic predisposition to depression and the second is maleness.

The biological basis of depression has been well established, and it is clear that individuals differ in their predispositions to develop crippling depression. Some individuals, because of a biological predisposition, may become significantly depressed with little or no environmental pressure, whereas others experience depression only under the most extreme stress. If Akiskal and McKinney (1973) are correct, however, regardless of the genetic inheritance of predispositions or thresholds and regardless of the

environmental, psychological, or cognitive factors fueling depres
sion, at some point all depression is expressed biologically. Clin
ical depression is, at least in part, a manifestation of a biological
change that affects the chemistry of the brain. It is through this
"final common pathway" that the body expresses its outrage at
the insults that it has suffered. Thus, as we have seen in the
preceding chapters, depression is a factor common to suicide across
the life span and depression is either rooted in biological predis
positions or translated into biological expression by chemical
changes in the brain.

A second biological factor that predisposes individuals of all
ages to suicide is maleness (i.e., being of the male sex). Simply
put, males of all ages are at higher risk for suicide than are females.
This fact appears to be true across cultures and throughout his
tory. It is impossible to know if maleness by itself predisposes
individuals to suicidal behavior or if the higher suicide rates occur
because of the commonalities in male socialization over time and
across cultures. However, we believe that the increased risk of
suicide is most likely a result of the interaction between biology
and socialization as these are mediated by a male's cognitive
processes and become incorporated into his self-concept. Higher
levels of male aggression and activity are well documented from
birth onward (Stillion, 1985). Building on these possibly inherited
tendencies, males learn lessons of competence, success, self-re
liance, and emotional isolation. The psychological world of the
male is one in which strength is valued, winning is important,
and admitting weakness or doubt is verboten. If we wanted to
write a prescription for increasing suicide risk, we could not im
prove on the traditional male socialization pattern. Take one male
child, who has higher levels of aggression and activity than his
female peers. Put the child into competitive situations. Tell him
he must win at all costs. Teach him that to admit fear or doubt
is weakness and that weakness is not masculine. Complete the
vicious circle by assuring him that his worth is dependent on his
winning games, then salary and promotion competitions, and you
have the perfect recipe for enhanced suicide risk.

Psychological risk factors, the second category in our model
suicide trajectory, are defined as those internal feelings and pat
terns of behavior that contribute to suicidal ideation. There are
at least five specific psychological characteristics that contribute
to suicide risk in every age group. The first is psychological depres
sion. We have stated that there is a biological component in most,
if not all, severe depression. Nevertheless, depression must also
be discussed as a psychological risk factor. Depression tends to
be perceived by those suffering from it as a psychological rather
than a physiological syndrome; that is, depressed people talk about
their feelings rather than their physiological symptoms. Further
more, evidence exists that in deep depression, when feelings of
hopelessness become pervasive, suicidal risk becomes elevated.

TABLE 8.1   Commonalities and Differences in the Suicide Trajectory Across the Life Span

Age group	Biological risk factors	Psychological risk factors	Cognitive risk factors	Environmental risk factors	Warning signs	Triggering events	Suicidal behaviors
Life cycle commonalities	Genetic predisposition to depression Maleness	Depression Helplessness Hopelessness Low self-esteem Lack of coping skills	Rigidity of thought Overgeneralization Selective abstraction Inexact labeling	Negative experiences in the family Loss Negative life events Presence of firearms & other means of self-destruction	Verbal threats Self-injurious behavior	"Final straw" life event	Higher rate for males Males use more lethal methods
Childhood (5–14)	Impulsivity Hyperactivity	Inferiority Expendable child syndrome	Immature views of death Concrete operational thinking	Abuse and neglect Parental conflict Family role definitions Inflexible family structure Parental suicidal behavior Repeated failure	Truancy Poor school performance Increased anxiety Sleep disturbance Aggression Low frustration tolerance Poor impulse control	Minor life events	Impulsive Highly lethal Males attempt and complete more suicides Greatest incidence of failed suicides Lowest completion rate
Adolescence (15–24)	Puberty Hormonal changes	Identity crisis Fluctuating mood states	Formal operational thinking Idealistic thinking Increased egocentrism Illusion of invulnerability Imaginary audience	Parental conflict Drug or alcohol abuse Poor peer relationships Anomic families	Self-mutilation Change in habits Truancy Poor School performance Preparations for death	Suicides by peers Suicides by famous people Failure experiences Problems with peers, parents, opposite sex, siblings	Largest rate of increase in past 30 years Most dramatic sex difference in attempts Vulnerable to cluster and copycat suicides

Young adulthood (25–34)	Postpartum depression	Lack of intimate relationships	Re-evaluation of life choice (catch 30)	Presence of children (W)* Marital problems (W) Occupational problems (M)** Drug and alcohol abuse (M) AIDS	Precipitous multiple life changes	Occupational setback Marital difficulty AIDS diagnosis	Small reduction in rate in past 5 years Peak suicide rate for blacks and American Indians
Middle adulthood (34–65)	Menopause (W) Climacteric (M) Decline in physical abilities and attractiveness	Loss of youthful dreams Increased inferiority Feelings of stagnation & self-absorption	Change in time perspective Midlife evaluation	Deaths of significant others Empty nest Fewer activities Fewer interpersonal activities Accumulation of negative life events Alcoholism			Peak suicide rate for women
Old age (65 and over)	Physical decline Organic mental decline Chronic illness Chronic pain	Increased passivity Loneliness Feelings of despair	Declining learning Declining retrieval Growing acceptance of death	Widowhood Retirement Inactivity Financial problems Cumulative loss Negative social attitudes toward the elderly	Physicians visits Putting affairs in order	Terminal illness	Highest rate of all groups Largest sex difference in completions Highest male completion rate Highest lethality level

*W = Women
**M = Men

Feelings of helplessness, often associated with depression and hopelessness, further exacerbate depression. Low self-esteem, as we saw previously, is a fourth psychological factor common to suicide at any age. Finally, individuals who have not acquired adequate coping skills (sometimes also viewed as ego defense mechanisms) also experience higher risk.

Commonalities also exist across the life span in the category of cognitive risk factors. Because growing intellectual capability shapes our self-concepts and our view of the world, this category is of major importance. People of all ages use their cognitive skills to evaluate and reevaluate life choices and to reinforce their positive or negative self-concepts. Therefore, cognitions may play a major role in leading an individual toward or away from suicide as a method of coping with life's problems.

Evidence is accumulating that suicidal individuals tend to become more rigid and dichotomous in their thinking and to narrow their cognitive focus to suicide as the best and only answer to their current problems. Three distinct elements seem to contribute to suicidal cognitions. The first is a tendency to overgeneralize. Like Jason in Chapter 4, suicidal individuals who experience the ending of a relationship tend to believe that all relationships will turn out the same way. They are unable to view an event as unique, and they tend to group all experiences together and settle on the most negative interpretation. The second element is selective abstraction. Like Marian, the nurse in Chapter 2, suicidal people tend to ignore positive experiences and selectively recall only negative episodes. They continually engage in negative self-talk, which promotes and perpetuates very low self esteem. The third element contributing to suicidal cognition is inexact labelling. Drawing on one or more experiences, suicidal individuals place on themselves negative labels that exclude the positive attributes they may have. Like overgeneralization, this type of cognition leads to a negative view of the self.

Completing the common risk factors across the life span are those that exist in the environment. Research clearly shows that negative family experiences increase the risk of suicide (Bock & Webber, 1972, February; Garfinkel, Froese, & Hood, 1982; Stephens, 1985). While the nature of those negative experiences may differ de pending on developmental status, there is no question that the family is the most important environmental factor in protecting against or increasing the risk of suicidal behavior. Negative life events, especially when they accumulate rapidly or occur out of the expected sequence (e.g., the death of a child), also become part of the environmental conditions that may predispose an in dividual to suicide. Loss of all kinds has consistently been shown to be related to suicide in every age group. The experience of loss, of course, is related to the psychological development of depres sion. Loss sets in motion a predictable grief sequence, one stage of which is depression. Depression, as we have seen, if deep

enough and protracted enough, is manifested biologically. In extreme cases, it may also cause suicidal behavior. Finally, the easy
access to instruments of self-destruction, especially firearms, is
another environmental factor that increases the likelihood of a
suicidal act.

All four of the background risk categories discussed lend
their weight to the development of suicidal ideation. Once suicidal ideation begins, individuals may find themselves in a cognitive downward spiral. Their negative self-perceptions gain in
intensity, and they begin to develop specific details of a suicide
plan. The suicidal thoughts frequently take on an obsessive quality. They intrude at unexpected times in the middle of daily functioning. Individuals who reach this point in the suicide trajectory
often experience feelings of helplessness in the face of their own
cognitions. One suicidal woman confided that she "couldn't shake"
her suicidal thoughts. She described her thought processes as follows: "I'll be making a cake and right in the middle of cracking
an egg, I'll think about driving my car over a cliff. I don't want
to think about it. It just happens. It's as though someone or some
thing sends me these thoughts against my will. I have no control
over them. They make me anxious, but they also promise relief
from my misery."

This woman's suicidal ideation had reached a point at which
it lost all rationality. She felt herself a victim of her own obsessive
thoughts and experienced a kind of thinking that bordered on
paranoia (i.e., someone or something was making her think that
way). She visualized how and where she would commit suicide
with ever-increasing clarity. While the obsessive quality of her
thinking was undoubtedly more dramatic than that of many suicides, the feeling that one is helpless to control one's own thinking
seems to be widespread when individuals have entered the stage
of active planning. Such feelings probably play a role in developing
the assurance that suicide is the best solution to the current
situation. The process of suicidal ideation seems to be common
across the life span, although the context may vary in richness
and detail depending on the individual and on the time in the
individual's life.

Suicidal ideation, as we have seen, may cause individuals to
exhibit some signs warning of their suicidal inclinations. Such
warning signs, if recognized by caring people, may lead to intervention, which may decrease the risk. It is important to note that
certain warning signs, such as verbal threats and self-injurious
behavior, are common to all age groups, whereas others may vary
with age.

The last two columns in Table 8.1 list triggering events and
suicidal behaviors. We have seen that triggering events are "final
straws" that upset the balance between thanatos and eros and
result in suicidal behavior. Two commonalities in suicidal behavior across the life span are that males exhibit higher rates of

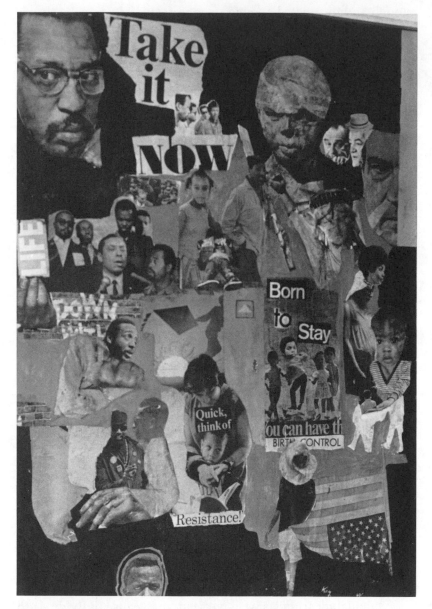

Take it Now, Kay Brown, 1969–1971. Collage, 42 × 32 in.
(Photograph by Roy Lewis Photography.)

suicide and that males of all ages generally use more lethal methods in their suicide attempts.

While it is important to note commonalities in the suicide trajectory, it is far more illuminating to examine the differences that are related to age and developmental stage.

Table 8.1 shows that during the childhood years (ages 5–14), there are two risk factors for suicide that may be rooted in biology. The first is a tendency toward impulsivity. Although the material reviewed in Chapter 3 clearly indicates that childhood suicide almost always occurs as a result of a history of problems, the act itself tends to be more impulsive in childhood than in any other age period. A child who has suffered over a long period of time from abuse or neglect will jump in front of a car without prior warning. Another child may run from the room in the midst of a parental argument, find the father's gun, and shoot him- or herself almost in one movement. Hyperactivity also seems to play a role in childhood suicide, adding to the apparent impulsivity of the act. Hyperactive children are unable to sit for a long time or to consider in detail the repercussions of an action. They have a bias for action and seem to move almost anxiously from one situation to another. Hyperactivity by itself does not predispose a child to suicide. However, if the predisposition to depression is there or if there are sufficient other psychological, cognitive, or environmental risk factors present, hyperactive children may have less protection against suicide than others who can contemplate more fully alternative solutions to problems.

There are two major psychological factors that increase children's risk of suicide. The first, explained well by Erikson, is a sense of inferiority. Children who feel inferior to others develop poor self-concepts and low self-esteem. They frequently act out in ways that confirm their low opinion of themselves and increase the likelihood that they will receive negative feedback from significant others. In this way they act so as to maintain or enhance their negative self-concepts, which may eventually lead to depression and possible suicidal behavior. The second psychological risk factor specific to childhood is the expendable child syndrome, which was discussed in Chapter 3. The expendable child experiences loss of love in the most extreme form. Parents of these children communicate very low regard for, hostility toward, and even hatred of them on a daily basis. These children believe they are unworthy and "expendable," that their deaths will not matter to anyone (Sabbath, 1969).

The cognitive risk factor most closely associated with childhood suicide is the immature view of death children have. Many children, especially in the early years of childhood, do not comprehend the finality of death. Because they tend to view death as a temporary and reversible state, children may be less likely to give it the respect it deserves. This cognitive factor, combined with a tendency toward impulsivity, may put certain children at much higher risk for suicide. Children between the ages of 5 and 12 also evidence concrete operational thinking, which involves an inability to see the multiple dimensions of morality. Concrete operational thinking resembles in many ways the characteristically rigid thought patterns associated with suicide at later ages. However, the developmental level of the child makes this type of thinking normative, which prospective helpers should keep in mind. Children simply are not able to envision multiple possi-

bilities for the future and are therefore likely to experience hopelessness when they are in a negative life situation.

The major environmental risk factors specific to childhood
are centered in the family and school. The literature shows that
abuse or neglect, parental conflict, unclear family role definitions,
an inflexible family structure, and parental modeling of suicidal
behavior all contribute to childhood suicide. In addition, repeated
experiences of failure in school and with peers can fuel a child's
sense of inferiority.

Warning signs in childhood include truancy and poor school
performance. Children may also demonstrate depression differ-

Anxiety, Edvard Munch, 1896. Lithograph. (Munch-museet, Oslo
Kommunes Kunstsamlinger, Norway.)

ently from adults. As discussed in Chapter 3, depressed children may manifest increased anxiety, sleep disturbance, aggressive behavior (which is acted out), low frustration tolerance, and poor impulse control.

More so than at any other period of life, triggering events may be minor occurrences. Because impulsive children are at higher risk for suicide, a seemingly tiny incident may trigger an impulsive, highly lethal act.

Suicidal behavior in childhood is characterized by its impulsivity and high level of lethality. Unlike all other periods except old age, in childhood males both attempt and complete suicide more often than do females. In addition, children are more likely than those in other age groups to fail in their suicide attempts. They also have the lowest overall suicide rate.

Turning to the adolescent years (ages 15 to 24), we again note risk factors that are specific to this age group. In the biological sphere, the onset of puberty, triggered by increased production of hormones, brings about sexual maturation. The process of maturation occurs over a period of years but has its most climactic effects in the early part of adolescence. These biological changes add their weight to the tumult of this age period, increasing suicidal risk.

In the category of psychological risk factors, the establishment of a sense of identity is a major developmental task of adolescence. Teenagers who develop some consistent understanding of who they are and who they are becoming will have a foundation of competence for dealing with the stresses of this period. In contrast, unfortunate adolescents who struggle with their identities are much less prepared to cope with these challenges. Identity crisis is a significant psychological risk factor for suicide among adolescents. Young people in the midst of an unsuccessful struggle to better understand their identity have few resources for dealing with other problems. A second psychological risk factor is the fluctuation of mood states. This moodiness, which is experienced by all adolescents, is partially rooted in the biological changes of the period. However, when it becomes extreme, it increases the risk of suicide. Since it is experienced as an emotional state, it is listed among the psychological risk factors.

In the cognitive realm, adolescents are also undergoing rapid change. As they become capable of formal operational thought for the first time, they are like children with new toys. They try out their newly acquired skills, creating in their minds worlds that have never existed. For the first time, they understand at a personal level the implications of such constructs as equality and justice. This may result in idealistic thinking—tinged with a sense of tragedy as they see the distance between their idealized worlds and what really exists. They may also have difficulty in accepting their own mortality; the result is an illusion of invulnerability, which contributes to higher risk taking among adolescents. In addition, adolescents experience a renewed period of egocentrism, as they believe that they are the first ones to really understand the world from their new perspective. This egocentrism fuels their sense of performing for an imaginary audience and increases their feelings of self-consciousness, making small embarrassments seem like major traumas. In this way, the pain of daily living is increased for adolescents. All of these factors may play a role in enhancing the risk of suicidal behavior.

The literature is clear on environmental risk factors in adolescence. In addition to conflict between parents in the home, adolescents are also at higher risk for suicide if their peer relationships are turbulent or nonexistent, if they abuse drugs or alcohol, and if their families have a pattern of anomic behavior.

Warning signs in adolescence include self-mutilation, changes in habits, truancy, poor school performance, and behavior that implies preparation for death, such as giving away prized possessions. Since the teen years are characterized by mood swings, spotting these warning signs may be difficult. It is not uncommon for people closest to a teenager to remark, following a suicide attempt, "I knew he was acting strangely, but I thought that was typical behavior for an adolescent."

Certain triggering events appear to be more common in adolescence than in other age periods. For example, suicides of other people seem to trigger suicidal behavior more frequently among teens than among others. Perhaps this phenomenon is related to the fact that adolescents are trying out new identities and therefore are more open to imitation and modeling. Also, the suicide of a peer or of a well-known public figure may act as a permission-giving device for adolescents. Whatever its effect, it is clear that publicized acts of suicide trigger more copycat and cluster suicides among adolescents than among those of any other age group. Other triggering events common to adolescence include experiences of failure and interpersonal problems.

Suicide among adolescents has had the highest rate of increase in the past 30 years. Another fact about adolescent suicidal behavior is that the attempt:completion ratio for females is almost a perfect mirror image of the ratio for males. Ninety percent of all suicide attempts in adolescence are made by females, whereas 80% of all completed suicides are by males (Berman & Carroll, 1984).

Among young adults, there are several indicators of suicide risk that differ from those for other age groups. In the biological arena, a special risk for suicide—for a small percentage of women—is the experience of postpartum depression. It should be noted that women who suffer from depression after their first birth are at higher risk for depression after subsequent births. Thus, postpartum depression may also be a risk factor for some women during the first decade of middle adulthood.

In the category of psychological risk factors, young adults are working on the task of establishing intimacy and avoiding isolation, and they are also beginning to achieve generativity or suffer from psychological stagnation. At this stage of life, there is a heightened risk of becoming psychologically isolated from others. The suicide statistics show higher rates of suicide among single people of both sexes. Young adulthood seems to be a critical time for forming bonds of intimacy with mates and friends that will protect against isolation and the accompanying sense of loneliness.

In the cognitive arena, young adults tend to face the first in a series of re-evaluations of life choices. Whether called "the age 30 transition" or "catch 30" (Sheehy, 1976), this process calls for a cognitive examination of all aspects of life to date, including occupation, marital choice, and parenting decisions, and it frequently leads to a reconceptualization of life goals. The process surely involves feelings as well as cognitions, but it is included under this category since it is experienced and described essentially as a thought process.

Environmental variables that increase the risk for suicide in young adulthood include, for women, the presence of young children in the home and marital problems. For men, the environmental risk factors appear to be related to occupational problems and to drug and alcohol abuse. A new factor increasing the suicide rates among young adults is AIDS.

Common triggering events among young adults include quarrels or physical fights with spouses and occupational setbacks. Recent research has shown that a new triggering event for young adults is a positive diagnosis of AIDS.

There has been a small reduction in the suicide rate for young adults over the past 5 years. Also, young adulthood is the period in which suicide rates for blacks and American Indians reach their peak.

During middle age, several biological changes may heighten the suicide risk. For women, one important event is menopause; for men, climacteric. Both of these involve changes in the ability to reproduce. Menopause is of course far more visible than the climacteric, because it results in the cessation of menstruation. However, both are triggered by the body's producing lower levels of hormones than at any time since puberty. Once again, individuals find their behavior and moods influenced by biology. In a culture as youth oriented as ours, any decline in physical abilities or attractiveness is likely to increase feelings of anxiety, inferiority, and depression.

In the psychological arena, many middle-aged adults experience the loss of their youthful dreams when they realize they have gone as far as they are going in their careers. While some middle-aged adults are able to become reconciled to the vanishing of their hopes for outstanding occupational accomplishment, others experience great pain and become highly vulnerable to depression and suicide. Another important psychological risk factor for middle-aged suicide is the increasing movement toward interiority. Interiority can be healthy if it promotes positive self-knowledge and increased satisfaction with one's life pattern. However, often the tendency toward interiority results in unhealthy ego absorption. As responsibilities to the family of procreation decline, the amount of daily interaction with one's children and with the individuals they bring into one's life also declines, resulting in the danger of cathectic impoverishment. As we discussed in Chapter 5, middle-aged individuals need to struggle against this natural tendency toward cathectic impoverishment in order to be productive and happy during midlife. Those who fail to do so begin to slip toward the stagnation pole of Erikson's continuum and increase their risk of isolation, depression, and suicide.

Cognitively, middle-aged adults experience a shift in their time perspective. They tend to change their focus from the amount of time already lived to the amount of time left to live, a shift which may trigger higher anxiety. It may also contribute to the onset of despair as middle-aged adults give up their youthful dreams and become convinced that there is not enough time left to begin anew. Many middle-aged adults also engage in a major cognitive evaluation of their life choices and patterns, often with such intensity that the term *crisis* is appropriate.

Increased environmental risk factors for suicide during middle age include the deaths of significant others, the loss of parental and filial roles, lower levels of activity and involvement, and an accumulation of negative life events. Alcoholism plays more of a role in the suicide of adults between the ages of 35 and 64 than for any other age group.

It should be noted that middle age is the peak age for suicides among women. From this age on, the rate of suicide among women actually decreases.

There is reason to believe that suicidal risk in old age is greatly exacerbated by biological factors. General physical and organic mental declines, combined with chronic illness and chronic pain, undoubtedly contribute both to the depression that is endemic to old age and to the high suicide rates among the elderly.

In the psychological sphere, elderly people experience increased passivity and loneliness. These feelings undoubtedly add to a growing sense of despair among a minority of older people. This sense of despair, the polar opposite to Erikson's sense of ego integrity, undermines both pleasure and meaning in life among some elderly individuals.

Cognitive risk factors in old age include a decline in cognitive functioning, both in the rate of learning new material and the rate of retrieval of information. Confronted by the cliche "You can't teach an old dog new tricks," many elderly persons stop trying to learn new material and withdraw further from involvement with the world. There is also some evidence that elderly people intellectually and emotionally reach a point of acceptance of death (Wass, 1979).

Environmental risk factors for suicide that have been shown to be important among the elderly include widowhood, retirement (especially for men), increasing inactivity, financial problems, and the experiencing of cumulative losses in a short period of time. A perception of being devalued or having outlived one's usefulness to society may also be introjected from the environment.

Warning signs among the elderly include visits to doctors' offices and visible indications of putting affairs in order. Suicide among the elderly is often triggered by the diagnosis of terminal illness.

The elderly have the highest rate of suicide of all age groups. In addition, this age group has the largest sex difference and the highest male suicide rate. Suicide attempts among elderly people are generally well planned and highly lethal, indicating a seriousness of purpose more developed than in other age groups.

Thus far in the chapter we have enumerated developmental principles, introduced a model suicide trajectory, and discussed commonalities and differences in suicide across the life span. The final section will examine the ways in which a life span perspective, added to the more traditional ways of viewing suicide, contributes to a more complete understanding of suicidal behavior.

RATIONALE FOR A LIFE SPAN PERSPECTIVE

When psychology began as a discipline over 100 years ago, its focus was on individual differences. The early pioneers (e.g., Wilhelm Wundt) established laboratories designed to explore the dimensions of individual behavior. They weighed, measured, counted, and observed every possible visible characteristic. The more they studied individuals, the more they knew about those individuals. Studying individuals separately and in depth is the basis of the idiographic method. The strength of the idiographic method is that it produces in-depth information about a few identified individuals. However, the knowledge gained about certain individuals is not easily generalizable to other individuals, and therefore it is not terribly useful in helping to understand individual differences or in predicting the behavior of other individuals.

In an attempt to help us understand behavior in a more general way, psychologists in the early part of this century developed the nomothetic method. This method involves measuring many individuals on one or more dimensions but reporting the results for groups rather than for individuals. This approach provides useful "milestones" of behavior and development. Perhaps the best-known early psychologist pioneering this method in the

United States was Gesell (1940), who provided many indicators
of child development, which allowed parents to compare their
children's progress with the "norm," or average child of the same
age. While this approach did provide useful information, it sometimes resulted in misleading conclusions. For example, when studies
were conducted with large numbers of the elderly, it was erro-
neously concluded that people became less well informed and less
intelligent as they age. The performance of elderly people in the
studies was compared to the performance of younger cohorts of
people who were more educated. Because of errors like this, researchers began to develop a new appreciation for the limitations
inherent in strict nomothetic studies. The truth is that, although
this type of study may yield useful information about groups, it
cannot be applied to individuals without a high risk of misrep-
resentation.

Growing out of both the idiographic and nomothetic methods is a third approach, which classifies or creates typologies for
certain behavioral responses. The reasoning behind such typologies is that they might provide a way to understand behavior in
a "shorthand" fashion. Categories of behavior based on normative
studies could be created, taught to prospective caregivers, and
used to help understand individual clients as well as to discuss
treatment approaches for individual clients with other professionals. In Chapter 2, we reviewed one of the first classifications
of suicide, which was created by Durkheim (1897/1951) in the
late 19th century. Since that time, many more systems have been
suggested. Shneidman (1985) recently reviewed five additional
classification systems and concluded that "these classifications,
taken singly or together, have either an arbitrary, esoteric, or ad
hoc quality to them. They do not seem impressively definitive.
I know for a fact that the best known of them is of practically no
use in the clinic, where the task is saving lives" (p. 29). Shneidman
went on to reject the typology approach to understanding suicide,
at least for the clinician working with suicidal patients. He believed that a "personology" approach was most appropriate.

The personology approach suggested by Shneidman is based
on the work of Henry Murray (1938). Murray believed that human
behavior could be understood as a product of the needs of the
individual as they were expressed in an environment that exerted
certain "presses" on the individual. Thus, suicidal behavior could
be understood as an attempt to meet one or more major needs in
a particular stressful environment. The emphasis in this model
is on the fit between the kind and amount of press that the environment imposes on individuals and their abilities to express
their dominant needs. Inherent in this view is the realization that
suicidal behavior can best be understood as the result of an interaction between internal and external forces acting on an individual.

In understanding suicidal behavior, the personology approach may indeed be more valuable than either the idiographic or nomothetic approaches alone. However, we maintain that for the beginning student of suicide each of these approaches is valuable. Each sheds light on the topic of suicide from a different perspective and each adds its weight to our growing understanding of this complex subject. Thus, reading case studies of suicidal people, particularly those who were treated successfully, helps beginning professionals gain understanding from an idiographic perspective. Examining the statistics of suicide for different age groups, clearly an example of the nomothetic approach, helps beginning professionals become aware of patterns in suicidal behaviors that may help them predict suicidal risk for specific clients more accurately. Classification systems may introduce beginning professionals to some of the commonalities that do exist in suicidal behavior, whereas the personology approach permits helping professionals to focus on the fit between the individual and the environment. All of these approaches can increase our ability to discuss suicide with other professionals, to raise appropriate issues with suicidal people with whom we work, and to feel more comfortable in dealing with suicidal people in general.

However, we believe that understanding the idiographic, nomothetic, typology, and personology approaches to suicide is not enough. We believe that, especially for young professionals, studying life span development is also essential. The addition of a life span perspective broadens our general understanding so that we come to view individuals as "moving targets" against a background of life's predictable stages, opportunities, accidents, and stresses. Furthermore, we come to recognize that these moving targets carry within themselves an ever-increasing accumulation of life experiences as filtered by their unique biology and perceptual styles. In espousing a life span development approach to understanding suicide, we are suggesting that age and the developmental characteristics associated with age are important background variables to be considered when working with suicidal individuals. For example, a young male counselor working with a 55-year-old woman might not understand her despair if he did not realize that a shift in time perspective is very common during middle age. Her lament that her life is over—that there is not enough time remaining to make a new beginning—might be construed by the young therapist as a manifestation of the cognitive rigidity that marks suicidal ideation rather than as a legitimate perception that is typical of middle-aged people. In like fashion, an understanding of the peer orientation of adolescence helps to forewarn beginning professionals about the impact an adolescent suicide might have on other adolescents.

At the very least, knowledge of developmental principles, milestones of development, and predictable themes and losses of the various age periods provides a more detailed context for understanding individual suicidal behaviors than the usual normative approaches and also adds a meaningful dimension to the usual idiographic approaches. At its best, a broad understanding of life span psychology makes us aware that warning signs, suicidal themes, and contributing factors are different for different age groups and must be responded to differently. Adopting a life span approach to suicide also expands our power of empathy, because it helps us to understand the frame of reference or worldview of suicidal persons of different ages. Finally, understanding life span principles helps us to predict types of suicides at different ages. For example, we might be more alert to the suicide risk among impulsive and angry children than among those who are more passive and sanguine, even given similar home and school circumstances. We might expect a rash of suicides among adolescents following the suicide of a teen idol. We would not predict the same number of suicides among a middle-aged population should a middle-aged star commit suicide. In understanding the high rate of suicide among the elderly, we might be more likely to recognize the very real factors of loneliness, cumulative loss, chronic pain, and imminence of death as contributors to distress. The approach we take in working with a child, an adolescent, a young adult, a middle-aged adult, or an elderly person will vary according to our ability to comprehend the realities of the individual's world as they interact with the developmental level that that individual has attained.

In summary, the life span perspective adds a richness to our understanding. It helps us to see suicide as a product of an individual's reacting to the particular stresses and life events of his or her personal history as they are mediated by biology and coping skills at a particular developmental period of life. Attending to the principles inherent in life span development, as well as understanding the special stresses of each period in the life cycle, may enable us to work more effectively with all individuals who are considering making premature exits from the stage of life.

SUMMARY

Our understanding of suicidal behavior is enriched by approaching this topic from a life span development perspective. In this chapter we have reviewed seven principles which are inherent in a life span development approach to the study of any behavior. The first principle is that genetic factors are important influences in all aspects of behavior in any age group. The second principle is that change is constant across the life span, and the third principle is that development, which involves organized movement from the simple to the complex as well as entropy toward the end of life, is also constant. The fourth principle is that development occurs as a result of imbalance or tension between the individual and the environment. The fifth principle pertains to the development of the self as the central organizing force within the individual. The self constitutes, among other things, an individual's identity, and it filters perceptions of the world in a manner consistent with the self-concept. The sixth principle is that a mature understanding of self, called individuation, will occur only in later years—after a great deal of life experience and self-exploration. The final principle is that cohort differences are important factors influencing behavior throughout the life span.

A model suicide trajectory was presented in order to delineate the many factors that, together with complex interactions, contribute to a suicidal act. The elements of the trajectory include biological, psychological, environmental, and cognitive factors that contribute to suicidal ideation. Suicidal ideation often leads to warning signs that a suicidal act may occur. Such acts are sometimes elicited by triggering events.

The suicide trajectory model was used to discuss both commonalities and age-related differences in suicidal behavior throughout the life span. Among the commonalities discussed were the biological risk factor of a genetic predisposition to depression, the psychological factor of helpless and hopeless feelings, the environmental factor of loss, and the cognitive factor of rigid, dichotomous thinking. All of these, as well as other factors, have been shown to be associated with suicide among all age groups. Age-related differences in suicidal behavior were also detailed. Important factors to consider regarding suicide among children include impulsivity, feelings of inferiority, immature views of death, child abuse, and school failure. Specific adolescent suicide factors include the biological changes of puberty, identity concerns, the idealism of adolescents, and family conflict. Special concern was expressed for the impact of other suicides as triggering events for this age group. Among the idiosyncratic factors that contribute to young adult suicide are postpartum depression, problems involving intimacy and child rearing, and occupational stress. Also important is the review of major life decisions which usually occurs around age 30. Middle-age factors include physical loss, occupational leveling, and movement toward interiority within the context of a changing time perspective. Finally, suicide factors especially important in old age include cumulative losses in physical, cognitive, occupational, and interpersonal spheres.

The importance of a life span perspective, in addition to idiographic, nomothetic, typology, and personology approaches, for fully understanding suicide was discussed in detail. We concluded that the insights about suicide that are provided by a life span development perspective will enable helping professionals to work more effectively with suicidal individuals of all ages.

REFERENCES

Akiskal, H. S., & McKinney, W. T. (1973). Depressive disorders: Toward a unified hypothesis. *Science, 218,* 20–29.

Bandura, A. (1977). *Social learning theory*. Englewood Cliffs, NJ: Prentice-Hall.

Berman, A. L., & Carroll, T. A. (1984). Adolescent suicide: A critical review. *Death Education, 8*, 53–64.

Bock, E. W., & Webber, I. L. (1972, February). Suicide among the elderly: Isolating widowhood and mitigating alternatives. *Journal of Marriage and the Family*, pp. 24–31.

Brazelton, B. (1969). *Infants and mothers*. New York: Delacorte Press.

Durkheim, E. (1951). *Suicide* (J. A. Spaulding & G. Simpson, Trans.). Glencoe, IL: The Free Press. (Original work published 1897.)

Ellis, A. (1962). *Reason and emotion in psychotherapy*. New York: Lyle Stuart.

Erikson, E. H. (1959). *Identity and the life cycle*. New York: International Universities Press.

Garfinkel, B. D., Froese, A., & Hood, J. (1982). Suicide attempts in children and adolescents. *American Journal of Psychiatry, 139*, 1257–1261.

Gesell, A. (1940). *The first five years of life*. New York: Harper.

Gould, R. L. (1978). *Transformations: Growth and change in adult life*. New York: Simon & Schuster.

Holmes, T. H., & Rahe, R. H. (1967). The social readjustment rating scale. *Journal of Psychosomatic Research, 11*, 213–218.

Jung, C. G. (1960). *The structure and dynamics of the psyche* (R.F.C. Hull, Trans.). In G. Adler (Ed.), *The collected works of C. G. Jung* (Bollingen Series 20, Vol. 8, pp. 749–795). Princeton, NJ: Princeton University Press.

Kelly, G. A. (1955). *The psychology of personal constructs*. New York: Norton.

Kohlberg, L. (1976). Moral stages and moralization: Cognitive-development approach. In T. Lickona (Ed.), *Moral development and behavior: Theory, research, and social issues* (pp. 31–53). New York: Holt, Rinehart & Winston.

Lecky, P. (1973). *Self-consistency: A theory of personality*. Fort Myers Beach, FL: Island Press.

Levinson, D. J., Darrow, C., Klein, E., Levinson, M., & McKee, B. (1978). *Seasons of a man's life*. New York: Knopf.

Meichenbaum, D. (1985). *Stress inoculation training*. Elmsford, NY: Pergamon.

Murray, H. A. (1938). *Explorations in personality*. New York: Oxford University Press.

Sabbath, J. C. (1969). The suicidal adolescent: The expendable child. *Journal of the American Academy of Child Psychiatry, 8*, 272–289.

Sheehy, G. (1976). *Passages: Predictable crises of adult life*. New York: Dutton.

Shneidman, E. S. (1976). The components of suicide. *Psychiatric Annals, 6*, 51–66.

Shneidman, E. (1985). *Definition of suicide*. New York: Wiley.

Stephens, J. B. (1985). Suicidal women and their relationships with husbands, boyfriends and lovers. *Suicide and Life-Threatening Behavior, 15*, 77–89.

Stillion, J. M. (1985). *Death and the sexes: An examination of differential longevity, attitudes, behaviors, and coping skills*. Washington, DC: Hemisphere.

Terenzini, P. T. (1987, November). *A review of selected theoretical models of student development and collegiate impact*. Paper presented at the meeting of the Association for the Study of Higher Education, Baltimore.

Wass, H. (1979). Death and the elderly. In H. Wass (Ed.) *Dying: Facing the facts*. Washington, DC: Hemisphere.

References

Ackerly, W. C. (1967). Latency-age children who threaten or attempt to kill themselves. *Journal of the American Academy of Child Psychiatry, 6*, 242–261.

Adam, K. S., Bouckoms, A., & Streiner, D. L. (1982). Parental loss and family stability in attempted suicide. *Archives of General Psychiatry, 39*, 1081–1085.

Adams-Tucker, C. (1982). Proximate effects of sexual abuse in childhood: A report in 28 children. *American Journal of Psychiatry, 139*, 1252–1256.

Akiskal, H. S., & McKinney, W. T. (1973). Depressive disorders: Toward a unified hypothesis. *Science, 218*, 20–29.

Alsop, R. (1984, April 24). As early retirement grows in popularity, some have misgivings. *The Wall Street Journal*, p. 1.

Alschuler, R., & Hattwick, L. B. W. (1947). *Painting and personality: A study of young children*. Chicago: University of Chicago Press.

Alvarez, A. (1970). *The savage god: A study of suicide*. New York: Random House.

American Humane Association. (1987). *Highlights of official child neglect and reporting 1985*. Denver: Author.

Angle, C., O'Brien, T., & McIntire, M. (1983). Adolescent self-poisoning: A nine year follow up. *Developmental and Behavioral Pediatrics, 4*, 83–87.

Aquinas, T. (1975). *Summa theologica* (Vol. 38). London: Blackfriars. (Original work written 1265–1272.)

Aries, P. (1981). *The hour of our death*. New York: Knopf.

Asberg, M., Nordstrom, P., & Traskman-Bendz, L. (1986, December). Cerebrospinal fluid studies in suicide. *Annals of the New York Academy of Sciences, 487*, 243–255.

Asberg, M., & Traskman, L. (1981). Studies of CSF 5-HIAA in depression and suicidal behavior. *Experiments in Medical Biology, 133*, 739–752.

Asberg, M., Traskman, L., & Thoren, P. (1976). 5-HIAA in the cerebrospinal fluid: A biochemical suicide predictor. *Archives of General Psychiatry, 33*, 1193–1197.

Atchley, R. C. (1976). *The sociology of retirement*. New York: Halstead Press.

Axline, V. A. (1947). *Play therapy: The inner dynamics of childhood* (L. Carmichael, Ed.). Boston: Houghton Mifflin.

Baker, P. M. (1985). The status of age: Preliminary results. *Journal of Gerontology, 40*, 506–508.

Baker, S. P., O'Neill, B. D., & Karpf, R. S. (1984). *The injury fact book*. Lexington, MA: Heath.

Bandura, A. (1977). *Social learning theory*. Englewood Cliffs, NJ: Prentice-Hall.

Banki, C. M., & Arato, M. (1983). Amine metabolites, neuroendocrine findings, and personality dimension as correlates of suicidal behavior. *Psychiatry Research, 10*, 253–261.

Baron, C. H. (1980, April). Termination of life support systems in the elderly. Discussion: To die before the gods please: Legal issues surrounding euthanasia and the elderly. Paper presented at a Scientific Meeting of the Boston Society for Gerontologic Psychiatry.

Barraclough, B. M. (1971). Suicide in the elderly. In D. W. Kay & A. Walk (Eds.), *Recent developments in psychogeriatrics*. (pp. 89–97). Kent, England: Headly Brothers.

Barraclough, B. (1987). *Suicide: Clinical and epidemiological studies*. London: Croom Helm.

Barraclough, B., Bunch, J., & Nelson, B. (1974). A hundred cases of suicide: Clinical aspects. *British Journal of Psychiatry, 125*, 355–373.

Barrett, C. J. (1979). Women in widowhood. In J. H. Williams (Ed.) *Psychology of women: Selected readings*. (pp. 596–506). New York: Norton.

Barry, B. (1984). Perceptions of suicide. *Death Studies (Supplement), 8*, 17–26.

Battin, M. P. (1984). The concept of rational suicide. In E. Shneidman (Ed.), *Death: Current perspectives* (3rd Ed., pp. 297–320). Palo Alto, CA: Mayfield.

Beck, A. T. (1967). *Depression: Clinical, experimental, and theoretical aspects*. New York: Hoeber.

Beck, A. T., Kovacs, M. & Weissman, A. (1979). Assessment of suicide ideation: The scale for suicide ideators. *Journal of Consulting and Clinical Psychology, 47*, 343–352.

Beck, A. T., Rush, A., Show, B., & Emery, G. (1979). *Cognitive therapy of depression*. New York: Guilford Press.

Beck, A. T., Steer, R. A., Kovacs, M., & Garrison, B. (1985). Hopelessness and eventual suicide: A 10-year prospective study of patients hospitalized with suicidal ideation. *American Journal of Psychiatry, 142*, 559–563.

Benjaminsen, S. (1981). Stressful life events preceding the onset of neurotic depression. *Psychological Medicine, 11*, 369–378.

Benson, R. A., & Brodie, D. C. (1975). Suicide by overdose of medicines among the aged. *Journal of the American Geriatrics Society, 23*, 304–308.

Berardo, F. M. (1968). Widowhood status in the United States: Perspective on a neglected aspect of the family life-cycle. *The Family Coordinator, 17*, 191–203.

Berardo, D. H. (1988). Bereavement and mourning. In H. Wass, F. M. Berardo, & R. A. Neimeyer (Eds.), *Dying: Facing the Facts* (pp. 279–300). Washington, DC: Hemisphere.

Berger, M. (1984). Intervention with potential suicides. In N. Linzer, (Ed.), *Suicide: The will to live vs. the will to die* (pp. 55–70). New York: Human Sciences Press.

Berglund, M. (1984). Suicide in alcoholism—a prospective study of 88 alcoholics: The multidimensional diagnosis at first admission. *Archives of General Psychiatry, 41*, 888–891.

Berman, A. L. (1987, November). *Suicide prevention: A critical need and a critical perspective*. Paper presented at the First National Conference on Suicide Prevention and the Public Schools, Orlando, FL.

Berman, A. L. (1988). Playing the suicide game. *Readings: A Journal of Reviews and Commentary in Mental Health, 3*, 20–23.

Berman, A. L., & Carroll, T. A. (1984). Adolescent suicide: A critical review. *Death Education, 8*, 53–64.

Blackwell, P. L., & Gessner, J. C. (1983). Fear and trembling: An inquiry into adolescent perceptions of living in the nuclear age. *Youth and Society, 15*(2), 237–255.

Blum, J. E., Clark, E. T., & Jarvik, L. F. (1973). The New York State Psychiatric Institute Study of Aging Twins. In L. F. Jarvik, C. Eisdorfer, & J. E. Blum (Eds.), *Intellectual functioning in adults: Psychological and biological influences* (pp. 13–20). New York: Springer.

Blumenthal, S. J., & Kupfer, D. J. (1986). Generalizable treatment strategies for suicidal behavior. In J. J. Mann & M. Stanley (Eds.), *Psychobiology of suicidal behavior* (pp. 327–340). New York: New York Academy of Sciences.

Bock, E. W., & Webber, I. L. (1972a). Social status and relational systems of elderly suicides: A reexamination of the Henry-Short Thesis. *Suicide and Life-Threatening Behavior, 2,* 145–159.

Bock, E. W., & Webber, I. L. (1972b, February). Suicide among the elderly: Isolating widowhood and mitigating alternatives. *Journal of Marriage and the Family,* pp. 24–31.

Boldt, M. (1982). Normative evaluations of suicide and death: A cross-generational study. *Omega, 13,* 145–157.

Bollen, K. A., & Phillips, D. P. (1982). Imitative suicides: A national study of the effects of television news stories. *American Sociological Review, 47,* 802–809.

Borg, S. E., & Stahl, M. (1982). A prospective study of suicides and controls among psychiatric patients. *Acta Psychiatrica Scandinavica, 65,* 221–232.

Brazelton, B. (1969). *Infants and mothers.* New York: Delacorte Press.

Breed, W. (1963). Occupational mobility and suicide among white males. *American Sociological Review, 28,* 179–188.

Breed, W., & Huffine, C. (1979). Sex differences in suicide among older white Americans: A role and developmental approach. In O. J. Kaplan (Ed.), *Psychopathology of Aging* (pp. 289–309). New York: Academic Press.

Bromberg, S., & Cassel, C. K. (1983). Suicide in the elderly: The limits of paternalism. *Journal of the American Geriatrics Society, 31*(11), 698–703.

Brown, G. W., & Harris, T. (1978). *Social origins of depression.* London: Tavistock.

Brownmiller, S. (1983). *Feminity.* New York: Linden Press and Simon & Schuster.

Buhler, C. (1961). Old age and fulfillment of life with consideration of the use of time in old age. *Acta Psychologica, 19,* 126–148.

Butler, R. N., & Lewis, M. I. (1977). *Aging and mental health: Positive psychological approaches.* St. Louis, MO: C. V. Mosby.

Butler, R. N., & Lewis, M. I. (1982). *Aging and mental health: Positive psychosocial and biomedical approaches* (3rd ed.). St. Louis: Mosby.

Cain, A. C. (Ed.) (1972). *Survivors of suicide.* Springfield, IL: Charles C Thomas.

Cain, A. C., & Fast, I. (1972). Children's disturbed reaction to parent suicide: Distortions of guilt, communication, and identification. In A. C. Cain (Ed.), *Survivors of suicide* (pp. 93–111). Springfield, IL: Charles C Thomas.

Calhoun, L. G., Selby, J. W., & Faulstich, M. E. (1980). Reactions to the parents of the child suicide: A study of social impression. *Journal of Consulting and Clinical Psychology, 48,* 535–536.

Calhoun, L. G., Selby, J. W., & Faulstich, M. E. (1982). The aftermath of child suicide: Influences on the perceptions of parents. *Journal of Community Psychology, 10,* 250–254.

Canada. (1987). Suicide in Canada: Report of the National Task Force on Suicide in Canada. Ottawa: Department of National Health and Welfare.

Cantor, P. (1987, November). *During and after a suicidal crisis: What educators need to know.* Paper presented at the First National Conference on Suicide Prevention and the Public Schools, Orlando, FL.

Cassem, N. H. (1980, April). Termination of life support systems in the elderly: Clinical issues. Paper presented at the Scientific Meeting of the Boston Society for Gerontologic Psychiatry.

Centers for Disease Control. (1986). *Mortality and Morbidity Weekly Report, 35*(22).

Clarkin, J. F., Friedman, R. C., Hurt, S. W., Corn, R., & Aronoff, M. (1984). Affective and character pathology of suicidal adolescents and young adult inpatients. *Journal of Clinical Psychiatry, 45*(1), 19–22.

Clausen, J. A. (1981). Men's occupational careers in the middle years. In D. H. Eichoun, J. A. Clausen, N. Haan, M. P. Honzik, & P. Mussen (Eds.), *Present and past in middle life* (pp. 321–351). New York: Academic Press.

Cohen, J. (1961). A study of suicide pacts. *Medical Legal Journal, 29,* 144–151.

Cohen-Sandler, R., Berman, A. L., & King, R. A. (1982). Life stress and symptomatology: Determinants of suicidal behavior in children. *Journal of the American Academy of Child Psychiatry, 21,* 178–186.

Cohn, H. (1976). Suicide in Jewish legal and religious tradition. *Mental Health and Society, 3,* 129–136.

Coleman, L. (1987). *Suicide clusters.* Boston: Faber & Faber.

Connell, H. M. (1972). Attempted suicide in school children. *Medical Journal of Australia, 1,* 686–690.

Corder, B. F., & Haizlip, T. M. (1984). Environmental and personality similarities in case histories of suicide and self-poisoning in children under ten. *Suicide and Life-Threatening Behavior, 14,* 59–66.

Corder, B. F., Shorr, W., & Corder, R. F. (1974). A study of social and psychological characteristics of adolescent suicide attempters in an urban disadvantaged area. *Adolescence, 9,* 1–16.

Cox, H. (1984). *Later life: The realities of aging.* Englewood Cliffs, NJ: Prentice-Hall.

Curphey, T. J. (1961). The role of the social scientist in the medicological certification of death from suicide. In N. L. Farberow & E. S. Shneidman (Eds.), *The cry for help* (pp. 110–117). New York: McGraw-Hill.

Curran, D. K. (1987). *Adolescent suicidal behavior.* Washington, DC: Hemisphere.

Darbonne, A. R. (1969). Suicide and age: A suicide note analysis. *Journal of Consulting and Clinical Psychology, 33,* 46–50.

David, D. & Brannon, R. (1976). The big wheel: Success, status, and the need to be looked up to. In D. David & R. Brannon (Eds.), *The forty-nine percent majority* (pp. 89–160). Reading: MA: Addison-Wesley.

Demi, A. S., & Miles, M. S. (1988). Suicide bereaved parents: Emotional distress and physical problems. *Death Studies, 12,* 297–307.

Derryberry, D., & Rothbart, M. K. (1984). Emotion, attention, and temperament. In C. E. Izard, J. Kagan, & R. B. Zajonc (Eds.), *Emotions, cognition and behavior* (pp. 132–167). Cambridge: Cambridge University Press.

Domino, G., Moore, D., Westlake, L., & Gibson, L. (1982). Attitudes toward suicide: A factor analytic approach. *Journal of Clinical Psychology, 38*(2), 257–262.

Donne, J. (1982). *Biathanatos* (M. Rudick & M. P. Battin, Trans.). New York: Garland. (Original work published 1644.)

Dorpat, T. L., Anderson, W. F., & Ripley, H. S. (1968). The relationship of physical illness to suicide. In H. L. P. Resnik (Ed.), *Suicide: Diagnosis and management* (pp. 209–219). Boston: Little, Brown.

Dorpat, T. L., & Ripley, H. S. (1960). A study of suicide in the Seattle area. *Comprehensive Psychiatry, 1,* 349–359.

Doyle, J. A. (1983). *The male experience.* Dubuque, IA: William C. Brown.

Dunn, R. G., & Morrish-Vidners, D. (1987). The psychological and social experience of suicide survivors. *Omega, 18,* 175–215.

Durkheim, E. (1951). *Suicide* (J. A. Spaulding & G. Simpson, Trans.). Glencoe, IL: The Free Press. (Original work published 1897.)

Eisenberg, L. (1980). Adolescent suicide: On taking arms against a sea of troubles. *Pediatrics, 66,* 315–321.

Ekerdt, D. J., Bossé, R., Levkov, S. (1985). An empirical test of phases of retirement: Findings from the normative aging study. *Journal of Gerontology, 40,* 95–101.

Elkind, D. (1967). Egocentrism in adolescence. *Child Development, 38*, 1025–1034.

Elkind, D., & Bowen, R. (1979). Imaginary audience behavior in children and adolescents. *Developmental Psychology, 15*, 38–44.

Ellis, A. (1962). *Reason and emotion in psychotherapy.* New York: Lyle Stuart.

Ellis, A. (1974). *Humanistic psychotherapy: The rational-emotive approach.* New York: McGraw-Hill.

Erikson, E. H. (1959). *Identity and the life cycle.* New York: International Universities Press.

Erikson, E. H. (1968). *Identity: Youth and crisis.* New York: Norton.

Erikson, E. H. (1980). *Identity and the life cycle.* New York: Norton.

Farberow, N. (Ed.). (1975). *Suicide in different cultures.* Baltimore, MD: University Park Press.

Farberow, N. L., & Moriwaki, S. Y. (1975, August). Self-destructive crisis in the older person. *The Gerontologist,* pp. 333–337.

Farberow, N., & Shneidman, E. (1961). *The cry for help.* New York: McGraw-Hill.

Fillenbaum, G. G., George, L. K., & Palmore, E. B. (1985). Determinants and consequences of retirement among men of different races and economic levels. *Journal of Gerontology, 40*, 85–94.

Fox, R. (1984). The Samaritans: An alternative approach to suicide prevention. In N. Linzer (Ed.), *Suicide: The will to live vs. the will to die.* (pp. 43–53). New York: Human Sciences Press.

Frankl, V. E. (1963). *Man's search for meaning: An introduction to logotherapy* (I. Lasch, Trans.). New York: Washington Square Press.

Frederick, C., & Resnik, H. (1971). How suicideal behaviors are learned. *American Journal of Psychotherapy, 25*, 37–55.

Frenkel-Brunswik, E. (1963). Adjustments and reorientation in the course of the life span. In R. G. Kuhlen & G. G. Thompson (Eds.), *Psychological studies of human development.* (pp. 554–564). New York: Appleton-Century-Crofts.

Freud, S. (1953). *The standard edition of the complete psychological works.* J. Strachey (Ed.). London: Hogarth Press.

Freud, S. (1961). *Mourning and melancholia.* In J. Strachey (Ed. and Trans.). *The standard edition of the complete psychological works of Sigmund Freud* (Vol. 14, pp. 243–258). London: Hogarth Press. (Original work published 1917.)

Freud, S. (1961). *The ego and the id.* In J. Strachey (Ed. and Trans.). *The standard edition of the complete psychological works of Sigmund Freud* (Vol. 19, pp. 3–66). London: Hogarth Press. (Original work published 1923.)

Freud, S. (1961). *Beyond the pleasure principle.* In J. Strachey (Ed. and Trans.). *The standard edition of the complete psychological works of Sigmund Freud* (Vol. 18, pp. 7–64). London: Hogarth Press. (Original work published in 1920.)

Freud, S. (1961). *Civilization and its discontents.* In J. Strachey (Ed. and Trans.). *The standard edition of the complete psychological works of Sigmund Freud* (Vol. 21, pp. 64–145). London: Hogarth Press. (Original work published in 1930.)

Fryer, J. (1987). AIDS and suicide. In J. D. Morgan (Ed.) *Suicide: Helping those at risk,* Proceedings of the Conference, May 28–30, pp. 193–200.

Garfinkel, B. D., Froese, A., & Hood, J. (1982). Suicide attempts in children and adolescents. *American Journal of Psychiatry, 139*, 1257–1261.

Garland, A. (1987, November). *Prevention programs: Evaluation guidelines.* Paper presented at the First National Conference on Suicide Prevention and the Schools, Orlando, FL.

Gartley, W., & Bernasconi, M. (1967). The concept of death in children. *Journal of Genetic Psychology, 110*, 71–85.

Gendreau, P., & Suboski, M. D. (1971). Intelligence and age in discrimination conditioning of eyelid response. *Journal of Experimental Psychology, 89*, 379–382.

Gesell, A. (1940). *The first five years of life*. New York: Harper.

Gibbs, J. P., & Martin, W. T. (1964). *Status integration and suicide*. Eugene, OR: University of Oregon Press.

Gibbs, J. T. (1984). Black adolescents and youth: An endangered species. *American Journal of Orthopsychiatry, 57*, 6–21.

Glick, I. O., Parkes, C. M., & Weiss, R. (1975). *The first year of bereavement*. New York: Basic Books.

Goldberg, E. L. (1981). Depression and suicide ideation in the young adult. *American Journal of Psychiatry, 138*, 35–40.

Goldberg, H. (1977). *The hazards of being male: Surviving the myth of masculine privilege*. New York: New American Library.

Goldney, R. D. (1981). Attempted suicide in young women: Correlate of lethality. *British Journal of Psychiatry, 139*, 382–390.

Goldney, R. D. & Katsikitis, M. (1983). Cohort analysis of suicide rates in Australia. *Archives of General Psychiatrym 40*(1), 71–74.

Goode, T. L. & Brophy, J. E. (1984). *Looing in classrooms*. New York: Harper & Row.

Goodwin, D. (1973). Alcohol in suicide and homicide. *Quarterly Journal of Studies on Alcohol, 34*, 144–156.

Gould, M. S., & Shaffer, D. (1986). The impact of suicide in television movies: Evidence of imitation. *New England Journal of Medicine, 315*, 690–694.

Gould, R. E. (1965). Suicide problems in children and adolescents. *American Journal of Psychotherapy, 19*, 228–245.

Gould, R. L. (1978). *Transformations: Growth and change in adult life*. New York: Simon & Schuster.

Gray, D., & Hudson, L. (1984). Formal operations and the imaginary audience. *Developmental Psychology, 20*, 619–627.

Green, A. H. (1978). Self-destructive behavior in battered children. *American Journal of Psychiatry, 135*, 579–582.

Greuling, J., & DeBlassie, R. (1980). Adolescent suicide. *Adolescence, 15*, 589–601.

Guze, S. B., & Robins, E. (1970). Suicide and primary affective disorder. *British Journal of Psychiatry, 117*, 437–438.

Haan, N. (1981). Common dimensions of personality development: Early adolescence to middle life. In D. H. Eichoun, J. A. Clausen, N. Haan, M. P. Honzik, & P. Mussen (Eds.), *Present and past in middle life*. (pp. 117–151). New York: Academic Press.

Hall, G. S. (1904). *Adolescence* (Vol. 1). New York: D. Appleton.

Haas, A. P., & Hendin, H. (1983). Suicide among older people: Projections for the future. *Suicide and Life-Threatening Behavior, 13*, 147–154.

Harmet, A. R. (Ed.), (1984). *The World Book Encyclopedia* (Vol. 18, p. 770). Chicago: World Book.

Hawton, K. (1982). Annotation: Attempted suicide in children and adolescents. *Journal of Child Psychology and Psychiatry, 23*, 497–503.

Hirschfeld, R. M. A., & Blumenthal, S. J. (1986). Personality, life events, and other psychosocial factors in adolescent depression and suicide. In G. L. Klerman (Ed.), *Suicide and depression among adolescents and young adults*. (pp. 213–254). Washington, DC: American Psychiatric Press.

Hirschfeld, R. M. A. & Cross, C. K. (1982). Epidemiology of affective disorders: Psychosocial risk factors. *Archives of General Psychiatry, 39*, 35–46.

Holinger, P. (1979). Violent deaths among the young: Recent trends in suicide, homicide and accidents. *American Journal of Psychiatry, 139*, 1144–1147.

Holinger, P., & Offer, C. (1982). The prediction of adolescent suicide: A population model. *American Journal of Psychiatry, 139*, 302–307.

Holmes, T. H., & Rahe, R. H. (1967). The social readjustment rating scale. *Journal of Psychosomatic Research, 11*, 213–218.

The Holy Bible. (1949). (King James edition). New York: American Bible Society.

Horn, J. L. (1982). The theory of fluid and crystallized in relation to concepts of cognitive psychology and aging in adulthood. In F. J. M. Craik and S. Trehub (Eds.), *Aging and cognitive processes.* New York: Plenum.

Hostetter, C. (1988, April). AIDS: Its impact on the nation, the community, the family, and the individual. Paper presented at the meeting of the Association for Death Education and Counseling, Orlando, FL.

Hudgens, R. W. (1983). Preventing suicide. *New England Journal of Medicine, 308,* 897–898.

Hull, D. (1979), Migration, adaptation, and illness: A review. *Social Science and Medicine, 13A,* 25–36.

Hume, D. (1929). *An essay on suicide.* Yellow Springs, OH: Kahoe. (Original work published 1783.)

Hutton, C. L., & Valente, S. M. (1984). *Suicide: Assessment and intervention* (2nd ed.). Norwalk, CT: Appleton-Century-Crofts.

Illfeld, F. W. (1977). Current social stressors and symptoms of depression. *American Journal of Psychiatry, 134,* 161–166.

Inhelder, B., & Piaget, J. (1958). *The growth of logical thinking from childhood to adolescence.* New York: Basic Books.

Jaco, R. M. (1987). Suicide-proofing youth: A survival technique for the eighties. In J. D. Morgan (Ed.), *Suicide: Helping those at risk. Proceedings of the Conference* (pp. 103–111). London, Ontario: King's College.

Jacobs, J. (1971). *Adolescent suicide.* New York: Wiley Interscience.

Jacobziner, H. (1960). Attempted suicide in children. *Journal of Pediatrics, 56,* 519–525.

Jaques, E. (1965). Death and the mid-life crisis. *International Journal of Psycho-analysis, 146,* 502–514.

Jennings, C., Barraclough, B., & Moss, J. (1978). Have the Samaritans lowered the suicide rate? A controlled study. *Psychological Medicine, 8,* 413–422.

Jobes, D. A., Berman, A. L., & Josselsen, A. R. (1986). The impact of psychological autopsies on medical examiners' determination of manner of death. *Journal of Forensic Science, 32* (1), 177–189.

Joffe, R. T., & Offord, D. R. (1983). A review: Suicidal behavior in childhood. *Canadian Journal of Psychiatry, 28,* 57–63.

Jorgenson, D. E., & Neubecker, R. C. (1981). Euthanasia: A national survey of attitudes toward voluntary termination of life. *Omega, 11,* 281–291.

Jung, C. G. (1960). *The structure and dynamics of the psyche* (R. F. C. Hull, Trans.). In G. Adler (Ed.), *The collected works of C. G. Jung* (Bollingen Series 20, Vol. 8, pp. 749–795). Princeton, NJ: Princeton University Press.

Kalish, R. A. (1963). Variables in death attitudes. *The Journal of Social Psychology, 59,* 137–145.

Kalish, R. A. (1975). *Late adulthood: Perspectives on human development.* Monterey, CA: Brooks/Cole.

Kalish, R. A., Reynolds, D. K., & Farberow, N. L. (1974). Community attitudes toward suicide. *Community Mental Health Journal, 10,* 301–308.

Kart, C. S. (1981). *The realities of aging.* Boston: Allyn & Bacon.

Kazdin, A. E., French, N. H., Unis, A. S., Esveldt-Dawson, K., & Sherick, R. B. (1983). Helplessness, depression, and suicidal intent among psychiatrically disturbed inpatient children. *Journal of Consulting and Clinical Psychology, 51,* 504–510.

Kelly, G. A. (1955). *The psychology of personal constructs.* New York: Norton.

Kiev, A. (1984). Suicide and depression. In N. Linzer (Ed.), *Suicide: The will to live vs. the will to die* (pp. 23–34). New York: Human Sciences Press.

Kleemeier, R. W. (1962). Intellectual change in the senium. *Proceedings of the Social Statistics Section of the American Statistical Association* (pp. 290–295).

Kohlberg, L. (1976). Moral stages and moralization: Cognitive-development approach. In T. Lickona (Ed.), *Moral development and behavior: Theory, research, and social issues* (pp. 31–53). New York: Holt, Rinehart & Winston.

Koocher, G. P. (1973). Childhood, death, and child development. *Developmental Psychology, 9,* 369–375.

Kosky, P. (1982). Childhood suicidal behavior. *Journal of Child Psychology and Psychiatry and Allied Disciplines, 24,* 457–467.

Kubler-Ross, E. (1969). *On death and dying.* New York: Macmillan.

Lampert, D. I., Bourque, L. B., & Kraus, J. F. (1984). Occupational status and suicide. *Suicide and Life-Threatening Behavior, 14,* 254–269.

Lecky, P. (1973). *Self-consistency: A theory of personality.* Fort Myers Beach, FL: Island Press.

Leenaars, A. A., Balance, W. D., Pellarin, S., Aversano, G., Magli, A., & Wenckstern, S. (1988). Facts and myths of suicide in Canada. *Death Studies, 12,* 195–206.

Lester, D. (1969). Suicide as a positive act. *Psychology, 6*(3), 43–48.

Lester, D. (1970). The concept of an appropriate death. *Psychology, 7*(4), 61–66.

Lester, D. (1971). The evaluation of suicide prevention centers. *International Behavioral Scientist, 3*(2), 40–47.

Lester, D. (1986). Genetics, twin studies, and suicide. In R. Maris (Ed.), *Biology of suicide.* New York: Guilford Press.

Lester, D. (1987). Preventing suicide: Past failures and future hopes. In J. D. Morgan (Ed.), *Suicide: Helping those at risk. Proceedings of the conference* (pp. 69–78). London, Ontario: King's College.

Lester, D., Beck, A. T., & Mitchell, B. (1979). Extrapolation from attempted suicides to completed suicides: A test. *Journal of Abnormal Psychology, 88,* 78–80.

Levenson, M., & Neuringer, C. (1971). Problem-solving behavior in suicidal adolescents. *Journal of Consulting and Clinical Psychology, 37,* 433–436.

Levinson, A. J. (1980, April). Termination of life support systems in the elderly: Ethical issues. Paper presented at the Scientific Meeting of the Boston Society for Gerontologic Psychiatry.

Levinson, D. J., Darrow, C., Klein, E., Levinson, M., & McKee, B. (1978). *The seasons of a man's life.* New York: Knopf.

Limbacher, M. & Domino, G. (1985). Attitudes toward suicide among attempters, contemplators, and nonattempters. *Omega, 16,* 319–328.

Linehan, M. M. (1981). A social behavioral analysis of suicide and parasuicide. Implications for clinical assessment and treatment. In J. F. Clarkin & H. I. Glazer (Eds.), *Depression: Behavioral and directive intervention strategies.* New York: Garland Press.

Linnoila, R., Erwin, C., Ramm, D., Cleveland, P., & Brendle, A. (1980). Effects of alcohol on psychomotor performance of women: Interaction with menstrual cycle. *Alcoholism: Clinical and Experimental Research, 4,* 302–305.

Lopata, H. (1973). Self-identity in marriage and widowhood. *The Sociological Quarterly, 14,* 407–418.

Lowenthal, M. F., Thurnher, D. C., & Associates (1975). *Four stages of life.* San Francisco: Jossey-Bass.

Lyons, M. J. (1984). Suicide in later life: Some putative causes with implications for prevention. *Journal of Community Psychology, 12,* 379–388.

Maccoby, E. E., & Jacklin, C. N. (1974). *The psychology of sex differences.* Stanford, CA: Stanford University Press.

MacMahon, B., & Pugh, T. F. (1965). Suicide in the widowed. *American Journal of Epidemiology, 81,* 23–31.

Maris, R. W. (1971). Deviance as therapy: The paradox of the self-destructive female. *Journal of Health and Social Behavior, 12,* 113–124.

Maris, R. W. (1981). *Pathways to suicide: A survey of self-destructive behaviors.* Baltimore: John Hopkins University Press.

Marks, A. (1977). Sex differences and their effect upon cultural evaluations of methods of self-destruction. *Omega, 8,* 65–70.

Marshall, J. R. (1978). Changes in aged white male suicide: 1948–1972. *Journal of Gerontology, 33,* 763–768.

Marzuk, P. M., Tierney, H., Tardiff, K., Gross, E. M., Morgan, E. B., Hsu, M., & Mann, J. J. (1988). Increased risk of suicide in persons with AIDS. *Journal of the American Medical Association, 259,* 1333–1337.

Maslow, A. H. (1954). *Motivation and personality.* New York: Harper & Row.

Maslow, A. H. (1971). *The farther reaches of human nature.* New York: Viking Press.

Masters, W. H., & Johnson, V. E. (1966). *Human sexual response.* Boston: Little, Brown.

Mathieu, J., & Peterson, J. (1970, November). Some social psychological dimensions of aging. Paper presented at the annual meeting of the Gerontological Society, Ontario, Canada.

Matter, D. E., & Matter, R. M. (1984, April). Suicide among elementary school children. *Elementary School Guidance and Counseling,* pp. 260, 267.

McAnarney, E. R. (1979). Adolescent and the young adult suicide in the United States—a reflection of social unrest? *Adolescence, 14,* 765–774.

McBrien, R. J. (1983). Are you thinking of killing yourself? Confronting students suicidal thoughts. *The School Counselor, 31,* 75–82.

McClure, G. M. G. (1984). Recent trends in suicide amongst the young. *British Journal of Psychiatry, 144,* 134–138.

McConkie, B. R. (1966)., *Mormon doctrine* (2nd ed.). Salt Lake City: Bookcraft, Inc.

McDowell, E. E. (1985). Sex differences in suicidal behavior. *Forum Newsletter, 8,* 9–11.

McGinnis, J. M. (1987). Suicide in America: Moving up the public health agenda. *Suicide and Life-Threatening Behavior, 17,* 18–32.

McIntire, M. S., & Angle, C. R. (1971). Suicide as seen in a poison control center. *Pediatrics, 48,* 914–922.

McIntire, M. S., & Angle, C. R. (1973). Psychological "biopsy" in self-poisoning of children and adolescents. *American Journal of Diseases of Children, 126,* 42–46.

McIntire, M. S., Angle, C. R., & Struempler, L. J. (1972). The concept of death in midwestern children and youth. *American Journal of Diseases of Children, 123,* 527–532.

McIntosh, J. L. (1983). Suicide among the elderly. *American Journal of Orthopsychiatry, 55,* 288–293.

McIntosh, J. L. (1984). Components of the decline in elderly suicide: Suicide among the young-old and old-old by race and sex. *Death Education, 8,* 113–124.

McIntosh, J. L. (1985). Suicide among the elderly: Levels and trends. *American Journal of Orthopsychiatry, 35,* 288–293.

McIntosh, J. L., Hubbard, R. W., & Santos, J. F. (1981). Suicide among the elderly: A review of issues with case studies. *Journal of Gerontological Social Work, 4,* 63–74.

McIntosh, J. L., Hubbard, R. W., & Santos, J. F. (1985). Suicide facts and myths: A study of prevalence. *Death Studies, 9,* 267–281.

McIntosh, J. L., & Jewell, B. L. (1986). Sex difference trends in completed suicide. *Suicide and Life-Threatening Behavior, 16,* 16–27.

McRae, R. R., & Costa, P. T., Jr. (1983). Psychological maturity and subjective well-being: Toward a new synthesis. *Developmental Psychology, 19,* 243–248.

Mehta, D., Mathew, P., & Mehta, S. (1978). Suicide pact in a depressed elderly couple: Case report. *Journal of the American Geriatrics Society, 26,* 136–138.

Meichenbaum, D. (1985). *Stress inoculation training.* Elmsford, NY: Pergamon.

Memory, J. M. (1988). *Juvenile suicides in secure detention facilities: Correction of published rates.* Unpublished manuscript.

Merian, J. (1763). Sur la crainte de la mort, sur le mepris de la mort, sur le suicide, memoire [About the fear of death, about contempt for death, about suicide, recollection]. In *Histoire de l'Academie Royale des Sciences et Belles-Lettres de Berlin* (Vol. 19).

Miles, C. (1977). Conditions predisposing to suicide: A review. *Journal of Nervous and Mental Disease, 164,* 231–246.

Miller, M. (1978a). Geriatric suicide: The Arizona study. *The Gerontologists, 18,* 488–495.

Miller, M. (1978b). Note: Toward a profile of the older white male suicide. *The Gerontologists, 18,* 80–82.

Miller, M. (1979). *Suicide after sixty: The final alternative.* New York: Springer.

Minkoff, K., Bergman, E., Beck, A. T., & Beck, R. (1973). Hopelessness, depression, and attempted suicide. *American Journal of Psychiatry, 130,* 455–459.

Morrison, G. C., & Collier, J. G. (1969). Family treatment approaches to suicidal children and adolescents. *Journal of the American Academy of Child Psychiatry, 8,* 140–153.

Murphy, G. E., Armstrong, J., Hermele, S., Fisher, J., & Clendenin, W. (1979). Suicide and alcoholism. *Archives of General Psychiatry, 36,* 65–69.

Murphy, G. E., & Wetzel, R. D. (1982). Family history of suicidal behavior among suicide attempters. *Journal of Nervous and Mental Disease, 170,* 86–90.

Murray, H. A. (1938). *Explorations in personality.* New York: Oxford University Press.

Mussen, P. H., Conger, J. J., & Kagan, J. (1974). *Child development and personality* (4th ed.). New York: Harper & Row.

Nagy, M. (1948). The child's theories concerning death. *Journal of Genetic Psychology, 73,* 3–27.

National Center for Health Statistics (1965). *Vital statistics of the United States 1965 supplement: Mortality data.* Washington, DC: U.S. Government Printing Office.

National Center for Health Statistics (1987, August 28). *Monthly vital statistics report,* vol. 36, no. 5 (DHHS Publication No. [PHS] 87-1120). Washington, DC: U.S. Government Printing Office.

National Center for Health Statistics (1988, September 30). Advance report of final mortality statistics, 1986. *Monthly Vital Statistics Report* (DHHS Pub. No. [PHS] 88-1120). Washington, DC: U.S. Government Printing Office.

Nelson, F. L. (1984). Suicide: Issues of prevention, intervention, and facilitation. *Journal of Clinical Psychology, 40,* 1328–1333.

Neugarten, B. L. (1968). The awareness of middle age. In B. L. Neugarten (Ed.), *Middle age and aging: A reader in social psychology* (pp. 93–98). Chicago: University of Chicago Press.

Neugarten, B. L., Havighurst, R. J., & Tobin, S. S. (1961). The measurement of life satisfaction. *Journal of Gerontology, 16,* 168–174.

Newman, A. (1987, October–November). The bomb and adolescent anxiety. *The High School Journal,* pp. 1–4.

Noyes, R. (1970). Shall we prevent suicide? *Comparative Psychiatry, 11,* 361–370.

Noyes, R., Frye, S. J., & Hartford, C. E. (1977). Conjugal suicide pact. *Journal of Nervous and Mental Disorders, 165,* 72–75.

Orbach, I. (1984). Personality characteristics, life circumstances, and dynamics of suicidal children. *Death Education, 8,* 37–52.

Orbach, I. (1988). *Children who don't want to live: Understanding and treating the suicidal child.* San Francisco: Jossey-Bass.

Orbach, I., Feshbach, S., Carlson, G., & Ellenberg, L. (1984). Attitudes towards life and death in suicidal, normal, and chronically ill children: An extended replication. *Journal of Consulting and Clinical Psychology, 52,* 1020–1027.

Orbach, I., & Glaubman, H. (1979). The concept of death and suicidal behavior in young children: Three case studies. *Journal of the American Academy of Child Psychiatry, 18,* 668–678.

Orbach, I., Gross, Y., & Glaubman, H. (1981). Some common characteristics of latency-age suicidal children: A tentative model based on case study analyses. *Suicide and Life-Threatening Behavior, 11,* 180–190.

Osgood, N. J. (1985). *Suicide in the elderly: A practitioner's guide to diagnosis and mental health intervention.* Rockville, MD: Aspen.

Osgood, N. J., Brant, B. A., & Lipman, A. (1988–1989). Patterns of suicidal behavior in long-term care facilities: A preliminary report on an ongoing study. *Omega, 16,* 69–77.

Osterweis, M., Solomon, F., & Green, M. (Eds.) (1984). *Bereavement: Reactions, consequences, and care,* Washington, DC: National Academy Press.

Parkes, C. M. (1972). *Bereavement: Studies of grief in adult life.* New York: International Universities Press.

Paulson, J. J., & Stone, D. (1974). Suicidal behavior of latency-age children. *Journal of Clinical Child Psychology, 3,* 50–53.

Pavlov, I. (1927). *Conditioned reflexes.* London: Oxford University Press.

Paykel, E. S., Prusoff, B. A., Myers, J. K. (1975). Suicide attempts and recent life events: A controlled comparison. *Archives of General Psychiatry, 32,* 327–333.

Peck, R. C. (1968). Psychological developments in the second half of life. In B. L. Neugarten (Ed.), *Middle age and aging: A reader in social psychology* (pp. 88–92). Chicago: University of Chicago Press.

Pettifor, J., Perry, D., Plowman, B., & Pitcher, S. (1983). Risk factors predicting child and adolescent suicide. *Journal of Child Care, 1,* 17–50.

Pfeffer, C. R. (1981a). Suicidal behavior of children: A review with implications for research and practice. *American Journal of Psychiatry, 138,* 154–159.

Pfeffer, C. R. (1981b). The family system of suicidal children. *American Journal of Psychotherapy, 35,* 330–341.

Pfeffer, C. R. (1982). Intervention for suicidal children and their parents. *Suicide and Life-Threatening Behavior, 12,* 240–248.

Pfeffer, C. R. (1984). Death preoccupations and survival behavior in children. In H. Wass & C. A. Corr (Eds.), *Childhood and death* (pp. 261–278). Washington, DC: Hemisphere.

Pfeffer, C. R. (1984a). Recognizing and treating suicidal youngsters. In N. Linzer (Ed.), *Suicide: The will to live vs. the will to die* (pp. 87–100). New York: Human Sciences Press.

Pfeffer, C. R. (1984b). Death preoccupations and suicidal behavior in children. In H. Wass & C. Corr (Eds.), *Childhood and death* (pp. 261–279). Washington, DC: Hemisphere.

Pfeffer, C. R. (1986). *The suicidal child.* New York: Guilford Press.

Pfeffer, C. R., Conte, H. R., Plutchik, R., & Jerrett, I. (1979). Suicidal behavior in latency-age children: An empirical study. *Journal of the American Academy of Child Psychiatry, 18,* 679–692.

Pfeffer, C. R., Conte, H. R., Plutchik, R., & Jerrett, I. (1980). Suicidal behavior in latency-age children: An outpatient population. *Journal of the American Academy of Child Psychiatry, 18,* 703–710.

Pfeffer, C. R., Plutchik, R., & Mizruchi, M. S. (1983). Suicidal and assaultive behavior in children: Classification, measurement, and intervention. *American Journal of Psychiatry, 140,* 154–157.

Phillips, D. P. (1979)., Suicide, motor vehicle fatalities and the mass media: Substantive and theoretical implications of the Werther effect. *American Sociological Review, 39,* 340–354.

Phillips, D. P., & Carstensen, L. L. (1986). Clustering of teenage suicides after television news stories about suicide. *New England Journal of Medicine, 315,* 685–689.

Piaget, J. (1926). *The language and thought of the child.* New York: Harcourt Brace.

Piaget, J., & Inhelder, B. (1969). *The psychology of the child.* New York: Basic Books.

Powell, E. H. (1958). Occupation, status, and suicide. Toward a redefinition of anomie. *American Sociological Review, 23,* 131–139.

Rachlis, D. (1970, Fall). Suicide and loss adjustment in aging. *Bulletin of Suicidology*, 7, 23–26.

Rando, T. A. (1985). *Loss and anticipatory grief*. Lexington, MA: Lexington Books.

Raphael, B. (1983). *The anatomy of bereavement*. New York: Basic Books.

Ray, L. Y. & Johnson, N. (1983, November). Adolescent suicide. *The Personnel and Guidance Journal*, 131–135.

Reich, T., Rice, J., & Mullaney, J. (1986). Genetic risk factors for the affective disorders. In G. L. Klerman (Ed.) *Suicide and depression among adolescents and young adults* (pp. 77–104). Washington, DC: American Psychiatric Press.

Resnik, H. L. P., & Cantor, J. M. (1970). Suicide and aging. *Journal of the American Geriatrics Society*, 18, 152–158.

Richman, J. (1981). Suicide and the family: Affective disturbances and their implications for understanding, diagnosis, and treatment. In M. R. Lansky (Ed.), *Family therapy and major psychopathology* (pp. 145–160). New York: Grune & Stratton.

Rifkin, J., & Howard, T. (1980). *Entropy: A new world view*. New York: Bantam.

Robins, L. N., West, P. A., & Murphy, G. E. (1977). The high rate of suicide in older white men: A study testing ten hypotheses. *Social Psychiatry*, 12, 1–20.

Rockwell, D., & O'Brien, W. (1973). Physicians' knowledge and attitudes about suicide. *Journal of the American Medical Association*, 225, 1347–1349.

Rogers, C. R. (1961). *On becoming a person*. Boston: Houghton Mifflin.

Rosenberg, P. H., & Latimer, R. (1966). Suicide attempts by children. *Mental Hygiene*, 50, 354–359.

Rosenn, D. W. (1982). Suicidal behavior in children and adolescents. In E. L. Bassuk, S. C. Schoonover, & A. D. Gill (Eds.), *Lifelines: Clinical perspectives on suicide* (pp. 195–224). New York: Plenum Press.

Rosenthal, M. J. (1981). Sexual differences in the suicidal behavior of young people. *Adolescent Psychiatry*, 9, 422–442.

Rosenthal, P. A., & Rosenthal, S. (1984). Suicidal behavior by preschool children. *American Journal of Psychiatry*, 141, 520–525.

Roy, A. (1982). Risk factors for suicide in psychiatric patients. *Archives of General Psychiatry*, 39, 1089–1095.

Roy, A., & Linnoila, M. (1986). Alcoholism and suicide. In R. Maris (Ed.) *Biology of suicide* (pp. 162–191). New York: Guilford Press.

Rubenstein, D. H. (1983). Epidemic suicide among Micronesian adolescents. *Social Science Medicine*, 17, 657–665.

Rudestam, K. (1977). Physical and psychological responses to suicide in the family. *Journal of Consulting and Clinical Psychology*, 45(2), 162–170.

Rudestam, K., & Imbroll, D. (1983). Societal reactions to the child's death by suicide. *Journal of Consulting and Clinical Psychology*, 51, 461–462.

Rushing, W. (1969). Suicide and the interaction of alcoholism (liver cirrhosis) with the social situation. *Quarterly Journal of Studies on Alcohol*, 30, 93–103.

Rygnestad, T. K. (1982). A prospective study of social and psychiatric aspects of self-poisoned patients. *Acta Psychiatrica Scandinavica*, 66, 139–153.

Sabbath, J. C. (1969). The suicidal adolescent: The expendable child. *Journal of the American Academy of Child Psychiatry*, 8, 272–289.

Sainsbury, P., Jenkins, J., & Levy, A. (1980). The social correlates of suicide in Europe. In R. D. T. Farmer & S. R. Hirsch (Eds.), *The suicide syndrome* (pp. 38–53). London: Croom Helm.

Santrock, J. W. (1985). *Adult development and aging*. Dubuque, IA: William C. Brown.

Santy, P. A. (1982). Observations on double suicide: Review of the literature and two case reports. *American Journal of Psychotherapy*, 36, 23–31.

Schaie, K. W., & Willis, S. L. (1986). *Adult development and aging* (2nd ed.). Boston: Little, Brown.

Schildkraut, J. J. (1965). The catecholamine hypothesis of affective disorders: A review of supporting evidence. *American Journal of Psychiatry, 122,* 509–522.

Schonfield, A. E. D. (1980). Learning, memory, and aging. In J. E. Birren & R. B. Sloone (Eds.), *Handbook of mental age and aging.* Englewood Cliffs, NJ: Prentice-Hall.

Schoonover, S. C. (1982). Crisis therapies. In E. L. Bassuk, S. C. Schoonover, & A. D. Gill (Eds.), *Lifelines: Clinical perspectives on suicide* (pp. 49–57). New York: Plenum Press.

Seiden, R. H. (1981). Mellowing with age: Factors influencing the nonwhite suicide rate. *International Journal of Aging and Human Development, 13,* 265–284.

Seiden, R. H. (1983). Death in the West: A spatial analysis of the youthful suicide rate. *Western Journal of Medicine, 139,* 783–795.

Sendbuehler, J. M., & Goldstein, S. (1977). Attempted suicide among the aged. *Journal of the American Geriatrics Society,* 245–248.

Seligman, M. E. P. (1975). *Helplessness: On depression, development, and death.* San Francisco: Freeman.

Selkin, J. (1983). The legacy of Emile Durkheim. *Suicide and Life-Threatening Behavior, 13*(1), 3–14.

Serafin, J. D., Thornton, G., & Robertson, D. U. (1988, April). The social stigma of suicide. Paper presented at the meeting of the Association for Death Education and Counseling, Orlando, FL.

Shaffer, D. (1974). Suicide in childhood and early adolescence. *Journal of Child Psychology and Psychiatry, 15,* 275–291.

Shaffer, D., & Fisher, P. (1981). The epidemiology of suicide in children and adolescents. *Journal of the American Academy of Child Psychiatry, 21,* 545–566.

Shaughnessy, M. F., & Nystul, M. S. (1985). Preventing the greatest loss—suicide. *The Creative Child and Adult Quarterly, 10*(3), 164–169.

Sheehy, G. (1976). *Passages: Predictable crises of adult life.* New York: Dutton.

Sheskin, A., & Wallace, S. (1976). Differing bereavements: Suicide, natural and accidental death. *Omega, 7,* 229–242.

Shneidman, E. S. (Ed.). (1967). *Essays in self-destruction.* New York: Science House.

Shneidman, E. S. (1971). Suicide among the gifted. *Suicide and Life-Threatening Behavior, 1,* 23–45.

Shneidman, E. S. (1976). A psychological theory of suicide. The components of suicide. *Psychiatric Annals, 6,* 51–66.

Shneidman, E. S. (1984). Postvention and the survivor-victim. In E. Shneidman (Ed.), *Death: Current perspectives* (3rd ed., pp. 412–419). (Reprinted from Shneidman, E. S., *Deaths of Man,* 1973).

Shneidman, E. S. (1985). *Definition of suicide.* New York: Wiley.

Shneidman, E., Farberow, N., & Litman, R. (1961). The suicide prevention center. In N. Farberow & E. Shneidman (Eds.), *The cry for help* (pp. 6–18). New York: McGraw-Hill.

Silver, M. A., Bohnert, M., Beck, A. T., & Marcus, D. (1971). Relation of depression of attempted suicide and seriousness of intent. *Archives of General Psychiatry, 25,* 573–576.

Skinner, B. F. (1953). *Science and human behavior.* New York: Macmillan.

Slater, J., & Depue, R. A. (1981). The contribution of environmental events and social support to serious suicide attempts in primary depressive disorder. *Journal of Abnormal Psychology, 40,* 275–285.

Smith, K., Eyman, J., Dyck, R., & Ryerson, D. (1987, December). *Report of a survey of school-related suicide programs.* Paper prepared for the American Association of Suicidology, Denver, CO.

Speece, M. W., & Brent, S. B. (1984). Children's understanding of death: A review of three components of a death concept. *Child Development, 55,* 1671–1686.

Stafford, M. C., & Weisheit, R. A. (1988). Changing age patterns of U.S. male and female suicide rates, 1934–1983. *Suicide and Life-Threatening Behavior, 18*, 149–163.

Stenback, A. (1980). Depression and suicidal behavior in old age. In J. C. Birren & R. B. Sloane (Eds.), *Handbook of mental health aging*. Englewood Cliffs, NJ: Prentice-Hall.

Stephens, J. B. (1985). Suicidal women and their relationships with husbands, boyfriends, and lovers. *Suicide and Life-Threatening Behavior, 15*, 77–89.

Stillion, J. M. (1984). Women and widowhood: The suffering beyond grief. In J. Freeman (Ed.), *Women: A feminist perspective* (pp. 282–296). Palo Alto, CA: Mayfield.

Stillion, J. M. (1985). *Death and the sexes: An examination of differential longevity, attitudes, behaviors, and coping skills*. Washington, DC: Hemisphere.

Stillion, J. M. (1985). *Exploring coping techniques among ninth grade academically gifted students*. Unpublished raw data.

Stillion, J. M. (1986). Examining the shadow: Gifted children respond to the nuclear threat. *Death Studies, 10*, 27–41.

Stillion, J. M., Goodrow, H., Klingman, A., Laughlin, M., Morgan, J. D., Sandsberg, S., Walton, M., & Warren, W. G. (1988). Dimensions of the shadow: Children of six nations respond to the nuclear threat. *Death Studies, 12*(3), 227–251.

Stillion, J. M., McDowell, E. E., & May, J. H. (1984). Developmental trends and sex differences in adolescent attitudes toward suicide. *Death Education, 8*, 81–90.

Stillion, J. M., McDowell, E. E., & Shamblin, J. B. (1984). The suicide attitude vignette experience: A method for measuring adolescent attitudes toward suicide. *Death Education, 8*, 65–80.

Stillion, J. M., McDowell, E. E., Smith, R. T., & McCoy, P. A. (1986). Relationships between suicide attitudes and indicators of mental health among adolescents. *Death Studies, 10*, 289–296.

Stillion, J. M., & Wass, H. (1979). Children and death. In H. Wass (Ed.), *Dying: Facing the facts* (pp. 208–235). Washington, DC: Hemisphere.

Stillion, J. M., White, H., McDowell, E. E., & Edwards, P. (in press). Ageism and sexism in suicide attitudes. *Death Studies*.

Streiner, D. L., & Adam, K. S. (1987). Evaluation of the effectiveness of suicide prevention programs: A methodological perspective. *Suicide and Life-Threatening Behavior, 17*, 93–106.

Sudak, H. S., Ford, A. B., & Rushforth, N. B. (1984). Adolescent suicide: An overview. *American Journal of Psychotherapy, 38*, 350–363.

Swain, B. J., & Domino, G. L. (1985). Attitudes toward suicide among mental health professionals. *Death Studies, 9*, 455–468.

Swain, H. L. (1979). Childhood views of death. *Death Education, 2*, 341–358.

Syer-Solursh, D. (1985, April). Suicide in Canada—task force report summary. Paper presented at the Conference of the American Association of Suicidology, Toronto, Canada.

Szasz, T. (1986). The case against suicide prevention. *American Psychologist, 41*, 806–812.

Taylor, S. (1982). *Durkheim and the study of suicide*. New York: St. Martin's Press.

Terenzini, P. T. (1987, November). *A review of selected theoretical models of student development and collegiate impact*. Paper presented at the meeting of the Association for the Study of Higher Education, Baltimore.

Teuting, P., Kaslow, S. H., & Hirshfeld, R. M. A. (1981). Special report on depression research. In *Science reports*. Rockville, MD: National Institute of Mental Health.

Thomas, R. M. (1979). *Comparing Theories of Child Development*. Belmont, CA: Wadsworth.

Tishler, C. L., & McKenry, P. C. (1983). Intrapsychic symptoms dimensions of adolescent suicide attempters. *Journal of Family Practice, 16,* 731–734.

Tishler, C. L., McKenry, P. C., & Morgan, K. C. (1981). Adolescent suicide attempts: Some significant factors. *Suicide and Life-Threatening Behavior, 11,* 86–92.

Toolan, J. M. (1962). Suicide and suicidal attempts in children and adolescents. *American Journal of Psychiatry, 118,* 719–723.

Toolan, J. M. (1975). Suicide in children and adolescents. *American Journal of Psychotherapy, 29,* 339–344.

Topol, P., & Reznikoff, M. (1982). Perceived peer and family relationships, hopelessness, locus of control as factors in adolescent suicide attempts. *Suicide and Life-Threatening Behavior, 12,* 141–150.

Toynbee, A. (1984). The relationship between life and death, living and dying. In E. S. Shneidman (Ed.), *Current perspectives* (3rd ed., pp. 8–14). Palo Alto, CA: Mayfield.

Turkington, C. (1983, May). Child suicide: An unspoken tragedy. *APA Monitor,* p. 15.

U.S. Bureau of the Census. (1956). *Statistical abstract of the United States: 1956.* Washington, DC: U.S. Government Printing Office.

U.S. Bureau of the Census. (1977). *Statistical abstract of the United States: 1977.* Washington, DC: U.S. Government Printing Office.

U.S. Bureau of the Census. (1985). *Statistical abstract of the United States: 1984.* Washington, DC: U.S. Government Printing Office.

U.S. Bureau of the Census. (1987). *Statistical abstract of the United States: 1986.* (10th Edition). Washington, DC: U.S. Government Printing Office.

U.S. Bureau of the Census. (1988). *Statistical abstract of the United States: 1987.* Washington, DC: U.S. Government Printing Office.

U.S. Department of Justice, Office of Juvenile Justice and Delinquency Prevention. (1985). *Children in custody: A report on the 1977 and 1979 censuses on juvenile detention, correctional, and shelter facilities.* Washington, DC: U.S. Government Printing Office.

Useui, W. M., Keil, T. J., & Durig, K. R. (1985). Socioeconomic comparisons and life satisfaction of elderly adults. *Journal of Gerontology, 40,* 110–114.

Vaillant, G. E. (1977). *Adaptation to life.* Boston: Little, Brown.

Van Fossen, D. (1985, June). Preventing youth suicide. *Health Link,* pp. 7–10.

Victoroff, V. M. (1983). *The suicidal patient: Recognition, intervention, management.* Oradell, NJ: Medical Economics Books.

Viorst, J. (1986). *Necessary losses.* New York: Fawcett.

Walker, W. L. (1980). Intentional self-injury in school age children. *Journal of Adolescence, 3,* 217–228.

Walsh, P. B. (1983). *Growth through time: An introduction to adult development.* Monterey, CA: Brooks/Cole Publishing.

Warren, L. W., & Tomlinson-Keasey, C. (1987). The context of suicide. *American Journal of Orthopsychiatry, 57,* 41–48.

Wass, H. (1977). Views and opinions of elderly persons concerning death. *Educational Gerontology, 2,* 15–26.

Wass, H. (1979). Death and the elderly. In H. Wass (Ed.) *Dying: Facing the facts.* Washington, DC: Hemisphere.

Wass, H. (1984). Concepts of death: A developmental perspective. In H. Wass & C. A. Corr (Eds.), *Childhood and death* (pp. 3–24). Washington, DC: Hemisphere.

Wass, H., & Stillion, J. M. (1988). Death in the lives of children and adolescents. In H. Wass, F. M. Berardo, & R. A. Neimeyer (Eds.), *Dying: Facing the facts* (pp. 201–208). Washington, DC: Hemisphere.

Webb, N. B. (1986). Before and after suicide: A preventive outreach program for colleges. *Suicide and Life-Threatening Behavior, 16*(4), 469–480.

Weisman, A. (1972). *On dying and denying: A psychiatric study of terminality.* New York: Behavioral Publications.

Weissman, M. M. (1974). The epidemiology of suicide attempts, 1960 to 1971. *Archives of General Psychiatry, 30,* 737–746.

Weissman, M. M. (1978). Psychotherapy and its relevance to the pharmacotherapy of affective disorders: From ideology to evidence. In M. A. Lipton, A. DiMascio, & K. F. Killam (Eds.), *Psychopharmacology: A generation of progress.* New York: Raven Press.

Weissman, M. M. (1974). The epidemiology of suicide attempts 1960–1971. *Archives of General Psychiatry, 30,* 737–746.

Weissman, M. M. (1986). Being young and female: Risk factors for major depression. In G. L. Klerman (Ed.), *Suicide and depression among adolescents and young adults* (pp. 105–130). Washington, DC: American Psychiatric Press.

Westermark, E. (1906–1908). *The origin and development of the moral ideas.* London: MacMillan.

Wetzel, R. D. (1976). Hopelessness, depression, and suicide intent. *Archives of General Psychiatry, 33,* 1069–1073.

White, H. & Stillion, J. M. (1988). Sex differences in attitudes toward suicide: Do males stigmatize males? *Psychology of Women Quarterly, 12,* 357–366.

Wiley, J. (1987). *Report to the Children's Services Commission regarding teenage suicide.* Unpublished report of the Missouri Children's Services Commission, Columbia, MO.

Worden, J. W. (1982). *Grief counseling and grief therapy: A handbook for the mental health practitioner.* New York: Springer.

Wrobleski, A. (1984). The suicide survivors grief group. *Omega, 15,* 173–184.

Yalom, I. (1975). *The theory and practice of group psychotherapy* (2nd ed.). New York: Basic Books.

Young, D., Rich, C. L., & Fowler, R. C. (1984). Double suicides: Four model cases. *Journal of Clinical Psychiatry, 45,* 470–472.

Subject Index

282

SUICIDE ACROSS THE LIFE SPAN

sex differences, 165–166
  underreported, 165
  young old and old old by sex/race, 168 (figure)
elderly in U.S. for males/females, 1985, 166t
elderly rates selected countries by sex/age, 164t
international, 111–112, 128
middle aged, 128, 130, 254
middle aged by age, sex, race, 130t
middle aged for selected countries by sex/age, 129t
mobility, 98
1986, 18
not reported, 20
racial differences, 111, 130, 253
selected countries by sex/age, 16–18
selected countries by sex/age, 17t
sex and race, 1986, 18t
sex differences, 22, 111, 128–130
underreporting, 67
years of potential life lost (YPLL), 19–20, 20 (figure)
young adult, 111–112, 253–255
Stereotypes, 23
Storm and stress, 207
Suicidal ideation, 241–243, 247
Suicide:
  in secular society, 9–16
  pacts, 180
  penalties for, 7
  prevention center, 11–13, 217
Suicide trajectory, 240 (figure), 240–255
  commonalities, 242–255t
  risk factors, 240–241
  suicidal ideation and, 241–242
  triggering events and, 242
  warning signs and, 241–242
Suicidogenic, 114
Superego, 30–32
Support groups:
  elderly, 219
  survivor, 200

Survivors, suicide, 221–226
  children, 224
  grief, 68
  social support and, 68–69
Survivor's grief work, 222
Suttee, 8

Television, 96–97
Terminally ill, 183, 216
Thanatos, 8, 28, 30, 89, 191
Therapeutic paternalism, 190
Therapeutic techniques:
  art, 206, 208
  dream, 206
  family, 208
  group, 214
  individual, 214
  play, 206
  reminiscence, 219–220
  support groups, 219
Time perspective, 102, 133, 216–217, 254
Topography of the mind, 28
Touching, 218–219
Transitional stages, 110
  coping, 111
Transpersonal psychology, 43
Triggering events, 241–242, 247–248, 251, 252, 253
Typology for classifying, 11

Unconscious, 28, 30

Warning signs, 241–242, 255
Widowhood, 178–180
  males vs. females, 178–179
  poverty, 180
  (see also Loss)

Young adulthood, 107–116, 213–214, 252–253
  (See also Cognitive theory; Depression; Development; Psychoanalytic theory; Risk factors; Statistics)

Name Index